THE CIVILIZATION OF THE AMERICAN INDIAN SERIES

On the Trail of the Arawaks

On the Trail
of the Arawaks

by Fred Olsen

With a Foreword by George Kubler

and an

Introductory Essay by Irving Rouse

University of Oklahoma Press : NORMAN

Library of Congress Cataloging in Publication Data

Olsen, Fred, 1891–
    On the trail of the Arawaks.

    (The civilization of the American Indian series, v. 129)
    Bibliography: p.
    1. Arawak Indians—Antiquities.   2. West Indies—
Antiquities.   I. Title.
F2230.2.A7047   970.3   73-7416
ISBN 0-8061-1137-2

To Florence Q.

who has never counted the cost of her effort, sympathy, and support—my love and appreciation.

Foreword, by George Kubler

Aᴛ this moment in the summer of 1973 Fred Olsen has left his pleasant house at the quarry on Long Island Sound to spend three months with Irving Rouse and a group of students in the excavation of a major site near English Harbour. In Connecticut his Arawak collections delight the professors and at Antigua his creation of the Mill Reef Museum educated many vacationers who never expected to become absorbed. Trained as a scientist, he became a humanist, as these pages show, during his long quest to retrace the Arawak migration. For many years his life has rotated from Connecticut to Antigua, and in this seasonal migration, he brought the library to the island, and the island to the Connecticut house.

Arawak treasures now fill the house: the stones and wood and pottery make a bridge for Yocahú and Atabeyra, while at Mill Reef other bridges were made for Antiguans today on their own island.

On the Trail of the Arawaks belongs in the large family of the stories of treasure hunt, but this one transcends its class in the irenic nature of the chase, and in the poverty of the treasure. No one dies violently, no one is defrauded, no one loses his fortune, and no one gets more than he deserves. It is a treasure without jewels, and a hunt without death, like the fabled quests of those scientists and scholars who find only in searching, and whose finds are incommensurable, that is, both worthless and beyond value, both real and ideal.

Gᴇᴏʀɢᴇ Kᴜʙʟᴇʀ

New Haven, Connecticut
June 3, 1973

ix

Acknowledgments

DURING the past decade and a half I suppose more books have been published on archeological subjects than ever before, so why another one, particularly one that concerns itself with such a little known group of human beings as the Arawaks? Perhaps the best answer is that because the Arawaks are so little known. Certainly during the fifteen years of our amateur digging we were all too conscious that there was not much literature to which we could turn for information about the Arawak. Nevertheless we did find people willing to be of help, and I think it only proper to acknowledge their aid. From the number of times Professor Irving Rouse is mentioned in this book it will be clear that I owe much to his counsel. To Professor George Kubler I could always go to refresh my feeling for the esthetic attributes of these ancient people.

Where I really needed help was in the organizing of the material in preparation of this book, and I am grateful to the generous guidance of Elizabeth Lawrence Kalashnikof and John Fischer. Mary Taylor and Elizabeth Kyburg have spent countless hours and much devoted effort in preparing the manuscript.

Much of the drawing of maps and artifacts was done by Lauren Brown and James Guy. My thanks go to all of these helpful persons for their fine work.

FRED OLSEN

Guilford, Connecticut
August 14, 1973

xi

On the Meaning of the Term "Arawak," by Irving Rouse

IN this book Fred Olsen tells the story of his search for the origins of the first Indians encountered by Christopher Columbus when he discovered the New World. These Indians, who lived in the Greater Antilles, are now known as "Arawaks," but they themselves did not use that name, nor did Columbus and his contemporaries ever come across it, as far as is known. Accordingly, Fred has asked me to explain how the subjects of his search came to be called Arawaks and to discuss the meaning of that term.

What Columbus actually found in the Greater Antilles was a series of local chiefdoms, each of which had its own name. Since these chiefdoms were independent, there was no need for an overall tribal name, and the Indians had none. However, they did supply Columbus with one such name, Carib, and told him that it applied to the Indians further south, in the Lesser Antilles. Intrigued by their story, Columbus sailed south into the Lesser Antilles during his second voyage and found the Caribs to be cannibals, accustomed to obtaining human flesh by raiding their less warlike neighbors in the Greater Antilles. Apparently, they used the term "Carib" to distinguish their own local groups, which were not subject to raiding, from the chiefdoms in the Greater Antilles, which were.

The phrase "Caribbean" is, of course, derived from the Caribs' name for themselves. That sea could not have been called "Arawakan" because the term was unknown to the early explorers.

"Arawak" does not appear in the literature until exploration of the Guianas began in the late 1500's, almost a century after the discovery of the New World. Then Juan Lopéz de Velasco (1894, pp. 153-4) noted the presence of people who called themselves

Arawaks on the Guiana coast, southeast of the island of Trinidad, and commented that a group of them had intruded into Trinidad. Sir Walter Raleigh (1928, pp. 12, 39) confirmed these statements and included the "Aruacos" in a list of the five Indian "nations" that inhabited Trinidad at the time.

The Arawaks of Trinidad have long since become extinct, but the Arawaks of Guiana survive, as Fred Olsen illustrates in this volume. Anthropological linguists have paid particular attention to their speech, and consider it to be typical of an entire family of languages, for which they have coined the term "Arawakan" by adding the suffix "-an" to the Arawaks' name for themselves. They have found that the Arawakan family of languages extended in the time of Columbus all the way from the upper Amazon Basin, in the present country of Peru, to Venezuela, the Guianas, and the West Indies.

Early in the course of this linguistic research, Daniel G. Brinton (1871) compared the few word lists that have survived in the Greater Antilles from the time of Columbus with the modern language of the Arawaks in the Guianas, and came to the conclusion that the Greater Antilleans, too, spoke an Arawakan language. He applied the phrase "Island Arawack" to the Antilleans (p. 436), later abbreviating this to "Arawack" (p. 440). Some subsequent authors have preferred the phrase "Insular Arawak" or the term "Island-Arawak" (e.g., Lovén, 1935, p. 2).

When I first began to work in the Antilles before World War II, I used the abbreviated name "Arawak" to refer to the local Arawakan speakers and merely stated in a footnote that "Island" or "Insular" is customarily used to distinguish those speakers from the Arawak proper in the Guianas (Rouse, 1948, p. 495). I have since come to believe that this was a mistake (Rouse, 1964, pp. 451–2). By using the abbreviated name I created the impression that the Island-Arawaks of the Greater Antilles and the Arawaks proper in the Guianas spoke the same language, which they did not. The two languages were no more alike than, say, French and English within the Indo-European family of languages. I also created the false impression that the Island-Arawaks and the Arawaks proper constituted a single ethnic group, which they did not, any more than the English and French together constitute such a group. I now think it advisable, therefore, to distinguish the Arawakan speakers in the Greater Antilles from those in the Guianas by employing the term "Island-Arawak" for the Greater Antilleans.

Geographically speaking, the distinction between Island-Arawak and Arawak proper is further justified by the fact that the two groups were separated in the time of Columbus by the Carib in the Lesser Antilles. The two were not in contact at that time, so far as we know.

In my early research I further applied the term "Arawak" to all the prehistoric remains in the Antilles, except those which lacked pottery (Rouse, 1948, pp. 507–17). I have since come to believe that this, too, was a mistake (Rouse, 1964, pp. 512–13). It resulted from a failure on my part to think through the problem how far into the past one can trace the Island-Arawaks.

This problem can best be approached by an analogy. The present inhabitants of southern Great Britain call themselves "English," and recognize that their ethnic group, the English people, is the product of a series of migrations from the continent of Europe into the British Isles, beginning with various prehistoric peoples and continuing with the Celts, Angles, Saxons, Vikings, and Normans of protohistoric time. Since the English people is a fusion of all these ethnic groups, one cannot trace that people back further than A.D. 1066, when the Normans, who were the last of the migrants, invaded Britain.

Just so, we must limit the term "Island-Arawak" to the period following the arrival in the Greater Antilles of the last of the Indian groups which migrated there from South America. Unfortunately, there is disagreement about this. I have concluded that the last migrants were the Saladoid people, who reached the Greater Antilles about the time of Christ (Rouse, 1964, p. 512), and Fred Olsen so assumes in the present volume. However, Rainey (1940, pp. 182–3) and Alegría (1965, pp. 248–9) believe that the Ostionoid people, who succeeded the Saladoids in the Greater Antilles, also migrated from the mainland, in which case we would have to say that the Island-Arawaks did not come into existence until the Ostionoids arrived in the islands about A.D. 1000 and fused with the Saladoids, just as the Normans fused with the Anglo-Saxons and Vikings to form the English people at about the same time.

If Fred and I are correct, we can trace the Island-Arawaks back to the time of Christ, when the last migration from the mainland took place, but if Rainey and Alegría are correct, that migration did not take place until A.D. 1000, and the Island-Arawak cannot therefore have existed before 1000. Our 1973 excavations at Indian Creek in Antigua, to which Fred refers in an appendix, favor the A.D. 1 date, for reasons I cannot go into here (Rouse, 1974). Nevertheless, I personally prefer to play safe and to limit the term "Island-Arawak" to the period after A.D. 1000 in the Greater Antilles, about which there is no controversy.

Had I written this book, therefore, I would have entitled it "On the Trail of the Island-Arawaks" in order to make it clear that the Greater Antillean and Guianan Arawaks are two separate ethnic groups, and I would have referred to the Saladoid and Barrancoid peoples as "ancestors of the Island-Arawaks," instead of simply calling the two peoples "Arawaks." This would not have materially changed the basic conclusions reached in the book, which are in my opinion eminently reasonable, given the present state of our knowledge. But it would, I believe, have made the conclusions more accurate and less controversial.

Contents

Maps

Illustrations

An index of figures begins on page 399. An eight-page section of color photographs follows page 140.

On the Trail of the Arawaks

I

Guanahani—Friday, October 12, 1492

I T is well documented that on the morning of Friday, October 12, 1492, Columbus landed on the island of San Salvador and discovered a New World. The friendly natives he encountered there he called Indians. Today we know they were Arawaks.

It was one of history's most momentous encounters. Not only did it open up new continents to a flagging Western Civilization, but it marked the beginning of the end of numerous indigenous cultures of the western hemisphere. The Aztecs, the Incas, the North American Indians—all eventually were subjugated, but none so rapidly and completely as the Arawaks. Within a hundred years of Columbus' landing these peaceful people, who had numbered perhaps two to three million in 1492, became extinct in the Antilles, victims of the cannibalistic Caribs, the white man's diseases, and Spanish greed. History records few such systematic exterminations.

Columbus had said, "To the first island which I found I gave the name San Salvador, in remembrance of His Heavenly Majesty, Who marvelously hath given all this; the Indians call it 'Guanahaní.' "

Then he sailed on and never returned to Guanahaní.

The actual meeting of Columbus with the Arawaks must have been filled with deep drama for both parties. Certainly the Arawaks, who had never seen such huge ships with so many spreading sails, or white men with their amazing clothes and armor, must have been awed and perplexed. And Columbus must have been stirred and heartened by the sight of land and of other human beings.

For days he had been desperately uneasy. Fear and despair had seized his crew, whose eyes told them they were in the center of an endless disk of ocean. They had come looking for land to the west—but perhaps there was no land there. The straining of eyes to see land which never materialized had filled them with disappointment. Disappointment turned to fear, and fear to terror. A fury surged through the crew and they rebelled. Columbus had calmed their fears for several days, but in their torment they became mutinous. Now thoroughly uneasy himself, Columbus promised that he would return to Spain if land were not sighted in two or three days. Even more eagerly, all eyes searched for signs of land, but as each day wore on this infinity of ocean remained terrifyingly empty. But not completely empty: some fish were seen. But fish were of the sea and gave no hint of land. Then there were birds. Perhaps they were land birds! Once there was a floating branch with berries on it. Columbus scrutinized every sign, prayerfully hopeful, but there is a tinge of despair in the terseness of this portion of his Journal.

Archibald MacLeish has translated these laconic statements of tiny specks of prophecy that land might be in the offing into his poem, "America Was Promises":

America was always promises.
From the first voyage and the first ship there were promises—
"The tropic bird which does not sleep at sea"
"The great mass of dark heavy clouds which is a sign"
"The whale which is an indication"
"The stick appearing to be carved with iron"
"The stalk with roseberries"
"and all these signs were from the west"
"and all night heard birds passing"

The tension had been heightened by the Crown's offer of 10,000 maravedis (approximately $70 in U.S. currency, and about one years' pay for a seaman) to the first man to sight land. An indication of his own state of nervous excitement may be gained by Columbus' claim of the prize for himself on the evening of Thursday, October 11, when he announced he could see lights ahead in the darkness, lights that he said went up and down and then flickered out.

This historic meeting between the Old and the New Worlds—a meeting that would change the course of history—is particularly vivid to me. I have stood on the very spot where Columbus landed on Long Bay (at least as close as intelligent research has been able to suggest), and it is not difficult to visualize the Santa Maria, the

4

Pinta, and the Niña lying at anchor perhaps less than a mile offshore, to see the long boats being rowed in and pulled up on the
beach, and then Columbus himself stepping out of the boat surrounded by his officers and men on the white coral sand. Already
a band of natives had gathered, eagerly crowding around such
extraordinary strangers. Who could these people be? He had no
idea who they were, nor could he understand a word they said.

In the Prologue of his Journal Columbus had written, "I thought
to write down upon this voyage in great detail from day to day all
that I should do and see, and encounter, as hereinafter shall be
seen." So what does he set down after the excitement of his first
glimpse of human beings in the land his eyes had strained to see
for so many despairing days? What was his impression of these
people of the New World?

*They all go quite naked as their mother bore them; and also the
women, although I didn't see more than one really young girl. All
that I saw were young men, none of them more than 30 years old,
very well built, of very handsome bodies and very fine faces; the
hair coarse, almost like the hair of a horse's tail, and short, the hair
they wear over their eyebrows, except for a hank behind that they
wear long and never cut . . . and they are the color of the Canary
Islanders, neither black nor white . . . . They are generally fairly
tall and good looking, well built.*

Columbus and other mariners from Spain or Portugal had
journeyed to Africa on their earlier voyages and had seen native
tribes there. They had learned that the best approach to unknown
people, with whose language they were completely unfamiliar, was
to make them small gifts of beads or other ornaments. In accord-
ance with that practice the natives were given

*red caps and . . . glass beads, which they hung on their necks, and
many other things of slight value, in which they took much pleasure. They remained so much our [friends] that it was a marvel,
later they came swimming to the ships' boats in which we were,
and brought us parrots and cotton thread in skeins and darts and
many other things, and we swopped them for other things that we
gave them, such as little glass beads and hawks' bells.*

The friendliness and generosity of the Arawaks deeply impressed
Columbus. "They are so ingenuous and free with all they have,
that no one would believe it who has not seen it: of anything they

5

possess if it be asked of them they never say no; on the contrary they invite you to share it and show as much love as if their hearts went with it. . . . I forbade that they be given things so worthless as broken bits of crockery and of green glass, lace-points [brass tips for shoelaces], although when they could get them they thought they had the best jewel in the world."

But even as he stood in amazement watching their magnanimity, he felt an uneasiness at the cupidity of his fellow Spaniards and made a gesture of rebuking them for giving worthless bits of broken glass for the things they wanted. Ironically, no one would betray these people more than Columbus himself, whose obsessive greed for gold would plunge them into slavery.

But what did the Arawaks think of the Spaniards? The first expression comes two days later, on Sunday, October 14, when Columbus took three ships' boats north along the leeward side of San Salvador, as he said

to see the other side, which was the eastern side, . . . and also to see the villages; and soon I saw two or three, and the people who all came to the beach, shouting and giving thanks to God. Some brought us water, others, other things to eat. Others, when they saw that I didn't care to go ashore, plunged into the sea swimming, and came out, and we understood that they asked us if we had come from the sky. And one old man got into the boat, and others shouted in loud voices to all men and women, 'Come and see the men who come from the sky, bring them food and drink.' Many came and many women, each with something, giving thanks to God, throwing themselves on the ground, they raised their hands to the sky, and then shouted to us to come ashore. . . .

Reading his Journal we ask ourselves how Columbus could have understood what they were saying. It had been only forty-eight hours since his first contact with the natives of Guanahaní (Island of the Iguanas), much too short a time to develop even a smattering of one another's tongues. True, Columbus had an interpreter aboard. Anticipating language difficulties, and on the then generally accepted premise that Arabic was the mother of all languages, he had brought with him one Luis de Torres, who spoke Hebrew as well as some Arabic. But Arawakan is, of course, totally unrelated to Hebrew or Arabic, so de Torres' linguistic ability was useless. Neither would Spanish make any sense to an Arawak. But the language of pantomime is universal, as is the spirit of friendliness and generosity so unmistakeably conveyed by the Arawaks in their actions.

We should remember, too, that Columbus was a devout man. Under his command services were held every day at which the Pater Noster, Ave Maria, and Credo were recited, and vespers ended each evening with the singing of Salve Regina. So when Columbus wrote that "the people who all came to the beach, shouting and giving thanks to God," he was attributing to the Arawaks what would have been the normal Spaniard's response instilled by generations of the Church's ritual disciplines.

What a turmoil of thought must have raced through the Admiral's mind as he saw these naked people. These were not the kind of men he had expected to see, because Columbus believed himself to be in the Japanese Islands—either there or, if he had missed Cipangu, heading for Cathay. He carried letters from Ferdinand and Isabella to the Grand Khan of China. He was looking for palaces heavily plated with gold and courtiers dressed in the finest silks and brocades, wearing pearls and precious stones, all according to the Book of Ser Marco Polo, with whose writing he was thoroughly familiar and a copy of which he probably carried with him.

What ran through his mind as he viewed these naked natives of Guanahaní?

"They—had—nothing" is the bitter comment he set down in his Journal. Nor were there any orchards, gardens, or herds of cattle to provide sumptuous banquets. In the Arawak villages he saw only palm-thatched huts and scattered patches of a plant we know as manioc, whose roots provided the starch for the bread these naked people had brought him. No jewels, no gold, no riches anywhere!

This must have brought great disappointment to the usually buoyant and optimistic Admiral. For ten years he had been telling the merits of a quick passage to Asia, the Indies as it was then called. He personally had approached King John of Portugal and King Charles VIII of France, while his brother Bartholomew had seen Henry VII of England. Before all these monarchs had been spread the lure of the vast wealth to be obtained from China and Japan, whose kings or emperors would, he said, be glad to recognize the sovereignty of a European ruler. For six years he had waited in Spain for support from Ferdinand and Isabella, promising treasure so abundant that Ferdinand would be able to lead his troops to the recovery of the Holy Sepulchre.

That gold was much upon Columbus' mind is evident from his earliest statements. On Saturday, October 13—his second day at San Salvador—he wrote:

And I was attentive and worked hard to know if there was any gold, and saw that some of them wore a little piece hanging from a thing like a needlecase which they have in the nose; and by signs I could understand that, going to the [south], . . . there was a king there who had great vessels of it and possessed a lot. I urged them to go there, and later saw that they were not inclined to the journey. I decided to wait until tomorrow afternoon and then depart to the [southwest], since, as many of them informed me, there should be land to the [south], [southwest], and [northwest], and that they of the [northwest] used to come and fight them many times . . . .

Columbus had not reached China or the Indies as he believed, but merely a tiny island in a great ocean, a forerunner of what was to prove to be two large continents which he and hundreds of other explorers would need lifetimes to discover. With such a totally unknown task ahead, he "decided to wait till tomorrow afternoon" before starting.

However, the information the natives had given him proved correct. To the south lay Hispaniola, later found to be the main source of gold on his first voyage. The island to the southwest would be Cuba. As to the land to the northwest, whence people "used to come to fight them many times"—could this be Florida?

This first meeting, how portentous it was! In retrospect how far beyond the imaginations of its participants. It was truly a meeting of East and West, an encounter that almost doubled the size of the known world and opened to the people of three continents a new home, incredibly greater than the kingdom of Ferdinand and Isabella.

But for the people of Guanahaní, and for the Amerinds of all the Caribbean islands, the future was to bring utter extinction. For them the drama that began that day was to end in total tragedy.

Not a single Arawak is alive today on any Caribbean island.

As the years passed and the existence of a New World to be had for the taking became general knowledge in the Old World, the Caribbean islands were settled by Europeans; even the smaller and less attractive ones became occupied. Often the new inhabitants neither knew nor cared what Columbus had named the particular island. Moreover, by that time the Arawaks, in their effort to escape enslavement, had deserted these smaller islands, so that none was left to identify Guanahaní or other islands and different names were adopted.

Historically, the island we now call San Salvador was shown on John Thornton's chart of the Bahamas in 1700 as Watling's Island, named for some buccaneer about whose existence there now seems to be doubt.[1] Actually, over the course of the centuries the real location of Columbus' landfall on San Salvador had become lost. Controversies arose as to which of the many islands of the Bahamas was the precise spot where Columbus first landed. It was only through the efforts of the Reverend Chrysostom Schreiner that the name of San Salvador was "restored" to the island in 1926, by the assent of the British government, and the name Watling's Island abandoned. However, this decision was hotly argued and rival claims were made for the name by nearby Rum Cay and even by the Caicos and Turk's Islands two hundred miles to the southeast.

Also suspicions were advanced about the reliability of Columbus' statements. Quite a point was made about his "hallucinations" when he claimed to have seen flickering lights on the evening of October 11, 1492, under conditions which some people declared to be impossible. No one, they said, could see a light he described as being like a little wax candle falling and rising and then flickering out, when he was so far out at sea. His detractors point out that since land was actually sighted four hours later, at 2 A.M., Friday, October 12, his ship would have been about thirty miles offshore at 10 P.M. on Thursday, October 11, a distance far too great to permit seeing the flame of a candle.

In June, 1966, I attended an archeological conference in San Salvador on ancient cultures of the Caribbean area at which Ruth Durlacher Wolper was hostess. The controversy about the identification of San Salvador and the nature of the flickering light had attracted Mrs. Wolper's interest when she came to the island some ten years earlier. She is a persistent woman, and it is easy to see behind her pleasant smile a quite determined spirit. It is much to her credit that she has painstakingly demonstrated that every one of the statements made by Columbus in his Journal, covering the four days he was at or near San Salvador, can be applied precisely to geographic features readily identifiable on the San Salvador of today. She has described her findings in a Smithsonian publication

9

entitled "A New Theory Identifying the Locale of Columbus's Light, Landfall and Landing" (No. 4534, Sept. 11, 1964).

The conclusions reached by Ruth Wolper have been checked by no less a navigator and scholar than Admiral Samuel Eliot Morison. She also obtained from the American Museum Hayden Planetarium in New York the time at which the position of the rising moon would duplicate the exact conditions Columbus had encountered on October 11, 1492. This, the Planetarium said, would occur on October 21, 1959, a time of year comparable to the arrival of Columbus. Mrs. Wolper obtained a launch, the 110-foot *M. V. Drake*, through the kind cooperation of Sir George W. K. Roberts, president of the Bahamas Legislative Council, and took up positions at sea corresponding to those that Columbus would have taken 467 years earlier.

The *M. V. Drake* first chose a spot about thirty miles east of San Salvador at 9:30 P.M., about half an hour earlier than the time at which Columbus had seen the flickering light, presumably from about the same position. It was pitch dark; the moon, six days beyond the full, had not yet risen, and all aboard strained their eyes to see if anything would be visible. Cooperative natives had agreed to place lights on the top of High Cay and other spots along the nearby coast, where the elevation is about one hundred feet above sea level.

A few seconds after 9:45 P.M., Ruth Wolper and others aboard saw two flashes of light pierce the darkness and then flicker out. This occurred several times during the next hour. Thus she had not only demonstrated that a light could be seen twenty-five to thirty miles away from San Salvador, but also had been successful in duplicating the phenomenon of the flickering and disappearing light that Columbus had reported.

Just what was the cause of the flickering?

Mrs. Wolper had noticed that at night, before going to bed, the natives lit smudge fires to drive off the sand flies and mosquitoes. Periodically they added a few palmetto leaves to the fires. The wax on the leaves caused the fires to burn up brightly, then the flame quickly subsided and the smoke spread through the air, partly discouraging the sand flies. I watched this technique in operation during my stay on the island and was grateful for its partial efficiency, for nowhere in the West Indies have I encountered such vicious insect attacks as on San Salvador. Probably both the topography of the island and the spot where we were located were responsible; the numerous inland lakes provide made-to-order breeding places for mosquitoes and the lee shore exposure accounts for the sand fly hordes.

As demonstrated, it was the bright flash that occurs when the waxy palmetto leaves are intermittently added to the fire, followed by a smoky and therefore dark period, that furnish a plausible explanation for the flashing and dying light that Columbus saw at 10 P.M. on October 11, 1492. It is of interest that Columbus did not say he saw the light of a little wax candle rising and falling when he was some thirty miles offshore. What he did say was that it *looked* like the flame of a little wax candle. What he saw was the flare-up and dying down of a fair-sized fire; it was the palmetto wax that caused flashes to reach perhaps two or three feet above the fire. Columbus had been an accurate observer of this phenomenon.

Mrs. Wolper's observation cruise gave added substantiation to the recordings of the Admiral of the Ocean Sea. The launch continued on its course through the blackness of the night toward High Cay on the southeastern tip of San Salvador. At 11 P.M. on October 21, 1959, the *Drake* was seven and a half miles from the island and the face of High Cay began to glow like a long narrow lens shape from the reflected light of the recently risen moon, shining from behind the stern of the ship. The white cliff face of High Cay is 114 feet above sea level and more than half a mile long, and since the similar but lower islands of Pokus Cay and Middle Cay are so close and in line with High Cay, they would probably appear to be about two miles of continuous coastal white cliffs when viewed from approximately eight miles out at sea.

It was this reflected moon glow from High Cay and its neighbors that the seaman Rodrigo de Triana had seen from the mainmast of the Pinta. His call of "Tierra! Tierra!" promptly brought Columbus on deck to observe the land which he saw as a "White Head of Sand." The cautious Admiral ordered most of the sails lowered and commanded the ships to jog until daybreak, which would have been three hours later, about 5 A.M.

Mrs. Wolper meticulously identified the capes and bays along the south and west sides of the island and showed that these follow the descriptions given by Columbus. She located his first landing at Long Bay on the west coast of San Salvador. At this point she erected a simple concrete cross with a memorial plaque that says: ON OR NEAR THIS SPOT, CHRISTOPHER COLUMBUS LANDED, OCT. 12, 1492.

11

II

How We Discovered the Arawaks

My first active encounter with Arawak culture took place nearly five hundred years after Columbus had met them on San Salvador. It occurred on Antigua, a Caribbean island the Admiral never visited. For his purposes a landing there would have been time wasted. He would have found no gold or hints of any, and the everyday possessions of the people there—objects which we have spent painstaking years excavating in the form of artifacts—would have been spurned by him as trash. It was the chance discovery of just such trash, a handful of broken bits of pottery, that set me on the trail of the Arawaks.

Antigua, one of the Leeward Islands of the West Indies (Map 1), lies in the corridor of the northwest trade winds, latitude 17° north, longitude 62° west. A north-south line drawn through the island would pass through Nova Scotia, near Halifax two thousand miles due north, and through Argentina, near Buenos Aires three thousand miles due south. The same line would run through Trinidad five hundred miles to the south. West of Antigua, on the seventeenth parallel, lies Oaxaca in Mexico, and much further west, Hawaii and Luzon. To the east, halfway around the globe, lie the fabled cities of Timbuktu, Khartoum, and Bombay.

Antigua is oval shaped, twelve miles wide and sixteen miles long, roughly the area of Brooklyn and Manhattan. But there the resemblance ends, and even the impression of size conveyed by the analogy is deceptive because so much is crowded into New York—people, skyscrapers, activity—that it seems larger. Seen from an airplane, which is how I first saw it in 1954, Antigua looks quite small, like a pearl that has rolled off a broken strand into the clear waters of the Caribbean. On closer approach to Coolidge Field, the island's landing strip, a fringe of coconut palms appears against the blue sea beyond, and then in a few seconds the same palms are silhouetted against the sky of a slightly paler blue.

A silhouette against the distant horizon is all that Columbus saw of Antigua as he sailed about thirty miles west of it on his second voyage of discovery in 1493. He had guided his caravels through Dominica Passage, which separates the Leeward from the Windward islands, and was scudding along the inside arc of the Lesser Antilles, which curves like a great scythe from Grenada, just north of Trinidad, to Puerto Rico, the beginning of the Greater Antilles. He named the islands he sighted after the shrines of the Virgin as he remembered them in Spain. The large island north of the Passage he named Santa Maria de Guadeloupe after the Virgin at Estremadura; the next one, a tiny island thirty-three miles to the northwest, he named Santa Maria de Montserrate after the monastery near Barcelona where Ignatius Loyola later dedicated himself to the Virgin; and the low silhouette to the northeast he called Santa Maria la Antigua after the miracle-working Virgin in the Cathedral of Seville.

Columbus sailed on westward and the warring European nations in general neglected Antigua until 1632, when the British established a colony there. For about three hundred years it was a sugar-growing island, like most of the other Antilles, but the climate is too dry for good sugar crops and today Antigua is primarily a winter resort. It is also the site of a tracking station for following Apollo missions to the moon.

It was the climate that first attracted me to Antigua. For some years my wife and I had been looking for a warm January vacation spot. Arizona, Bermuda, and Florida had all proven too cold and Jamaica too humid and full of tourists. Cuba, in the 1953 pre-Castro days, we found delightful, but the January gales sweeping down from the north, locally called "Nortes," ruled out swimming several times in the month and left the beaches strewn with stinging Portuguese men-of-war.

The following year I learned that Adlai Stevenson had just returned from the Mill Reef Club in Antigua where, he said, he had had a perfect rest. From his description it sounded like a splendid winter haven for what I thought was an overworked executive, and we arrived there on December 1, 1954. It was all Mr. Stevenson had said and more. We have returned every year, and since my retirement in 1957 have been about six months of each year at Mill

Reef (Map 2), spending the better part of my time excavating and trying to reconstruct the story of the island's Arawak aborigines.

Before coming to Antigua the term "Arawak" was known to me only through occasional, sketchy references in archeological publications and from museums where I had found the pieces labeled "Arawak" interesting, although much more primitive than the Mayan and Aztec material with which I was more familiar. An interest in primitive cultures had occupied my nonbusiness hours for several years, and it was this interest that prompted me to ask, during our first week at Mill Reef, "Who were the aborigines who used to inhabit Antigua and the Lesser Antilles?"

"Caribs," was the general answer, but no one seemed to know or care when the Caribs were there or from whence they had come. And I certainly never dreamed of the effort, study, and travel in strange places that would be necessary to answer those questions!

Like every visitor to Antigua, I visited English Harbour (Map 2) where Nelson's fleet had been outfitted before the battle of Trafalgar. The Admiral's house and other buildings in the dockyard have been restored. In the small museum were a few stone axes and potsherds labeled "Carib" (all of which later turned out to be Arawak material). The labels described the capture of the governor's wife by raiding Caribs in the seventeenth century, and her alleged reluctance to leave the Carib chieftain and his thatched hut in Dominica, a hundred miles to the south. The map of Antigua (Map 2) shows an "Indian-town Point" and an "Indian-town Creek" but a brief visit revealed no evidence of Indian occupation. The present inhabitants guessed that the "Caribs" might have lived there and repeated the tale of the governor's fickle wife.

After returning to Connecticut, I gathered a few books on the history of the West Indies and learned that Arawaks had inhabited the islands of the Antilles and that the warlike Caribs had driven them out of the Lesser Antilles "some time before the coming of Columbus." At the Museum of the American Indian in New York City the scholarly and friendly Frederick Dockstader furnished references to the Arawaks and showed artifacts from the West Indies, most of which were labeled "Arawak." One piece, an attractive pottery bowl, had actually come from Antigua. On our second trip to Antigua in 1955, I arrived well supplied with books.

The pleasant Mill Reef Club is the product of the foresight of Robertson Ward, an internationally known architect whose beautifully designed houses are famous throughout the Caribbean.

"Happy" Ward had known the islands before World War II and in 1947, looking for the perfect spot for a winter home, made a reconnaissance of the Virgin Islands and the British West Indies from Grenada to St. Kitts. Antigua was his choice, but before making his final decision he flew around its coastline and selected the stretch of lovely bays along the southeast shore as offering the best possibility for attractive homes and excellent swimming. There are five bays, all protected by coral reefs, with fine white-sand beaches backed by hills which provide dramatic sites for houses facing into the breeze of the prevailing trade winds. About fifteen hundred acres were secured and the Mill Reef Club was organized. The name was suggested by an old conical sugar mill at the entrance to the property (now the Old Mill Arawak Museum) and by the reefs that make swimming attractive and comfortable.

Happy and I had touched briefly on the island's history and prehistory the year before. Therefore on my return in 1955, I told him of the museum visits, the displays I had seen, and the books on Caribbean history I had brought to Antigua. Happy was sure the Arawaks had been in Antigua and neighboring islands, although he knew of no artifacts identifiable as Arawak having been found there. It was strange that I had brought up the subject of Arawaks, he said, because only the day before the name had come up at a party he had attended in St. Croix. Among the guests was Henry Gross, the water dowser about whom Kenneth Roberts had written.

"You're a long way from Kennebunkport, Henry," Happy said. "What's a Maine man doing in St. Croix?"

"Looking for water."

"They need it here," Happy admitted. "So do we in Antigua. Tell me, Henry, how do you go about finding water? I don't mean the way the rod twists in your hands to point down to an underground vein. Just how do you·know where to walk with your wand?"

"Go by the map," Henry said laconically.

"Will you show me how you do it?" Happy spread out a map of the Mill Reef area. Gross studied it silently and said, "Try here, and here. And over here." He drew a cross at each designated spot.

Happy acknowledged his appreciation by pouring another round of drinks. Then he asked, "Henry, can you dowse for anything other than water?"

"Such as what?"

Happy said there had been Arawak Indians on many of the

Caribbean Islands and he wondered if they'd ever got to Antigua. And if so, whether any buried relics could be found. Henry nodded, took the map, and retreated into himself. Finally he indicated another location.

"Dig here. And over there," he said, marking the spots this time with circles.

Happy tucked the map into his pocket and the talk drifted to other subjects. "Let's have a look at Henry's markings," he said, showing me the map. The marked locations were only a few minutes' walk from where we sat. "I'm going to turn this over to my son-in-law, Oggie Starr," he said. "Oggie's the most enthusiastic of the English Harbour regimental button collectors. Maybe he'd like to give Henry's Indian sites a try."

The next afternoon Happy and a very excited Oggie appeared at my house carrying a handful of bits of broken pottery. "Believe it or not, Gross's marks have led us to something!" Happy said. "See what Oggie has found. I don't know if they're Arawak, but they look old to me."

They poured the pottery bits out before me and I examined them one by one. "They're old, all right," I agreed, "and they certainly look like the sherds I've seen in museums labeled as Arawak." Now I was as excited as Oggie and we all hurried off to the site of the discovery. There we checked the map. These were indeed marked sites, but wasn't there something wrong?

"Good heavens, Oggie!" Happy said. "You've dug at the places Henry Gross cross-marked for water instead of those he circled for Indian remains!"

Thus in this unscientific manner we stumbled on the trail of the Arawaks, misreading a map and digging for artifacts where a dowser had indicated we would find water.

Early next morning, while it was still cool, Happy and I set out to do a bit of digging on our own. I was anxious to explore because I couldn't accept the idea of a water dowser knowing where to find artifacts. Kenneth Roberts had created a wide reputation for Henry Gross. I hadn't read his books, but had heard friends discuss Gross's alleged ability to detect a spring, perhaps a hundred feet below ground, by some "force" the flowing water was able to exert on a Y-shaped witch-hazel rod, making it turn downward in his hands. I just couldn't believe in such mysterious powers of divination.

Later, when I read Roberts' books, I was amazed at the accumulation of data on Gross's activities. Without a doubt he had been a great help to many people in locating supplies of underground water. He told them where to dig and he was often right. Not always, but he made no claims of one hundred per cent performance. In fairness I had to admit that even when drawing on the strictest scientific methodology and wide geological knowledge, our great oil companies don't always strike gas or oil. They drill many dry wells. I don't know whether their performance surpasses that of Henry Gross, but I do understand a little of the reasoning behind their selection of spots to test. I can also see the logic behind some of Gross's choices, but for the life of me I can't see what the Y-shaped stick has to do with it. I know of no scientific principles by which a source of water, twenty or a hundred or five hundred feet below ground, can convey any message or transmit any force to a human being carrying a wand on the surface.

I was thinking in this vein as we walked along the island road leading to Gross's circled digspots and wondering also about Happy's reaction to dowsing for artifacts. He is a brilliant architect with a sure eye for the right place to build. He is very much of an individualist and reacts as a creative artist does to challenge or irritation. I have seen him reject a suggestion, regardless of its apparent merit, and then come up with a better idea. The suggestion had been the irritant that set his mind working. Now, how would Henry Gross's suggestions about excavation sites affect him?

As though he were reading my mind he said, "I doubt if Henry knows where to look for Arawaks. Let's find our own places to dig." We had arrived in a dip where the road crosses a sort of V-shaped trough that continues on either side. "Here's the spot," Happy said. "There might have been water here before they felled all the trees."

It intrigued me that Happy had selected another place that Gross had X-marked as an underground water location. Of course the Arawaks would have needed water, and probably would have chosen village sites where it could be readily obtained.

"It was perhaps a bit swampy when the first inhabitants were here," I said. "Let's move up the slope a bit."

It was a gentle slope, and when we had gone perhaps a hundred feet and reached ground about ten feet higher than the low place, we began to dig a small pit about a foot square. In the top six inches we came upon a few pieces of broken pots. "They look old and just like the ones Oggie found yesterday," I said. "Perhaps these are Arawak."

Happy made no comment, but paced off fifty feet and started another pit. Same results: potsherds right near the surface! We looked at each other, grinned, and made two more excavations at fifty-foot intervals.

"Seems like there are potsherds everywhere," said Happy. "Let's take a look for the most likely place where people would have lived." His architect's eye was choosing a site. Eventually he indicated a place a hundred yards or so to the east, a still higher location commanding a view of the sea. "That's where the Gould house is located," he said. "Maybe the Arawaks would have liked that spot too." Happy is proud of that site. The house has a fine view of the sea both to northeast and southeast, and these are also the directions of the trade winds which keep the house cool even in midday sun. He turned to me, and from the poise of his head, with its thatch of hair reminding me of that other great architect, Frank Lloyd Wright, I knew I was about to receive a lecture.

"The Arawaks probably weren't interested in esthetics," he said, "but here they would have a clear view of the sea in case of enemy approach."

I had spent forty years as head of a research organization and knew the best tactic with creative people was to raise just enough minor objections to act as prods, a technique developed long ago by that greatest of gadflies, Socrates.

"But Happy," I said, "I doubt if the Arawaks saw one canoe load of strangers every ten or twenty years. Island hopping hadn't been discovered."

"Oh, yes, it had," he snapped. "How do you think all these islands of the Caribbean were populated if they didn't hop from one to another?"

I tried another barb. "They probably had no clothes and wouldn't have liked the night wind blowing on their naked bodies as they slept." I launched that one because Happy had chosen for his own homesite at Mill Reef a location in the lee of a hill.

"It is cool when you lie uncovered at night, even with the temperature at 78°," he granted. Actually, the daytime temperature throughout the year is between 80° and 84°. You are not conscious of much difference between the weather in January and July unless the trade winds die down, which occasionally happens. The coldest night I have experienced was when the thermometer dove to 70°.

"But there's a tiny hill between the sea and where we stand," he said. "And it's only a hundred yards or so to Little Deep Bay where they could have hauled their canoes."

On the basis of this reasoning we selected for our first excavation site a flat place at the top of the slope and spread out our paraphernalia. At that time I had never seen a "dig" in operation, but my summer's reading had indicated what we would need, and to the thinly veiled indignation of our household staff I had assembled a motley but efficient kit from the kitchen equipment.

Happy, of course, is never without his measuring tape. With this he laid out a series of three-foot squares. Then, armed with cutlasses—as the machete is called in the English islands—we cleared away the prickly brush and cactus and started digging our respective squares. I had requisitioned a trowel from the gardener and Happy had a real mason's trowel. Cautiously we began to pry up the soil an inch at a time, removing by hand the bits of pottery that appeared immediately and placing them in a plastic basin.

In a few minutes there were a dozen or more sizable sherds in each container, and from the curvature of some of the pieces Happy judged them to be fragments of a pot about twenty inches in diameter.

"Quite a big circular pot," he said.

"The outer surfaces are blackened," I pointed out. "Probably a cooking pot."

A hand lens is as inevitable a part of my pocket equipment as a tape measure is of Happy's. Studying the sherds with its help I could see bits of shell and grains of sand on the broken edges, evidently part of the tempering material used to give body to the clay mass. The sherds looked much alike, except for one that had a bright red surface.

"Wonder why they painted the pot red on the outside," Happy said. "Was it just for looks?"

"I would guess that this was a water-storage vessel, since the sherd shows no blackening of the outside," I suggested, "and that the red oxide was rubbed into the pores to make the object more water-tight."

Happy agreed. He was trying to fit several sherds together. "They ought to belong to the same pot," he said. "They are the same color and you can see that they have the same curvature because one lies inside the other pretty closely. But when you put them edge to edge, they don't match."

"You've got a real jigsaw puzzle, Happy, and a lot of the pieces are missing."

He kept on trying and in a minute gave a whoop of delight, holding up two fragments that did match. "You see? The edges mesh perfectly. But most of these sherds don't belong to this pot because, even though they look alike, they are not of the same thickness. You can easily feel the difference. Your finger sense is more accurate than your eyesight."

Next we turned to the task of rubbing the accumulated soil through the galvanized iron-mesh sieve I had improvised. I was proud of that sieve. It looked exactly like those I'd seen in a book picturing a group excavating in Mesopotamia. As we rubbed the soil over the mesh surface a cloud of dust arose, covering us with a layer that formed a sticky paste on sweat-soaked arms, faces, and clothes. We shifted to windward and continued until nothing was left on the screen but a few roots which we tossed aside, a few rough stones, and some broken shells. We examined each stone, but saw nothing to indicate that any had been used by man. They were apparently just pieces of natural limestone from the rock formation that outcropped in several nearby spots. We discarded them.

I don't know shells, but Happy said that the dozen or more fragments on the screen were pieces of what the natives of Antigua call *wilks*. "They may be what we would call whelks."

At this moment Mrs. Erl Gould, owner of the nearby house, drove up and stopped. "What on earth are you two doing?" she called. "Looking for pirates' gold?"

"Digging for Arawaks," I answered.

"Are you finding anything?"

"Come and see," we invited, and she picked her way between the pits and over our tools and plastic pails. I dropped a couple of the curved gray sherds into her outstretched hand and she studied them with interest.

"How do you know they come from Arawak pots?" she asked.

"We don't," I admitted, "but we think they may have been ancient cooking vessels because they don't look like any modern pottery."

"Could they be from slave days of an old plantation?"

"I doubt it," Happy said. "This would have been a dry part of the island even back in plantation days and the land doesn't look as if it had ever been planted in cane. But you are a shell expert, Kate. What kind of shells are these?"

21

Fig. 1. *Eventually we acquired about half a bowl (Florence, wife of author, sorting sherds).*

Kate Gould is an enthusiastic sheller and has one of the best collections in Mill Reef. She placed our specimens immediately. "Oh, they are from the West Indian Top Shell, so named because it's shaped like a top. *Cittarium pica* I think the scientific name is." She wished us good luck and we returned to our digging.

As we dug we discussed a suitable name for our first excavation site. We settled on Brooksite, after the hypothetical stream that might have run at the bottom of the slope several hundred years ago when the land was heavily forested (Map 2). It would have been the Arawaks' source of water.

We had set ourselves the stint of finishing our 3 x 3 foot squares, three inches deep, but when the sun reached its zenith it go too hot to dig. We were about to quit when Happy struck another cache of red sherds. "Here's more of the red stuff and two pieces mesh," he said. In a minute he had four pairs whose edges coincided perfectly and one group of three that fitted. I was about to say he was lucky, but refrained since I was beginning to suspect that Happy's eye for this sort of puzzle was much better than mine. As if to confirm my suspicions he looked over my lot, now risen to about fifty sherds, and indicated two pieces.

"Try them," he said. "They will fit." Indeed they did, and I felt a bit abashed at not having recognized them as mates. Eventually we acquired about half a bowl (Figure 1).

We had almost finished our squares when I had my own lucky find—a red sherd on which curved lines had been scratched to form an open spiral design. I couldn't have been more pleased. To me this was *real* buried treasure! It was our first contact with the esthetic sensitivity of the Arawaks and we decided it was a perfect time to quit for the day.

We collected our finds and tools and made our way home with more than a hundred potsherds. Quite a haul, we felt, but a dirty one, and we proceeded to take ourselves and our sherds into the sea for a communal bath. It was hard to say which were the more dust-encrusted—the potsherds or ourselves. But freed of the soil of centuries the pottery bits were soon gleaming brightly in the sunshine and a long swim in the lively waters relaxed our muscles, cramped by hours of stooping and bending. We were thirsty too, and corrected this with a long gin and tonic.

Happy picked up my red potsherd and, taking off his spectacles, held it close to his eyes to examine it better. "The line is not very cleanly drawn. Maybe they scratched it with a stick," he said. "But it's kind of a nice sweeping curve. It's simple. Our Arawaks had good taste."

Friends arrived and we displayed the results of our morning's work. Most of the group were only mildly interested and turned to discussion of the long putt sunk on the second green or the lucky out from the sand trap on the eighth fairway. But two were curious and handled the sherds with interest.

"When are you going again?" one asked.

"Tomorrow."

"I'd like to go too," the second volunteered. "What time?"

They were on hand the next morning and soon we were joined by three more, two men and a girl who had heard about digs at a dinner party. We assigned a 3 x 3 foot plot to each, and soon all were busily scraping the soil. In half an hour everyone was hot, damp, and dirty-faced, but evidently having a wonderful time. After our previous day's experience Happy and I were regarded as experts and expected to explain everything that was found. The newcomers' plots yielded more of what we had unearthed the day before: broken shells and plain potsherds. But now Happy and I were down to the six-inch level and conch shells were appearing in numbers. There were many other kinds of shells—scallops, turkey wings, mangrove oysters, keyhole limpets, periwinkles, and some which none of us recognized. We would have to make a collection of ancient Arawak shells. Fishbones were common too, and so were land-crab claws, but we threw these out. Later, when Clayton Ray, a Harvard biologist, showed us how much data about the Arawaks' food habits we were discarding, we became much more interested in collecting the bones. Indeed, one of the lessons we were slowest in learning was the necessity of saving everything we dug and recording the position where each item appeared in the midden. A discarded rock might be a hearthstone.

By now we had learned to recognize rim-edge pieces and to notice that there were variations in the shape of the rims. By the end of the second day's digging we were automatically separating plain from colored sherds and further grouping them into rims, bases, and rounded walls of the pots.

Lucy Brody, the girl in the group, came up with a sherd that puzzled us all. It was a rim, but obviously not from a pot or bowl since it was quite flat. The rim was only a quarter inch above the inside level of the dish. We couldn't imagine what a dish with a rim like this could have been used for. Then two other rim pieces turned up which meshed with the first. They suggested a very large flat plate, possibly thirty inches in diameter judging by the very slight curvature of the rim.

We were stumped. Then the bright young lady turned to me. "Didn't you say the Arawaks lived mainly on cassava?" she asked. "Well then, couldn't these be pieces of a griddle on which they baked cassava bread?"

Taken aback by this clean reasoning, we agreed that Lucy's theory was plausible. Even Happy, who in his eagerness to explain things frequently squelches other peoples' suggestions, bought this one. "By God, Lucy, I believe you're right!" he applauded. "Let's find the rest of it." But that was all of the griddle we turned up that day.

We examined the sherds more closely and noticed that the flat face, where presumably the cassava cake would have lain to bake, was quite smooth. The under side was rough. All this fitted Lucy's theory, for the fire would have licked up under the lower side and there would have been no need for it to be smooth. The shallow rim, we decided, probably held the cassava meal and governed the thickness of the disk of bread.

At the end of the second day we had accumulated about 350 sherds to be taken home and washed. Not so many per person as the first day, but the haul included the griddle sherds and these were destined to play an important part in our later studies.

That evening Happy spent some time fitting together the sherds and holding them in place with a little glue. In the morning he displayed a dozen or so examples, one being almost a third of a pot about ten inches in diameter, an aggregate of ten sherds. He pointed out that the inside surface of this bowl showed a series of ridges, clearly indicating that it had been made by coiling a long cylindrical "rod" of clay.

After that we dug every day. With our headstart Happy and I kept a few inches farther down than the others, and in a day or so we reached a depth of twelve inches. At this level we found more colored pottery and some interesting shapes began to appear. "The quality gets better the lower we go," Happy observed cheerfully. Then we came on a two-inch layer particularly rich in fishbones and what appeared to be bird-leg bones. Below this was a gray layer of ash which indicated a cooking hearth with stones sur- rounding it, presumably for supporting cooking vessels.

By this time I was beginning to feel uneasy that, in our archeo- logical ignorance, we might be spoiling an important site. I asked Happy what he thought about my writing to Professor Irving Rouse, of the Department of Anthropology at Yale, telling him what we were doing and inviting him to come down to see our finds and check our procedures. I knew Professor Rouse only slightly, but I was well aware of his standing as an archeologist and as the leading authority on the Caribbean prehistoric culture. He had begun his field studies in the Greater Antilles some thirty years earlier, publishing his work on Haiti in 1939, on Cuba in 1942, and on Puerto Rico in 1952. For more than a decade he had collabo- rated with Professor José M. Cruxent in Venezuela and also with Professor J. A. Bullbrook in Trinidad. If anyone could guide us and prevent us from error he could.

Happy agreed and I sent an airmail letter to Professor Rouse, describing what we had found and asking him to pay us a visit. The letter arrived at a fortunate time, the start of the Christmas holidays, and I was delighted to receive a cabled reply that he would arrive about New Years' and could spend ten days with us.

25

As I waited for Professor Rouse I became more and more uneasy about his visit. He was a busy scholar, and here was I, a rank amateur in archeological excavation, inviting him to fly 1,783 air miles to look at what might be Arawak artifacts—or equally well might be trash from the garbage midden of long-abandoned slave quarters.

Professor Rouse had published material about Arawaks in the Greater Antilles, but had not mentioned them in the Lesser Antilles. On the other hand, I reasoned that since Arawaks had been found in both Trinidad and Puerto Rico they either went south from Puerto Rico or north from Trinidad. Either way, they would have had to pass through the Lesser Antilles. And I couldn't believe that anyone in a dugout canoe would travel such distances without stopping at each island—including Antigua. Then, too, there were the griddle sherds. It all sounded plausible, but we couldn't be sure.

Professor Rouse arrived and immediately captivated Mill Reef with his modesty, consideration, and patience. A tall strapping man, he has a gentle but quizzical smile. He looked at the sherds and, to my immense relief, said, "Yes, these look like the Arawak sherds I have dug in other places." Then, to my delight, he added, "These are part of a cassava griddle and that is pretty good evidence of Arawaks."

"How old do you think they are?" asked one of our crew.

"Oh, I would say 1000 to 1500 A.D. But let's all go out in the morning to see what else we find."

Next morning Happy and I, with a large complement from our digging group, escorted Professor Rouse to Brookside. Happy and I were now down to a depth of three feet. Ben, as we soon were calling our mentor, was instantly on his knees examining the walls of the cut we had made. He exclaimed at the quantity of shells exposed in the walls, then studied the dump where we had pitched shells already dug.

"There are more shells than fishbones," he said. "Shellfish may have been the main source of protein to supplement their carbohydrate cassava diet. I don't see any animal bones, but animals would have been unlikely on such an isolated island. No animal could swim here from anywhere. The only animals possible would have been those that chanced to float here on logs or those brought deliberately by the Arawaks in their canoes."

He staked out another 3 x 3 foot square plot and began digging, while we watched every movement he made. To our comment that he dug a little faster and more vigorously than the rest of us, he replied, "This is exploratory digging, and from what I see of the sherds and other material you have turned up there isn't too great a chance of damaging anything important. It is good to get, first of all, a complete cross-section of the midden, so I am anxious to see the bottom. Also, I have to dig faster than you and Happy because, judging by the contour of the midden, you may have only another foot or so to go."

So we all dug a little faster, but still as gently as possible. Ben, keeping an eye on our progress, called our attention to a number of small stones we had been discarding.

"I think I would keep those," he said tactfully. "They are flint. Some of them are knives, like this piece." He held up a flattish, oval-shaped stone. "See, it has a long sharp cutting edge. Then, too, it fits the fingers nicely, perhaps for cutting fish. There is a flat place on top where the index finger could rest to give power and guidance to the cutting operation. At the base you can feel a place where the thumb and second finger fit conveniently to hold the knife firmly."

Each of us tried the operation, and discovered the flint was just right as a knife.

"This other flint may have been a chisel," Ben said, picking up a narrower stone. "Possibly even hafted to a wooden handle to permit better guidance and more forcible cutting action." Again we tried the stone, agreeing as to its efficiency. We felt a degree of wonderment at how a knowledgeable person could "bring to life" these bits of stone.

"This one was perhaps a scraper," Ben continued, selecting another stone from our discard pile. "The user would seize it at the broad wedge end. See, this is the rounded and smooth part of a flint pebble which an Arawak may have picked up in a stream, then cracked into these chips. With thumb on one side and first two fingers on the opposite, he had a strong and quite effective scraping tool."

"For scraping what?" someone asked.

"Oh, scales off a fish. Meat out of the carapace of a turtle or off the bones of a pelican or gull. Or even to fashion wood into a slender, smooth spear."

"But we thought the Arawaks were peaceful people!"

27

"Not for fighting, but to spear fish, or even birds, though they may have used a slingshot. Have you seen any small stone or pottery balls that might have been used as slingshot?"

We hadn't. But a couple of years later we would, and still later, in the Surinam jungle, I was to see Arawaks who could bring down a flying bird with a spherical stone about the size of a walnut.

Examining the flints, one of the diggers asked Ben, "Where would the Arawaks get their flint?"

"On an island with this kind of geology there is probably an abundance of it," Ben replied. And this is so, because later, in the limestone area of the island, we saw places where quantities of flint pebbles could be picked up.

The digging went on quietly, but every now and then Ben was shown a piece and asked about its purpose. His answers were always clear and simply expressed. After a while someone came upon a red sherd with white lines painted on it.

"I've been waiting to see if that would show up," Ben said. "It's quite typical of late Saladoid pottery." This was a term I heard for the first time that day, but one I was destined to hear a great deal later on. "It is pottery that was first painted red, or perhaps it would be more correct to say it was burnished by rubbing red ochre on the surface of the vessel with a smooth stone," he explained. "Then a simple geometric design in white was painted on the red background, probably with a thin flexible stick or possibly a band of palm frond cut to the width of the desired line."

The white, he said, was probably a clay, like bentonite, or one of the white marls to be found in the limestone portion of the island. It may have been mixed with cactus juice, which even today is used as the slightly sticky vehicle for applying "Bermuda pink" colors to house walls, so often seen in the tropics.

"This white-on-red potsherd is rather crude compared with pottery the Arawaks had produced much earlier," Ben continued. "As you go deeper, watch out for thinner pottery, so well fired that it is hard enough to give a ring when struck. When the white-on-red design is painted with much better craftsmanship, you will have evidence that the quite early Arawaks were here."

Two or three days later Ben spotted a sherd that Happy had just dug from the forty-eight-inch level. It was thin and hard, but not painted. He struck one sherd against the other and a metallic clink was heard. "That's the early Saladoid pottery, but not the white-on-red variety. Notice that the sherds are scarcer at this depth. You may be near the bottom, below which you will find only sterile ground. That is, there will be no artifacts."

We wanted to know how old the hard, thin piece was. But Ben hesitated about giving a date as there were no carbon-14 datings from the Lesser Antilles. "You may have noticed pieces of charcoal as you dug through various hearth layers. You can see them in the vertical walls of your plots. That's what you need to get carbon-14 datings."

We had seen scattered pieces of charcoal, but had paid no attention to them. This embarrassed me, since I had read about radioactive carbon-14 and knew that it had been used for dating archeological sites, although at the time the technique was quite new and the bits we had met seemed too small to bother about.

Now at the fifty-inch level I resumed my digging, inwardly lamenting our carelessness. Then Ben called, "Look, Fred, here's some charcoal now. Be careful how you dig it, and particularly make sure that it is not contaminated with charcoal dropping by chance from a higher level. Get a clean small box and dig the charcoal with a pen-knife."

He watched as, painstakingly, I picked up each bit of charcoal, even those the size of a pinhead, and placed them in a little metal box. "There seems to be quite a good sized patch here," he said. "Don't worry about a bit of clay mixing with it. It's only the carbon in the charcoal that counts."

I spent an hour or more extracting an ounce of charcoal. Ben went back to his digging. He, too, was down to the fifty-inch level. Then he called that he had hit charcoal at the same depth. I watched him meticulously transferring the bits to another small box. Finally he had collected what I guessed was well over an ounce. He measured the pit depth and the position of the charcoal in the 3 x 3 foot square and recorded it on a label he attached to the box. I copy-catted his actions, noting also that my sample was five feet from Ben's and at the same level.

"I will send my sample to the Geochronometric Laboratory at Yale," he said. "Where can you send yours?" I didn't know offhand, but I proposed to ask Morgan Davis, president of the Humble Oil Company, who had a home at Mill Reef and is a close friend. His company would undoubtedly have laboratory facilities for making carbon-14 datings.

These events and discoveries became the talk of the cocktail circuit at Mill Reef. I doubt if an evening passed when the subject of the Arawaks didn't come up. Undoubtedly the presence of the illustrious Yale professor added dignity and glamor to our proceedings. In any case, the enthusiasm grew and we had five to ten diggers per session. Every day cars stopped at the side of the road and people got out to ask about our progress. Everyone wanted to see the latest finds. Even the golfers dropped by to dig after they had finished their rounds, and some even missed a game to be there. We dug every afternoon, Sunday included, missing only one day out of 108, and then only because of rain.

By the time March rolled around digging had become as popular as golf, even luring the ladies from their afternoon bridge games. At least half the diggers were women, despite the fact that excavating in the dust-dry, wind-blown soil of a tropical island is not recommended cosmetically.

As we worked we talked about our long-ago Arawak predecessors. We had learned a little about their household possessions and their food sources. But as they changed in our minds from shadowy long-dead Indians into people who, like us, had lived and worked and, it is hoped, played on this lovely island, we became increasingly eager to know more about them as people.

The past fifteen years have brought the answer to some of these questions, although many still are, and perhaps always will be, lost secrets. Such answers as I have been able to learn are taken up in the chapters that follow.

III

We Meet the Arawaks in Surinam

As the digging progressed and the accumulation of artifacts became large, interest shifted from the classification of the objects to their interpretation. By the time a hundred thousand potsherds had been recovered, about two dozen shapes of vessels had been defined. The largest were apparently for storage, being as wide as two feet in diameter, with strong rims and flat bases but without decoration. Several were not blackened on the outside, so they were not cooking pots. Indeed, they appeared too large for cooking vessels and would have been too heavy to carry when full of water, but they might have been for water storage, filled by successive trips to the brook with smaller pots.

Other types of artifacts included stone axes. It seemed easy to picture their use in cutting trees and making dugout canoes. But what about the hundreds of flint chips caught in the sieves as trowel-loads of dust were screened? Some were knives or scrapers, used for scaling and cutting fish, but I had no idea what sort of wooden household objects the Arawaks might have made with the flints.

J. Walter Fewkes had pictured many stone artifacts from various islands, but nothing like them had been encountered on Antigua. Perhaps this was too small an island to have attracted many of the wandering Arawaks, so my curiosity quickly developed to visit other islands of the area. St. Kitts (Map 1), to the north, was only a few minutes' flight and Antigua friends had suggested going to the sugar plantations there where surface finds might well have been collected. This proved to be correct, and I soon heard about a collection referred to as "Carib stones," but these were later found to be Arawak artifacts. They had been gathered by a planter fifty

31

years earlier and were now taking up space in the home of the third generation, to whom they were of no interest whatever. They were mostly stone axes of all shapes and sizes and a number of conical stones with a rounded base polished by much grinding.

On Montserrat, the next island to the southwest, there had been no systematic excavation. Again, a sugar plantation superintendent had picked up "curios" as he inspected his cane fields, and again had lost interest in them. Asked about a necklace of stone beads with a jade frog pendant, he said the individual beads had been found one at a time over about forty years, always in the same twenty yards of furrows. I guessed there had been some graves in that part of his field. He said he had never found any complete pots, just broken pieces, and had saved only a few of the "prettier" ones. These included some early Saladoid white-on-red sherds very much like those dug at Mill Reef.

It was much the same story along the chain of islands: Guadeloupe, Martinique, St. Lucia, St. Vincent, and each of the lovely little islands of the Grenadines down to Grenada itself (Map 1). I chose to visit these islands the pleasant way and chartered a fifty-six-foot ketch, *Viking II*.

Each island demonstrated that the same kind of Arawaks had lived all through the Lesser Antilles. They made the same kind of pottery, fabricated the same tools, and all had cultivated manioc as evidenced by the numerous griddle sherds. All told, I went ashore on twenty-nine islands, many of them just briefly, and found Arawak artifacts on twenty-two. But although a great many new artifacts had been encountered I was still unable to associate them with the Arawaks who had used them. To further understand the relationship I felt it was necessary to come face to face with actual living Arawaks.

I knew from Professor Rouse that there were remnants of Arawaks still living in South America, but he had warned me the places where Arawaks might still be practicing some of their ancestral habits would be in the jungles of Surinam, Guyana, or Venezuela and probably difficult to reach.

Flying to Trinidad, we took a two and a half days' sail on the Alcoa bauxite boat from Port of Spain to Paramaribo (Map 1), the capital of Surinam which is still part of the Netherlands. Dutch architecture and Dutch cleanliness are much in evidence, but it takes only a trip to the central market to see one of the most complex racial mixtures. There is strong East Indian influence and the colorful Indonesian costumes are everywhere. However, since the objective was to find Arawaks, I was intent on spotting their Mongoloid characteristics. They were not difficult to find. Professor Geijskes, curator of the Paramaribo Museum, said that in Surinam there were about three thousand Caribs, less than one thousand Arawaks, and perhaps four thousand Amerinds belonging to other tribes. Professor Geijskes said it would be necessary to keep away from the towns to make the best contacts with Arawaks.

The Paramaribo Museum had relatively few Amerind exhibits. There were a few reconstructed pots, but they were of poorer quality than most of the material found in the Antilles, so I assumed they were of late manufacture, perhaps dating to about the time of the Carib invasion of the islands. Professor Geijskes' map of Amerind distribution showed that the Arawak village of Bernardsdorp (Map 1) was not far from Paramaribo, and although I had specific directions and mileage data I did have trouble finding it. The tiny settlement was screened from the road by a fringe of trees, and I only reached it by using a garbled mixture of sign language and poor French and German, the latter being my nearest approach to Dutch. Later I learned that all natives of Surinam speak "Tacki-Tacki," a mixture of Dutch, French, Spanish, English, and Amerind, with a possible sprinkling of Chinese and Hindu, a combination quite beyond my meager linguistic ability.

Bernardsdorp comprised a dozen or so Arawak huts, which at first sight looked like large rectangular haystacks. Two strong vertical poles, fifteen to twenty feet high, with a connecting ridgepole, formed the main support for a steep roof of palm-leaf thatch, with several posts framing the "walls" of the hut. Usually there was no thatching on the vertical walls, the roof sloping down to within four feet of the ground, protecting the people inside from prying eyes and at the same time permitting ample ventilation.

Wandering into the village, I was a little uncomfortable at intruding until a group of children appeared. At first they were shy in spite of their curiosity about a stranger, but they responded immediately to a few hard candies, tearing off the cellophane wrappings and popping the sweets into their mouths with evident relish. One of them, a little girl of perhaps eight or ten, sensed that I did not know which way to turn and with shy graciousness took me by the hand, leading me to a house where a woman was peeling manioc tubers. Here was exactly what I had come to see—an Arawak woman in the process of preparing cassava which Professor

Rouse had said was their chief food. With neither Arawakan nor Tacki-Tacki at my disposal, I needed an interpreter. So I smiled, dispensed a few more candies, and departed for the city to make new arrangements.

Next morning I returned with a guide, a young Creole named Frank who spoke Tacki-Tacki and some Arawakan and who said he knew just what I wanted to see and would be able to interpret for me. Characteristically, his present enthusiasm was driving a recently acquired secondhand automobile faster than the state of the road dictated.

When we reached Bernardsdorp, I decided the correct approach would be to call formally upon the Arawak chieftain, offer him a gift for the tribe, and, the amenities over, ask permission to take photos and visit the homes of his village to see how cassava was processed. I had been told that he was "very old" and that his name was Sabajo (Sah-bah-*ho*), but I had no notion of what sort of person he was nor even if he would receive me. We found him so easily that I suspect he had anticipated my visit. He was a fine looking man, with an independent glint in his eye and an inherent dignity in every movement. As for his age, he was perhaps five years younger than I. He wore a faded but neat suit, with a leather patch on each elbow of the jacket. Noticing that these pads had caught my attention, he moved both elbows with evident pride so they would show to greater advantage. Sabajo accepted my scrutiny as being a quite proper recognition of his jacket as a status symbol. I was presented to his wife, a handsome lady with a dignity even more accentuated than that of her husband. She sat with a definite solidarity, as if permanently occupying the throne of Mother Earth. I asked her name, and in a clear voice, with a certain regality, she replied "Elise Jabetana" (Aye-*lee*-say Hab-aye-*tah*-nah).

She and her husband were the grandparents of the Arawakan clan at Bernardsdorp; apparently all the houses were occupied by members of the Sabajo family. Grandfather Sabajo took me to see the arrows he was making, explaining that they were used mainly for hunting fish and were equipped with sharp sawtooth-like barbs which converted the arrow into a harpoon. Apparently the men are very skillful, since he said they rarely lost an arrow. Asked about the arrows with blunt heads, he said in Tacki-Tacki, which Frank volubly translated, that there were used to stun birds wanted for their bright feathers. Since we had already seen and heard parrots and macaws in the woods, I could readily guess the source of the little piles of colored feathers lying on his bench. He seemed to surmise my thought. "Yes," he said. "These are parrot and macaw feathers. But this pile of bright red ones comes from the cock-of-the-rock (*Rupicola rupicola*). They are very hard to get."

Motioning toward another part of his workshop, he showed a ceremonial headdress, the main part of which was like a bonnet made of plaited palm fronds to which feathers had been sewn. There were squares of yellow contained in a zig-zag band of blue feathers, with carefully placed accents in the form of red disks made from feathers of the cock-of-the-rock. Although incomplete, it was quite elegant and looked a good deal like the Peruvian feather mantles. The geometric designs were sufficiently alike to make me wonder about a possible origin of the Arawak culture in that distant Andean land. I tried to purchase the headdress, but Sabajo wouldn't sell it because it was unfinished and therefore did not fully represent his artistic competency. He did let me have a quiver full of his arrows.

Asked if anyone was making cassava, he called to a little girl who had been watching the whole episode. I recognized her as the youngster who had guided me the day before. She was a granddaughter of the chieftain and once more took me by the hand. We went directly to her home. Again I met the woman whom I now knew was her mother. In introducing me to Elaine Sabajo, Frank told of my interest in Arawak customs. Apparently her daughter's confidence had pleased the mother.

In an instant I was watching the operation I had been anxious to witness for a long time: the extraction of the poisonous juice from the grated manioc. She had just finished the grating operation and had put aside the grater, whose jagged surface had been made by punching hundreds of nail holes in a flattened sheet from an oil can. A layer of cassava had already settled in the bottom of a large basin with an inch or so of clear juice on top. Elaine poured off the liquid into another bowl and unhooked a long tube of plaited palm fronds from the rafter. The tube was open at the upper end and closed at the lower, with a strong loop attached to each end. Resting the lower end of the tube on the ground, she pushed down the upper end, thereby contracting the length of the tube from about seven feet long to five feet. I noticed that this contraction enlarged its diameter from about four to six inches. The tube was called a *matapi* (mah-tah-*pee*), Elaine said. She began scooping wet cassava into the open end and continued until

Fig. 2. *Arawak children seesawing to extract poisonous juice from grated manioc in a matapi.*

the tube was full. Lifting the matapi, she hung the upper loop over a peg in the rafter. Next she inserted a pole into the woven heavy loop at the bottom until about two feet of pole was on one side of the loop and eight feet at the other (Figure 2). The short end was placed under a joist of the hut and Elaine gave a low whistle, the signal for her three children—the little girl and two smaller boys— to sit on the long end. This applied considerable downward pressure, lengthening the tube and squeezing the wet cassava pulp inside it. The liquid ran freely from the bottom of the tube into a basin. I had given each youngster a candy, which they were chewing with delight, grinning at me while they gently seesawed in a way to produce just the right rhythmic pressure for the extraction of the juice.

I didn't time the operation, but would guess the children kept up their giggling and seesawing for about five minutes. Mama was busy at a nearby trough fixing a screen for the next operation, but she kept her eye on the matapi. When the juice ceased to drip she removed the pole from the lower loop, lifted the matapi from the roof peg, and contracted the tube, which expanded the woven mesh to free the inner core of white starch, now compressed into a firm cylinder. As Elaine removed this in chunks from the matapi I saw that each cylinder bore the strong impression of the criss-cross weave of the tube (Figure 3). The contents were emptied into a nearby wooden trough. Each chunk was broken by hand and the pieces rubbed through a woven screen called a *manari* (man-*are-*ee). The damp crumbs, collected in a wide bowl, were now ready to be baked into cassava bread. But before turning to the baking Elaine needed a bigger stock of the cassava "flour," so I would have to wait for another time for further steps in the processing of manioc.

I was delighted to have witnessed this essential step in cassava making, the removal of the poisonous juice from the grated manioc. I had not realized how much juice manioc tubers contained, but the catch basin held two or three quarts of liquid. I noticed that Elaine did *not* throw away the poisonous juice, but poured it into a large blackened cooking pot. She explained that she would boil it down to a thick sauce, which she called *cassareep* (*cas-*sah-reep), the basic ingredient of the dish known all through the Caribbean as West Indian pepper pot, a very piquant stew of whatever meat was available together with cassava, potato, yam, or eddoe. Actually the boiling of the juice evaporates the poisonous hydrocyanic acid

Fig. 3. Cylinders of cassava starch bear a strong impression of the weave of the matapi.

and the concentrate becomes a sort of soy sauce which is said to tenderize meat. It certainly gives it a delightful flavor.

I thanked Elaine and went to say goodby to her father, Sabajo. He suggested I might like to visit the Carib village across the road. We made our way to pay our respects to the Carib chieftain Kaytawari (Ky-tah-*wah*-ree), who was seated peacefully weaving a basket. Indeed, he had the same contented look that a woman has when she is knitting.

Kaytawari was a handsome man with the characteristic high cheek bones, long, thick black hair, and the slightly slanting eyes of the Mongoloid race. There was certainly nothing pugnacious about him to suggest a warlike Carib. He permitted me to photograph him at work on his basket, while he engaged in a slow tempo conversation with two friends, who looked as if they might belong to some other tribe. I was introduced to the older man, Anapaike (Anna-*pye*-kee), who turned out to be chief of the Wayana (Woi-

yah-nah) tribe. I was told that Anapaike was politically minded and had gone to Paramaribo to try to get government recognition of himself as head of all the tribes surrounding the Lawa River and as boss of virtually all the Amerinds of south central Surinam. A year later I learned he had been unsuccessful in his political aspirations.

I asked Kaytawari if any pottery was being made and he directed me to a hut down a side road where I was surprised to find a young man busily at work. I had understood that only women made pottery. He was making a water jar, rolling out a long smooth strand as thick as his little finger and coiling it skillfully as he built up the wall. Next he took a smooth flat stone and rubbed the outside wall until the plastic coils had thoroughly welded together and there were no ridge marks showing, although some ridges were visible on the inside, which he had not worked so thoroughly. The top of the jar was finished with a rim on which he rubbed a dark red color, presumably a finely pulverized iron oxide to which enough water was added to form a creamy paste. This and a wavy red band on the bulge of the jar were the only decoration. He described laying the sun-dried vessels on the brush pile, covering them with more faggots, and then setting fire to the pile. If it looked as if more baking were needed, additional fuel was thrown on the pile. There was no such thing as a kiln.

Returning to Kaytawari, I asked if any cassava bread was being made. He looked up from his weaving, gave me the slightest of grins, and said, "Yes, I can smell it baking." He pointed toward another hut. There I found an old woman making bread. She had a large bowl of white cassava meal into which she dipped a palm-leaf scoop to pick up a rapidly gauged charge of crumbs, which she dropped on a nearby griddle. Her eye had been accurate and the crumbs covered the surface to a depth of about a quarter of an inch (Figure 4). The griddle, a well-scoured head of a steel oil drum, was obviously much more serviceable than the fragile pottery disk of her ancestors. I learned later that a burnished oil-drum head was one of the most prized possessions of an Arawak or Carib woman.

Under the griddle was a small fire. I timed the cooking as seven minutes, up to the moment she took her palm leaf and flipped over the disk of cassava to reveal a golden-brown surface. Six more minutes and the cassava bread was baked. The resulting disk was quite firm and I guessed that the residual juice, which had kept the

Fig. 4. Leveling cassava crumbs on the griddle.

crumbs damp, probably contained sugars that had not been converted into starch during the ripening of the tuber. It was the caramelization of these sugars that had given the golden-brown color and also had glued the crumbs into a quite strong cake. The disk was carried outside and placed on the thatched roof to dry in the sun for several hours (Figure 5). In this dried condition the cassava bread may be kept for six months or more.

All these operations had been photographed without apparently being noticed by the cook. Suddenly she spotted the camera and disappeared. I feared she was displeased at being photographed without her permission. Fortunately only her vanity had been disturbed, for she soon reappeared wearing her best dress hastily donned over her working clothes. Then, with true grandmotherly pride, she called several nearby children and posed with them.

Thus are cassava cakes made today, and thus they had been made by the Arawaks who had given them to Columbus at San Salvador.

Fig. 5. Disks of cassava sun-drying on the roof.

This process had been practiced perhaps for a couple of thousand years prior to that time.

Though I felt that I now had a fair picture of the process, I realized that there were many complexities I still did not understand. Such a technology must have evolved very slowly. I knew that these cassava bread techniques were old because the griddle sherds found by Professor Rouse in the Arawak middens of Venezuela dated as far back as 1010 B.C. What I had seen were only the finished steps, painstakingly worked out over many centuries of cut-and-try experiments. The beginnings were still a mystery.

But what about other artifacts that might throw light on the cassava process? Obviously, the nail-pierced oil-can graters are a recent innovation. What were their predecessors? At museums in Trinidad and Paramaribo I had seen manioc graters, or rasps, made of wood, with a solidified gum resin surface into which tiny needle-pointed fragments of flint had been imbedded. But none of these were in any huts in Surinam, although I inquired for them everywhere.

Of ancient matapis, screens, or palm-leaf scoops, no trace remains. These certainly would have rotted away in the tropical climate. So we have no tangible, datable evidence of how early the matapi was discovered.

However, I was fortunate in getting another installment of the manioc process before leaving Paramaribo. I had asked Frank if he knew of any place where manioc was being grown, since I wanted to see the plant in its natural state. He had a girlfriend, he explained, who had her own manioc patch just down the road. When we reached the house he gave a shrill whistle and out came a good-looking Bush Negro girl who greeted Frank with enthusiasm. There followed a rapid cross-fire of Tacki-Tacki, at least part of which must have related to my question about manioc because the girl started off on a trail into the bush. Frank said she would bring a manioc plant, so we waited and waited. We were about five degrees north of the equator, it was noon, the sun was beating down mercilessly, and the dense jungle cut off any cooling breeze. Finally the girl reappeared and Frank called, "Me denk Sie lassen." This seemed translatable as "I thought you were lost," and I felt hopefully that Tacki-Tacki would eventually be understandable. But in the next few weeks I acquired only two or three more words.

The manioc plant was a little higher than the girl, who was about five feet tall. It had a curiously knobby stem, due to big leaf scars left by the falling of each large leaf with its five radiating fingerlike leaflets. At the bottom of the stem were three dark brown tubers looking a bit like sweet potatoes, but when the skin was peeled off the white core of cassava was revealed.

Through Frank's interpretation the girl told me that her mother was busy grating manioc. We went into the hut where the mother was leaning over a wooden tub rubbing the white cores of manioc tubers against a grating board. Hundreds of nails had been driven through the board so that the points projected about an eighth of an inch, making a very effective rasp.

These tubers were also rich in juice and the pulp formed a watery slurry in the tub. I asked what the woman would do with the wet cassava and the daughter explained that this cassava would not be used for baking, but for laundry starch to be sold in the Paramaribo market. Both women were glad to show me part of the starch-making process. The excess juice was poured off and the pulp transferred to a large wooden mortar. Actually it was a log of a tree a little more than a foot in diameter with a hole about fifteen inches deep and ten inches in diameter dug out of the upright end. With a three-foot pole, whittled in the form of a pestle with a five-inch knob at the base, the mother pounded the cassava pulp for several minutes and then washed the starch through a screen with water. The slurry was allowed to settle, the water poured off, and the starch spread in the sun to dry. The pounding had evidently broken up the sacs of cassava starch granules, releasing the fine powder which is the familiar laundry starch. It was too dark in the hut to photograph the pounding operation and the mortar was too heavy to move to the door, but she did move her grating board to the entrance so I could photograph her rasping the tubers.

As we drove back to our hotel I felt I had learned several steps in the manioc technology, but what was even more important I had seen living Arawaks—and Caribs too—going about their daily chores. They were clearly living close to their environment and were well adjusted to it. They had probably found in Surinam as fine a place as any their ancestors had come across in thousands of years of wandering. Their jungle has an almost constant temperature the year around, much of the time hovering only a few degrees above 80° in the shade. It feels comfortably cool at night even if it is 77°. The land is plentiful, fertile, and moist enough to grow manioc, yams, sweet potatoes and eddoes, as well as such fruits as bananas, coconuts, and the delightful mangoes. For proteins the sea and rivers are rich with fish and shellfish. And the bush yields meat such as deer, agouti, laba, and peccary. An excellent home for Arawaks!

Although Professor Geijskes map showing distribution of groups of Amerinds indicated that most were deep in the jungle and required extensive travel to reach, there was one exception, Powakka, an Arawak settlement which was quite isolated yet might be approached by a road which went within five miles of the village (Map 1). The remaining distance surely must be traversable by trail. From the superintendant of the bauxite plant closest to Powakka it was learned that his assistant Gerrit Loor knew the place and would take me there. I was warned that only a jeep could navigate the road, which was only a poor wagon trail.

Our driver assured me he could get just the car we needed, but next morning he brought not a jeep but a new Volkswagen. "Much better than a jeep," he asserted with finality. "It is light and will go anywhere."

When Loor saw it he shook his head. But Frank was positive, and to prove how superior the car was we traveled the normal road at such a clip that we passed everything in sight. When we turned onto the trail, which was not even marked on the map, I could see trouble ahead. It was hardly more than a path newly cut through the bush, with stumps and roots everywhere. No rocks (thank Heaven!), but a dry, white-sand surface which made us slow down to less than ten miles an hour. Even at that speed we were stuck at times, but were able to push the light car out of trouble and creep along a little farther. We had not gone more than half a mile when one wheel dropped into a hole and this time we couldn't budge. Frank spun the wheels until the bottom of the car was flat on the sand. We put branches under the wheels and tried prying with poles, using logs for a fulcrum. The morning sun was beating down fiercely. There was no breeze and the white sand seemed to reflect more heat. By the end of half an hour I was exhausted, and in another quarter of an hour so were Loor and Frank. But nothing was accomplished, so I decided the only thing to do was to walk the trail until we found the Arawak village and hope for help there. Reluctantly the others agreed and we set off. The sand was so soft it was even difficult to walk. No wonder the car hadn't a chance.

I have done a lot of trail hiking in my time and guessed we were doing two miles an hour, but my stop watch said only one and a half. I was twenty-five years older than Loor and forty-five years older than Frank, so was not able to match their pace. The sun was nearing the zenith and we could feel its reflection from the white sand. With neither shade nor breeze it grew so unbearably hot that I had to rest nearly every quarter mile. By the time we had trudged three hours I felt I could go no farther. The trail seemed endless and no change in the topography suggested the location of the village. Loor and Frank, too, were feeling the pull of the slipping sand on their leg muscles. During rest periods we strained our ears for any sound of human beings. Finally Frank heard something, and soon it was evident to all of us that we were listening to the rhythmic blows of an ax. Aroused to new energy we came in another ten minutes upon the woodsmen—and Arawaks they were. They understood Loor's mixture of Tacki-Tacki and Arawakan

44

and told him Powakka was about a mile farther. We made the last mile without a stop.

I was delighted with the village. It was a good-sized community of about fifty houses. Indeed, it was quite spectacular. A large rectangular plot had been cleared for a space of about six hundred by two hundred feet. Along each edge of the clearing, which was clean white sand, was a line of neatly built thatched huts. In most cases there were no walls, the roofs sloping down to about three feet from the ground for better ventilation. Entrance was from either end of the huts, and instead of doors there were canopies of thatch over the openings, giving a nice architectural note. Dogs, chickens, and an occasional monkey walked in and out of the houses. Sometimes three or four cassava disks were sun-drying on a roof.

We were directed to the chieftain's hut where we found Arma-keto (Ar-ma-*kay*-to), a solidly built, fine-looking man with a friendly manner (Figure 6). I made the customary gift and asked permission to take photographs. This was granted by a sweep of the hand suggesting "anywhere you like." Told of our trouble with the stuck car he agreed to see that we got help.

They were making no pottery, I was told. The clay was not good quality and it was too far to Paramaribo to make it worth while carrying such pots there for trading. Instead gourds were used for containers and calabashes cut for spoons and cups. There were one or two cooking pots, but the wide bowls for holding ground cassava and the juice from the matapi were all enameled basins. I wondered what they took into town to trade for the basins, the blue overalls the men wore, and the women's cotton dresses. "Live parrots and monkeys," they said, "and laundry starch."

I visited several houses, accompanied by chattering youngsters delighted with our unusual visit. In none of the huts was cassava processing underway, but the disks on the roofs indicated that the day's baking was already finished. There was no weaving going on, but I saw one woman spinning cotton thread. Other women were in the nearby fields getting a new supply of manioc tubers. They worked in groups probably because they enjoyed being together for a daily chat.

The village was primitive and almost spotlessly clean. The people lived almost entirely on cassava, with a few fruits and nuts. Peccaries and monkeys supplied the scanty protein portion of their diet. I asked about fish, but they said the river was eight miles away, too far to walk, so they did little fishing.

45

Fig. 6. Armaketo, Arawak chieftain of Powakka.

46

Armaketo appeared with two men as strong as himself and a couple more for good measure. There was a shorter trail through the bush, he explained, that would save a couple of miles. With the whole group of youngsters forming the long tail of the procession, we started back to the stranded car. The trail was a well-beaten path through the heavy jungle and only when an occasional break occurred in the canopy of branches was there light enough for a photograph. I wondered about the nearness of jaguars and anaconda snakes, but I have been in the bush enough to know that all animal inhabitants would be well aware of such a large group, so even if they were only a few feet away they would conceal their presence while probably watching us with alert curiosity. We saw and heard parrots, macaws, and an occasional monkey, but as far as my senses were aware the forest was empty of all other living creatures, even insects.

We were walking in swampy land. This was evidently a well-used trail since they had placed logs across each stream, sometimes even stretching a thin pole to serve as a hand rail. There were also logs wherever the swamp would not permit a man to carry a load, some of them sufficiently narrow to make me dubious about my balance. Here the children delighted in running and dancing across the log to show me how easy it was, and often, with friendly pride, would take my hand and steady me across.

The trip back to the car was not only shorter but comfortably cool, and was made without any rest periods. The men literally picked the car up and turned it around onto firmer ground in a matter of minutes. When I asked the charges Armaketo smilingly suggested a figure which I doubled, and we parted in good will.

I returned to Paramaribo well satisfied with the day's excursion. My first meetings with Arawaks, who were presumably little influenced by contacts with the West, had been pleasant and instructive. It suggested that they were the same friendly cooperative people about whom Columbus had written so glowingly.

IV

The Story of Manioc—the Bitter
from the Sweet

U NQUESTIONABLY, the pieces of the manioc story were being
fitted together. In the jungle villages of Surinam I had seen
the essential steps which the Arawaks had developed for extracting
the edible starch cassava from the poisonous manioc tuber. Nevertheless, the primary question how an aboriginal tribe would persist in the use of a poisonous root once they had discovered its
harmful nature—still had to be answered. Surely if a plant caused
sickness or death it would be shunned by primitive people—indeed, become immediately taboo. What then could be the explanation of its acceptance?

The conversion of a poisonous root to a food staple is very complicated and undoubtedly would be a slow process. How slow might
be gleaned from noticing that in many ancient cultures the transi-
tion from hunting to food gathering to agriculture required a long
time. Even under apparently favorable circumstances it took three
thousand years (from 9000 B.C. to 6000 B.C.) to domesticate wheat
and barley in the Fertile Crescent, the western Asiatic "cradle of
civilized man." The task of establishing an economy based on agriculture that utilized a poisonous root would be truly formidable.

Yet it happened. And a long time ago, as proven by the cassava
griddle sherds in the earliest layers at Saladero, about 1010 B.C.
Indeed, the association of Arawaks with griddle sherds was so consistent that I began to wonder if the Arawaks might not have been
the inventors of the cassava process. But how did they break the
taboo? Presumably it would have to tie into one of their deeply
rooted practices, and my hunch was that it grew out of their skills
in fishing.

49

It has long been a habit among many South American tribes to use poison in catching fish. Over a period of several generations, while their fishing skills were being developed, primitive people must have tested all kinds of baits and poisons obtained from bark, roots, and berries. The circum-Caribbean area is rich in plants containing narcotics, frequently alkaloids, affecting the nervous and other physiological systems of animals. If a crushed mass of a plant containing a suitable narcotic, poison, or paralyzing agent is added to a pool, the fish may be temporarily immobilized. It is only by continuous movement that a fish can extract, through its gills, essential supplies of fresh oxygen dissolved in the water through which it is swimming. If it can't swim to fresh supplies of oxygen, the fish suffocates and floats to the surface. The natives pick it out of the water and apparently there are no ill effects when the fish is cooked and eaten.

Ecologist Carl O. Sauer has suggested that the use of such devices for stunning fish may have first arisen during the making of fish-nets, when fibers were obtained by pounding and retting the bark of certain trees in pools of water. Some of the vegetable glues holding the fibers together were either poisonous or had strong detergent properties that adversely affected the absorption of oxygen by the gills and yielded the netmakers an unexpected supply of stunned fish. Likewise, observing the poisonous effect of manioc on humans who attempted to eat it would naturally suggest its being tried as a fish poison. Presumably, the experiment of throwing manioc into a pool was highly successful.

Thus we can visualize a situation in which a stock of crushed manioc had been prepared as fish poison. Some of it had been used successfully, but part of the supply may have stood in the sun long enough for the hydrocyanic acid to evaporate. Next day the fishermen, putting the same crushed manioc into the pool, noticed that the fish were not paralyzed as expected. The people, puzzling over its loss of power, eventually might connect this failure with its dryness due to too long exposure of the manioc to the sun. Or perhaps a hungry child ate some of the dried manioc, initially to the horror of the parents and later to their amazement when no ill came to the child. If ground manioc hurt neither fish nor child after it had been exposed to the sun for a long time, they may have reasoned that it was safe to eat because it had lost its juice. They may have also concluded that the evil spirits that harmed humans and fish resided in the juice. Then they might have eliminated the juice by squeezing it out of the root. But how did they hit upon the device of the matapi? Perhaps watching an anaconda squeeze its victim to death gave these jungle people the idea of weaving their own snakelike matapi tube.

The botany of manioc, however, suggests that the process by which manioc became a food staple may have been somewhat different. Some varieties of manioc are poisonous and others harmless; they are referred to, respectively, as "bitter" and "sweet" manioc.

Many Antiguans are not very clear about the distinction, so I consulted available published sources on the subject. Most were singularly lacking in definite information. The most comprehensive statement was in *Agricultural Origins and Dispersals* by Carl O. Sauer, the eminent American ecologist, who says of manioc:

Its native climate is that of the savanna with the rainless season longer than the rainy one . . . . The bitter or poisonous varieties of yuca (manioc) have been distributed in Atlantic drainage basins from Cuba to South Brazil. They were unknown in Central America, most of Colombia, and on the Pacific Coast of South America. The manner of preparation follows a fairly standard pattern of grating, pressing, and washing, to remove the hydrocyanic acid, followed by baking into admirable and long keeping flat bread called cazabi (cassava).

The sweet varieties appear to be grown wherever bitter manioc is. Sweet manioc is mainly boiled or baked without grating, and rarely is the staple food that the bitter forms commonly are.

It was a beginning, but only that. I wrote for information to Professor Edgar Anderson, of the Missouri Botanical Gardens in St. Louis, with whom my wife and I had studied elementary botany thirty years ago. Professor Anderson referred me to a former pupil, David Rogers, head of taxonomy at the New York Botanical Gardens, saying he had been studying manioc for ten years and probably knew as much about the plant as anyone.

Professor Rogers sent a copy of his paper on manioc.[1] It gave a fine review of Central and South American locations where *wild* manioc occurs today, from which the cultivated varieties might have developed. I studied the article and arranged an appointment with its author at his office in Bronx Park.

First I asked Professor Rogers to clarify a point of nomenclature, since I had noticed several different botanical names for manioc which suggested different species, namely, *Manihot esculenta,* *Manihot utilissima,* and *Manihot manihot.* Professor Rogers said that they are all names of the same species. The first, *Manihot esculenta,* is the one currently acceptable to most botanists. *Utilissima* should be discontinued and the *Manihot manihot* designation was erroneously applied and should also be discarded. The word "manihot," he suggested, was probably just a local variation of the Tupi-Guarani word "manioc."[2]

Asked how he distinguished the bitter and sweet manioc plants visually, Professor Rogers said he could not tell the difference by looking at the plants. He showed photographs of plants designated sweet and bitter by the Indians who had grown them. I could not see much difference between the pictures nor could he.

While stationed in British Guiana, Professor Rogers had grown some twenty plants, roughly half sweet and half bitter, as brought to him by Amerind growers, privately labeling each sweet or bitter as the Indians had designated. Later he asked other Indian farmers to name the plants for him. Usually each farmer started out quite briskly, naming this one sweet and that one bitter. But after about half a dozen plants had been identified, the Indians became hesitant and even confused. The net result, he said, was that there was no consistent agreement as to which were sweet and which were bitter.

I told him of my experiences in the jungle of Surinam seeing Arawaks make small clearings by felling the trees, burning the slash, and as soon as the rains came planting manioc between the logs and stumps. A short cutting of a manioc stem was stuck in the ground wherever it was convenient to make a hole. No attempt was made to plant in rows.

"The same thing is found in British Guiana also," said Professor Rogers.

I mentioned my puzzlement about the complicated technology of removing the poisonous juice to make cassava bread. "Do you think it possible," I asked, "that hydrocyanic acid develops slowly in manioc and is not detectible in early tubers of, say, six months' growth, so that the young plant is called sweet, but that after a year and a half or two years the hydrocyanic content is high enough so that the manioc tastes bitter?"

Professor Rogers did not know.

I asked if measurements of the hydrocyanic acid content of manioc roots had been made at, say, three month intervals. Professor Rogers knew of no such published analyses.

Since we would be returning to Antigua within a few weeks I decided that my next move would be to study at firsthand the manioc practices of the island.

Manioc is an important crop in Antigua and numerous patches can be spotted as you drive around the island. The natives raise it mainly for home consumption, but also sell it at local markets. It is grown scientifically at the Antigua Experiment Stations conducted by the Department of Agriculture. Franklin Margetson, the horticulturalist at Mill Reef, had previously been in charge of experimental work for the department, and as soon as we were back on the island I called on him.

Frank offered to guide me on a tour of manioc plantings on the island. Our first visit was to a fairly large manioc patch in the lush southwestern part of Antigua, owned and cultivated by a woman who had worked for Frank some years ago. In reply to my question about the difference between bitter and sweet manioc, she said she would be happy to identify them for us. (In Antigua, the plant is called cassava instead of manioc.)

The distinction seemed fairly clear as she picked them out. The bitter cassava had tall gray "sticks" (the island term for the main stalk), whereas the sticks of sweet cassava were greenish gray and their leaf scars were less prominent and not so closely spaced as on the bitter (Figure 7). At the top of the bitter cassava stick was a spreading crown of leaves, dark green and shiny, with seven radiating long, narrow, sharply pointed leaflets (Figure 8). In the case of sweet cassava the leaves were light green, not so shiny, and with three, five, or seven shorter, broader, and more rounded leaflets. It was the shape, color, and number of the leaflets that distinguished the bitter from the sweet.

So far so good. It seemed as though a little light was dawning. But might not these be merely local, perhaps superficial, distinctions as developed on an isolated island?

We went next to the Claremont Irrigation Project where recently constructed dams were impounding rainwater to irrigate experimental plots. George Weaver, who had worked under Franklin Margetson's supervision but who was now foreman of both the Claremont Project and the Cade's Bay Experiment Station, offered to take us to Cade's Bay on the middle of the south coast of the island. Weaver explained that the station's large field of manioc included bitter and two varieties of sweet cassava, which he called White Stick and Black Stick. To me the differences between these

53

*Fig. 7. Leaf scars of bitter manioc are prominent and closely spaced.
(Franklin Margetson, Antigua.)*

54

Fig. 8. Bitter manioc leaf has seven radiating leaflets. They are long, narrow, sharp-pointed, dark green, and shiny.

two types of sweet manioc were certainly not great. The stems were by no means white and black, but merely lighter and darker shades of green. The leaves of the two types seemed indistinguishable, both having large light green leaves with three, five, or seven radiating leaflets. But I did notice that the petioles of Black Stick were deep purple-red throughout their length, whereas the petioles of White Stick were light green with just a touch of red at the base. This seemed like a minor distinction, but perhaps it was diagnostic.

Weaver said the peasants have no preference between the White and Black Stick sweet varieties. Both are used as a starchy vegetable simply by boiling the peeled tubers. Both varieties can also be used for cassava bread. But the bread made from bitter manioc keeps longer, he said.

By now I felt I could distinguish sweet from bitter cassava (manioc) fairly well by the differences in their foliage. But how did one differentiate between tubers? I recalled that Jane in the market at St. Johns, from whom we buy fruit and vegetables, said she could not tell the tubers of sweet from those of bitter manioc, but had to rely on the peasants bringing her the right kind. She sells only sweet cassava, not wanting to risk selling the poisonous product. If, after twenty or more years' experience in selling vegetables, Jane couldn't tell sweet from bitter, how did the peasants keep the distinction clear after the tubers had been dug, regardless of how positive they might have been about the growing plants?

When the Cade's Bay workers, a number of whom had gathered around us, were asked if they could tell bitter from sweet cassava just by the looks of the tubers, they said that they could. They began scraping away the soil to reveal tubers (Figure 9). Scratching the brownish skins, they pointed to color differences which frankly were beyond my ability to recognize. I was most eager to observe the distinction, but it was too subtle for my eyes.

"Can you smell any difference?" I asked, anticipating that free prussic acid might have a detectible odor. I also realized that in the living plant there might be no free hydrocyanic acid, since the cyanide would probably be chemically combined with a glucose base to form a complex organic glucoside. The hydrogen cyanide would be released only by such agencies as heat, water, or enzymes. One of the workers explained that when bitter cassava is being scraped you can smell it as you come near the place.

I asked what it smelled like. Evidently the smell was difficult to describe. The workers looked at one another, puzzled. Then one finally said, "Oh, sourlike," which is probably a good answer.

"Does sweet cassava have any smell?" I asked.

"No," very definitely.

"Even if it is an old tuber?"

"Makes no difference. No smell."

I asked them about the taste of sweet cassava.

"It's sweet," said a worker.

"Like sugar?"

"No, not that sweet. Hardly any taste."

"Does an old tuber of sweet cassava taste sweet?"

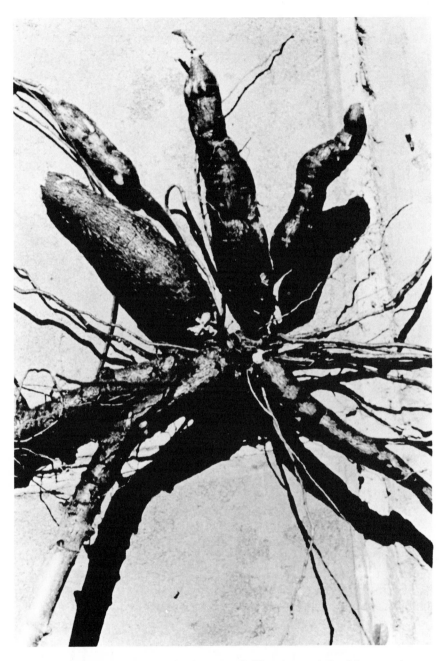

Fig. 9. Sweet manioc tubers look so much like those of the bitter variety that I could not tell them apart.

"Just the same as a young one."

"What is the taste of bitter cassava?"

"Ah don' taste it. It piesen."

So much for that. I tried another tack. "Why do you grow sweet cassava?" I asked.

"It's good starch vegetable."

"Then why do you grow bitter cassava?"

"Gives bigger yield an' bread keeps better."

I had noticed, as the men were bringing specimens of the different varieties, that the White Stick and Black Stick varieties were growing together with bitter cassava in what appeared to be a haphazard arrangement. I asked the reason for this, but got no coherent answer. However, I have lived long enough in the islands to sense when the peasants don't know the answer or when they don't want to give the information. So I rephrased the question.

"Why do you plant White Stick and Black Stick and bitter cassava all mixed up?"

I believe the man intuitively recognized my awareness of his reluctance, for he gave me a quizzical smile and replied, "Well, dey is some people steals cassava at night, but dey carn' see which is which in da dark, and is sure to pick some piesen plants. Den get turrible sick to da stummick. Dat teach him not to steal."

This sounded like a real deterrent, but it implied that when bitter cassava was boiled as a vegetable it still was poisonous enough to cause illness.

We continued around the southwestern corner of the island to the village of Bolans, where we noticed a girl working in her cassava patch. I could now recognize the White Stick and Black Stick varieties of sweet cassava, but the girl introduced a third variety which she called Butter Stick. To me it was indistinguishable from the White Stick, but she insisted it was butter-colored inside. Scratching off the outer cambium layer of the stem, she pointed to the thin inner layer which was admittedly a bit more yellowish than in the White Stick type. People who work every day with plants, breaking the stems or cutting them for planting, become acquainted with such subtle distinctions.

"It's sweet cassava, just like the others," she added.

Arriving home with my labeled samples, I photographed them and tabulated the characteristics of each specimen.[3] On the basis of the data from the ten samples I had gathered, plus observation of several hundred specimens in the field, I reached the following conclusions:

The variety of *Manihot esculenta* that the natives of Antigua call bitter cassava is readily distinguished visually from sweet cassava.

	Bitter Manioc	Sweet Manioc
Shape of leaflets	Sharp-pointed, long, narrow	Rounded, shorter, broader
Color of leaves	Dark green, shiny	Light green, not shiny
Stem color	Dark gray stick	Lighter green-gray stick
Leaf scars	Very prominent, closely spaced	Not so prominent, much more widely spaced

The varieties of sweet cassava which are called White Stick, Black Stick, and Butter Stick are not so easily differentiated from one another. The Black Stick is perhaps the easiest to spot by its dark purple-red petioles and the darker green color of its stem, if these actually are diagnostic features.

I have chewed the brilliant white cortex of the sweet cassava tuber. It tastes sweet but leaves a faintly bitter aftertaste, which may be related to a very small cyanide content. The natives say that sweet cassava tubers a year or more old have no bitter taste.

Does the hydrocyanic acid content of bitter manioc vary with the age of the plants? And is there any difference in the cyanide content between the bitter and the sweet varieties of manioc? H. A. L. Francis, head of the Antigua Department of Agriculture, agreed to make analytical tests that may answer these questions. Meanwhile, my own glimpses into the ecology of manioc have suggested further clues about the lines along which manioc may have developed as the food staple of a wide range of people, originally in South America but now adopted widely in Africa and southeastern Asia.

From my own journeyings it became evident that manioc was the principal food of the aboriginal tribes not only of the Greater and Lesser Antilles, but also of the whole Guiana Coast from French Guiana and Surinam into eastern Venezuela. This was proved by the ubiquitous griddle sherds at ancient sites. It is still the staple food for many of the present inhabitants of these lands.

A north-south line drawn through Caracas would roughly divide the manioc-growing tribes of lowland eastern Venezuela from the maize-growing people of the higher western half of the country. This division line has an ecological rather than a political basis. Maize grows better on the higher lands of western Venezuela, and manioc prefers the eastern low-lying llanos, where a short rainy season is followed by a long, hot, dry period.

From the reports of Professors Rouse and Cruxent there is also archeological evidence for the longtime existence of this north-south division line through Caracas. Excavations east of this line reveal cassava griddle sherds in the lowest layers of about three thousand years ago. Similar digging to the west shows the presence of stone implements such as *metates* and *manos* commonly associated with the grinding of maize, but not at so early a date. Maize-growing may have diffused into western Venezuela either from Peru to the southwest or from Mexico by way of Colombia. Maize-grinding tools are found occasionally in excavations to the east of this north-south line, hinting at possible intrusion by maize-eating Amerinds from the west. Perhaps the migrant tribe from the west abandoned the attempt to grow maize on land more suited to the cultivation of manioc, or accepted the corn cultivation being diffused to them from the west, abandoned the maize and returned to manioc. The latter seems the more likely explanation, based on ecologist Carl O. Sauer's generalization that grain-eaters tend to stick to grain and root-eaters to roots.

Sauer refers specifically to two distinct types of agriculturist: those who grow plants by seeding and those who propagate them by cuttings. Maize is the outstanding example in the Americas of growing from seed. Potatoes and manioc are propagated by cuttings, or, as Sauer says, by vegetative methods. In potato culture the tuber is sliced to give at least one "eye" from which a new plant can be started. With manioc the stem is cut into short lengths, each containing two leaf scars; these are planted vertically in the ground at the time of the rains.

Although not an ecologist I understand that any food plant becomes popular, and hence domesticated, because it thrives naturally in a particular environment. Potatoes grow better at higher altitudes and in cooler climates than does maize; therefore the culture of the tribes in the high Andes was based on potatoes. The tribes in the valley of Mexico found that maize flourished in areas of middle elevation, so maize became their staple. For the same reason the tribes along the lowlands of the Orinoco grew manioc.[4]

Since these speculations take us back into the early Neo- and Meso-Indian eras, there is little or no possibility of knowing the names of the tribes that made these early agricultural experiments. About all we can say is that the discovery of each of these crops established an economy that permitted the development of early cultures.

However, wheat and barley is associated with the rise of Sumer and the Mesopotamian cultures, and somewhat later with the rise of Egypt. Similarly, maize is linked with the rise of the Maya and associated groups in Central America and perhaps parts of Peru. Potatoes we tie to some of the Peruvian cultures at higher elevations of the Andes.

But whom are we going to name as the people whose rise depended upon manioc? I suggest as a working hypothesis that the Arawaks may have developed the technology of winning cassava from manioc, that by this solution of their food economy they grew to be a major tribe with sufficient vigor and numerical strength to populate parts of eastern Venezuela and later Trinidad and the islands of the Antilles.

The Arawaks were fortunate in their selection of this tuber as their main source of food, because manioc produced a higher yield of starch per acre than any other crop available three thousand years or more ago, including maize and potatoes, or even wheat and barley. With the problem of their food supply solved the Arawaks could then divert their energy from hunting or food gathering to the development of pottery, basketry, weaving, and perhaps even to ballgames and drinking of chicha-type beer made from cassava. Indeed, many of their rituals may have originated as fertility rites in connection with the new agricultural practices of producing manioc. Among the Arawaks, like other people, responsibility for ceremonial practices would probably be placed in the hands of men who could be relieved from some of the burdens of securing daily food. It would be these men, shamans, who cultivated the esthetic interests out of which developed the arts of painting, sculpture, dancing, and finally what is perhaps the ultimate expression of esthetics, religion. They were free also to try the difficult but engrossing steps of becoming civilized.

As for the hypothesis that the Arawaks were the people who developed cassava processing and established a manioc economy—what evidence supports this theory? First, every ancient Arawak site contains cassava griddle sherds throughout each occupation layer; equally early sites of non-Arawak tribes usually have no griddle sherds. At Saladero no pottery or other artifacts exists below this 1010 B.C. level, and at the moment we have no evidence of Arawak sites earlier than this anywhere. Actually we have no proof that the tribe living at Saladero about 1000 B.C. was Arawak. Professor Rouse is chary about attaching the tribal names of historic peoples to prehistoric pottery types. He prefers that the makers of the well-known white-on-red sherds be called Saladoid people rather than Arawaks.

Who, then, are the Arawaks? Perhaps the way out of this difficulty is to say that by Arawaks, I mean the people Columbus first met at San Salvador and Hispaniola. The name Arawak might then be extended to cover their ancestors and their descendants—indeed, those I met in Surinam called themselves Arawaks.

The next step is to ask if the Amerinds whom the Spaniards met were from the same stock as those who had left the white-on-red pottery at Saladero nearly three thousand years ago. The answer seems to be that they were, because the early middens on all the islands from Hispaniola to Trinidad contain material similar to that at Saladero. The stratigraphy of the middens, according to Rouse, reveals only a normal and gradual modification of pottery design or technology. Moreover, cassava was used throughout this period, and the griddle sherds present in each layer on the whole range of islands show only a logical development, such as changes of the rim that held the cassava crumbs in place or in the size and shape of the pottery legs that raised the griddle above the fire. These changes were not only slight, but were gradual over a period of more than a thousand years.

I believe, therefore, that cassava-eating by Arawaks, as I have defined them, has been a continuous process from 1000 B.C. onward and over a sweep of territory from the delta of the Orinoco to the Greater Antilles. But where is the original home of manioc, the hearth from which it sprang? This we do not know yet.

Another question equally perplexing is whether bitter manioc or sweet manioc was the parent plant. Is there any evidence that wild varieties of each developed in different localities? The present answer is "no." Or, is sweet manioc merely a cultivated variety arising from man's selection of fast-growing types, to accommodate the shorter growth cycle demanded by annually flooded lands? The available data lean toward a "yes" answer.

With respect to the hearth where manioc originated Rouse himself admits that he has no evidence of the Saladoid people prior to their appearance in the delta. He believes they probably came *down* the Orinoco. If, at this time, we cannot trace the origin of manioc through the known artifacts of the Arawaks, perhaps we can trace it by exploring those places where it might have flourished. The main clue to manioc cultivation seems to be in the essential feature of the plant. Manioc requires a wet period at the beginning of its growth, followed by a long dry period during which starch is produced and stored in the tuber, so that the plant can start new vigorous growth when the rains or floods bring the needed moisture. These conditions are met in the llanos of Venezuela.

I am, therefore, much interested in the hypothesis that sometime prior to 1000 B.C., perhaps as early as 2000 B.C., a group of Amerinds came down the Rio Apure from Colombia, or down the Amazon from the Peruvian or Ecuadorian Andes, and finally reached the upper Orinoco. They may have had only a very primitive knowledge of agriculture and perhaps only a smattering of pottery-making. If they had come from Peru they might have known about potato cultivation and therefore about making vegetative cuttings for planting, although there is still some question as to how early the potato was discovered. When they reached the llanos of Venezuela they would naturally have pulled up plants to see if any bore usable tubers, and in some such manner discovered manioc.

V

Was the Orinoco the Early Trail
of the Arawaks?

ALTHOUGH the visit to Surinam had given not only a firsthand contact with living Arawaks, it had also helped me to understand
the significance of some artifacts dug in Antigua. Particularly was
this the case in the processing of manioc, which perhaps had played
as important a part in the daily life of the Arawaks a thousand years
ago as it obviously did today.

Since manioc processing had probably originated in Venezuela,
where its very early use by Arawaks had been demonstrated by
Rouse and Cruxent to have occurred at Saladero, a visit to the
Orinoco was arranged. It was hoped that something might be
learned of the hearths from which manioc might have sprung, the
most likely location being the llanos of Venezuela.

Passage was arranged on the Netherlands Shipping Line freighter
S. S. Poseidon, which sailed in May, 1965, from Port of Spain,
Trinidad, to Ciudad Bolívar (Map 3), a river port about a hundred
miles or so up the Orinoco. This route gave an opportunity to see
the Gulf of Paria, in whose sheltered waters the Arawaks most
likely had learned their navigational skills while living in Trinidad
for several hundred years before migrating to the islands of the
lesser Antilles. We left the Gulf of Paria by way of the Dragon's
Mouth to sail around the north and east coasts of Trinidad. After
twelve hours in clear turquoise water, the color of the sea began to
change to a pale green hue. The captain pointed out to me on his
charts the westward flowing current, originating as a discharge
from the Amazon some five hundred miles to the east. Mud was
being transported this incredibly long distance and geologists had
shown it to contain minerals peculiar to the Amazon, though pos-

sibly augmented by material from the rivers of Surinam and Guyana. As we sailed farther into this current the color changed gradually from green to light brown. Finally when the boat reached the sediment-laden current from the Orinoco there was quite an abrupt change to a Mississippi-like mud.

The powerful steamer lost two knots' speed when the full force of the Orinoco was encountered. This was the current which presumably had carried the Arawaks northward along the east coast of Venezuela to Trinidad. At sundown the *Poseidon* reached Punta Barima at the mouth of the Orinoco and a Venezuelan pilot climbed aboard to take us upstream to Ciudad Bolívar.

The Orinoco is an impressively large river. Its banks are low-lying, like the coastline of Venezuela. Dense trees flank its banks, but we could see that there was no sign of habitation or cultivation for mile after mile up the river. This land would be flooded at high water season every year, and from the elevation of the ship's bridge no high land was visible in the background to which a farmer might escape at flood time. Land that was almost completely unoccupied today would in all probability have been equally unacceptable to Arawaks two or three thousand years ago. The only tribe in the delta lands for many centuries was the Warrau, a backward and shy people.

After a full day's slow travel upstream we reached Ciudad Bolívar, where we were joined by Brad Endicott, a longtime digging associate at Mill Reef and president of the Antigua Archeological Society at that time. A delay in the starting of the Venezuelan government boat, which would go upstream as far as the Orinoco was navigable, gave an opportunity to visit Saladero, only fifty miles downstream. However, there was no direct road of any kind or any small boat available for charter. The only way was to fly a long round-about circuit of small air strips to Maturín, a hundred miles north of Saladero. From Maturín there was a good road to Barrancas (Map 4), of which Saladero is a suburb and which a rented auto did in two hours, giving a better feel of the llanos than that obtained from the air. It reminded me of driving through the drier parts of Kansas. I was quite conscious that this might also be a route by which the Arawaks could have migrated north from Saladero to the Gulf of Paria and Trinidad, if they had taken a land route instead of the water journey down the Orinoco and then north along the Venezuela coast to the Serpent's Mouth and Trinidad (Map 3). The land route would have been fairly simple since there are small rivers every few miles that would have provided adequate drinking water and would also have been easy to cross. Game was probably fairly plentiful on the prairies, at least to competent hunters. I wondered whether a tribe like the Arawaks, living for many generations on a river and using it as their major supply of protein, would be able to break away from their customary riverine habits. Could they change to a land-roving tribe and wander the considerable distances across land leading to Trinidad and the Gulf of Paria? Even though there were no major physical barriers, the llanos might have appeared endless and forbidding to a tribe accustomed to living near water.

Barrancas is a small river port (Map 4) with a number of small boats, mostly dugouts, many equipped with outboard motors. Brad looked up Pedro, whom he had known on a previous trip and who had also been with Rouse and Cruxent during their digging fifteen years earlier. Pedro, an alert and likable man, soon took things in hand. A launch was hired to take us to Saladero, a mile upstream, and in a few minutes we were scrambling up the forty-foot bank (Figure 10) whose contour was familiar through Professor Rouse's meticulous descriptions in his "Archeological Chronology of Venezuela." A recent fall had broken loose a couple of tons of dirt from the bank and sherds were spread out over the ground. We picked up several characteristic Saladoid and Barrancoid sherds.

The road along the top of the bluff was just as Ben Rouse had described it. He had provided a sketch showing each wattle-and-daub house—all nineteen of them—that composed the "village" of Saladero, and had given the name of the "ranchero" living in each house. When I reached a house and identified it as the ninth "rancho" from the west end of the path, I checked the list of names and walked to the door, calling in a cheerful voice, "Ola, Señor Pablo Silva." An astonished man came out wondering who this visitor might be, but broke into smiles when I said I was an "amigo de Señor Rouse." All of these people remembered the kindly Professor Rouse, almost all having worked at the excavation during 1950. They were delighted to hear about him.

Soon Pablo Silva's wife appeared with a half calabash full of sherds and I sorted out the ones in which I was interested. Pedro stood watching, asking from time to time, "¿Todos?" When I indicated that I was finished, he counted, "Uno, dos, tres," touching each one I had selected, and announced the final total, "Doce," as if the great computing machine had successfully completed its

*Fig. 10. Steep bank of the Orinoco at Saladero. Brad Endicott finds
Saladoid sherds in recent landslide.*

task. Then he promptly asked the owner, "¿Cuanto?" The owner hesitated. She well knew that the going price was one or two bolívars apiece (roughly twenty-five to fifty cents), but some were nicer pieces and might bring four or five bolivars. So she tried "Cinquenta B's." A look of incredulity came over Pedro's face, tinged with the proper amount of scorn to impress his principals in the deal. I indicated that I wanted the pieces, so Pedro offered "Treinta." Immediately she countered with "Cuarenta." Glancing at me out of one corner of his eye, Pedro said "Treintacinco" with finality, and already the pieces were being gathered into his paper bag.

Now the son appeared, perhaps twelve years old. He had four or five pieces. Then two daughters, one six the other three. We bought sherds from each of them. Finally a naked baby boy just able to toddle came over to me. He carried in his chubby little hand a small pot handle in the form of an animal head. "Mi cabeza, mi cabeza," he chirped in imitation of his brothers and sisters who had shown their handfuls of pottery heads. He held it out to me and I examined it. It wasn't of any significance, but I wouldn't have disappointed him for the world. "Uno B," said his six year old sister in support of the young merchant. I handed him a shiny silver bolívar, which he promptly put in his mouth—the safest place he knew.

This was repeated at other houses, each group following us down the row of houses until there was quite a troop of adults and dancing, giggling youngsters making a fiesta out of our visit.

From this performance it was obvious that since 1950 the digging and saving of *adornos*, as these decorated potsherds are called, had become a thriving business at Saladero. Ben Rouse had taught these peasants to dig carefully, so that every promising looking sherd appearing in any of their garden plots had been saved to offer visitors. When the wages earned from the official excavation had ceased, their income had been sharply reduced. Months would pass and no tourist or visitor would appear. But when one did, he was understandably welcomed as a possible source of revenue.

This performance had been fun, but actually I was looking for sherds that would help me understand the series of pottery decoration technics that had been employed. Very few early decorated Saladoid pieces were among the sherds offered, probably because they had not dug down to the Saladoid levels, but had gathered only what had turned up during gardening or in superficial scratching of the surface.

Going down the only pathway a patch of ground came in sight, perhaps a hundred feet square, in which a number of irregular holes had been dug. Potsherds were lying all over the place. Obviously this was where some of the cabezas had come from. I was puzzled about the holes, however. Could this have been a burial ground? Rouse had described the nine excavations he had made to "sample" the entire site of Saladero and had specifically commented on the absence of burial urns. Inquiring if any complete pots had been found, they said one had been dug the day before, the informant pointing to one of the holes. The pot was a big one, he said, and had been obtained at a depth of one meter, indicating that this was really quite deep. Someone offered to get the pot and it was brought to us. It was a beauty, and quite large—seventeen inches in diameter and thirteen inches deep—with two fine loop handles, each bearing a well-carved head (Figure 11). The base was cracked, but otherwise it was in perfect condition.

The pot looked like the burial urns shown in photographs which Rouse had published from other parts of Venezuela. I inquired if there had been anything inside. "Nothing but a bunch of old bones," they told me. Asked where they were, they replied with a grimace of horror, "Oh, we threw them away, immediately!" Obviously this was a burial urn. I checked the map of Ben's excavations. Four of his sites actually ringed this burial spot and one was only sixty feet away. It was thus by the sheerest bad luck that he had missed the burial site. I am convinced that this burial site should be dug because the casual excavations have gone to a depth of only one meter, whereas Saladero-style pottery is found at its best nearly two meters deep.

Further questioning revealed that several large bowls had been found, but they were still in hiding at a ranch whose owner was not at home. I left the suggestion that any new finds should retain the bones since the pots would then be more valuable.

Pedro volunteered the information that someone had come down from Caracas and tried to prohibit the digging and sale of the artifacts, even attempting to confiscate the pieces on hand (without offering to pay for them). But these people have a fierce sense of possession. It is their land and they resent any interference. So successful was their protest that the fracas died down and they went back to their occasional digging. They pointed out with considerable logic that the river had been eating into the bank and at

Fig. 11. The pot was a beauty, and quite large.

every flood stage great slabs of earth fell into the river with the total loss of the sherds.[1]

By this time it was one o'clock and the launch took us downstream about two miles to the little settlement called Apostadero (Map 4), which is Spanish for "naval station" and seems an unlikely name for such a small group of huts. However, a signboard with "Tome Pepsi-Cola" was a welcome sight, since we were thirsty, but no thirstier apparently than the tiny baby who was helping

71

himself ecstatically from a very pretty woman with sculptured breasts like those of the exotic Hindu beauties carved on the temples at Khajuraho and Konarak. My attention was eventually diverted (the light not being good enough for photographs) by a man carrying on his head a huge pile of what looked like cassava bread. These golden-brown disks were thirty inches in diameter. He had emerged from a thatched hut bearing the sign Panadería— Teodoro Továr.

We walked over to the bakery and one glance was enough to identify the tools for processing manioc as being the same as those we had seen in Arawak huts in Surinam. Teodoro Továr, the baker, was dancing from one processing step to another with almost hummingbird alertness and precision. He welcomed us and was eager to answer questions. I found immediately that most of the names were different. Manioc was called *yuca* in Venezuela; peeled and unpeeled tubers of yuca were lying around the little bakeshop. The grater, which he called a "rayo," was made from the wall of an oil can punched with holes, just as in Surinam. It was clogged with yuca starch and fibers. The tube for extracting the poisonous juice had been called a matapi in Surinam and here was known as a *sebucan*. It was hanging from a rafter and juice was draining out of the tube. Cylinders of yuca starch were lying in a trough and broken chunks were being sifted through the screen, which he said was a *manari*, to give crumbs of cassava (yuca) starch. A large disk of the bread, which he called *casabe*, was baking on an iron griddle; disks were sun-drying on the thatched roof and on every other available flat surface. It was interesting that although they used the Arawak word "yuca" instead of "manioc," they had retained "cassava" in the form of "casabe," the common interchange of *b* and *v*.

Teodoro was performing each task himself and couldn't have been busier. He was a sprightly, talkative fellow, and every answer was accompanied by a smile as he flitted from one job to another.

"Do you use both sweet and bitter yuca?" I asked. This seemed to puzzle him. Evidently, I was not using the correct word for "bitter." Brad came to my assistance. Teodoro caught on immediately, explaining that there were two kinds of yuca; *yuca dulce* and *yuca amarga*. I tried again.

"Are you using yuca dulce or yuca amarga in your bread?"

"Solamente amarga," he replied with definiteness and pride.

I asked him to show me the tubers he was using. He picked up some. They had a light reddish skin, rather than the dark brown skin I had learned to associate with bitter manioc in Antigua. I asked to see the stems or "sticks" of the plants from which the tuber had come. Teodoro, who was having a wonderful time as the principal actor upon whom all attention was being lavished, went to a nearby pile of yuca stems, which he said were being saved for planting. I examined the stems and saw instantly that they were the sweet variety. They had the same smooth, light-green surface and the widely spaced leaf scars which, in Antigua, we would call the White Stick variety of sweet manioc.

"But these are dulce, not amarga," I said.

Teodoro looked crestfallen for a moment. Then, with a flashing smile he said, "Si, señor, correcto. We are using dulce today because the bread is to be eaten right away by customers here in Apostadero. When we ship the casabe bread we must use only yuca amarga."

This is in exact agreement with the well-known superior keeping qualities of bitter cassava. It was a crucial point, and I couldn't let it pass.

"Why do you use the sebucan with the dulce when it is not poisonous?" I asked.

"You can't make bread with wet yuca," replied Teodoro with finality.

As a baker he knew from long experience that the crumbs must be dry enough to spread evenly on the griddle with tiny air spaces between them. It is equally important that the crumbs not be too dry. There must be just enough dampness so that the plant sugars in the residual juice will caramelize during baking, binding the crumbs into a firm disk. If the unsqueezed grated yuca were poured onto the griddle, it would form a liquid slurry that would stick to the griddle and not form a disk of bread.

It was clear that the sebucan was the device needed to give the crumbs the right *texture* for baking. This was true for the sweet as well as for the poisonous variety of yuca. It was only incidental to the mechanical operation that the poisonous juice was removed when yuca amarga was used for breadmaking.

Casabe from yuca amarga commands a better price because it can be kept for months. Teodoro had probably said he was using yuca amarga when actually he was using dulce not because of any propensity to untruth, but because of an innate pride in producing the higher quality of casabe for shipment to outside markets. It was merely by chance that I was witnessing production of the dulce variety for local consumption.

Fig. 12. An elegant animal head, or adorno—the handle of a pot.

While wandering around Apostadero, I was shown a hole, about four feet in diameter and four feet deep, where three pots had recently been found. These were burial urns since they had contained bones, but even more exciting there were gold ornaments. Our informant had not seen the gold, only heard of it in local conversation, and could give no statement about its form. Burial urns holding bones and gold suggest an early connection with Colombian gold fabricators and give a hint of possible Arawak origins.

Returning to Barrancas, I was taken to a man who had a large garden from which he had extracted a number of decorated sherds, one a nice large animal head, the handle of a pot (Figure 12). It had been broken in three pieces, but the fragments fitted easily to give about a 90 per cent complete adorno. It was Los Barrancos style.

Our visit to Saladero and its associated sites had been well worth while for I had acquired specimens illustrating all of the styles that Professor Rouse had dug there—Saladero, Barrancas, Los Barrancos, Guarguapo, and Apostadero (Map 4). Returning to Ciudad Bolívar we found the Venezuelan government boat S. S. *Apure* anchored in the river—not docked, because there was no dock. The

Fig. 13. The strong Orinoco current biting relentlessly into the banks. Amerind habitations well above flood line.

banks were fairly steep and I was glad that it had been sunny most of the day; otherwise we would have slid rather than walked down the bank. We boarded gingerly, walking up two wobbling planks.

The *S. S. Apure* was a good-sized river boat, 180 feet long. The space below deck was filled with cargo of all sorts, including cattle, pigs, and chickens. On the deck were eight two-person cabins, each no larger than a clothes closet. Quite a number of passengers were coming aboard so I walked aft to see where they were all going. There were no cabins aft, but forty hammocks were hung everywhere at all angles and heights.

We got underway about midnight in bright moonlight. The next morning I experimented with a shower bath which delivered muddy water pumped from the river.

It was pleasant on deck, with the temperature about 80° and a gentle breeze blowing. The banks on both sides of the river were low—not more than ten to twenty feet above the water level—for at least three quarters of the way. The strong Orinoco current

Fig. 14. Mile after mile of flatland came right to the edge of the river.

was relentlessly biting away at the banks (Figure 13). Fresh land-falls were evident everywhere. Indeed, two or three times a day we saw great hunks of the bank sliding into the river. Mile after mile of flat land came right to the edge of the river (Figure 14), fre-quently with a band of trees close to the water. Only rarely were hills seen in the background, usually several miles away. This was the llanos country and almost uninhabited. Only when the banks rose more than twenty feet above the river were there any signs of human life. Then thatched huts appeared, much like the Surinam jungle huts but not so well built. Through binoculars I could distinguish people, evidently Amerinds, standing immobile against their houses.

Throughout the morning I watched the shoreline, photograph-ing everything that might contribute to a picture of life along the Orinoco: the style of the houses, the people, and particularly the nature of the crops—almost invariably manioc, or yuca as I should call it in Venezuela. Only once did I see a house on low land and noticed that the Indian was already dismantling it in anticipation of the coming high water. The palm-leaf side walls were being removed, leaving the bare pole supports. Pots and other meager possessions were already stacked up, presumably to be carried to the hills a mile or two back from the river.

The *S. S. Apure* was making its way slowly—about twice as fast as a man can walk—up this great river. I kept thinking that this was perhaps the route by which the Saladoid potters had come downstream from some unknown point of origin in the west. This was partially supported by the fact that Saladoid pottery had been found at two locations upstream: Ronquín, near Parmana (Map 5), which we should reach in a couple of days, and Cotua, near Puerto Ayacucho, the end of our boat trip. Unfortunately, neither Ronquín nor Cotua pottery styles had been dated by carbon-14 tests. Professor Rouse had suggested that Ronquín might be earlier than Saladero, but Cotua he felt must be much later (Map 6).

The presence of Saladoid potsherds is generally agreed as being indicative of Arawak occupation. Four other sites of Saladoid pottery have been found in northeastern Venezuela: Irapa, found on the Paria Peninsula which points at Trinidad; El Mayal and Chuare, both sites about sixty miles west of Irapa, near Carúpano on the north coast; and El Agua, on the northeast tip of Margarita Island. The pottery at all four of these sites displays the same white-on-red designs that occur at Saladero, Ronquín, and Cotua.

These four pottery styles—Irapa, El Mayal, Chuare, and El Agua —have been shown to be later than the Saladero style, having carbon-14 dates about A.D. 1 to 300. Hence these could not be places from which the Saladoid potters at Saladero originated, but might be places to which they had migrated. Only Ronquín remains as a possible point of origin. If Ronquín is redug and charcoal samples give dates earlier than 1010 B.C., then it could be postulated that the Ronquín potters had gone downstream to Saladero.

The only ceramic material in Venezuela earlier than 1010 B.C. is that found at Rancho Peludo (Map 7), northwest of Maracaibo. It is dated 1970 B.C. and comprises bowls with decoration of appliqued strips bearing punctation marks. One example has a roughly incised head and the base of one bowl shows fabric impressions. None of these features is found in Saladero pottery, and therefore it seems quite plausible that the potters who made such vessels at Rancho Peludo in 1970 B.C. could have developed their skills by 1010 B.C. to make the more sophisticated Saladoid pottery. Furthermore, the trip from Maracaibo to the Orinoco delta could have been made by crossing the llanos on foot or coming down the Rio Portuguesa, which joins the Rio Apure a little west of Ronquín. Obviously we would hope to find pottery transitional between Rancho Peludo and Saladero to establish the line of migration or diffusion.

The *S. S. Apure* was heading due west, and after watching the sun set the short twilight gave way to pitch blackness, since the moon would not be up for several hours. I could distinguish no shoreline anywhere, nor could any of the passengers, but there must have been better eyes on the bridge. In answer to my query, the captain said the ship had no radar, and as it was "getting pretty dark" we would have to stop until the moon came up. A sounding showed the depth to be six feet, which he said was fine, since the boat drew only five feet. The anchor was dropped and we did not get under way again until midnight when the moon, beginning its last quarter, rose over the stern.

Next morning we were still in the Mississippi-like river with low banks and an occasional mud flat. It was just six degrees north of the Equator and quite warm. There was no thermometer, but it felt 90°, with no breeze, even though we were supposed to be doing nine knots. A thin edging of trees grew along the south bank of the river and through an occasional hole in the fringe I could see a few acres of recently cleared land. The trees were lying in all directions as they had been slashed and burning was taking place. Manioc planting would begin as soon as the high water receded. It had been rising for several days and had eight or ten feet to go before reaching flood level, as judged by the paint marks showing the levels of the past four or five years on the occasional outcropping rock. Some of these rocks had been smoothed into strange shapes by the endless washing of the river.

At noon we reached Las Bonitas (Map 6), the anchor was dropped, and several passengers went ashore to join waiting friends. It was now overcast and pleasantly cool—about 80°—then a few drops of rain, and finally a good downpour. The rain brought out swarms of grasshoppers and they were all over. I had been familiar with various sorts of locusts during the twenty-five years we had lived on the banks of the Mississippi, but these were like no grasshoppers I had ever seen. I didn't actually catch one and measure it, but I strongly supported someone's estimate of eight inches. This was, as we soon learned, the warning that more insects were to come.

About a dozen huts, several hundred yards apart, were visible on the north bank. Through binoculars we could see thatched roofs, so they were probably Indian. Each had a small clearing and I suppose it was manioc they were growing, though the distance was too great to positively identify the plants.

As we passed Parmana, I watched the banks carefully, knowing that the Ronquín site was just west of that small town. The banks were well above flood line, which fitted the requirements for a major Arawak site. It could have been reached by people coming down the Rio Apure or its major tributary the Portuguesa from the Maracaibo and Valencia sections of western Venezuela or even from northern Colombia. Or, since we were now close to the big bend of the Orinoco, the Arawak ancestors could equally well have come north up the main stream from either southern Colombia, from the still more western land of Ecuador, or even from Peru. If Ronquín is redug and if it should turn out to be earlier than 1010 B.C., then the next obvious step would be to test sites on the high banks along the upper Orinoco, the Rio Meta, the Rio Apure, and the Rio Portuguesa to see whether or not the earlier migrants who became the Arawak potters at Saladero came from Peru, Ecuador, or Colombia (Map 5).

Only a few miles farther upstream from Ronquín was a river port, Caicara (Map 6), at which the *S. S. Apure* was to anchor overnight. We decided to go ashore and explore the country.

We learned that there were several tribes of Indians living within twenty miles of Caicara. The hunting was still quite good and they all grew yuca, bringing casabe to town when they wanted to purchase something. At a small store were several piles of bundles wrapped neatly in palm leaves. "Casabe pan," said the dealer, noticing my interest. Each was a circular package about thirty-six inches in diameter and ten inches high containing twenty disks of cassava bread each weighing a kilo. Caicara, he told me, was the center of a large yuca amarga production by the Indians.

We were still anchored next morning at breakfast time. Raul, the purser, who was very friendly and helpful, came with what was obviously good news, but he talked so fast in Spanish that I couldn't catch the cause of his excitement. Patiently he slowed down, writing for me the words I didn't understand, since I have a much better visual than audial understanding. Some Indians, he said, had just come aboard "con regalos." I went aft with him to find three men, each wearing only a breach clout and looking more

79

Fig. 15. Panares Indians with manari screens.

surly than most Indians. They belonged to the Panares tribe and
had walked twenty miles to Caicara to obtain cash for some un-
specified purchases. The older and most severe looking man said
he was the chieftain of the tribe and was named Esteban. The two
young lads were his sons.

I had wondered what the purser meant by saying the Indians had
"regalos." The word signified "gifts" to me, but that didn't make
sense. No Indian would come aboard bearing gifts to unknown
people. It was slowly made clear that "regalos" also meant "something special or elegant." The "elegant" things turned out to be

three large basketry trays, circular in shape (Figure 15), about thirty inches in diameter. They were decorated with an artfully contrived pattern of alternating squares of light and dark strands of tiriti palm fronds, so skillfully woven that the four quarter segments gave the impression of being separately made and then fitted into a disk form. They were manaris for screening the yuca as it came from the sebucan. The men wanted fifteen bolívars for the three screens, about one dollar each. I thought of all the work that had gone into their fabrication, and with a feigned look of ignorance gave them twenty bolívars, which they accepted with an undisguised grimace of incredulity. They allowed me to photograph them, but would not permit any one else to take their pictures.

Also they told me something new about the poisonous yuca amarga juice. In Surinam the juice was boiled down to a thick syrupy sauce called cassareep for use in making pepper pot stew. In Venezuela it was named *cumache* and they added what they called ant butter, which the ants produced after "milking" the aphids they were using as "cows." If the ant butter contained any of the formic acid or other stinging elements associated with them, it might well add to the piquancy of the sauce.

As we lay at anchor at Caicara a school of large fish which the purser called Tonina, each about five feet long, were playing in the water like porpoises. I learned that the "fish" was actually a mammal, Tonina del Orinoco (*Inia geoffroyensis*), a fresh-water dolphin. There must have been thirty or more, and they put on an entrancing ballet around the ship. It was one more piece of evidence that the tropical rivers provided a rich source of protein for the Arawaks.

Shortly after weighing anchor we reached the junction of the Rio Apure and the Orinoco (Map 8). This is where the Orinoco makes its big turn east after its long flow north from Brazil. The Rio Apure, with its main tributary the Rio Portuguesa, drains much of northeastern Colombia and is therefore one of the probable migration routes into Brazil and Venezuela for Indians entering South America through the Isthmus of Panama. Two mud flats form good-sized islands, illustrating the sedimentation that occurs when the rate of flow of silt-laden currents is slowed down by the meeting of two opposing currents.

Having passed the mouth of the Rio Apure we were going due south, heading upstream for La Urbana (Map 6). The banks were still lowlying but several outcroppings of rock were beginning to appear. Hills were more common and small farms frequent. Manioc was still the main crop at each homestead. La Urbana would, in my opinion, be a promising place to look for ancient sites of Arawaks who had migrated from Colombia down the large Orinoco tributary, the Rio Arauca.

For some unclear reason insects were on hand in great numbers. There were no mosquitos or biting insects, but hundreds of varieties of bugs and beetles. In the shower bath—still muddy water—bugs crawled up legs and body by the hundreds and a water jet strong enough to sting the body did not deter the bugs in their climb. The only effective means of dispersing them was a shot of DDT from a spray gun. Birds were in great numbers too, but obviously not enough to cope with the excessive insect population.

On a nearby bank, above La Urbana, we noticed a stark tree that had shed its leaves. Roosting in it were eight large birds with striking red, black, and blue colorations. They were easy to identify as macaws (*Guaca maya roja* in Venezuela) of the species *Ara macao*. Two of them were fighting noisily, the others sitting and watching the squabble. Some were even hanging by their beaks from branches in their excitement at the fun. Apparently to get a closer view of the fight, they would leave their perches and fly to a better vantage point. Green parrots (*Loro real*), much smaller than the macaws, flew into the tree presumably to be in on the fight, but they were soon chased off as impudent intruders.

Huge herons were everywhere, wading at the edge of the mud banks, stately birds with black shoulders which showed up vividly against white plumage. Whenever they decided to move to a place a bit too far for walking they took to the air, so slowly and seemingly clumsily that one expected them to drop at any moment. Every now and then they did drop to earth, but no doubt it was just where they wanted to be.

Occasionally monkeys were seen swinging among the trees, chattering volubly. In addition to the dolphins the river seemed well stocked with large fish (measuring twelve to fifteen inches) traveling in huge schools. It was evident that the food supply was plentiful and may have been even more so in early Arawak days.

The river continued to narrow rapidly. It now appeared to be only about a quarter of a mile wide, but at times it was difficult to tell whether you were looking at the bank of the river or the bank of a long island. Rocks appeared in the river which at times seemed to be a series of rapids, and sand bars were frequent. We passed at least a dozen places where huts had been abandoned and others were being dismantled. The framework was standing and everything would be washed clean when the flood came—with a nice new rich garden deposited on top of the old one. Some houses were still being occupied, but their level was evidently judged safe by the Indians, who knew from experience what to expect from the flooding waters. At almost every homesite a few manioc fields were still standing, and from the light green stems it was apparent the plants were all yuca dulce. Newly slashed forest and the smoke of burning trees showed they were preparing the ground for planting a new manioc crop when the flood receded.

Whereas for several hundred miles the Orinoco had lacked a variety of scenery to the point of monotony, the land now was accented by hills and even mountains in the distance. Occasionally the outcropping rock was quite beautiful in form and color. At one particularly striking spot a stretch of several hundred yards of black rock lay about twenty feet above the level of the river. These rock surfaces had been modeled by time and the elements into fantastic shapes. Their scored surfaces suggested glacial action, but at four degrees above the equator and only a few hundred feet above sea level that seemed improbable.

We were now heading toward Puerto Paez and the river widened to a mile or more. The banks were again low and this condition lasted for about twenty miles. I could not see beyond the heavy fringe of trees on the river bank, but I supposed the llanos stretched for many miles since no hills were visible.

There were still no lights or markers on the river, but we kept chugging along in the inky blackness until 11 P.M. The captain said there were rapids ahead and we would have to stop soon. I heard the anchor being lowered and then silence until 5:30 A.M., when there were sounds of activity. By the time I reached the deck there was just enough light to see that the river ahead was studded with rocks. The boat had anchored a hundred yards from the beginning of the rapids. And rapids they really were! Soon the boat was being maneuvered around rocks in a way that I found really exciting. It was a superb job of taking a 180-foot boat on an almost slalomlike passage. Fortunately the rocks were now clearly visible with none submerged in the channel, but I realized that the captain had somehow known enough to stop in total darkness the night before, just a bare hundred yards short of the first rapids.

It was only an hour's run to Puerto Paez at the mouth of the Rio

Meta, a large tributary of the Orinoco separating Venezuela from Colombia, which it penetrates almost to Bogota and the Rio Magdalena. Puerto Carreño, the port on the Colombian side, could be seen clearly from where we were mooring. It looked like a large and thriving town, in contrast to the small and not too well kept Puerto Paez, which has about a thousand inhabitants. Looking upstream along the Rio Meta it was evident that the same pattern of low banks with occasional higher spots existed for miles. This region should also be searched for old sites of Arawaks migrating from Colombia.

It was only a six-hour run from Puerto Paez to Puerto Ayacucho, the last port up the Orinoco. We could see from quite a distance that we were approaching the first well built Venezuelan town since Ciudad Bolívar. In some respects it was even better equipped, since there were fine docking facilities here where none had existed in Ciudad Bolívar.

My interest in Puerto Ayacucho was to see the first major change in topography of a country in which about a thousand miles of llanos had given way to terrain hilly or rocky enough to change the smooth river into a series of rapids that could be traversed only by pushing or hauling canoes over the difficult spots. Also I hoped to see some present-day Indians living where the ancestors of Arawaks might have lived had they come from Ecuador or Peru, by traveling on any of the eastern Andean streams feeding the Amazon. It was said that at Puerto Ayacucho there were missionaries who maintained small-airplane contact with various tribal villages in remote jungle spots of the Amazonas territory to the southeast.

I sought out the pilot, who said he could not reach the only tribe speaking Arawakan on the Rio Negro (Map 5). It was a canoe trip and would need three or four *curiaras* (Venezuelan term for dugout canoes) with two competent rivermen in each—a two month trip. As I was not prepared to tackle such a major undertaking I visited a nearby tribe of Piaroa Indians, but all we could see was a single conical-shaped thatched hut occupied by a missionary with no Piaroa associates. As a longer stay at Puerto Ayacucho seemed unprofitable I took a Venezuelan plane to Caracas.

The plane took only sixteen minutes to go to Puerto Paez, a distance that had taken us six hours on the boat, then fifty minutes to Caicara, as against the fourteen hour boat trip, not counting the overnight anchorage. I was glad to be able to visualize from the air the vast area of the llanos north of the Orinoco and particularly to continue about a hundred miles up the Rio Apure to San Fernando. This was still llanos country, stretching for almost two hundred miles upstream, to the foot hills of the Cordillera Mérida, the eastern branch of the Andes. It had been the mountain barrier to early migrants from northern Colombia and Panama.

From San Fernando we flew to Caracas where I met Brad Endicott, who was anxious for me to visit John Odehnal, a professor of biology with a fine collection of Amerind artifacts from all over Venezuela. Included were several potsherds from the Arauquinoid series, to which the Guarguapo style belongs, giving another clue to the possible migration of Barrancoid potters from the region of Lake Valencia a few miles southwest of Caracas.

Professor Odehnal also showed several kinds of sebucans, which indicated that some of the tribes had modified the Arawak device for extracting the juices from yuca. One was a very narrow sebucan, only about three inches in diameter, used for squeezing a cooking oil out of crushed palm nuts. Another was a much wider tube, about six inches in diameter, employed to remove the juice from the core of the moriche palm to yield an edible starch. Evidently the sebucan device has had a wide application for pressing liquids from pulpy material.

This led to a discussion of manioc and Professor Odehnal furnished the interesting information that in the upper Orinoco, above Puerto Ayacucho, some of the tribes do not make cassava bread out of yuca but take the product from the sebucan, boil it in water, and drink it as a gruel. Sometimes after screening the yuca is dried as a powder instead of being baked, and is then known as *mandioca*.[2]

On the way back to Antigua I kept turning over the events of the three weeks' trip. Perhaps the outstanding feature was the vivid picture of the huge network of the Orinoco system that forms the drainage for the llanos of Venezuela and adjoining parts of Colombia. Here seems to lie the secret to the possible routes the Arawaks may have traveled, if their prior base was Colombia, Ecuador, or even Peru. The water routes are very complex, but the possible lanes of migration can be unraveled. Actually the Amazon River basin is even more extensive, but it is intimately tied into the Orinoco basin because its Rio Negro tributary is joined during flood time with the Casiquiare (Map 5), tributary of the Orinoco, and the two great river basins are mutually traversable.

What is needed is a careful examination of potsherds from all sites in Peru, Ecuador, and Colombia to see if any show stylistic

Fig. 16. Terraces of the Orinoco exposed as the land rose gradually.

features which might be related to Arawak pottery styles, especially
of the Saladoid or Barrancoid series. If any such relationships are
indicated the search must be continued for similar sherds from
locations lying on possible connecting routes by which the Arawaks
might have reached Saladero from Peru, Ecuador, or Colombia.[3]

The trip up the Orinoco did not provide the factual data needed
to answer the pressing question as to Arawak origins, but it did
provide a backdrop against which to formulate plausible hypotheses
as to migration routes.

As I have pointed out, two thirds of the Orinoco banks is under
water at flood time. It seems reasonable to assume that the migrant
Arawaks would have settled first on land high enough to escape
flooding, or at least at spots subject to only slight inundation. From
photographing the banks every few miles I gained the impression
that the *entire land level of the Orinoco basin is slowly rising.*
Figure 16 shows several levels of the bank and suggests that the

three or four terraces shown are areas of the bank successively exposed as the land rose gradually. If this is so the lower terraces would be the most recently exposed and hence artifacts found on lower terraces would tend to be later than those found on upper terraces. If this reasoning is correct, any land lower than that being occupied at present would probably have been too low to escape flooding two or three thousand years ago. Hence the presently occupied high land is perhaps the only part worth examining for ancient sites.

Undoubtedly nearby areas of lower land would have been planted in manioc, but they would not likely have been living sites. Hence we would not expect to find griddle sherds there. Moreover, on such low areas it would be yuca dulce (sweet manioc) that would be planted. The farmer using flooded land would very quickly have learned to save stems from those plants that had produced the earliest and largest tubers and would have made cuttings from them to plant on the lower ground. It is also quite easy to judge which lands had been flooded because along the side of the river occasionally there are black rocks on which the high-water marks show as lines of mud or debris. When exceptionally high water occurs, as happened in 1960, a line has frequently been painted on a prominent rock with the date of the flood stage.

I estimated that at least two thirds of the land through which we were passing on the S. S. *Apure* in May and June, 1965, was about ten feet below the 1960 high mark. The flooded area in 1960 must have seemed like a huge inland sea. Moreover, since the water was rising rapidly at the time of our journey, it might be only a week or so until much of the banks would again be under water.

It is entirely possible that this annual flooding of the llanos is the real explanation of the differentiation of yuca into sweet and bitter varieties. Perhaps the metabolism of those plants which mature early favors rapid starch synthesis at the expense of the production of the poisonous cyanide-glucoside combination. After hundreds —even thousands—of years in which the stems of the fastest growing tubers were saved for vegetative cuttings, sweet manioc may have developed, a consequence of persistent selective breeding. This would support the idea that bitter manioc was the parent plant.

There are literally hundreds of places where the Arawaks might have lived along the banks of the Orinoco.[4] Some day these high spots will be scientifically investigated and charcoal from ancient hearths will reveal the direction in which the migration moved.

Somewhere along the banks of the Orinoco or its great tributaries, the Rio Apure or the Rio Meta, archeologists may find pottery older than 1010 B.C. from which the Saladoid pottery could have been derived. The associated griddle sherds will attest their earlier use of manioc. Friends have suggested that in still earlier sites griddle sherds may give way to flat stone slabs on which cassava bread was baked before the invention of the pottery griddle. Such stones would probably herald the beginnings of vegetative agriculture in South America. I know of no such stone slabs, but we have not yet found any Arawak sites earlier than Saladero. Professor George A. Kubler asks where such stone slabs might be found in the rock-barren llanos. It may prove to be very difficult to carry the story of manioc growing any further back than Saladero.

VI

The Arawak Religion — the Cult of Yocahú

THE first time we found a piece of stone with a pointed cone everyone at the Mill Reef site stopped digging and began a guessing contest. The first comment was that it looked like a sombrero (Figure 17), but that stimulated no enthusiasm. A skeptic suggested it was just a nicely shaped pebble some Arawak had picked up off the beach, but the hand lens revealed the pecking marks of a tool used in forming the prominent cone. Human hands had determined the shape.

As we continued digging similar stones came to light, all with the same conical hump (Figure 18). We felt they must be things of special significance, but what? Then Don Marshall, retired editor of *The New York Times*, discovered a piece about twice as large as those found previously. It would have been a full six inches long if an inch or so had not been broken off one end—back in Arawak days since it was an ancient break. But this stone was different. It had clearly marked decoration on the hump and an oval ring surrounding a concave base (Figure 19). These objects seemed to comprise a series, Don observed, all of a definite pattern, but this latest one more elaborate than the rest. He was willing to bet they were ceremonial objects.

That evening I consulted J. Walter Fewkes's *The Aborigines of Puerto Rico* (Smithsonian Institution Report 1903–04) which showed several illustrations of similar stones found in various Caribbean islands. Some were a foot long, often elaborately carved with a human head at one end and at the other animal legs drawn up as if to kick backward. These pieces, said Fewkes, were called "three-pointed stones." To me the designation seemed inept since there was only one real point—the prominent cone which sug-

Fig. 17. The first conical stone found at Mill Reef.

gested a humpbacked figure lying on its belly with head in front and legs behind. These must be figures of importance, perhaps pertaining to religious rites.

My interest in these objects greatly increased when I acquired a

Fig. 18. As we continued to dig more conical stones came to light.

Fig. 19. Don Marshall came up with a larger conical stone—decorated.

number of Arawak artifacts collected over a period of sixty years by Miss Cecil Stevens.[1] They included a dozen fine specimens of the humpbacked stones. Some were beautifully carved, one about a foot long having a strong male head with wide-open mouth like several in the Fewkes article, and one wearing ear ornaments (Figure 20). I recalled reading in Sven Loven's *Origins of the Tainan Culture, West Indies* (p. 599) a statement by Columbus regarding houses where their idols, which they called zemies, were kept. The shaman took a hollow cane that had two branches which he placed in his nostrils and snuffed up the dust. I learned later that the dust was a narcotic which threw the shaman into a trance and the words he uttered were the message the deity wished to convey to those present.

Were these conical stones the zemies to which Columbus had referred? If so, why did they have the prominent hump and what had inspired this strange shape? The prototype must have been

Fig. 20. A strange, partially human figure, apparently lying on its belly (Puerto Rico, ca. A.D. 1200).

related to something of tremendous significance to the Arawak way of life, and as none of the conical stones had been discovered on the South American mainland whence the Arawaks had come this hump must have been of deep concern only to island Arawaks.

The answer to my puzzle literally appeared to me one day when I was cruising the Lesser Antilles aboard the ketch *Viking II*. Sailing southwest from Barbuda (Map 1) we were temporarily out of sight of land. Then the volcanic peak of Mt. Misery on St. Kitts appeared, a speck on the horizon. As the *Viking II* spanked along before the northeast trade wind the speck of land became a cone, the surrounding lowland created by some long-ago volcano flow became a base, and the composite became the humpbacked deity I had been studying. The illusion vanished as we neared land, but for an hour or so I had experienced what a canoe-load of Arawaks, paddling into unknown waters, would have seen as they approached each new island. Land, god-given, revealed to them by the conical peak of the volcano.[2] Even the smallish eminence of Antigua's Boggy Peak would have been part of the miracle to Arawaks struggling northward through rough waters from Guadeloupe. How natural, then, for them to have associated the volcanic shape with the powerful deity who had guided them there. And how logical, as they migrated through the Antilles, welcomed from island to island by the ever-present pointed mountain, to have created their principal god in the form of a volcanic cone.

This seemed particularly reasonable when I recalled that the Arawaks had lived on the flat prairielike llanos of the Orinoco River basin of Venezuela before taking off through open water for the islands. When they reached the Antilles it must have seemed like a new world of limitless ocean, with tiny specks of land appearing in the wide expanse of empty sea. Particularly impressive would have been the volcanos rising starkly out of the water. Actually, the Lesser Antilles comprise a very thin line of islands, with no land within reach of early man either to east or west. But fortunately, in clear weather, each island in the chain is visible from its nearest neighbor—sometimes not from sea level, but from hills on each island the cone of the one beyond can be sighted, assuring seafarers of land ahead.

At some point during their wanderings the voyagers may well have been startled and awed by the sight of a volcano in eruption, perhaps Mt. Pelée on Martinique or Soufrière on Guadeloupe. To these riverine and prairie people the violence of a mountain pouring out fire and lava would have been a terrifying experience. Surely only gods could belch forth flame and molten rock! The transfer would have been easy to make. The volcano must be their own great and powerful deity, or perhaps the place where their supreme being lived. Probably this was the god that had brought them out of their prairie home on the llanos along the Orinoco, beckoning them onward from island to island.

The Arawaks developed the cone-shaped deities only after they had encountered cone-shaped volcanos. I know of no other aboriginal tribe that has adopted the simple but powerful form of the volcano for the sculptural embodiment of their principal deity. In their early days on the Venezuelan llanos (1000 B.C. or earlier) the Arawaks may have revered a deity, or at least a cult hero, who had given them the all-important manioc. However, there are no traces in any Arawak excavation sites along the Orinoco of any stone or pottery effigies which might be considered as religious symbols. Even during the first Arawak years on the Antillean islands, I assume that only a spirit or legendary cult hero existed and that he was without any physical embodiment.

My thinking had advanced thus far when I met Professor José Juan Arrom, professor of Spanish literature at Yale. As he was much interested in the religion of the Arawaks we arranged a meeting at my gallery in Guilford, Connecticut where the zemi collection was on display. He walked straight to the great humpbacked, open-mouthed figure (Figure 20), picked it up with a grin, and with increasing excitement slowly turned it around and over. "It's a beauty," he said. "You know who he is, of course?"

I admitted my ignorance. "You mean you know his name?"

"Indeed I do. He is Yocahú, the great Arawak male deity. The giver of manioc. The *yoca* part of his name is the same as in the word manioc and the suffix *hu* means "giver of.""

Professor Arrom gingerly handed the figure to me, and although I always handle artifacts carefully this time I touched the deity with a sense of awe as I respectfully returned him to his stand.

"How do you know his name?" I asked. Professor Arrom explained that in the Beinecke Library for Rare Books at Yale he had come across an old Spanish manuscript written about 1525 by Hernán Pérez de Oliva. Oliva had given his manuscript to his friend Fernando Colón, son of Christopher Columbus. The last part of the book described and named three of the Arawak deities.

"The manuscript had been lost for about four hundred years," Professor Arrom said, "so I have written a book about it and would be pleased if you would accept a copy." It is from Professor Arrom's book that I have obtained my information about Yocahú and two other members of the Arawak pantheon.[3]

I was gratified to learn that my hypothesis—that the Arawaks might have been the discoverers and domesticators of manioc—was supported by the Arawaks themselves. They had named their chief

94

god Yocahú, giver of manioc, in recognition of the vital part manioc had played in the development of the tribe. Admittedly, I was curious as to what point in their wanderings through the islands Yocahú had taken this form. It would not have been in Antigua since there has been no active volcano there for perhaps thousands of years. Furthermore, Antigua was probably too small an island for such an event to have occurred. There would have been a much better chance for an important development in religious thinking or ritual practice to take place on a larger island, such as Guadeloupe or Martinique.

Guadeloupe is approximately six times greater in area than Antigua, and for hundreds of years Arawaks prospered on that lush and lovely island where fish were plentiful inside the coral reefs and the rich soil would have produced bountiful crops of manioc. The numerous griddle sherds in the early middens of Guadeloupe prove that Arawaks were cultivating manioc extensively. Not only is this island more fertile than rain-scarce Antigua, but the volcanic peaks are more impressive and have been more active. A firsthand study of its middens and artifacts recovered there was indicated.

I contacted my friend Edgard Clèrc, president of the Historical Society of Guadeloupe, and he invited me to visit their principal site at Morel. It is a large site (Map 9a), a few miles east of the town of Le Moule on the east coast of Grande Terre which, with the contiguous island of Basse-Terre, comprise Guadeloupe. The site lies right on the beach, and the lowest layer of Arawak occupation is now only a few inches above high tide line. In this latitude the daily tide is only about a foot, so except during storms the midden is above the action of the waves. The land has been slowly sinking for the past two thousand years, Clèrc said, adding that he had found artifacts on the flat rocks in sea water thirty feet or so from shore. The site comprises a large midden running along the shore for more than a hundred yards. It is now fifty feet or more in width and about ten feet deep at some places.

There are four distinct layers. Morel I, the lowest layer, is about a foot thick and lies on flat beds of sedimentary rock which remain bare at normal high tide. This layer yields characteristic white-on-red Saladoid pottery, showing that the Arawaks were still following the craft traditions of their earlier tribal existence in Venezuela. In this bottom layer I saw Z-I-C sherds (i.e., sherds with zoned [Z] areas of decoration containing incised [I] cross-hatching [C], indicating the Arawaks were living there about A.D. 100–300. Edgard Clèrc has obtained supporting carbon-14 dates of A.D. 170 and 190. Not a single zemi with the conical hump has been found in Morel I.

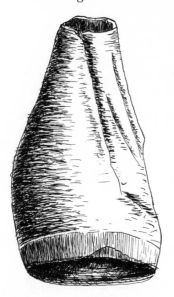

Fig. 21. The earliest conical zemi, made from a conch shell knob (Guadeloupe, A.D. 220).

The first zemies occurred in Morel II. The earliest one, found near the bottom of this layer, was of very simple structure, consisting of nothing more than one of the knobby protuberances of a conch shell (Figure 21). The point, about two inches long, had been cut off the shell, but its conical surface was not worked in any way. Its top had the characteristic shell depression which strongly suggests the crater of a volcano. The base had been flattened and shaped, somewhat crudely, in an oval outline. On this base was a concavity that revealed part of the original brilliant inner curved surface of the conch. Charcoal samples from the level of this conch zemi yielded dates of A.D. 220 and 240. Every conical zemi found in Morel II was fabricated out of conch shell.

The idea has already been advanced that the sight of an erupting volcano probably made such a deep impression on the Arawaks that they felt these mountains must be the home of their god Yocahú. But the question as to why the conch protuberance had been selected as the embodiment of the manioc deity had still to be answered. I suggest that the transfer from the volcanic peaks to the cone-shaped zemies may have taken place when some observant Arawak shaman chanced to look closely at a conch shell (*Strombus gigas*) which happened to be silhouetted against the sky. I had just such an experience while photographing a conch (Figure 22), and was surprised to notice how much the knobs on the shell looked like the mountainous skyline of Basse-Terre as seen from the distance of its neighboring island of Grande Terre, a correspondence probably indelibly sealed in the mind of the Arawak shaman who first observed it. Here, he pondered, was the way that he, the artist and mystic, could capture the power of the volcano. He would cut a knob from

Fig. 22. Close-up of conch shell whose silhouette resembles the moun-tainous skyline of the island of Basse-Terre as seen from the neighboring island of Grande Terre, Guadeloupe.

a conch shell and from it carve an image of a volcano, the housing for the powerful spirit of Yocahú who, he believed, must live in the mountain peak.

After visiting the caves of France and Spain in 1968, I realized that this making of an image to capture its internal power might be analogous to the attempted domination of a mammoth or bison by the Cro-Magnon artist who painted the animals on the walls or ceilings of the caves at Lascaux and Altamira. By making an *image* of the animal, he believed that magically he captured its *spirit*, with full confidence that in tomorrow's chase he and his associate hunters would bring down the actual bison by their spears directed against vital spots as illustrated in his paintings. The Arawak shaman had cut the knob of the conch so that it could stand on its own base and serve as the image of the volcano. He had performed the magic of making a zemi that would contain some portion of the power or spirit of Yocahú, who resided in the volcano and who would be forever available to him.

Fig. 23. Morel II yielded more symmetrical and stylized zemies, some of them elaborately decorated (Guadeloupe).

Not only did the zemies continue through Morel II, but they were made only from the knobby protuberances of the conch shell. The form became more symmetrical and stylized and the surface finish smoother, even to the degree of being polished. Some of the later ones were decorated elaborately with incised bands of punctation (Figure 23) presumably giving added distinction to the zemi. But in spite of these modifications they were still definitely representations of a volcano.

The top of Morel II has been carbon-14 dated at A.D. 560. It is interesting and significant that the Saladoid white-on-red pottery accompanied the conch zemies all through layer II, indicating three centuries of continued occupation of the site by the same kind of people.

The next highest layer, Morel III, revealed a notable change in the progression of the zemi. About A.D. 575, some daring Arawak sculptor broke with tradition and carved a zemi from stone. Perhaps he was a shaman who had noticed a stone on the beach, shaped by the sea somewhat in the shape of a conch zemi but appreciably larger. He conceived the idea of transforming it into traditional zemi shape by a little carving thus creating a god-form that would add distinction to his clan, perhaps by virtue of its increased size, impossible to achieve with the limited dimensions of the conch protuberances. This concept evidently caught on since the conch zemies gradually disappeared from Morel III to be replaced by zemies carved from limestone, andesite, agate, or coral.

The form expanded and the cone became more pronounced. The

98

Fig. 24. The largest stone zemi found in Guadeloupe, twelve inches long, with the face of Yocahú carved on the side.

cutting became precise and the surface frequently flawless. Strangely enough, the sculptors felt it necessary to preserve the hollowed base that had characterized the conch zemies. To date this concavity in the stone has no known significance. It is very likely a carryover of a long-familiar form.

The stone cone-shaped zemies persisted throughout Morel III, and the decoration that had embellished some of the small conch zemies was developed until finally the face of Yocahú appeared. By this time, about A.D. 900, the stone zemi had reached a foot in length and a height of six inches (Figure 24), as large as the stone zemies found in Puerto Rico and which date two or three hundred years later. The Guadeloupe zemies, however, never acquired the complexity of the stone Yocahú from Puerto Rico with the wide-open mouth and ear ornaments (Figure 20).

Thus over the period of three or four hundred years that the Arawaks occupied Morel III a full range of stone zemies was produced, differing in size and complexity, suggesting widely varied use, perhaps corresponding to the rank of the possessor. The smaller ones were probably carried to give personal protection to individuals. A slightly larger one would be kept in the home as guardian of the family. Others guarded the clan or the village. The largest and most elaborate would belong to the chieftain who, as indicated by Father Ramon Pané, maintained a shrine for the tribal Yocahú, perhaps with a coterie of shaman attendants to serve the deity. As the padre said, "All or the majority of the people have many zemies of different kinds." It would not surprise me if these zemies had also been involved in fertility rites to promote better manioc crops. Small ones may have been buried in the manioc fields, but these would rarely be found today.

Finally, in Morel IV there were *no* zemies. Edgard Clèrc attributes the sudden absence of this form of artifact to the arrival of the Caribs and their extermination of the Arawak males, who were most likely the sole carvers of zemies. At the interface between Morel III and IV many of the zemies were broken. Presumably the Caribs were familiar with these protective fetishes of the Arawaks and destroyed them at the same time they killed and ate their owners.

Consequently I suggest that the zemi cult in Guadeloupe lasted about eight hundred years, beginning shortly after A.D. 200 and being ended by the Caribs some time after A.D. 1000. Whether the zemi cult of Yocahú originated in Guadeloupe or in some other island will not be known until scientific excavations are made on other islands such as Martinique. But I feel that I have pinpointed the beginning of the zemi cult, traced its evolution over a period of several hundred years, and even demonstrated its termination at Morel IV when the Caribs invaded the island, killed off the Arawaks, and demolished the zemies, thus obliterating Yocahú from Guadeloupe.

From the lessons I had learned in the stratified, well-dated layers at the Morel site, it was natural that I should be anxious to see if the same sequence of Yocahú zemies could be found in Antigua. At Mill Reef I had not found sites where continuous occupancy could be as well established as at Morel. But at Indian Creek, a site a few miles west on the southern coast, it seemed obvious from the style of sherds lying on the surface that the five mounds existing there would prove to be of quite different datings. I was unwilling to dig these mounds as I expect Professor Rouse will shortly undertake definitive excavation of what appears to be the most extensive and important Arawak site on this island. Only on one mound were there found early Saladoid sherds exhibiting the negatively painted white-on-red designs and also the equally diagnostic zoned, incised, cross-hatched designs—the Z-I-C sherds. Consequently I confined my activity to an extensive surface examination of that large mound. It took a dozen visits, spaced over a period of two years, before I found what I sought: three small Yocahú zemies, all carved from the prongs of conch shells (Figure 25). There were no stone zemies on the surface of the mound, so presumably this localized area is similar to Morel II, and I am guessing that the same dates, roughly A.D. 220 to 560, may apply.

Since these conch zemies were all surface finds it is impossible to establish their sequence, but they closely parallel the Guadeloupe Morel conch zemies. The zemi shown in figure 25a is a beautifully shaped "volcanic cone." The crater is clearly shown at the peak and the base reveals a portion of the smooth inner concavity of the shell. There is no decoration on the outer surface of the cone, but the zemi in figure 25b does have some decoration. A groove had been cut around the cone near the base to give a definite "pedestal" for the zemi. Examination of the spiral markings of the base of 25b shows that the piece was cut from the front tip of the conch. Zemi 25c has the same kind of pedestal as 25b, but it has further decoration, namely a narrow groove halfway between the peak of the cone and the pedestal, with an incised cross segmenting this peak. The base has been flattened and again shows part of the smooth inner cavity of the prong of the conch. In the same area were three other shell pieces that I believe were also Yocahú zemies. One was a conch prong showing the crater top and hollow base, but with no evidence of any smoothing of the outside surface and quite closely resembling Edgard Clèrc's earliest conch zemi. The other two were very crudely worked with flat bases, one with a grooved band to provide a typical pedestal. They are, however, not from conch, but the cone of the American Top Shell, the only ones I have seen made from this shell.

My tentative conclusion, therefore, is that the same evolution of Yocahú, going through various stages of conch-shell decoration, occurred in Antigua as in Guadeloupe. I now feel confident that systematic excavation of the Indian Creek mounds will confirm this development of the conch zemies from the simplest cut prong to elaborately engraved conch zemies, all in a context of Saladoid pottery belonging to a range of approximately A.D. 200 to 600. In

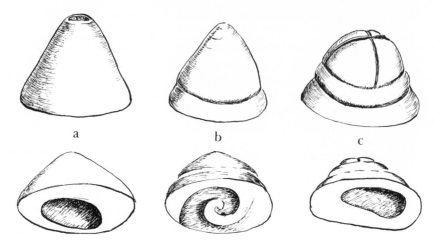

Fig. 25. Zemies: a (left): *Well-shaped volcanic cone. Base reveals the smooth inner concavity of the conch shell.* b (middle): *Has a groove cut around base. Spiral grooves of base show it was cut from front tip of a conch.* c (right): *Similar to 25b, but has an upper groove around cone and incised cross on top. Again base shows inner concave surface of shell.*

some later mound I fully expect that a whole series of stone zemies will be discovered, beginning with small ones and eventually ending with large carved figures showing a head at one end and feet at the other. A small amount of scratching in the soil of an arroyo cut by rain runoff through another Indian Creek mound has brought to light one stone zemi larger than any found at Mill Reef. The head had been knocked off, possibly by invading Caribs. In association with this piece were pottery sherds having elegantly executed designs resembling the "baroque" Los Barrancos style, hence perhaps about A.D. 1000 or later.

THE ARAWAK FERTILITY GODDESS—ATABEYRA

As discussed in the concluding pages of the Pérez de Oliva manuscript and as revealed by excavations of island Arawak sites, Yocahú stood first in the Arawak pantheon. Next in importance to him and in the number of sculptural representations that have been found was a female deity referred to as Atabeyra. Actually this goddess had several Arawakan names describing her functions: mother of moving waters—the sea, the tides, and the springs—goddess of the moon, and the fertility goddess of childbirth.

In my collection are six carved stone figures of Atabeyra which come from Puerto Rico. The largest shows her as a fertility goddess, squatting in the act of parturition (Figure 26). Her hands are holding her chin while her elbows press into her sides as she struggles in the labor of childbirth. Her eyes are fixed in a distant stare. Below is a bulging mass, the emerging babe. This powerful and evocative figure, with an estimated date of about A.D. 1200, was formerly in the Cecil Stevens collection.

A much smaller squatting figure comes from Haiti (Figure 27). Again Atabeyra's hands are tight against her chin. I am deeply impressed by the vividness of this sculpture. The open mouth and the heavy eyebrow ridge over wide-open eyes convey the intensity of her efforts in the throes of childbirth. Her legs are carved in a somewhat different position than on the larger figure. Evidently this position of the body was a difficult one for the Arawak artist to portray. The babe is not shown.

Arawak sculptors did, however, achieve some splendid results and no work exhibits their competence better than the superb figure from Puerto Rico (Figure 28). This goddess of fertility is a tour de force of the sculptor's art, a brilliant piece of abstraction that I feel sure would earn the admiration of Henry Moore. The head, breasts, and umbilicus are all concave and the total figure is of great simplicity. To me this ranks with the masterpieces of modern abstract sculpture, and I should like to honor her with the Arawakan equivalent of "Venus of the Arawaks."

From Antigua, the only fertility figure at all noteworthy is a clay figurine dug at Marmora Bay (Figure 29, Map 2). It may be a representation of Atabeyra. She has a large head, with heavy eyebrow ridge, stubby legs, but no arms.[4]

THE ARAWAK DOG DEITY—OPIYEL-GUAOBIRAN

The third member of the Arawak pantheon mentioned in the Pérez de Oliva manuscript is designated as a dog deity.

Several years ago, in a native hut on the island of Barbuda (Map 1), I came across an interesting stone piece. It was being used as a doorstop[5] and was covered with black paint which the owner said

Fig. 26. Atabeyra, Arawak fertility goddess, hands under chin in labor, babe emerging (Puerto Rico).

Fig. 27. Atabeyra (Haiti).

Fig. 28. Atabeyra in highly abstract form. A masterpiece of Arawak sculpture, "Venus of the Arawaks" (Puerto Rico).

106

Fig. 29. Ceramic Atabeyra (Mamora Bay, Antigua).

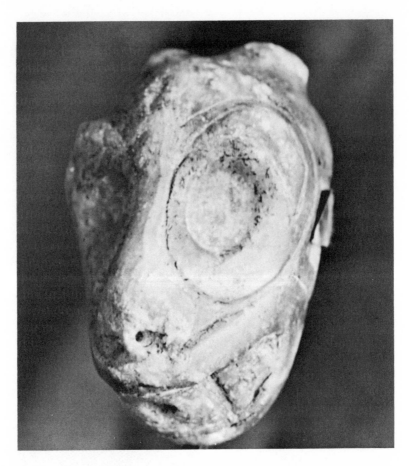

Fig. 30. Head of dog deity (Barbuda).

he had applied. When the paint was removed a splendidly carved
animal head was revealed (Figure 30). It had fangs bared for action
and the surface was smooth, except for the ear and eye sockets,
presumably left rough to retain some tree gum in which shell eyes
and ear ornaments had probably been imbedded.

A strange hole or passage commenced in the underside and continued upward through the head for about three inches, then divided to exit at the top in two perforated nubbins suggesting that
this Y-shaped passage through the head might be an elaborate form
of the tubes the Arawaks are known to have used to snuff narcotics
to induce a ritual trance. Perhaps the shaman had held it over some

narcotic such as cahoba dust, drawing deep breaths to bring on a state of religious narcosis. Trance induced through the head of a deity presumably would have had special authority for a believer.

Shortly thereafter Professor Arrom came again to Guilford to see my new artifacts. At sight of the Barbuda animal head his eyes widened. "It is the great dog deity Opiyel-Guaobiran, as named in the Pérez de Oliva manuscript," he said. "It's unique, the only deity I have ever seen that contained its own snuffing tube." He explained the meaning of the deity's formidable name. "Opiyel-Guaobiran is Arawakan for 'the dog deity who takes care of the souls of the immediately deceased and is the son of the spirit of darkness.' " It seemed to be somewhat like the Greek dog Cerberus, who guarded the entrance to the infernal regions.

One day in March, 1968, our houseboy, Christopher, came to me with the kind of friendly smile that betokens something of special interest. He has dug with me for eight years, is sharp-eyed, observant, and interested in the artifacts we have found. Now he had news of a find he felt was important. And indeed it was. "It's nice, Doc," he said. "You'll like it."

"Fine. But what is it?"

"A shell."

"I'm not interested in shells, Christopher. It's Mrs. Olsen who collects them."

"This one is different," persisted Christopher. "It's carved like a skull and it has funny lines on it."

"For Heaven's sake, *get* it," I urged.

He would get it that evening, he said, and told me about its discovery. A little boy in his village of Freetown, three miles northwest of Mill Reef, had been playing in his mother's cotton patch when he stumbled across a conch shell that caught his eye. It had two big strange holes in it. Rubbing off the soil, he saw that it was cut like a head and, delighted with his new plaything, he ran home with it. His mother took one look and drew back, raising her hands in horror.

"Don't touch it," she screamed. "It's evil. It's a Jumbie! Take it out of the house. Get rid of it."

Although disappointed at losing his new toy, the lad obeyed, ridding himself of the forbidden shell by giving it to an older boy, a neighbor of Christopher's. Knowing Christopher's interest in archeological fieldwork, the new owner showed it to his friend, who recognized it as something I would want to see.

The object arrived before breakfast next morning. At the first glance I was tremendously excited. It is indeed a shell, a conch shell beautifully worked into a head (Figure 31). The face is dominated by two huge eyes in the form of circular openings which suggest a skull. The teeth are incised with great precision on upper and lower jaws, and powerful fangs are emphasized. Across the forehead are two "ropes" of small incised dots which form upper and lower borders for intermediate oval bands of triple-incised lines terminating in large dots. I had seen the same kind of punctation decorating a shell necklace ornament in the collection of Edgard Clèrc in Guadeloupe, who dates his piece about A.D. 500. For the time being I suggest a similar date for the conch piece from Freetown, Antigua.

The more I handled the head, the more the teeth challenged me. The dentition was so explicitly delineated: at the center of each jaw four small incisor teeth, flanked at each side by huge fanglike canines placed to interlock when the jaws closed, then five molars. Aboriginal people frequently were meticulous in depicting specific features of animals or birds that would best serve their identification—the tusks of the mammoth in the Dordogne caves, for example. I wondered what animal has teeth like those so precisely carved on this conch creature. The fangs were obviously prominent, but what animal important to the Arawaks had canines like these?

My mind flashed back to the stone head from Barbuda. I had first thought it was a jaguar, then a monkey, and finally learned it was a dog. Actually *the* dog—Opiyel-Guaobiran. Was this another dog deity? Neither the Encyclopaedia Britannica nor any accessible biology or animal books gave any information on the dentition of dogs. But the next day, as I waited at Parham Harbor for a ferry to take me to a possible Arawak site on Long Island off the north coast of Antigua, I noticed a dog following a woman who had come to the dock to buy fish. I asked if I might pet him. She gave me a toothless grin and warned me to be careful. He was a biting dog, she said. I held out my hand. The dog stopped in his tracks, eyed me suspiciously, and snarled. I continued to hold out my hand, talking quietly. Slowly he advanced, and when I stroked his back he made it evident that this was the most pleasant feeling he had had in some time. Even more carefully I gently petted his head. Ecstatically he rolled his eyes—eyes large like the holes in the conch

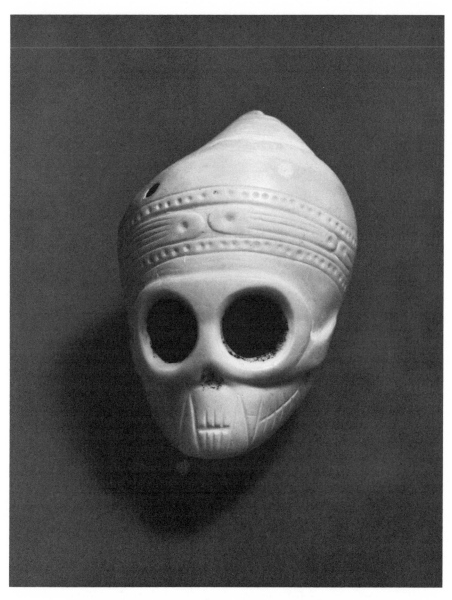

Fig. 31. Conch shell worked into dog's head (Antigua).

head. Gradually I touched his lip and raised it for a clearer look at the teeth. There were the small upper and lower incisors, tightly packed between closely fitting canines, and molars at each side, just as on the Arawak carved conch. I gave the dog a friendly pat and he trotted after his mistress, wagging his tail as he ran.

I feel pretty sure now that the conch head was intended as a dog's head, and that on Antigua, about fifteen hundred years ago, our Arawaks had a guardian deity to take care of their souls as soon as their bodies were deceased—the dog zemi, Opiyel-Guaobiran.

A year or so later I learned that Professor Paul Barker, head of the Anthropology Department of the University of Maine, who was about to retire, had some nice Arawak material he had dug in Haiti. I visited his collection and the first thing that caught my eye was a stone dog, obviously another form of Opiyel-Guaobiran (Figure 32). Erect on his hind legs, he was twelve inches high. Large hollows in the head, depicting the eyes, reminded me of the Antigua conch head, but there was no concern about the teeth. The dog had evidently been in a shrine supported against an upright tree trunk, as there was a hole just back of his forepaws through which a cord or thong could be passed to fasten the body to the tree. For additional security the cord fitted into two small grooves cut into the shoulders. That it was a male dog was clear from the erect penis, whose length of one and one half inches is "one eighth of the standing dog, a rather grossly abnormal appenditure," Professor Barker described it.

The most startling feature was that forepaws were placed beneath the chin in the same manner that the hands were placed in the two stone figures of Atabeyra during childbirth labor (Figures 26, 27). Evidently the Haitian sculptor had been so familiar with Atabeyra in this pose that he assumed the dog deity should hold his paws in a like manner.

The dog was discovered in the Trois-Rivières Valley of northwest Haiti. With it, buried in a manioc patch, were two other objects: a ten-inch stone roller with long conical points at each end, and an attractive stone parrot with wings folded over its breast.[6]

I have mounted these three pieces as part of an altar assemblage to represent a shrine of the dog deity. I picture the ritual to have been somewhat as follows. An Arawak who has just lost a relative promptly visits the shaman to ascertain the status of the departed soul. The ceremony begins with the shaman's cleansing himself externally by bathing in the sea, then internally by applying the

Fig. 32. A Haitian Arawak's sculptural concept of the dog zemi Opiyel-Guaobiran with other ritual shrine objects (left to right): *roller stone for crushing narcotic leaves; Y-tube; turtle bowl; swallowing stick; and parrot-shaped grinding stone. Y-tube and swallowing stick rest on Arawak wooden altar, probably for votive offerings.*

carved bone swallowing stick (Figure 33) to promote vomiting. Only with this thorough purification is he fit to appear before the deity. He enters the shrine where the dog deity is fastened to a vertical post (Figure 32). On a table below is the stone roller with which the shaman crushes dry tobacco leaves or the beans of a cahoba plant. This done, he takes the parrot-shaped grinder stone and uses the smooth, slightly convex back of the bird to pulverize the crushed leaves or beans. This dust is put in the small stone bowl shaped like a turtle and the single stem of the Y-shaped bone tube is placed in the narcotic powder while the two ends of the Y-tube are fitted to the shaman's nostrils. With a sharp intake of breath he sniffs the powder into his lungs and passes into a trance within seconds. The words he utters comprise the message the dog deity imparts about the soul of the deceased.

Obviously it will require further excavation on other islands before we can reconstruct the development of various Arawak religious rituals, and I shall not be surprised if the practices prove to have been somewhat different from island to island. From collections made in Puerto Rico it is evident that the development of Yocahú reached a greater degree of elaboration and refinement there than in the Lesser Antilles. Walter Fewkes, in his Smithsonian reports, describes about a hundred Yocahú zemies, but these are mostly the large carved figures. The smaller stone ones, so common in Guadeloupe and Antigua, are apparently quite scarce in Puerto Rico and Hispaniola, and I know of no conch-shell zemies from the Greater Antilles. In his ten years of excavation in Haiti, Professor Paul Barker did not find a single Yocahú zemi. This may suggest a change in emphasis of Arawak interest in the three principal deities. In Haiti there may have been a swing toward a greater popularity of the mother goddess Atabeyra, as evidenced by the large number of female figures found at the Cadet site in Trois-Rivières. Barker, in a personal communication, describes this site as being "probably the largest prehistoric town ever discovered in the Greater Antilles. It was most likely the seat of government under the powerful Arawak chieftain Guacanagarí. The town comprised approximately a thousand houses and was inhabited by five to fifteen thousand persons." This was presumably the town of Trois-Rivières to which Columbus, on December 13, 1492, sent nine sailors and an Indian interpreter. They reported it to be an immense village where they were well received and fed with fish and cassava bread. The sailors commented that the natives were more handsome than those on Cuba, "and among them they saw two wenches as white as they can be in Spain." On December 16, Columbus anchored at Port-de-Paix at the mouth of Trois-Rivières, and there entertained a young chieftain belonging to the court of Guacanagarí.

I give this background material because it was this item in the chronicles that had attracted Paul Barker when he was planning his first visit to Haiti. Apparently up to that time no one had sought out the town of the thousand houses mentioned by Columbus, and it seemed to him that no spot could be more desirable for excavation than the largest of the Arawak towns and the home of the great king Guacanagarí.

After many strange adventures Paul Barker located the site and dug there for a decade, bringing to light an amazing collection of Arawak artifacts. One of the most striking of his finds was a large cache of female figures carved from coral limestone. I surmise that these may represent the fertility goddess Atabeyra, and if so would support the idea of a major change of interest in the three principal Arawak deities.

Many of these figures are small and some of quite simple form, even of crude workmanship, suggesting that they were votive offerings (Figure 34).[7] Possibly they were made by individual petitioners, but at least one is of larger and more commanding proportions (lower left corner). She is 8 x 8 inches, with just enough carving to show eyes, nose, and mouth, and with the suggestion of a protruding pregnant form and the genitals to establish the sex. There are no breasts, but no Haitian—and indeed no Arawak figure of which I have knowledge—gives any prominence to the breasts, with the possible exception of the Atabeyra (Figure 28) whose concavities I have designated as head, naval, and breasts, although some have suggested the laterial cavities represent arms. No sculptor of my acquaintance who has studied the piece has rejected these as breasts.

The idea of a change to an interest in deities other than Yocahú is supported by four other examples found in the Trois-Rivières region of Haiti (Figure 35), which presumably, are representations of the dog deity.[8]

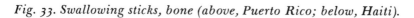

Fig. 33. Swallowing sticks, bone (above, Puerto Rico; below, Haiti).

Fig. 34. Limestone figures probably representing the fertility goddess Atabeyra, varying from small crude examples (perhaps votive offerings)

to the impressive 8 x 8 inch figure, lower left (Haiti).

Fig. 35. Amulets of conch in form of sitting dogs (Haiti).

SUMMARY

One of the most intriguing concepts derived from this study of the Arawak religion is that these people slowly invented a series of deities pertinent to their specific needs. They seem to have recognized their good fortune in having the bountiful manioc provided by their cult hero Yocahú. In the course of time they deified him, and as indicated at Morel in Guadeloupe they recognized the powerful volcanos of the Antillean islands as the logical habitation of their god.

If there is any merit in my hypothesis that some Arawak shaman noticed the resemblance between the conical protuberances of the conch shell and the conical peak of a volcano, we may have an unusually clear example of the actual creation of a deity. It was presumably an act of sympathetic magic to seize the power or spirit of the volcano by creating its image in the form of the carved conch cone. The first actual embodiment of Yocahú was in the form of the conch zemi. From that moment the Arawaks probably believed that they had personal possession of physical zemies which contained a portion of the very spirit of Yocahú. Moreover, we know the date when the embodiment took place in Guadeloupe, about A.D. 220. This was evidently a very significant achievement, judging by the large number of conical conch zemies that have been found, and also by the long span of 350 years during which the conch-zemi cult continued. After A.D. 575 the stone zemies were developed until they reached the complexity of the large ones with human heads, having wide-open mouths whose function perhaps was to crush rock to make soil for growing manioc. The variety and refinements of these large stone zemies suggest the growth of a hierarchy whose members possessed zemies compatible with their rank.

The Yocahú cult continued in the Lesser Antilles until the coming of the Caribs (perhaps some time after A.D. 1000), who destroyed both the zemies and the Arawaks who made them, and in the Greater Antilles until the conquest by the Spaniards, both of which events marked the termination of the religion of the Arawaks and of the gods they had created. We have thus evidence of the birth, development, and death of a deity that Arawak shamans invented.

The Arawaks had been sufficiently clear visioned to perceive the essential features of their ecological environment, that theirs was a manioc-oriented culture. Wherever they migrated they carried their manioc plants with them and introduced them to the new lands, since there seems to be little likelihood that manioc could have been indigenous to the Caribbean islands. With manioc they had solved their food economy and could expand their population enormously. They could also deploy their excess labor to many other activities, including the development of their religion.

Appropriate ministrations to their benign god Yocahú were demonstrably adequate to protect their food supply of manioc, augmented as it was by an easy access to a relatively illimitable quantity of protein in the form of fish and shellfish. Hence for many generations their need for the participation of divine agencies other than Yocahú was probably limited to protection against sickness and accidents, which the Arawaks blamed on the activities of malevolent spirits just as we are inclined to attribute them to almost equally mysterious agencies such as viruses and chance. The Arawak solution to the combatting of these adverse spirits was to call upon the beneficent spirits housed in their zemies. This is perhaps analogous to our bringing in our modern "shamans," doctors, who, possibly with a minimum of unintelligible incantation as shown in their prescriptions, administer their magic and equally mysterious antibiotics to us. Our greater lifespan is perhaps correctly interpretable in part to the greater efficiency of our shamans.

Thus the Arawaks were successful for the amazingly long period of a thousand years or more, until they met a superior force against which they had prepared no defense—predator man in the form of the Caribs in the Lesser Antilles and the Spaniards in the Greater Antilles. The Arawaks greatly outnumbered both of these invaders, but they had no previous experience that would allow them to develop either a combative spirit or the weapons by which to protect themselves. They had invented no deity whose zemi would be an effective guard against the malevolence of these two human aggressors.

VII

Petroglyphs

QUITE early in our studies of the Arawak culture I became interested in their petroglyphs, strange figures scratched onto the
surface of prominent rocks. Friends familiar with sailing in the
Lesser Antilles had told me of seeing pictures carved on stones on
St. Vincent and Guadeloupe. They said they resembled children's
playful drawings, although natives of the islands insisted they had
religious significance.

I was eager to see at firsthand if any of these petroglyphs resembled the Arawak male god Yocahú, their female fertility goddess Atabeyra, or the dog deity Opiyel-Guaobiran. It seemed as if
the most pleasant way of viewing the petroglyphs would be by
sailing to the various islands, making shore excursions from a yacht
that would provide not only transportation according to my own
schedule but also convenient housing at out-of-the-way locations.
So in April, 1959, we chartered the *Viking II*, a fifty-six-foot ketch,
and sailed south from Martinique to St. Vincent at the northern
end of the chain of small islands known as the Grenadines, re-
putedly one of the most delightful sailing areas in the Caribbean.

We anchored at Kingstown (Map 9b), the capital of St. Vincent,
went ashore, and drove up the west coast through some of the most
intensively cultivated valleys I have seen on any of the islands. We
passed many rich banana groves and fields of arrowroot, which at
an early stage of their growth resemble luxuriant lawns. The imposing cone of Mt. St. Andrea furnished a picturesque backdrop
for the lush tropical scenes.

St. Vincent had witnessed some of the laststand fights between
the Caribs and the British, long after the Arawaks had been ex-
terminated and forgotten, so when we reached the village of Layou

I inquired about the location of "Carib stones," even though I felt sure that any petroglyphs would be the work of Arawaks. Without much difficulty we met a Mr. Hendrickson, who knew just what I wanted. There was a "very big Carib stone" on his property, and in a friendly manner he directed us there.

We went along a small valley, following a clear stream as it bubbled over stones, changing its direction every few yards as some large boulder deflected it. Finally we reached a sort of grotto where the stream widened into a pool, above which the trees on either bank closed in to form a leafy canopy. It was a beautiful spot, just the kind of place to put romantic, or even religious, ideas into one's mind. The "very big Carib stone" was in the thickest part of the glen. I saw at a glance that the great smooth face of the rock (twelve feet wide by eighteen feet high) which sloped upward from the bank of the stream was covered with petroglyphs.

Moss and leaves hid much of the shallow grooves, making the design indistinguishable. With our fingers and a broom improvised from small branches we cleaned the face of the rock. Just as we finished a shaft of sunlight fell across the surface, throwing the ancient Arawak incised lines into clearer relief. However, there was still not enough contrast between the shallow lines and the base rock for a good photograph. The faint lines would have to be chalked in. The grade of the rock face was too steep for me to climb, but the much more agile Sten Holmdahl, owner and captain of the *Viking II*, made his way up the sloping face and commenced to chalkmark all the discernible incised lines. Soon the designs began to establish themselves and we could detect where previously indecipherable parts must be more thoroughly cleaned to complete the shapes. In the meantime I had crossed the stream and climbed a small leaning tree to reach a spot from which a ninety-millimeter lens could capture the pictures on the rock.

At first there seemed to be a bewildering mass of forms, most of which looked like human faces. However, closer examination showed that some of the natural cracks in the rock had unwittingly been included in the chalking process. On eliminating these it became clear that there was one principal face surrounded by several smaller ones (Figure 36). This dominant figure has a grotesque face with a bulbous nose and eyes consisting of double circles, each contained within an almond shape. The points of the almonds are connected by a long sweeping line curving above the nose. An elongated mouth is filled with teeth, and below the mouth

Fig. 36. Arawak petroglyph (Layou, St. Vincent).

a second curve terminates at each end in small spirals. Surrounding
the face is a triangular line, at the apex of which is a circle containing an obliquely set cross with a small circle in the lower
segment. On each side of the face is an oval with an oblique cross
and circle. These ovals may represent ear ornaments.

I was most curious about the identity of this "deity," but at that
time I could find no hint in the chronicles of Columbus, the current technical papers, nor from archeologist friends. It was not
until about ten years after that visit to Layou that the significance
of the grotesque triangular face was clarified. I was working with a

Fig. 37. Yocahú, chief male god of the Arawaks (Puerto Rico).

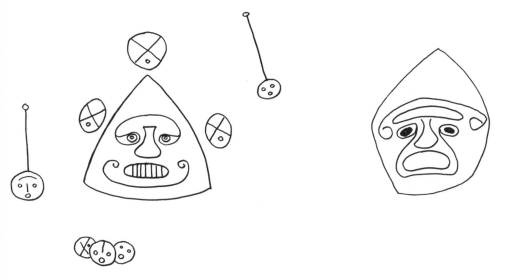

Fig. 38. Sketch showing resemblance between Figs. 36 and 37.

large Yocahú zemi, taking shots from various angles in an attempt
to get the most dramatic photograph. From a directly frontal and
almost horizontal position (Figure 37) I noticed that the hump of
Yocahú provides the same triangular outline of the face that appears on the Layou petroglyph. I have made a sketch of the two
figures to show the resemblance (Figure 38).

The figure on the Layou rock I now conclude to be the Arawak
petroglyph for Yocahú. I could well imagine that ancient Arawaks
participating in rituals at this outdoor shrine would have no trouble
in recognizing the triangle surrounding the face as representing the
"hump" of the zemi, the volcano home of Yocahú. As I continued
looking at the photographs I could appreciate the problem those
early artists encountered in depicting a three-dimensional conical
form on a two-dimensional rock surface. Also I suggest that the
date of this Layou petroglyph may be about A.D. 1200, since this is
the date attributed to the large stone zemies of Yocahú.

Going back to the total picture on the Layou rock (Figure 36),
I am still puzzled by the eight circular symbols accompanying the
central Yocahú figure. Two of these appear to be human heads, each
suspended on the end of a long cord. What are these hanging heads?
Anyone familiar with Peruvian art will wonder if they are related
to the "trophy heads" which hang so prominently from the hands

of warrior figures depicted on Paracas, Nazca, and Mochica artifacts. We have no evidence that the Arawaks practiced headhunting, but it is well to be alert to anything that could connect the Arawaks with earlier peoples from whom they might have been derived. Geographically, Peru is a possible point of origin, and these hanging heads merit consideration as hinting at a linkage of the Arawaks with that country.

I offer the suggestion that Yocahú, the main figure in the Layou petroglyph, the patron god of the Arawaks and giver of manioc, may have had rival deities to contend with, and that these hanging heads may represent hostile gods whom he had overcome during his ascendancy to the position of principal deity.

Leaving Layou we traveled north to Barrouallie (Map 9a), a small village where we had been told a "picture stone" could be found in a hillside garden. This turned out to be quite different from the Yocahú figure at Layou. Judging by the fringe that the figure wears as a headdress, it might be a petroglyph of the sun god (Figure 39a). At first glance the figure appears to have four eyes, but closer examination suggests that only the two upper circles are eyes and that the lower ones are probably spiral terminations of a long sweeping curve, possibly cheek ornaments but perhaps hinting at scarification. Paralleling the upper part of this curve is a second line whose ends come to a point forming the nose. An outer curved band contains thirteen points or rays. Perhaps these refer to the thirteen lunar months, although I know of no other example of Arawak concern for astronomical data.

More puzzling is the labyrinthine pattern in the lower part of Figure 39a. Is it just a chance arrangement of geometrical lines in contrast with the multiple curves of the head? To me this seems too elaborate a figure, with too much concern for detail, to warrant any such explanation as mere doodling. I recalled from my trip to Lascaux and other caves in the French Dordogne that the Aurignacian or Magdalenian artists were much concerned with symbols for the male and female organs. The vulva was painted on many of the cave walls, and I wondered if the artist who carved this Barrouallie symbol was unconsciously seeking an Arawak counterpart for the Cro-Magnon female organ (Figure 39b). Perhaps the T-form shown in the lower part of Figure 39a and the right-hand element of Figure 39b is the symbol for the male organ. If so the composite figure may represent the penetration of the one by the other, perhaps depicting the copulation of the Sun God of the

Fig. 39. a: *Sun God petroglyph (Barrouallie, St. Vincent).* b: *Arawak symbols in Fig. 39a, compared with Cro-Magnon male and female symbols in French caves.*

Female symbols

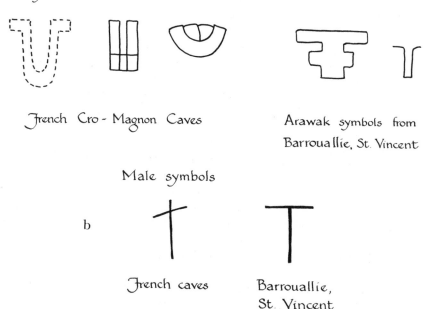

French Cro-Magnon Caves

Arawak symbols from Barrouallie, St. Vincent

Male symbols

b

French caves

Barrouallie, St. Vincent

Day and the Moon Goddess of the Night. It is a theme often used by those Peruvian "cousins" of the Arawaks, especially on Mochica pottery which might be roughly contemporaneous with these Arawak petroglyphs.

Returning to Kingstown, we learned of still another petroglyph, this one on the east coast of St. Vincent near the mouth of the Yambou River. A drive up the Mesopotamia Valley took us through the highly cultivated center of the island. Lacking any road map,

I was unable to find what two rivers bounded this beautiful valley, but when we reached its northern end we cut eastward through the mountains along what the natives call the Yambou Pass, a clear indication we were on the right road.

By following the rocky Yambou River we reached the sea, but could find no petroglyphs and none of the people along the road knew of any "Carib stones." Finally we met a helpful man working in his garden of yams and manioc who asked me, "Do you mean the figures on the Lourdes shrine?" I agreed this might be what we were looking for and followed his directions to turn inland until we reached a sheer cliff in about half a mile. As we approached the cliff I guessed it had been an ancient shoreline before some up-heaval raised the east coast of St. Vincent.

High up on the cliff face was a cut-stone shrine in the form of a niche where-in Our Lady of Lourdes was standing to receive visiting pilgrims. My eyes, how-ever, were quickly attracted by a group of four Arawak petroglyphs six to ten feet below the shrine. Sten Holmdahl prompt-ly climbed up and chalked the lines for me to photograph and sketch (Figure 40). These four heads, each about six to ten inches in diameter, were generally simi-lar to the small heads surrounding the Yocahú figure at Layou. Even after many viewings I have not been able to suggest any interpretation for these Yambou petroglyphs.

Fig. 40. Sketch of petro-glyphs on Lourdes Shrine (Yambou, St. Vincent).

The island of Guadeloupe, like St. Vincent, is famous for its petroglyphs. We sailed there in April, 1961, once again on the *Viking II*, this time from Dominica, following almost the identical route described by Columbus on his second voyage in 1493. His first landing in the Lesser Antilles was at the island he named Santa Maria la Galante, so we too stopped there en route to Guade-loupe, anchoring off the small port of St. Louis (the capital of what is now known as Marie Galante) in the same roadstead the Ad-miral had used. He had gone ashore for wood and water and his sailors had their first encounter with the manchineel tree, *Hip-pomane mancinella*, whose poison the Caribs used for tipping their spears and arrows. Later I was to experience the potency of manchineel poison when, camping under a tree, I was peppered by its dry dust. My body was badly blistered, including my eyes, and for a week I was blind and in great pain.

We landed on Marie Galante in hopes of finding some of the axes the Arawaks had used, perhaps only a hundred years or so before Columbus' arrival. I looked up the local priest, Père Barbotin, who had a nice collection of Arawak stone axes but was unwilling to part with any.

We sailed on to Guadeloupe, making an overnight stop at the lovely group of islands named "The Saints" because Columbus sailed past them on the day of Todos los Santos. At Guadeloupe I presented letters of introduction to M. Derussy of Trois-Rivières (Map 9a). He and his wife could not have been more hospitable. They took us for a long drive through the countryside, particularly to beaches that might have been Arawak landing sites, but I saw no middens.

"You would like to see the Carib rock drawings?" our host asked. Indeed we would. We went to a little wharf where boats leave for Les Isles des Saintes and then set off on foot along a path winding by a little mountain stream where women were washing clothes, until we reached a number of rocks bearing petroglyphs.

The attractive sylvan setting was reminiscent of the Layou location, but the petroglyphs are much more numerous and varied. One large rock, called Roche La Tortue, is about eight feet wide and twelve feet high and covered with small figures, many of them quite dissimilar from those at Layou. Again the density of the foliage made photographing difficult, but I did get pictures for record against which to check the quick sketches I made (Figure 41).

I find these petroglyphs quite baffling. The two upper right figures (Figure 41a) appear to be of the same style and maybe by the same artist. I hazard the guess that they are female figures, as indicated by the suggestion of breasts and vulva. The bottom right figure may be allied to the so-called sun god figure we saw at St. Vincent on the petroglyph at Barrouallie (Figure 39a). At the present stage of our ignorance about the interpretation of Arawak petroglyphs, there may be little we can do other than to continue collecting illustrations of these rock-face figures throughout the islands and build up a sort of dictionary of glyphs that will permit the formulation of hypotheses about the nature of the Arawak rituals.

On some of the nearby rocks were figures that appeared to be

a

b   c

Fig. 41. a (top), b (bottom left), c (bottom right): *Petroglyphs on Roche La Tortue (Trois-Rivières, Guadeloupe).*

wearing a headdress of plumes of feathers (Figure 41b). Again we spotted another figure whose "plumed" headgear was attached to an attenuated body of strange configuration (Figure 41c).

My next encounter with Arawak petroglyphs occurred in August, 1967, when I visited the Capá ceremonial plaza near Utuado (Map 10) in the central plateau of Puerto Rico. It was an attractive river valley location with a picturesque backdrop of mountains. The site had been meticulously restored by Professor Ricardo E. Alegría, of the University of Puerto Rico at San Juan and Director of the Instituto de Cultura Puertorriqueña. Since no middens have been found that would indicate this to have been a townsite or even a large village, I am inclined to think that this extensive lay-

Fig. 42. Ceremonial plaza, Capá site (Puerto Rico).

out of ritual and recreational sites was a mountain resort to which Arawaks repaired seasonally. I would guess that those ancient Arawaks must have felt it to be an esthetically satisfactory setting for large ceremonial gatherings, especially when ballgames could also be enjoyed in the main Ball Court and in the six adjoining practice courts.

The main plaza (Figure 42) is flanked on its east and west sides with a "wall" of vertical slabs of limestone 160 feet long. I counted more than fifty of these on the west side of the rectangle, with a dozen large stones, some of them six feet square and six inches thick probably weighing about two tons apiece in the center and grading down to smaller ones at each end. The north and south sides, 120 feet long, provided "sidewalks" about four feet wide, laid with smooth igneous rocks brought from the stony bed of the Rio Tanama, which runs northward through the site to join the

Rio Grande de Arecibo about six miles before it enters the Atlantic Ocean at Arecibo.

It is on the huge vertical slabs of the west wall that the petroglyphs occur. One of these (Figure 43a) was vociferously signaling for my attention. It is a vigorous figure with skinny, upraised arms, perhaps even with clenched fists. The head is almost heart-shaped, with large ears, eyes, and mouth. Even the nostrils are shown. But it was the egg-shaped body that eventually demanded attention. A large circular groove was shown on the upper part of the body with a small but prominent indentation which might be the "tummy-button." Someone had made the figure more clearly visible by marking the grooves in black, but as I examined these markings more closely I believe he had failed to notice the two dotted circles that formed ear ornaments and instead had represented them as the right and left fists of the figure. I therefore made a sketch of the petroglyph (Figure 43b), changing the position of the forearms to correspond to the outline clearly shown on the transparency when examined with a hand lens. Further examination of the slide strongly suggests that the circle below the squatting legs may be the head of the emerging babe. In my drawing I have perhaps overaccentuated the marks which I can discern on the stone, to show them as eyes, ears, and mouth of the babe. The position, however, reminds me of our Atabeyra figures from Haiti and Puerto Rico, squatting in the act of childbirth.

In the same central group of slabs is a large stone with a carefully incised, strangely complicated figure (Figure 43c). Again there is a well-defined, heart-shaped head with even more prominent circular ear ornaments, but also a quite elaborate headdress. The figure is squatting and the female genitals are clearly shown, so I regard this as another Atabeyra figure. Once more, a close examination of the transparency with a lens reveals lines on the stone that had not been marked with chalk. It may be that the circle in the center of the figure represents the head of the babe, still within the mother; indeed, when the slide is held upside down other lines are revealed that could be the body and legs of the baby (Figure 43d). Again, I admit to interpreting these marks on the stone to a degree which may not be completely warranted. I regret not being able to return to Capá for a careful surface washing of the stone and a more accurate interpretation of the figure, but I believe the identification of the Arawak deity Atabeyra to be a probable one. Since the three figures occurring in the west wall closely resemble available exam-

a

b

c

d

Fig. 43. a: Petroglyph of Atabeyra on wall at Capá, main plaza. b: Detail sketch of petroglyph shown in Fig. 43a. c: Another squatting Atabeyra figure at Capá. d: Sketch of Atabeyra shown in Fig. 43c.

Fig. 44. Ring of stones at northwest corner of plaza within which arietos were danced (Capá, Puerto Rico).

ples of Atabeyra, with no other figures appearing on that wall or on the opposite east wall, it would seem that this ceremonial plaza may have been dedicated to Atabeyra, the Arawak goddess of fertility.

As I stood in the plaza it was easy to picture rituals being conducted in this large rectangular area, with spectators seated on the north and south stone terraces. Marker stones protrude from near both ends of east and west walls, presumably indicating where participants turned in their marches or dances, but I could not help wondering if the women had left votive offerings before the central slabs of the west wall bearing the image of Atabeyra. Moreover, the close proximity of the circular ring of stones (Figure 44) just outside the northwest corner of the plaza might very likely have been the site where a chain of dancers performed their arietos around the large stone in the center of the ring.

While struggling with the interpretation of the petroglyphs at the Capá ceremonial plaza, I recalled that I had obtained three stones bearing petroglyphs in the Cecil Stevens collection, alleged

Fig. 45. Sun God figure (Capá, Puerto Rico).

to have been found at Capá. Obviously they were small enough to have been carried away from the area and I wondered from what part of the site they had come. They did not seem to belong to the walls of the plaza, but they might have been markers from the nearby ball courts.

The largest of the three stones is about two feet high and weighs seventy pounds (Figure 45). It is very simple in design, and under a raking light reveals a broad shallow groove around a natural bulge on the stone providing the outline of a face having two large cavities as eyes and a slight oval depression as mouth. Long linear grooves radiate above and below the head, perhaps representing the sun's rays and giving rise to the usual name of Sun God for the figure.

A smaller version weighs eighteen pounds (Figure 46). A heavy rounded ridge outlines the face, having two large oval eyes with shallow depressions but without expanding rays. Instead there are straight line grooves below the chin suggesting a beard—a strange device among beardless people—and stimulating the thought that what I have been calling sun's rays may have nothing to do with the sun. Indeed, the lines on the top of the large sun god (Figure

Fig. 46. A smaller version of the Sun God (Capá, Puerto Rico).

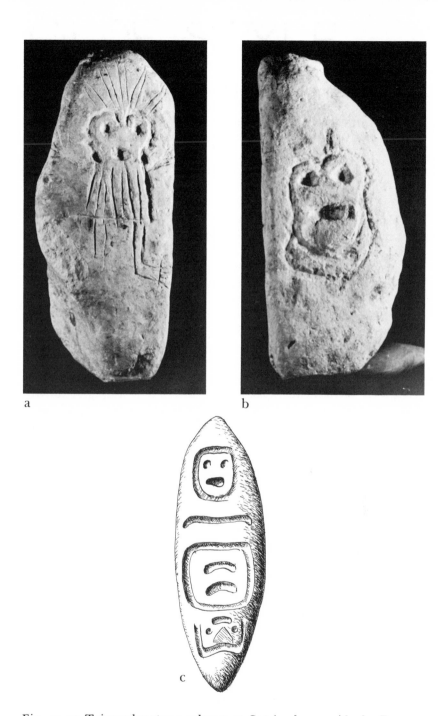

a

b

c

Fig. 47. a: *Triangular stone column at Capá; obverse side.* b: *Reverse side of column.* c: *Pillar column from Stevens collection, Puerto Rico.*

45) may represent a feathered headgear, similar to what we encountered on the petroglyphs at Guadeloupe (Figures 41b, c).

The third block of stone (Figure 47a, b) has a triangular cross-section with petroglyphs on two sides. It is a foot long and weighs eleven pounds. One side (Figure 47a) shows a figure with outstretched arms. Two grooves outline the face but stop short of the chin. They terminate in cavities which may represent ear ornaments. Ten incised lines on top of the head may be interpreted as five feathers of a crown since three of the pairs of lines definitely form points. (The other pairs may have been similarly joined since the stone shows damage that could have broken the points.) Below the face are eight somewhat heavier grooves which resemble the "beard" decoration shown in Figure 45, but the sharply cut horizontal line also suggests a cape or coat. The arms and legs are crudely drawn, each hand being provided with the requisite five fingers, but the one undamaged foot is indefinite as to the number of toes. The other side (Figure 47b) shows an equally primitive incised head with deeply gouged eyes and mouth. Below the chin there seems to be an ornament which may be a string of beads.

Another stone from the Stevens collection is long and narrow with pointed ends. The markings are shallow and difficult to photograph, so I offer a sketch (Figure 47c). Apparently it is a totemlike figure with one face at the top and another at the bottom but upside down, with a shieldlike decoration in the center. My guess is that this also is a "pillar column" from a ceremonial court, but have no suggestion as to an interpretation of the carving.

VIII

Thunderstones

As we go through the islands where Arawaks no longer remain, searching for evidence of their existence there a thousand years ago, we find strange parallels between ancient Arawak practices and those prevalent among the current descendants of the Negro slaves who were brought to the sugar plantations in the seventeenth and eighteenth centuries.

The shamans of the Arawaks had an elaborate paraphernalia of accessories for use in the rituals by which they served their sacred zemies. The function of these services was to conjure the aid of friendly spirits that would protect their clients, and perhaps of even greater importance combat the malevolence of the ubiquitous evil spirits.

The shaman of the Arawaks has been replaced by the practitioner of a new kind of ritual.

It is particularly interesting that some of the ancient artifacts of the Arawaks have been discovered by pure chance by these modern shamans. The significance of these objects is quite unknown to the new man of magic, but their very strangeness gives them an added quality and they are incorporated into the current rituals.

In all the Caribbean islands, the man of magic is all-powerful. He is an integral part of the uneasy lives of the people. The West Indian peasant is a happy, or rather a happy-go-lucky, individual. It is natural for him to sing, to dance, and to make music out of anything. We all know of his ingenuity and versatility with a cut-off oil drum. The steel drum bands are famous, and none more so than the Brute Force Band of Antigua. But if he hasn't a steel drum he will make rhythm by hitting a whiskey crate with the palms of his hands or by tapping a calabash. Every now and then, however, the music in him stops and a faraway look comes into his eyes. He is uneasy about something or someone. Jumbies are lurking about and can bring him a stubbed toe, a new pain somewhere—in the shoulder, in the back, in the leg, or in the stomach, which is the worst place. It is then that strange things happen. A new odor wafts back from the charcoal pot as some potent herb tea is concocted. The erstwhile gay and apparently sophisticated boy or girl disappears for a while, and if you have been careful to keep yourself out of sight you may see him driving a nail into the Pain Tree. "Poundin' ma ache into ole tree . . ." he murmurs. There are times, however, when remedies personally applied are of no avail. Then the aid and guidance of the modern Magic Man must be sought.

The most important man of magic whom I have met is Simeon Joseph, of St. Lucia. Father Jesse, of Castries, had told me of him, not as a practitioner but as the possessor of some nice "Carib stones." I made several attempts to see him, but he was elusive. At length, however, satisfactory arrangements were made by Father Jesse and we trundled off in the Father's jeep, going north from Castries to Babonneau. Entering the village I noticed a liquor store with the name Simeon Joseph over the doorway. Adjacent was a little dancehall with soft-drink facilities, also labeled Simeon Joseph. Evidently the gentleman was a successful entrepreneur. Half a minute's walk and we were in front of a very fine church.

Magic was already in the air because apparently from nowhere, and with no appreciable signal, children appeared from all over eager to cooperate in having their pictures taken. By this time an attractive girl had come up and recognized Father Jesse. She was Simeon Joseph's daughter and we were welcomed into the house.

Simeon was there to greet us, particularly Father Jesse, with great politeness. The Father explained that Professor William Haag, who had joined me in the expedition, was a great scientist interested in archeology and that Fred Olsen was the American for whom Simeon had promised to get some "Carib stones."

"And where are the stones?" asked Father Jesse.

"They're at my other daughter's house," replied Simeon.

"Well, send for her."

"Oh, no. She out working in the garden and we couldn't fine her."

"Come now, Simeon," said Father. "We made this appointment with you, and you said you'd have the stones. Aren't you a man of your word?"

A faraway look came into Simeon's eyes. It had started with the question, "Aren't you a man of your *word*?" I wondered. Was it

Fig. 2. Arawak children seesawing to extract poisonous juice from grated manioc in a matapi.

Fig. 4. *Leveling cassava crumbs on the griddle.*

Fig. 5. *Disks of cassava sun-drying on the roof.*

Fig. 8. Bitter manioc leaf has seven radiating leaflets. They are long, narrow, sharp-pointed, dark green, and shiny.

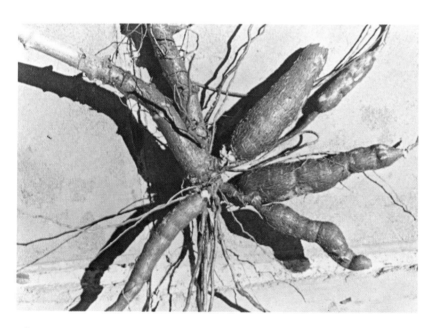

Fig. 9. Sweet manioc tubers look so much like those of the bitter variety that I could not tell them apart.

Fig. 10. Steep bank of the Orinoco at Saladero. Brad Endicott finds Saladoid sherds in recent landslide.

Fig. 12. An elegant animal head, or adorno—the handle of a pot.

Fig. 13. The strong Orinoco current biting relentlessly into the banks.
Amerind habitations well above flood line.

Fig. 24. The largest stone zemi found in Guadeloupe, twelve inches long, with the face of Yocahú carved on the side.

Fig. 43c: Squatting Atabeyra figure at Capá.

Fig. 110a: *Elegant specimens of W-O-R sherds from trench six, level five.*

Fig. 83. *The ball court at Copán, Honduras, is an architectural gem.*

the sound of "word" that had got him started? I know how the natives love repetition. They will take a phrase and repeat it over and over, with slight modifications or modulations. I had heard them make almost an anthem out of "In the beginning was the word, was the word, was the word. And the word was with God, with God, with God. Word was with God, with God. And the word was God, the word was God, the word, the word, the *word*. . . ." On and on endlessly, with a crescendo of excitement, until some climax was reached, and then a cadence until the last word was almost whispered: ". . . and the word, and the word . . . ." Hands waving, feet moving, hips swaying—part of some forgotten ancestral ritual.

I chose this moment to break gently into his consciousness. "Simeon, it's all right, but I am disappointed. I have waited a long time and have come a long way to meet you. I do so want to see one of your sacred stones."

I was careful not to use the term "Carib stones," but chose "sacred" instead. Simeon glanced slowly at me, but said nothing.

"Don't you have one of your stones in your house?" I asked.

"Yes, Ah does," he said to my surprise.

"Will you show it to me?"

Simeon called to his daughter, asking her to bring him "*the* stone." "An' some sewin' string," he added. She returned with "*the* stone" and a bobbin of thread. Evidently this was what was meant by sewing string.

Simeon motioned her to hand the stone to Father Jesse. He passed it to Professor Haag, who said, "Oh, it's a Carib ax."

"No, it ain't no Cry-eeb ax," said Simeon with some petulance. "It's a tunda stone. It were sent fum Heaven to ma gran'pap. He were big fightin' chief in Afreeka."

This was interesting. In Martinique you hear these stones called "pierres de tonneau," and in Puerto Rico or Santo Domingo, "piedras del rayo." They are thunderbolts, according to native belief, caused by lightning.

"Tell me, Simeon, about your grandfather's thunderstone," I asked.

"Yars an' yars ago da stone come fum Heaven an' kill coconut tree. Ma gran'pap fine it undah tree. It Sacred Stone."

I had read about these stones in J. Walter Fewkes's *A Prehistoric Island Culture Area of America* (Smithsonian Institution, 1912–13, p. 175): "They are supposed by the country people to be endowed with magic powers and are regarded as efficacious in healing diseases. They are likewise supposed to protect the natives from lightning, being frequently deposited for that purpose under the thatch forming the roof of their cabins. In St. Vincent and some other islands, they are placed in earthen jars to keep the drinking water pure and cool." Fewkes adds, "It is sometimes stated that they are found in trees struck by lightning, while others declare they penetrate the earth and come to the surface in seven years. A true thunder stone may, according to some informants, be determined by binding a thread around it and applying a lighted match. If the thread burns, the stone is genuine."

With this passage in mind I could hardly wait to see the thread test. But Father Jesse had taken up the conversation because of Simeon's reference to a "sacred" stone. "Now Simeon, you don't really believe the stone is sacred," he said. "The Church would not approve of that. You are a good Christian, aren't you?"

"Yes Father, Ah is. Ah's shure good Christian."

"Well, Simeon, what do you use the stones for?"

"Oh, jus' things, Father."

"But what kind of things?"

No answer.

"You use them outdoors, don't you?"

"Yes, Father."

"And you put flowers around them, don't you?"

"Yes, Father."

"Red and white flowers? Red and white? Isn't that so?"

"Yes, Father."

"And then you sing, don't you?"

"Yes, Father."

"And dance around them?"

No answer.

"Now, Simeon, you know the Church does not approve of that. That is not being a good Christian."

I was watching both Simeon and Father Jesse intently. Poor Father Jesse! He was so unhappy about it all. He is the kindest soul in the world, yet as the Church's representative he had to protest against these "pagan" practices. Simeon, on his side, was hurt by the suggestion that he was not a good Christian.

"But Ah *is* a good Christian! Nobody anywhere better Christian than Simeon. Ah *is* a good Christian." There was sorrow in Simeon's voice, but protest too.

Father Jesse continued. "But you do sing and dance around the red and white flowers, with the stone among them, don't you?"

"Y-e-s, Father."

I was puzzled by the reference to the red and white until I recollected that a white chicken was to be killed by the stone ax and the red blood caught in the hands and drunk. Sometimes the blood was touched to the sick person or thrown toward the distant enemy believed to be harming the supplicant.

"And then you get a chicken . . . ." But this was too much for Father Jesse to continue. He simply couldn't face all the gory details. But he couldn't drop the subject without letting Simeon realize the seriousness of his actions.

"Don't you know that the Church could excommunicate you for this?" he asked.

Simeon looked puzzled, then more puzzled, and finally resentful.

"Ain't nuthin' in the Ten Commandments 'gainst it," he declared with some indignation. This time Father Jesse was silent. Simeon didn't know what "excommunicate" meant, but it sounded dreadful. "You ain't goin' do me harm, Father?" he pleaded.

Father Jesse was almost in tears. "No, Simeon, I will do you no harm," he said with great compassion.

I thought this was a good time to change the subject. Turning to Simeon, I said, "I am tremendously interested in your Sacred Stone. Just what can it do that other stones can't do?"

Simeon was so relieved to have Father Jesse off his back that he turned to me with a smile and started to tie the thread around the smoothest part of the stone ax. I felt I had seen all this before. Actually I had never seen it, but I could visualize the procedure so clearly. I noticed he tied the thread quite tightly and then struck a match and held it next to the thread. Nothing happened. The thread did *not* burn.

I recalled Fewkes's statement, "If the thread burns, the stone is genuine." But that did not make sense. It would ordinarily be expected that the thread *would* burn. The magic would be when it did *not* burn. I guessed that Fewkes had never seen the magic test performed and had written without firsthand knowledge. But why didn't the thread burn? There seemed only one possible explanation. The mass of the stone was large and the heat from the flame of the match was quickly dissipated by conduction through the stone, to the degree that there was not enough heat to ignite the thread held so tightly against the smooth surface.

"Well, Simeon, that certainly looks like magic," I said. "But wouldn't the same thing happen to any stone?"

Simeon went immediately to the door, picked up a stone, and tied the thread around it. I noticed that the stone was not smooth like the ax he had used and that there was a slight air space under parts of the thread where the roughness of the stone held it a little away from the surface. The flame of the match immediately burned through the thread at one of these spots. Simeon smiled broadly, with the conscious pride of a successful magician.

"Do you mind if I try it?" I asked. Simeon nodded and I went to the door and selected the smoothest stone I could find. I tied the thread as tightly as I could. Then I struck the match and, admittedly with a little uneasiness, held it against a spot where the thread lay tight to the surface. The thread remained unburned. I wondered what would be Simeon's reaction. It was instantaneous. He roared with laughter, rolling from side to side and waving his hands at me.

"I knowed you was magic! I knowed you was magic too!"

Simeon had one more trick, however. He puffed on his cigarette, then pushed the glowing end of it against the thread of my stone. The thread burned through and fell off because now the heat was localized and in intimate contact with the thread. Simeon grinned.

"Okay, Simeon. Now take a good puff on your cigarette and touch the thread on your own stone."

He did. The thread burned and fell off. A wider grin, then he walked over to me, shook hands, and beamed, "What I get you to drink?"

"Rum and jelly water," I replied, which pleased him very much. A little boy was dispatched to climb a coconut tree and knock down some green nuts, "jelly nuts" in the native vernacular. The husk was cut from one end by a neat cutlass stroke and two holes poked in the eyes of the nut. Out came a stream of crystal-clear jelly water, which to me is the best diluent for rum. Simeon couldn't have been more hospitable, so I decided this was the time to turn to my original quest.

"You see now why I want one of your stones," I said. "I want one that came from Heaven."

"You kin have them." I noted the word, "them."

"How many can you let me have?"

" 'Bout six."

"And how much will they be?"

144

"Oh, they is val'ble. Very val'ble."

"Yes, I know. But how much?"

"Ten dollar each."

"All right. I'll give you fifty dollars for the six."

Simeon reflected. "But six tens ain't fifty!" he protested.

"It is, by my magic."

He grinned, and I handed the fifty dollars to Father Jesse. "Just give the six stones to Father Jesse and he will give you the fifty dollars."

Simeon went into his bedroom to emerge a moment later dressed in a much-faded, ancient, square-cut frock coat with long satin lapels. On his head was a gaudily decorated hat.

"Dis what Ah wear when Ah does ma dance 'fore da tunda stones," he beamed as he posed for his photograph.

We departed, and all the way back to the presbytery in Castries Father Jesse talked of the difficulty of eradicating the old magic practices of otherwise good Catholics.

A year later the good priest sent Simeon's stones from St. Lucia to Antigua by a friend. "They are fine axes," Father Jesse wrote, "and quite interesting from an archeological standpoint because they are black from innumerable rubbings during the rituals, and also tarnished by the smoke from the oil burned in front of the ax." This kind man is a sincere anthropologist.

These "Carib axes" are now mounted and make a fine display. Actually they are not Carib axes at all, but Arawak tools designed for felling trees and making dugout canoes perhaps a thousand years ago. But in the last ten or twenty years they have been transformed into "tunda stones." They have become sacred in old rituals practiced by present-day shamans. They have been darkened by hands rubbing sanctified oil into their stone surfaces. They have become sacrificial weapons used to release the magic blood of a chicken or goat that will relieve pains, remove fears, and counteract the harmful workings of malevolent forces.

The ancient Arawaks had wrought most potently.

IX

Tools and Weapons

WHEN we started digging at Mill Reef in 1955 we paid little attention to the bits of flint found in almost every pail of soil sifted through the screens. We supposed these fragments were merely part of the natural stony components of the soil. Occasionally a piece caught our attention, such as one having a long sharp blade which we suspected might be an artifact. Even then they did not arouse much enthusiasm because none resembled the nicely worked Indian arrowheads with which we were familiar from collections in the United States.

When Professor Rouse visited us he showed how one of these flint blades could be used as a knife and another as a scraper. Now we save every piece of flint and have accumulated more than five thousand. I tried various methods of classifying the flints and studied the available literature, but did not find much that helped in understanding the Arawak flint chips.

The illustrations in technical articles did show a steady progression in the design of stone tools from the earliest pebble choppers of Paleolithic man, perhaps a couple of million years ago in Tanzania and Kenya, through the hand axes of Acheulian man of 500,000 B.C. (Figure 48), to the spear points of Solutrean man[1] in the caves of France and Spain some twenty thousand years ago. I tried to make correlations between the Old World tools and those of early man in the Americas and was intrigued by the comparison between the elegant spear points of Clovis and Folsom man in North America ten thousand years ago and the "Laurel Leaf" projectile points of the Solutreans of Europe some ten thousand years earlier (Figure 49). It was an impressive record of man's slow but competent achievement in weaponry.

Arawak flint tools seemed to fit nowhere into this picture. They

147

a   b   c

Fig. 48. a: *Olduvai pebble chopper,* ca. *1,800,000 B.C.* b: *Acheulian-type hand ax, Olorgesaillie,* ca. *500,000 B.C.* c: *Acheulian-type cleaver, Olorgesaillie,* ca. *500,000 B.C.*

seemed to be just bits of flint crudely broken off available pebbles (Figure 50) and not fashioned into anything like the patterns of the elaborately worked flint tools of Cro-Magnon man. Moreover, the Arawak man whose tools were encountered in Antigua lived only a scant fifteen hundred years ago, not fifteen thousand or more as in the case of the makers of the superb flint tools in other parts of the world. What was the matter with the Arawaks? Were they so backward that even as late as A.D. 500 they had not caught up with European man of 15,000 B.C.?

I recalled the comment, in the book *Prehistory and the Beginnings of Civilization,* by Sir Leonard Wooley and Jacquetta Hawkes, that Pithecanthropus in Java and Southeast Asia had remained in a backward state for a hundred thousand years or more during the early Paleolithic stage, while man in western Asia and Europe had advanced "rapidly" toward civilization. Had this backwardness lingered in Asia until their Mongoloid descendants

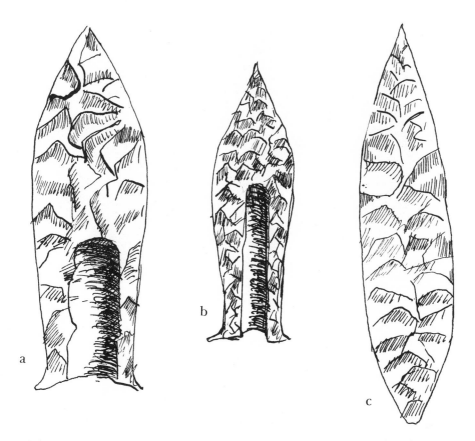

Fig. 49. a: *Clovis and* b: *Folsom flints from North America compare favorably with* c: *Solutrean flints from caves of France and Spain.*

crossed the Bering Bridge to the Americas to show up in a slower rate of tool development by the Arawaks? But this did not make much sense in the light of the great achievements of the Olmec and Maya Amerinds several hundred years B.C., or of the much earlier Clovis and Folsom men of Arizona and Texas.

This "structureless" feature of Arawak flints remained a perplexing obstacle for several years. Perhaps a better explanation might be forthcoming by making a comparison between the *functional* uses of tools made by Cro-Magnon man of ten thousand to

Fig. 50. Arawak flints fitted nowhere . . . .

fifteen thousand years ago and by the Arawaks. The former were big-game hunters, evidenced by the paintings of mammoth, bison, and rhinoceros on the cave walls of France and Spain. This kind of hunting was dangerous work and the success and safety of the hunters depended on the precision with which the projectile points entered the most vulnerable spots of the animals. Any special shaping and sharpening of spear points that would make a weapon more effective would be amply worth while. In contrast, the Arawaks had virtually no animals to hunt on the isolated islands of the Caribbean. A sharp splinter of flint on the end of a stick was good enough to spear the plentiful fish. The edge of a freshly broken flint would serve to scale and cut up fish, or for scraping wood to shape it into domestic articles. It might just be that the Arawaks did not have the need or the incentive to fashion their flints as precisely as did the Cro-Magnon hunters.

However, as I continued the attempts to classify our growing pile of Arawak flints it became apparent, on the basis of shape alone, that only about one third of them had the sharp edges or points which might allow the pieces to serve as useful tools, whereas two thirds of the flints showed no structural forms that might conceivably make them usable. I guessed that, in general, tools had been fabricated on the spot where they were being used and that most of the unshaped pieces were waste flint fragments, discarded in the process of making useful tools.

What I had collected, therefore, was a whole range of flints, from unbroken pebbles, which presumably the Arawaks had gathered as raw material, to the finished tools. The cores from which they had struck the sharp-edged and pointed flakes are clearly recognizable in the middens, and of course the waste chips are there in profusion.

Specifically, the sorting of several thousand flint pieces yielded the following results: 71 per cent unusable flint material, such as residual cores and waste chips; 29 per cent potentially useful flints, having sharp points or edges.[2]

The next step was an attempt to correlate the 29 per cent usable flints with the needs of the Arawaks. Since I did not know what their daily needs might have been, about all I could do was to guess how men and women might have accommodated themselves to the benign environment of these tropical islands, where protein in the form of fish and shellfish abounded in the reefs and lagoons and where carbohydrates could be obtained from the luxuriant growth of their adopted manioc plant.

Four main occupations seemed to provide for their daily needs and to account for the tools I had collected: food preparation; tree cutting and canoe building; making of household equipment; and fishing and hunting.

Tools for Food Preparation

In Surinam I had learned that manioc comprised 80 per cent of their food, hence the most urgently needed tools would have been: knives to peel the manioc tubers; graters to shred them; matapis to squeeze out the poisonous juices; manari screens to form the crumbs of cassava; and griddles to make the cassava bread or cakes.

Presumably the peeling knives would be the long, sharp-edged flint blades found in every midden (Figure 51). The manioc graters I had seen in Surinam were made from the walls of empty oil cans punched full of jagged nail holes. Obviously these graters were a modern version of the ancient wooden boards into which tiny pieces of flint (microliths) were inserted as teeth, examples of which

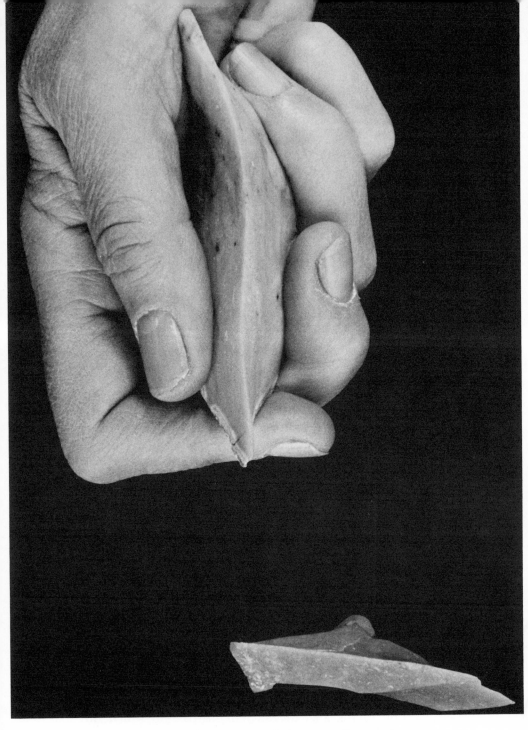

Fig. 51. Sharp-edged flint blades for peeling manioc.

are in many museums. In the Antigua middens a large number of coral fragments are found in all stages, from pristine pieces of spiny coral to those on which the spines have been worn smooth. I am guessing this coral was probably used for grating manioc (Figure 52).

The matapi, that most ingenious tube woven from palm fronds for squeezing the grated manioc, has already been described. We have no idea when or where this device was invented, and no trace of its early use is likely to be found because woven basketry could not survive the tropical climate. The same is true of the woven manari screens used for sieving the cassava crumbs prior to baking.

The griddles for cooking the cassava bread have a long history. They go back to the griddle sherds in the earliest Arawak middens at Saladero in 1010 B.C. and similar sherds are found plentifully wherever Saladoid Arawaks migrated.

The middens, however, give evidence of other foods. Shells of the conch (*Strombus gigas* and *Strombus pugilis*) and the West Indian Top shell (*Cittarium pica*) are prolific, almost all of them cracked open by what are commonly known as hammer stones (Figure 53). These look like ordinary stones and a frequent question is how we can know that these are tools. The answer is that these stones are not part of the geological makeup of the middens where they were found. They had been brought from the beach by Arawaks who had selected stones which fitted the hand conveniently. Evidence of usage is given by the pitting or pockmarks from continuous hammering.

Over a period of fifteen years I have acquired a collection of stone tools from several islands, particularly St. Vincent, St. Lucia, and St. Kitts in the Lesser Antilles, and Puerto Rico and Haiti in the Greater Antilles. In retrospect I realize that *no* hammer stones were included in these collections; presumably these ordinary-looking stones had been ignored by planters as they walked their cane fields. They only picked up stones of intriguing shape. Perhaps the most common were those with conical handles, easy to grasp and with a slightly convex base, polished smooth from long grinding of food materials (Figure 54).

A few grinders were shaped like animals, some carved so realistically that they were readily identified as bird, turtle, frog, etc. (Figure 55). Some of these so closely resembled the elaborate parrot grinder from Haiti (Figure 32) that I guessed the ornate ones had been used by shamans for pulverizing narcotics such as cahoba or tobacco.

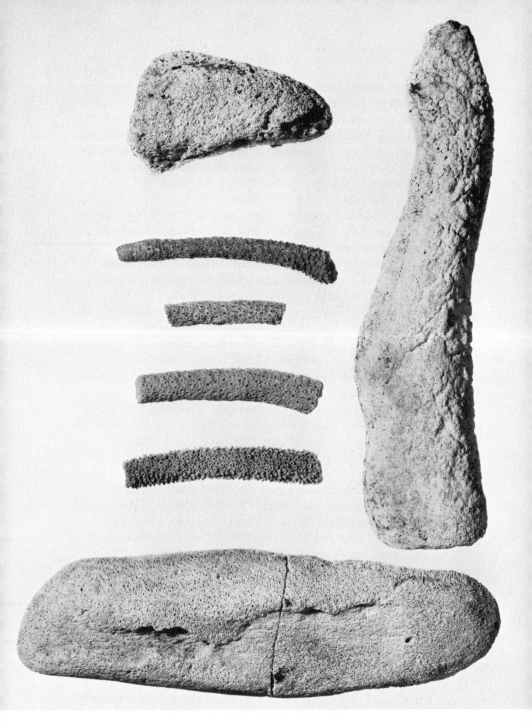

Fig. 52. Coral graters (Antigua).

Fig. 53. Hammer stones (Puerto Rico).

Fig. 54. Conical grinders, their bases smooth from grinding food stuffs (St. Kitts).

Fig. 55. A few grinders were shaped like animals (Haiti).

Fig. 56. Pestles, mortars, and grinding slabs (Puerto Rico).

Occasionally the grinders (Figure 56) look like the pestles used to this day for grinding pigments, and with these were found mortars quite like contemporary examples. Even more common than mortars are the grinding slabs whose surfaces were hollowed and of which twenty or more specimens have been found.

Two large flat grinding stones merit special description because they reveal the manner in which the Arawak housewife probably prepared the daily food. One is a three-legged carved stone from Puerto Rico (Figure 57), similar to a Mexican metate, commonly considered an implement for grinding corn but also used with meat and vegetables. I saw a Mexican woman at Comalcalco, in the state of Tobasco, working with one quite similar as she prepared the noontime stew.

Tools for Tree-cutting and Building Dugout Canoes

It seems probable that the occupation involving the closest co-operation among the men would have been the building of canoes. Columbus himself recorded how large some of these were—once in waters around Hispaniola during his first voyage in 1492, and again during his third voyage in 1498 while sailing westward along the northern coast of Venezuela. He mentioned canoes seventy-five feet long and five feet wide, carrying more than fifty people. To make such large canoes seems an amazing performance for people with only stone tools.

For felling trees, the tools would presumably have been stone axes, more than a hundred of which were collected from the same islands where the grinding stones were obtained. It soon became evident that these axes belong to two distinct categories: (1) highly polished, almond-shaped stones, generally known as "polished petaloid celts" (PPC) from their resemblance to the petal of a flower (Figure 58a); (2) stones shaped somewhat like a present-day steel ax, but ground to a matte surface (Figure 58b) instead of the gleaming polish of the PPC. They usually have lugs at the butt end around which strong cords were wrapped to hold the ax tightly to a wooden ax-handle.

Polished Petaloid Celts (PPC)

Almost everyone seeing these PPC is attracted by them and picks them up to feel their astonishingly smooth surface. They were made from igneous rocks such as basalt or andesite and are very hard and tough. Occasionally they are of jadeite, which takes a beautiful green polish. The more I studied these PPC the more I was struck by the uniformity of their shape and surface finish over

Fig. 57. "Metate" from Puerto Rico.

the whole range of islands from Grenada to Haiti. They were obviously the product of the same kind of people, and I am strongly inclined to attribute them to the Saladoid Arawaks since they are found in the territory occupied by them. Also, the A.D. 600 dating of the two large PPC from the "chieftain's hut" at Mill Reef is early enough to fit nicely into the time period of Saladoid occupancy.

Just how were these petaloid celts used? They fit the hand conveniently and could have been used in much the same manner as we picture the ancient hand choppers were wielded by Acheulian man in the Old World half a million or more years ago. Indeed, man's arm seems like a natural and satisfactory ax-handle. However, comparing a celt held in the hand with one hafted on an ax-handle will easily demonstrate that not only is the shock effect on the arm much less when the hafted ax is used, but the striking force is greatly increased. Consequently, I feel reasonably sure that all the larger celts, from ten or more inches in length, were hafted (Figure 59a).

Handles would most likely have been selected from such tough hardwoods as lignum vitae, mahogany, or purple heart, all readily available on most of the islands. Perhaps the Arawaks made holes or splits in young saplings which would heal and give tough cavities to accommodate the pointed end of a celt. It is apparent that each blow would tend to tighten the fit of the pointed celt in the hole of the shaft.

Fig. 58. a: *Polished petaloid celts (PPC) (Haiti).* b: *Ground matte-sur-faced stone ax, somewhat like a present-day ax (St. Vincent).*

It is worth noting that at least half of the **PPC** are small, three to five inches in length, and a number of these have blunt rather than pointed bases (Figure 60). This would hint that the shorter celts were hand-held as chisels or wedges whose blunt bases were struck with hammer stones (Figure 53). Occasionally the hammer stones are shaped so they could be hafted by using a shaft with a split end into which the neck of the hammer could be inserted and the outer ends of the split secured by thongs or cords (Figure 59b). These hammer stones run all the way from five pounds down to two ounces. The five-pounders could serve as mauls to drive heavy stone wedges for splitting logs. The two-ounce stones would make

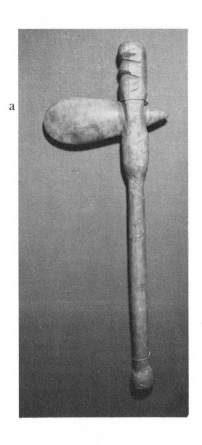

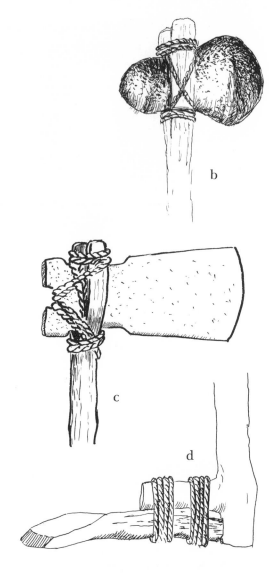

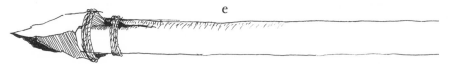

Fig. 59. a: *I feel reasonably sure that all large, polished petaloid celts (PPC) were hafted.* b: *Hafted hammer stone.* c: *Hafted lugged ax.* d: *Hafted conch adze.* e: *Hafted projectile point for spearing fish.*

Fig. 60. Half the small PPC have blunt bases.

light hammers, useful with stone chisels for working both stone and wooden objects.

The shapes of the hammer stones vary considerably, some looking like peening hammers (Figure 61). The range is so extensive as to suggest comparison with a modern artisan's tool kit.

Matte-surfaced Lugged Axes

Stone axes having a matte surface show an amazing spectrum of shapes. Most have projections in the form of lugs, some suggesting an almost compulsive interest in elaborate symmetry (Figures 62a, b), while others veer to the extreme opposite and are wildly asymmetrical (Figure 62c). Some observers have seen in certain axes an arrangement of the lugs which they liken to a crested bird's head

Fig. 61. Some hammer stones look like peening hammers.

(Figure 62d). Clearly all these lugs could have served as stops around which cords were wrapped to fasten the ax-head securely to the shaft (Figure 59c).

Some axes are carefully flattened on one face, suggesting their use as adzes. They would require a specialized hafting technique, perhaps as shown in the sketch Figure 59d. We can only guess at the form since no such adze handle has been found, nor is it likely to be unless one is discovered by chance in some such place as the Pitch Lake in Trinidad, where an adze might have been lost and the handle preserved in the tar for hundreds of years.

These two types of axes—the polished petaloid celts (PPC) and the matte-surfaced lugged axes—seem obviously the tools an Arawak

Fig. 62. a, b: Some axes suggest a compulsive interest in symmetry (St. Vincent). c: Others are wildly asymmetrical (St. Vincent). d: Some lugs resemble a bird's crested head (St. Vincent).

would have used in felling trees and making dugout canoes. I puzzled a long time over the technical details of these operations. Even to fell a tree that would yield a seventy-five-foot log perhaps three to four feet in diameter at its smaller end must have been a formidable task. I handled the stone axes, both the PPC and the matte-lugged axes, and felt their edges. Sharp, yes. But not really sharp. Admittedly, the polished axes were sharper than the ground axes, but not sharp enough to cut a finger run over the edge.

Years ago, as a young man, I worked for several winters cutting logs in Canadian lumber camps. Our steel axes were kept almost razor sharp. They could cut a finger carelessly touching the edge. It seemed to me that a stone axe would probably only mash the fibers of a tropical tree. I seriously doubted that it would cut one down, so I tried pounding a tree with a stone ax. All that was accomplished was to bruise the wood. It would seem an almost impossible task to fell a tree large enough to make a big canoe with a relatively blunt ax.

Fortunately, friends at Yale referred me to a two-volume book published in 1791 by Friar J. Gumilla regarding his travels in South America and his work with the Otomac tribe in Venezuela. Describing the felling of a tree for building a canoe, the padre wrote, "It took the Indians along the Orinoco two months to cut down a tree." Friar Gumilla explained that fires were kindled around the base of a tree and wet moss applied against the trunk to prevent the fire from spreading too far. At intervals axes and chisels were used to hack away the charcoal and the charred wood.

That makes sense! The stone axes could easily chop out the brittle, charred wood, even if they couldn't cut live fiber. More fire was then applied and more charred material gouged out until the tree toppled. With the tree on the ground and branches removed, a line of small fires was lit along the full length of the log. As the wood charred it was hacked out with adzes and chisels.

Trying to visualize this operation in detail, I could picture that if small fires were burning a few inches apart they would produce pits from which the charred material could be scooped. Wedge-shaped barriers would remain between the adjoining cavities, and this brittle wood could then be chopped out with a reasonably sharp-edged stone adze (Figure 59) or by a chisellike celt with a blunt base (Figure 60) and pounded by a hammer stone (Figure 59b), splitting off chunks of wood "with the grain."[3]

166

Previously I have mentioned that in the Antigua middens we have found only two polished celts (from the "chieftain's hut") and no matte-surfaced stone axes. However, we have obtained a great quantity of celts and chisels made from the heavy lip of the conch shell, *Strombus gigas*. These vary from broken fragments and partially formed pieces to complete sharp celts. Clearly these tools had been made on the spot where the woodworking operations were carried out. The conchs had been brought from the sea and a gash made in the side of the shell to sever the muscle fastening the edible body of the sea snail to the shell (Figure 63). The heavy lip was broken from the conch shell and chipped to the desired shape and size. Slabs of sandstone are encountered frequently in the middens with worn spots where the side edges of the celt had been smoothed, and also with curved cavities, showing how a sharp circular cutting edge had been formed by rubbing the celt with a swinging motion against the standstone.

Conch tools are found at their best in Barbados where fabrication techniques were more highly developed (Figure 64), perhaps because there is no hard igneous rock on Barbados and conch celts and chisels had to take the place of stone axes and adzes. On many islands, of which Antigua is a notable example, conch celts are found in abundance despite an inexhaustible supply of hard volcanic rock out of which PPC could have been made. Conch celts were probably made in large numbers because shell is easier to work than hard rock. They would be tough enough to remove charcoal or charred wood in the fabrication of canoes. Moreover, they are easy to resharpen.

In making a canoe by burning, chiseling, and sawing, an immense amount of woody material would have to be removed from the inside of the log until the canoe walls were suitably thin. The final smoothing of the wood might have been done with the rough skin of a man-killing shark, as mentioned by one of the chroniclers. I suggest also that coral rasps might have been used since a great many coral slabs (Figure 52), often ten inches long by three inches wide, are found in the middens, the spines worn smooth by use. It is easy to conjecture that familiarity with the use of coral for grating manioc would probably have transferred to the smoothing of wood. Unfortunately, Friar Gumilla did not say how long it took to make the canoe. Unquestionably it was a major operation.

167

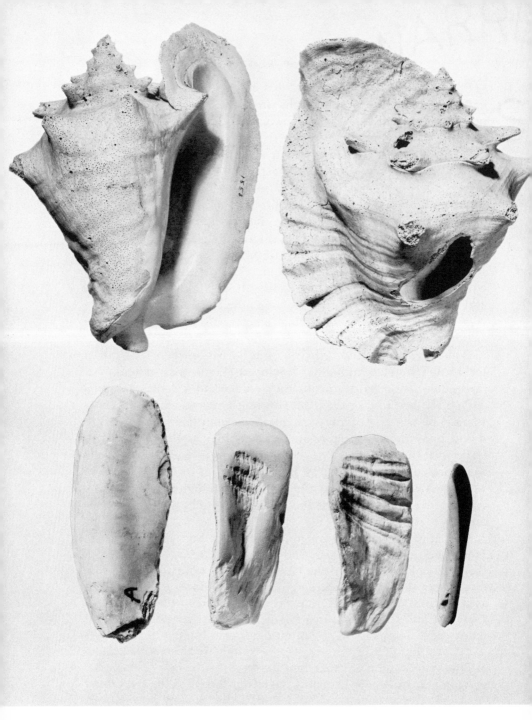

Fig. 63. Conch celts and the shells from which they were made.

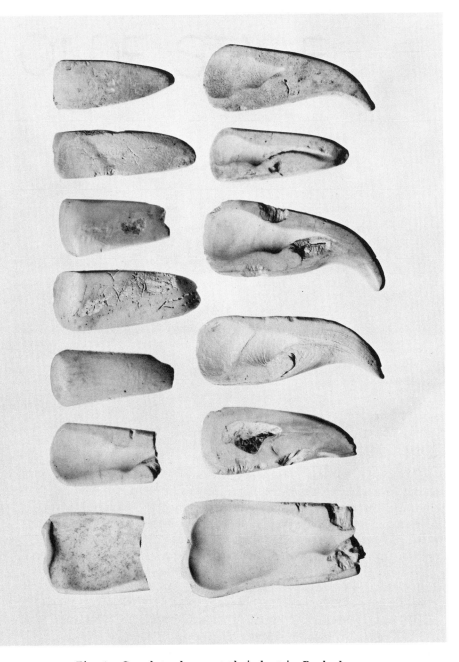

Fig. 64. Conch tools are at their best in Barbados.

169

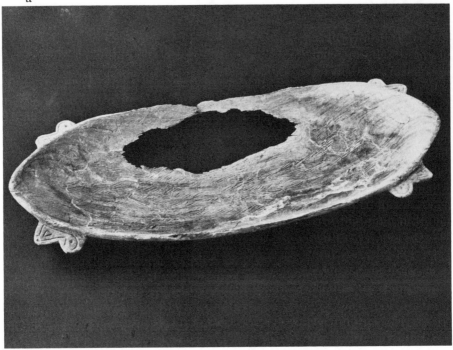

Fig. 65. a: *Arawak carved wooden tray (Haiti)*. b: *Arawak carved wooden seat or duho (Haiti)*. c: *Arawak carved altar of Yocahú (Haiti)*.

Tools for Making Household Equipment

It was not until I saw, in August, 1967, four wooden objects found in a Haitian cave that I realized what beautiful woodwork the Arawaks could do (Figures 65a, b, c). The tray (Figure 65a) has been much eroded after perhaps seven hundred years in a cave, but even today we would consider it elegant in design, and the craftsmanship shows mastery of the techniques of woodworking. Such articles may have been associated with an important personage and perhaps buried with him in the cave. Objects in Figures 65b, c are usually called *duhos*, an Arawakan word for "seat." I have read that a chieftain's personal duho was carried by a retainer to the ball court so that he could sit while watching the game. The duho in Figure 65c has been thought to be shaped like a turtle or even an alligator, but the study I have made of the various forms of

b

c

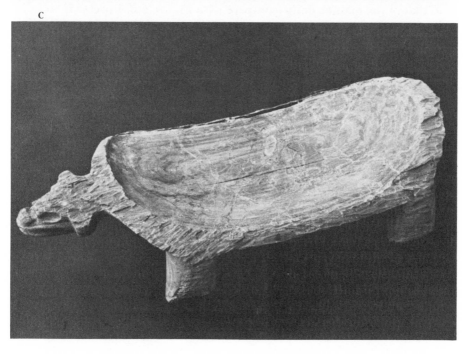

a

b

Fig. 66. a: *Square-faced chisel.* b: *Round-faced chisel.* c: *Scrapers. (All from Antigua.)*

Yocahú zemies convinces me that the head on this duho is the same as that of the manioc deity (compare with Figure 20). I prefer therefore to consider the piece to have been an altar for receiving votive offerings rather than a seat.

One can readily picture a whole series of wooden household objects such as benches, trays, platters, combs, etc. that might have been made by people possessing the skills of these Arawak craftsmen. That such a wide range of wooden objects may have existed

c

is supported by the presence of stone tools strongly resembling knives, chisels, or awls and by the large concentration of flint tools in the middens (Figure 66a, b, c). Examination of the tray (Figure 65a) with a hand lens suggests that flint scrapers (Figure 66c) were perhaps the commonest tools for creating the sweeping convex and concave surfaces of the tray. If a flint scraper is held with both

a   b

Fig. 67. a: Serrated edge of flint blade could be used as saw. b: Knife blade. (Both from Antigua.)

hands and the sharp edge given a strong sweeping drag over a piece of wood, it will be found an unexpectedly workable tool. Likewise, a flint knife or saw is satisfactory even when held directly in the fingers (Figure 67a, b). Fitted to a handle, it would be even more effective.

The decoration of the handle of the tray or that on the wooden

Fig. 68. Large flint burins (Antigua).

altar readily could have been scratched out with a sharp-pointed flint burin (Figure 68), as can be learned by experimenting with a few suitable pointed flint flakes. The Arawaks would appear to have been well equipped for shaping wooden articles with the wide array of flint tools found in the middens.

TOOLS FOR FISHING AND HUNTING

What the Arawaks ate is known mainly from the shells and also from the animal bones found in the middens, at least as far as the

protein part was concerned.[4] Sixty per cent of the bones at Mill Reef belonged to three creatures: parrot fish, 32 per cent; sturgeon fish, 14 per cent; and rice rat (*Oryzomys* genus), 14 per cent. A smaller amount were turtle, grouper, barracuda, shark, iguana, and guinea pig.[5]

Fish were most likely speared, using flint projectile points fastened into the ends of split rods (Figure 59e). However, they probably used nets and fishing lines, since spinning whorls (Figure 69) converted from waste potsherds are common.[6] In support of the use of fishing lines, one fish hook has been found, carved from a conch shell (Figure 70).

Basketry fish traps also may have been fashioned from many available vines, cut by hand choppers (Figure 71a), barked, split with flint knives (67b), and smoothed with flint scrapers (Figure 66c). Although no remains of baskets have been found, it seems probable that the Arawaks made them since basketry was an art practiced all over the world to provide containers for carrying and storing food. Recently, Desmond Nicholson, president of the

Fig. 70. Fish hook made from a conch shell (St. Kitts).

Antigua Archeological Society (1971), found griddle sherds on the bottom of which were impressions of matting, indicating that the potter had shaped the large griddle (Figure 72) while the plastic disk of clay lay on a mat of woven palm fronds. Since they knew how to make mats, they probably also made baskets.

The net result of this study of the four most likely occupations of the Arawaks—food preparation; tree-cutting and canoe-building; making of household equipment; and fishing and hunting—indicates that all these functions could have been carried out adequately with the types of tools we have unearthed. Moreover, I feel that the puzzlement about the crudity of Arawak flint tools can be resolved by the broad conclusion that elaborate secondary working of flint tools was not necessary or desirable in meeting these four main requirements of the Arawaks. The blades and flakes so easily obtained from the plentiful Oligocene flint are adequate. On the other hand, the very lives of Old World game hunters depended on the precision of their projectile points. Where occasion demanded, the Amerinds developed the necessary skills to work flint

Fig. 69. Spinning whorls (Antigua).

Fig. 71. a: *Flint hand chopper (Antigua).* b: *As held in hand.*

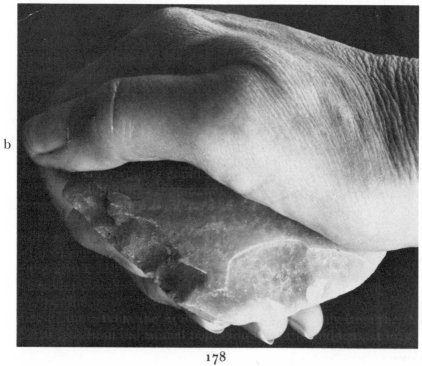

Fig. 72. Impression of woven mat on base of griddle sherd (Antigua).

179

more delicately, as shown by the Folsom and Clovis flint projectile points used in hunting the bison (Figure 49).

Apparently the Arawaks started with a very small kit of tools, since a few flint chips and one bone awl were all that Rouse and Cruxent found in the middens of the Arawak homesite at Saladero. These were in the lowest layers bearing typical white-on-red Saladoid pottery, dated 1010 B.C. Within a hundred years or so these Saladoid Arawaks were driven out by the encroaching Barrancoid people and we next learn of them in Trinidad, only a couple of hundred miles away from Saladero.

It was during their stay in southwest Trinidad, according to Professor Bullbrook, that the Arawaks made their first acquaintance with shaped stone tools. In the lowest layers of his excavation, in 1920 at Palo Seco, Bullbrook reported finding three stone celts, probably wedges or chisels since they were only three inches long, with blunt bases showing pockmarks where they had been struck with hammer stones, perhaps when being used in making a dugout canoe.

To the question of whether they invented them or acquired them in trade from some prior occupants of the area, we have no definite answer. It is known that Meso-Indian people lived in Trinidad (Map 11) long before the Arawaks arrived, tools from flint and celts from igneous rock having been dug from a preceramic site at Ortoire (with a carbon-14 dating of 800 B.C.). Consequently, the Palo Seco stone axes or chisels could have been obtained by the Arawaks from these Meso-Indians by trade or they might have learned tool-making techniques from them.

Professor Bullbrook, who was a geologist before he became an archeologist, stated that the igneous rock from which the Palo Seco celts were made was not indigenous to Trinidad. He described the rock as volcanic, perhaps andesite, which is the common igneous rock of the Lesser Antilles. It would seem likely that these Palo Seco or Ortoire celts had been made in the Lesser Antilles, hinting that Meso-Indians occupied the islands and exported the celts to their fellow Meso-Indians in Trinidad, who in turn traded them to the Arawaks at Palo Seco. But unfortunately, no Meso-Indian occupation sites are known in the Lesser Antilles.

However, Meso-Indians had long been known to have lived in the Greater Antilles, particularly in Haiti and Cuba, perhaps from about 1000 B.C. up to the time of Columbus. They were called Ciboney, perhaps because they lived in caves (Arawakan word *ciba,* meaning a rocky cave, and *eyeri,* meaning man) , and were described as fishers and food-gatherers, with no knowledge of pottery nor of manioc cultivation. In spite of these deficiencies they were evidently highly competent stone-workers, since Professor Rouse illustrates a series of their artifacts from Haiti and Cuba made of both flint and stone. These comprised double-bitted axes, "ceremonial" objects, even an elegantly carved pendant, together with flint knives and daggers.

Thus there were Meso-Indians in Trinidad at 800 B.C. and in the Greater Antilles as late as 1492, a tribal existence of more than two thousand years—quite a long stretch, both in time and distance. But since no Meso-Indian sites have been discovered in the Lesser Antilles, the manner of their migration between Trinidad and the Greater Antilles can not be established. Indeed, for the past thirty years the Meso-Indians have been considered as reaching the Greater Antilles by being storm-blown from Venezuela (perhaps from the vicinity of Margarita Island).

Recently (April, 1970), Professor Cruxent found that the Meso-Indian occupation of Trinidad could be pushed back still further, to about 3000 B.C. This unexpectedly early date was obtained for an extensive site at Banwari Trace, southwest of Fernando, where flint tools and celts were found. The flints were obviously made on the spot because a full range of cores and waste-flint chips were present. But there was no evidence of waste-stone chips, indicating that the celts had not been made there. Furthermore, the rock from which the celts were made was not native to Trinidad. So presumably these early celts had been obtained from somewhere outside Trinidad—again probably from the Lesser Antilles. Thus, once more, it would appear that Meso-Indians did occupy the Lesser Antilles, even if no trace of them has been found there.

Fortunately, we have been lucky in finding two sites on Antigua which appear to be Meso-Indian. In February, 1970, Desmond Nicholson and Morellen Wilson found some strange-looking pieces of flint on the Salt Pond at Deep Bay on the northwest coast of Antigua (Map 2). These tools were different from any Arawak flints, being of blue-gray chert, in contrast to the brown chert used by the Arawaks. Moreover, they were much larger tools, two to three times bigger than the flints made by the Arawaks (Figure 73). Still more important, they were more competently fabricated since they showed strong secondary working, which is quite rare with Arawak flints.

Fig. 73. a (left): *Ciboney flints are about twice as long as* b (right): *Arawak flints (Antigua).*

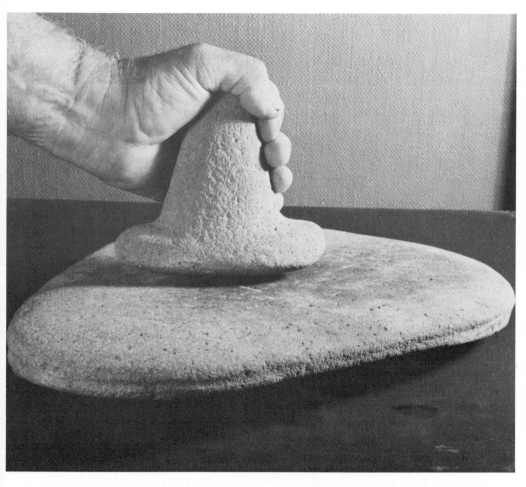

Fig. 74. Grinding slab, possibly a Ciboney artifact (Salt Pond, Antigua), with conical grinder from St. Kitts and probably Arawak.

The site was investigated immediately. It is a large midden, about five hundred feet long, littered with shells and gray-blue flint chips, but with *no* sherds. This complete absence of ceramic material was crucially important since it suggested a preceramic site—the first in the Lesser Antilles. We guessed the occupants might have been the Ciboney described by Rouse and Cruxent at Haiti and Puerto Rico.

At this same Salt Pond location Dorothy Butler found a heavy oval stone slab with a prominent groove around its edge (Figure

74). It was obviously a grinding stone. Presumably a rope had been held firmly in this groove with its front end perhaps looped, halter style, over the shoulders of a woman squatting while she worked. In this way she could have supported the stone in front of her, with the narrow end between her legs, and the stone slanting forward to allow the food being ground to fall into a large gourd (they had no ceramic pots). This type of grinding slab, as far as is known, is unique.

A year later, in 1971, a second and much larger preceramic site was discovered on Long Island off the northern coast of Antigua. Flint cores and waste chips were scattered in great profusion—by the tens of thousands—on what was obviously a "factory site" (Figure 75) where a considerable population of Meso-Indians, allegedly Ciboney, had prepared flint tools for perhaps several hundred years.

The geological formation is a weathered-down Oligocene limestone, deposited thirty to fifty million years ago in which countless cavities, scattered through the ancient shell deposits, had been filled with silicates crystallizing in the form of flint from a supersaturated solution. Large nodules of flint—cobblestones—can be seen in situ in the limestone at dozens of spots on the shore, being released slowly from the calcium carbonate matrix as the sea eats into the softer limestone (Figure 76). The original limestone bed may have been hundreds of feet thick and, as it eroded, the escaping flint nodules increasingly cluttered the vast exposed floor until today there is what is graphically described on the U. S. Geodetic charts as "Flinty Bay," the densest deposit of flint I have ever seen.

This "factory site" may have been the main source of flint tools for a long period. The best tools were probably removed from the site by the Ciboney and traded throughout the neighboring islands. The evidence for this removal is that the ground is littered with flint "caps," the rounded ends knocked off the cobblestones to form a flat platform from which the artificers skillfully struck off the long thin blades. These four-inch diameter caps would be the tops of oval stones five or six inches in diameter, each of which may have yielded dozens of knife blades or scrapers. The waste chips were scattered about in great quantities, and also many broken or poorly formed blades.

These flints were shown to Professor Rouse, who tentatively endorsed the finds as probably of Ciboney origin. We can now envision an early occupation of all the Lesser Antilles by the Ciboney,

Fig. 75. Ciboney "factory site" (Flinty Bay, Antigua, Cornelius Roosevelt).

185

Fig. 76. The sea releases cobblestones from ancient Oligocene limestone (Antigua).

whom the Arawaks could have contacted during their migration from Trinidad, perhaps as early as A.D. 100. It would have been these Ciboney Meso-Indians, obviously skilled in working flint and other stones, who could have served as the traders from whom the Arawaks obtained their stone tools or from whom they learned the technique of fabricating them.

However, the high quality of Ciboney tools does pose the question as to where and how *they* developed the talent of making such artifacts.[7]

Actually we have no idea when or from whom these Meso-Indians on Trinidad or the Antilles learned about polished celts, but in light of Professor Cruxent's date of 3000 B.C. for their presence on Trinidad it is conceivable that they may have been in the islands a thousand or more years before the Arawaks arrived there. This might have been ample time for them to learn how to make stone axes by grinding the basaltic rocks, polish them by extensive rubbing, and trade them with Meso-Indians on Trinidad and later with Saladoid Arawaks.

In the absence of charcoal from the Salt Pond or Long Island sites in Antigua, what reasonable date can be suggested for the Ciboney occupation of Antigua? I recalled the first visit of Professor Rouse in January, 1956, when he came to guide us in the early excavation of the Mill Reef location. At the lowest level he had called my attention to an ancient hearth and instructed me in the techniques of collecting a charcoal sample. Half an hour later he also found charcoal about five feet from where I had worked and at the same level. Professor Rouse sent his sample to the Yale Geochronometric Laboratory, which reported a carbon-14 date of 475 B.C. My sample went to the laboratory of the Humble Oil Company and yielded a similar date, 450 B.C. Professor Rouse considered these dates as being much too early for Arawak occupation and they were temporarily rejected. I am now suggesting that they should be reconsidered as perhaps indicating an earlier Ciboney campsite, the 450–475 B.C. being intermediate between the 800 B.C. date for the Ortoire preceramic site in Trinidad and the 300 B.C. for the Meso-Indian site at Krum Bay in the Virgin Islands.

Another thing meriting further study is a flint blade found in the same bottom layer at Mill Reef. Until recently I have regarded it as an Arawak flint, but as I notice its shape and the blue-gray color of the flint blade I now suggest that it might have been Ciboney. Obviously, further excavation of the Mill Reef site is needed to obtain more evidence of Ciboney artifacts.

The polished petaloid celts from the "chieftain's hut" at Mill Reef, dated A.D. 600, may be a thousand years later than the Ciboney flints in Antigua. This may have been a long enough time for the development of PPC by the Arawaks, but we still have no evidence as to who first produced PPC or when or where they were developed.

A similar uncertainty may exist about the beautiful PPC dug on Haitian Arawak sites, relatively close to Ciboney sites which continued into historic times. The extraordinary degree of fine workmanship displayed on these Arawak PPC bears close comparison

Fig. 77. Ciboney double-bitted axes (Haiti).

with the nearby elegant Ciboney double-bitted axes (Figure 77). Many are of such sensitive design that they have been considered ceremonial objects rather than useful tools. But a hand lens observation of these PPC shows many nicks along the edge such as would be expected on useful tools. One celt which shows no such nicks may have been a freshly made tool not yet subjected to actual work. It is still a possibility that these fine petaloid tools were acquired in trade from the Ciboney who made the axes shown in Figure 77. However, the workmanship and the sculptural quality of Arawak stone zemies and ball belts would seem to confirm their high competence. If indeed these PPC are actually of Arawak fabrication, we would conclude that they had mastered the technique of stoneworking to a degree equaling that of the Ciboney.

However, in comparing the work of these two groups of artisans there may be one important differentiation between their flint fabrication techniques. Arawak blades are about three inches long, while those of the Ciboney are more than twice that length (Figure 73), suggesting they may have been made by quite different methods. I recalled that about five hundred thousand years ago an important technical improvement was made, perhaps in Africa or Europe, by using a heavy anvil stone against which the flint cobble was struck, instead of hitting the cobble with a hammer stone. This anvil method produced *large* flakes. This suggests that the smaller Arawak flakes may have been made by striking near the edge of a flint platform with a hammer stone, whereas the much larger Ciboney blades may have been made by striking the flint cobble platform against an anvil. (Actually, the anvil stone permits larger cobbles to be used and hence produces the longer blades.) In this connection I wonder if the large flat rocks at Flinty Bay, instead of being, as I first assumed, convenient spots where Ciboney workers sat while they made flint blades, might not have been anvils against which they struck the cobbles. The same litter of cores, caps, and waste flakes would have surrounded these flat stones in either case. This brings up the point that if Ciboney flaking was done on an anvil and Arawak flints were flaked off by hammer blow, then it would appear that the Arawaks did *not* adopt Ciboney techniques, but obtained Ciboney tools initially by barter.

So far we have found no polished stone celts on the Ciboney sites of Antigua, but the grinding slab found by Dorothy Butler on the Salt Pond site does furnish evidence that the Ciboney of Antigua practiced the art of grinding stone artifacts and exhibited a workmanship comparable to that shown on Ciboney ground stone artifacts from Haiti. A nicely ground basalt pestle was also found on the Long Island site, offering further evidence of Ciboney familiarity with grinding techniques.

It is no easier to account for the origin of the unpolished celts. These are the matte-surfaced and lugged axes which are generally referred to as Carib axes, although I know of no direct evidence for their being a Carib product. True, these matte-surfaced axes are found almost exclusively in the Lesser Antilles, which, as is well known, were captured by the Caribs, perhaps about A.D. 1400. Moreover, specimens of these ground and lugged axes are rare in the Greater Antilles (which the Caribs never captured) and are usually considered as being made of stone found only in the Lesser Antilles and hence probably trade objects. Nevertheless, in the absence of any carbon-14 dates defining the date of these axes we are obliged to recognize the possibility that the ground axes might have been of Carib manufacture.[8]

Whether or not PPC are Arawak and ground stone axes are Carib, there is a vast *difference* in the techniques of making the two types of tools, enough to strongly suggest that these two kinds of axes were the products of separate tribes. The outstanding variation is, of course, the polishing. The polished petaloid celts are so smooth that occasionally they reflect light like glass, whereas the ground axes are worked only to a dull finish.

The shapes of the PPC and the ground axes also vary greatly, so it seems unlikely that the ground ax is a development of the PPC. Indeed, the differences between them are not of degree, but of kind, and seem to indicate the introduction of a new idea rather than the evolution of an old one. I suspect that the matte-surfaced stone ax was an intrusion. But by whom? And when?

The only hint I have encountered is a matte-surfaced ax from Colombia which closely resembles the matte axes from Guadeloupe or St. Kitts. It was found on the Cauca River, a tributary of the great Magdalena River. I know of no similar axes in the Guyanas, so the Colombian find may be an important clue to the problem of whence and by whom stone axes came to the Lesser Antilles. We have no carbon-14 datings for this ax, but at least it is from a location that could have been on the trail of the Arawaks.

In the years prior to A.D. 1400 there was probably a fairly brisk trade between the Lesser Antilles and the Neo-Indian lands around the Caribbean Sea. When Columbus and the succeeding Spaniards sailed westward from Trinidad along the Venezuelan coast they met traders coming from still farther west. Unfortunately, no Spanish chronicler stated what objects they traded, other than hinting they were ornaments of gold; nor did they say what the traders wanted in exchange for their gold. Presumably it would not have been food or any bulky material. Could it have been the beautiful jadeite, jasper, or amethyst beads made by the Arawaks? Frankly we don't know. But I suggest that some trader brought a hafted matte-surfaced ax from Colombia, possibly as a working tool to split dry driftwood for making fires for the evening meal. Perhaps this ax was so attractive to some Arawak—or possibly Carib—in Grenada or St. Vincent that he acquired it. His fellows observed its merits and the fabrication of ground stone axes commenced on the islands, the makers using the andesite and other igneous rocks so plentiful in the Lesser Antilles.

The technique seems to have spread to St. Lucia, Martinique, and Guadeloupe because matte-surfaced axes are common on those islands. It will require meticulous excavation in these places, and the gathering of charcoal from locations where these stone axes are found, to determine just when the ground stone ax was first introduced and how fast its use was accepted through the islands.

Apparently the matte-surfaced ax skipped Antigua, since we have found only PPC there.[9]

I have mentioned that the building of a dugout canoe was a very slow operation. So, too, must have been the making of the ground stone ax, which was first chipped into its general rough shape and then ground by hand-rubbing the stone against a hard surface. Chipping marks are observable on most matte-surfaced axes and even on several of the polished petaloid celts.[10]

I am uncomfortably aware that I have raised more questions about the PPC and the matte-surfaced lugged axes than I have answered.

WEAPONS

When we turn from tools to weapons the task is simpler. The Arawaks were peaceful people and we find few weapons. But those we do come across are so unusual that they invariably attract lively attention.

191

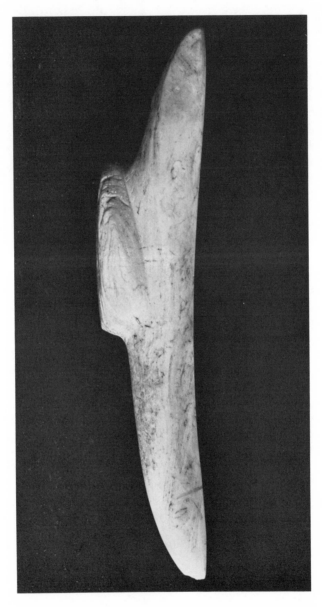

Fig. 78. Arawak conch dagger.

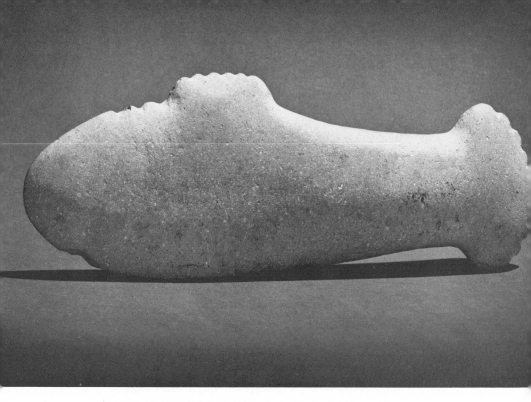

Fig. 79. Stone ax in form of a shark (St. Vincent).

First is an Arawak dagger (Figure 78). It is difficult to identify at first sight, but repeated handling shows that the object best fits the hand as a dagger, with the index finger placed over the protuberance to guide a powerful down stroke. It was cut from the lip of a conch shell and finished to a sharp point at each end. It has a fine sculptural shape and as far as I know is a unique specimen. So much has been heard about the peaceful nature of the Arawaks that I am inclined to regard this dagger as a protection against sharks rather than as a weapon against their fellow men.

The second piece is a lunate knife of gray basaltic stone obtained on St. Vincent. It has been suggested that crescent blades were used as sacrificial knives, but I know of no evidence to support the idea of blood rituals among the Arawaks.

The third item is a very fine hand ax in the shape of a shark (Figure 79), presumably designed with the idea that by "imitative magic" the power and swiftness of the shark would be added to the blow, thereby making it a very effective weapon. It, too, was obtained in St. Vincent and is cut from a piece of igneous andesite

Fig. 80. Carib war club (Guyana).

rock. Sculpturally it is a masterpiece from the hands of some Arawak Brancusi.

Finally, there is the pair of Carib war clubs made of extremely hard wood from Guyana known as purple heart (Figure 80). These are not, of course, of Arawak fabrication, but are included to show the kind of weapons the Caribs used in exterminating the Arawaks from the Lesser Antilles.

X

The Arawak Ballgame

LARGE oval rings, some weighing more than fifty pounds and beautifully carved from hard, igneous rocks, have been known in the Caribbean islands for about seventy years, ever since J. Walter Fewkes visited Puerto Rico in 1902. He had been sent by the Smithsonian Institution to collect "data and specimens that would shed light on the prehistoric inhabitants of this West Indian Island which has just come into the possession of the United States." Fewkes reported that "no archeological objects found in Porto Rico have attracted more attention and are more characteristic of the island than those rings made of stone that from their shapes are called collars or horse collars." He added that they were "of un-known use."

More than a hundred of these "horse collars" are in various mu-seums, about sixty in the United States and forty in Copenhagen, London, Paris, and Berlin. Five are in the collection of the writer (Figure 81).

It seemed impossible that they could be horse collars since the Arawaks knew no horses until Columbus brought them.[1] Their use remained unknown for about fifty years until Gordon Ekholm, in 1961, published his suggestion that these stone collars were belts worn by Arawak athletes playing their ballgame and were quite similar to the stone yokes associated with the ancient ballgame of Mexico. This viewpoint is now accepted by almost all archeolo-gists.[2] Even two of the rubber balls used in the Amerind ballgame have been found, one now on display in the Anthropological Mu-seum in Mexico City, the other in Copenhagen.

I willingly accepted Professor Ekholm's interpretation of these stone collars as ball belts, but I had no premonition of the vast

Fig. 81. Four so-called "horse-collars." The lower left is the fifteen-pound one; lower right weighs fifty-five pounds (Puerto Rico).

amount of time and effort that would be spent in researching the Arawak ballgame. It would mean going from island to island hunting for ball-court sites in the Lesser Antilles, where none as yet has been found, and into the mountainous areas of central Puerto Rico to the ball court at Capá. It would be these very "horse collars" and their related Mexican stone yokes that would entice me to the ancient ball courts of Mexico, Guatemala, and Honduras, looking for possible relationships between the game played by Mayans or Aztecs on the mainland and by the Arawaks on the islands of the Antilles.

A game using a rubber ball was played in the Americas perhaps more than a thousand years earlier than anywhere in the Old World. The first reference in Europe to a rubber ball was made by the Florentine ambassador to Spain, Giacciadini, who chanced to be on the dock one day in 1525 when a Spanish ship arrived from the West Indies. Some Indians debarked and, glad of the opportunity to stretch their legs on solid ground after the long voyage, began to play the Arawak game with "a ball that bounced," to the astonishment of the ambassador and doubtless of everyone else who watched the performance. Unfortunately, the ambassador did not describe the game, perhaps considering it too trivial for his notice. It was the novelty of the bouncing ball that absorbed his interest.

The first written description of the Arawak game, called Batey (bah-tay), was by El Capitan Oviedo, known as the official chronicler of "The Indies." He visited the New World in 1513 and spent more than thirty years in the Caribbean. He probably saw several ball courts in Hispaniola and published the first account of the game in 1535, but only sketchily. He stated that the ball was "struck with the shoulder, elbow or head, or more frequently with the hip or knee. The object was to put the ball across the other side's back lines."

Cortés and his followers, who landed in Mexico in March, 1519, saw a ballgame being played by the Aztecs, but this was perhaps more than twenty years after Spaniards on Hispaniola had seen the Arawak game. The Spanish chroniclers were frequently clerics, more disturbed by the "pagan" practices of the natives than interested in the techniques of their sport, so it is difficult to get a clear picture of the game from their writings.

To the statements of the chroniclers can be added the findings of archeologists who have unearthed more than two hundred ball courts, about sixty in Puerto Rico and Hispaniola, over a hundred in Mexico and Guatemala, and about forty in Arizona and other parts of the United States. The courts vary so greatly in structure that the game would seem to have been quite different in various locations, a view generally accepted. Most recent investigators of the Amerind ballgame have concerned themselves with the mainland version, probably because of the popularity of travel to archeological centers such as Chichén Itzá and Monte Alban in Mexico, or Tikal and Copán in Guatemala and Honduras (Map 1). At each of these sites are beautiful ball courts, the largest and most spectacular being at Chichén Itzá (Figure 82). It is an exciting experience just to walk through the field, examining at close range the magnificent bas reliefs and temples surrounding the court. However, the court in Copán in Honduras is my favorite (Figure 83). It is an architectural gem.

In contrast, the Arawak ball courts seem like very puny structures. The best court is at Capá (Figure 84, Map 10) in the central plateau of Puerto Rico, but it has none of the temples or other highly developed architectural features displayed at Copán or Chichén Itzá (Map 1). Consequently, for several years the general view has been that the sport diffused from the advanced cultures

Fig. 82. Ball court at Chichén Itzá (Yucatan).

of the Middle American mainland to the less developed Arawak islands.

In spite of the fact that the Arawaks were skilled in carving stone, as their zemies and other ritual artifacts demonstrate, they were not architects nor did they practice any masonry. Indeed, I know of no example where any Arawak had deliberately placed one stone upon another. Consequently, Arawak ball courts had no walls, but merely unjoined slabs of stone set vertically to mark the edges of the court. Between 1936 and 1938, Professor Rouse examined thirty-five ball courts in Puerto Rico, most of them in the hilly central part of the country. They were frequently located on ground commanding a good view, where enough flat land was available, even though at times this involved extensive movement of earth.

But what did these Arawak ball courts look like? The only available photographs had been taken in 1914 by J. Alden Mason when he investigated the Capá site. One picture showed most of the stone slabs lying as they had fallen into the playing area. However, in the early 1960's, Ricardo Alegría restored the Capá site, and this

Fig. 83. The ball court at Copán, Honduras, is an architectural gem.

is now regarded as the finest example of an Arawak ball court in the Caribbean area. I visited the site in 1967.

Capá is near Utuado, on a plateau several hundred feet above the Rio Tanamá, with a dramatic backdrop of mountains on all sides. It has been set aside as a national monument. The whole site is roughly rectangular, about eight hundred feet long by four hundred feet wide, the main feature being an extensive ceremonial plaza (see Chapter VI). To the north of this plaza is the large ball court (Figure 84), about two hundred feet long by fifty-five feet wide, flanked along the east and west sides with large limestone slabs. Some of these slabs are over six feet high and four to five feet wide (Figure 85). At each end of the court is a curved pavement of smooth stones. Spectators probably sat on these pavements while others stood along the sides of the court, peering over the vertical slabs or through the gaps between the tall stones.

Walking down the ball court, it was easy to visualize the ball being bounced back from the slabs by players advancing along the court, just as it would have been from the massive walls of the

Fig. 84. The ball court at Capá, Puerto Rico, flanked on opposite sides with slabs of limestone. At each end is a curved pavement of stones (foreground) where spectators sat.

Fig. 85. I could visualize the ball being bounced back from the huge limestone slabs that flank the main ball court at Capá.

courts at Copán, Palenque, or Chichén Itzá. If, however, the ball missed one of the slabs, it would be out of bounds and would have to be brought back, probably to be played by a member of the opposing team. Stones at each end of the court, set at right angles to the long sides, were evidently markers for goal lines. It was at these points that the pavement curved outward to an extent of about fifteen feet, providing a convenient space on which spectators sat. I recalled Oviedo's straightforward statement, "In its simplest form the player endeavors to knock the ball over the opponent's back boundary." The court itself echoes this remark.

Six other ball courts were scattered around the Capá site, most of them running north and south (Figure 86). These courts were smaller and I measured only two—one of them one hundred by forty-five feet, the other seventy-five by twenty-five feet. I guessed that all six of them were practice courts, since many were edged with smooth river stones instead of the imposing massive slabs and had no "pavement" ends for spectators.

There were no petroglyphs on any of these ball-court stones, but I suspect that originally there had been several, removed long ago as souvenirs because they were small enough to transport easily. In my collection are three small petroglyphs which were attributed to Capá by their former owner.

The overall impression is that the Capá site was a large ritual and recreational area. Since there was only one ceremonial plaza as contrasted with seven ball courts, it would seem that the ballgame must have rated quite high at the gatherings.

Quite early in these studies of the Arawak ballgame I had been attracted to the Middle American ball courts, particularly those at Chichén Itzá, Monte Alban, and Palenque in Mexico, and Copán in Honduras. I visited these locations, some of them several times, fortified with data compiled by several students of the game.[3]

Play on the Aztec courts was apparently lively and the excitement intense. We are told that the stakes were high. Chieftains and princes wagered their jewels, their wives, and their slaves. The lower orders gambled any or all of their possessions, while the lowest bet their freedom and went into slavery if they lost. The game was played by everyone who had the ability. Moctezuma, emperor of the Aztecs, was an accredited star, and the mythical Quetzalcoatl was of fabled skill. The gods were tremendously interested in mortals when they played, and they too indulged in the game. It was part of the innermost fabric of the people.

Fig. 86. One of six smaller ball courts at Capá, perhaps practice courts.

The bas reliefs of the huge court at Chichén Itzá show highly dramatic incidents of the game. The carvings are usually interpreted as depicting the sacrifice of the captain of the losing team, either by having his heart cut out with swift strokes of an obsidian knife or by being decapitated (Figure 87a and interpretative drawing Figure 87b). The severed head is plainly visible on the gray stone frieze of the lower bench of the court. Anyone viewing the reliefs can vividly, if vicariously, relive the fierce moments when the threat of defeat spurs the losing captain to superhuman effort. However, I know of no mention by the chroniclers of this practice of sacrificing the defeated captain and am inclined to seek another explanation for the episode depicted in these bas reliefs.

Unquestionably they do show a man kneeling on left knee and with his head cut off. Seven streams of blood gush from his severed neck, but closer scrutiny reveals that these streams have the form of serpents. The victim's head is held by a regal standing figure with a large knife, presumably an obsidian blade, in his right hand while blood also spurts from the head, but this time not in the form of serpents. The two opposing figures apparently represent ball players since each wears the characteristic protective pad on his

Fig. 87. a: Bas reliefs at Chichén Itzá, showing decapitated captain of the losing ball team. b: Sketch of Chichén Itzá bas relief, abstracting pertinent details of the decapitation.

right knee. However, the regalia of the standing figure is so elaborate as to suggest that he is ceremonially clad. His accoutrements include a long jade rod through his nose and a sweeping plume of quetzal feathers attached to his headgear. Even the decapitated head retains a long jade nose-rod and again the plume of quetzal feathers. Hardly suitable garb for a violent game!

The number seven plays an important part in these reliefs, implying magic. There are seven men on each team, seven streams of blood, and each stream a serpent. This would seem to be related intimately to the Aztec fertility goddess, Chicomecouatl (*chicome*, Aztec for seven and *couatl* meaning serpent). The blood apparently is fertilizing the earth, represented on the bas reliefs by the disk prominently placed between the executioner with his obsidian knife and the headless figure. The disk bears the features of the God of Death and signifies the close relationship between the deities of Earth and Death. From death there springs new life.[4]

The results of the fertilization of the earth are graphically shown by the flourishing lotus plant. Blossoms in all stages of florescence, from bud to flower, spring from the plant. Merely from an artistic viewpoint the meandering stem (or, more correctly, rhizome) is a tour de force of draughtsmanship, filling the whole background with an elaborate and beautiful design that integrates the leading action of the drama into the total composition of the relief.

Perhaps the game symbolized on these reliefs was the culmination of an elaborate program of rituals for bringing rain. We can imagine that the two greatest teams in the land would be selected for the final event.

It seems plausible that the Aztecs, accustomed to the sacrifice of thousands of victims[5] on the steps of their pyramid temples in order to ensure the coming of the reluctant spring rains, might also have staged a ballgame, decapitating the losing captain or even the whole team. But I doubt that such sacrifice was the fundamental reason for the existence of the ballgame. It seems more likely that these games were played throughout the land because they were the most enjoyable pastime the Amerinds had developed.[6]

In my opinion the most satisfactory explanation for the bas reliefs at Chichén Itzá is that the participants are not mortals, but, judging from the quetzal-feather ornaments, are the gods themselves. These gods are engaged in a fertility rite, using the ballgame as a device for providing the symbolism. The reliefs therefore tell the story of how the earth is fertilized by the very life-blood of the gods.

That the Mayans and Aztecs were deeply concerned with symbolism is shown by their extraordinary painted books, the Codices. Some of these Codices depict in great detail their efforts to interpret various astronomical phenomena. For example, the Codex Borgia explains the continuous alternation of day and night in terms of ballgames played between the god of the day and the god of the night. Daylight resulted from the victory of the day deity. Darkness similarly denoted the victory of the night deity.[7]

The Maya or Aztec priests were the elite, probably the only ones able to read and write the language of glyphs and understand the subtleties of the Mexican pantheon. To make contact with the people the priests used the familiar ballgame to depict, in easily recognizable form, the concepts they had developed concerning the heavenly bodies. In much the same way the medieval churches of Europe used sculpture and painting to bring to the people, most of whom were illiterate, an understanding of Church dogma.

Splendid as the Chichén Itzá ball court, with its bas reliefs, undoubtedly is, and intriguing as the Mexican Codices may be, I was frankly unable to extract any material that seemed relevant to the Arawak ballgame. Likewise, visits to the beautiful sites at Copán in Honduras, Monte Alban in Oaxaca, or Palenque in Chiapas are deeply rewarding—even thrilling—but they, too, gave no further clarification of the uses of the Arawak belts and elbow stones from Capá or the techniques of the game. However, a lucky find of a Nayarit model of a ballgame became available (now in the Yale collection) and I have spent countless hours with this extraordinary piece. Found in a deep grave chamber in Nayarit, western Mexico, it is a beautifully modeled ceramic work showing in considerable detail a game in progress by villagers of some unknown tribe, possibly Tarascan (Figure 88a). The audience is seated, about ten on each side of the court and four at either end. Two late arrivals are coming up a stairway flanking the court. Obviously it is an occasion for a pleasant family outing since a well-bosomed mother sits with her arm around a child at each side. To the right of this trio the father, wearing an elaborate headgear, bends solicitously toward the children. Two places to the left of the mother is a man with his demure but buxom girlfriend. Other recognizable figures are a mother holding her baby in her arms, pairs of young lovers sitting close together, and so on. Everyone is having a good time and the probability that the losing captain will be decapitated seems almost certainly nil.

The game is underway. Apparently there are three players on each team and an umpire in the central position (Figure 88b). One team wears white brimmed hats and white belts or caps. One player is at the end of the court and we judge him to be the one about to make the play since all the other players face him. His two team-mates are at the opposite end of the court, while the third member of the guarding team has placed himself in a position to intercept the ball before it can reach the two white-belt players.

This arrangement requires a totally different scheme of playing than that indicated by the description of the Aztec game. In the Aztec version the teams stay on their own side of the center line, just as tennis players keep to their own sides of the net. But in the Nayarit village game the players appear to cover the entire court, guarding the actions of the man making the play or seeking to

a

Fig. 88. a: *Model of ballgame found in grave chamber in Nayarit, Mexico (100 B.C.–A.D. 250). A pleasant family gathering, spectators seated at*

b

sides and ends of court (now at Yale University Art Gallery). b: *The game underway.*

intercept the ball from the player or his teammates. Presumably a player could hit the ball into the air and continue the play by striking the ball on the fly or after bouncing, slipping between the men guarding him or passing the ball to his two companions at the other end of the court.

What evidence of this can be extracted from the model? The most significant hint seems to lie in the five hemispherical blobs scattered along the floor of the court. Obviously they are not court markers since they are spaced so irregularly. My guess is that they represent successive points at which the ball bounced on the occasion of some spectacular play that had made the principal player famous. I am inclined to think that this model gives us a basis for the reconstruction of the game, more graphically than could be done by any Spanish padre's writing.

To try to clarify this play I have made a diagram of the players in the model (Figure 89) showing white-belt-and-cap team members as A-1, A-2, and A-3, while their opponents (no white belts or brimmed hats) are designated as B-1, B-2, and B-3. Perhaps the game went as follows:

1. A-1 first hit the ball into the air from Position 1.

2. Ball went over heads of B-1 and B-2 while A-1 immediately maneuvered between B-1 and B-2 and hit ball with head or elbow to Position 2.

3. A-1 continued play with a fast movement of ball from Position 2 to Position 3. Meanwhile B-1 and B-2 turned and pursued A-1.

4. Player A-1 continued his triumphal swing down the field. B-3 attempted to block A-1 by rushing toward ball at Position 3, but A-1 lobbed ball over B-3 to Position 4.

5. A-1 then dodged around the oncoming B-3 and knocked ball to Position 5 before B-3 could turn, which put A-1 in the clear to finish the play by bouncing ball to end of the court.

Presumably this successful navigation of the full length of the field by the flying A-1 constituted a spectacular scoring play which became famous through repetition of the story. Finally it was recorded in this clay sculpture to the eternal glory of the hero—A-1 —and buried with him upon his death.

Furthermore, I am inclined to agree with the view expressed by the late Miguel Covarrubias, the eminent Mexican artist, when I described this piece to him in a pleasant conversation in a little bistro in Mexico City. These Nayarit scenes, he said, were probably

Fig. 89. Diagram of action. Two teams of three players each, umpire at middle of court. Player A–1 with white belt is about to make play. Two opponents (B–1 and B–2) guard him. Two white-belt players (A–2 and A–3) are guarded by one beltless player (B–3). Hemispherical blobs on floor of court mark positions of ball in the spectacular play of Player A–1, whose fame was celebrated by this model buried with him.

the work of sculptors not later than A.D. 500. Our model may there-- fore represent a much earlier phase of the game than the "savage" version at Chichén Itzá, circa A.D. 1200. Whether or not this reconstruction of the Nayarit game is correct, it at least affords a picture of a ballgame that can be reasonably transferred to the Capá court.

The suggested date of A.D. 500 would also be early enough to be the source of the Arawak game in Puerto Rico, if evidence for diffusion from Mexico to the Greater Antilles should be established. An occasional scholar has suggested the game may have migrated in the opposite direction, from Arawak areas to Mexico. My own opinion is that a third hypothesis merits much further study, namely that both the Mexican game (called Pok-ta-Pok by the Mayas and Tlachtli by the Aztecs) and the island Arawak game (Batey) were derived from a common and very early source in South America. The evidence is by no means adequate, but the essential feature of both the Mexican and the Arawak game is a rubber ball, and it seems likely that rubber was brought into Mexico and Arawak lands from the south.

We have no proof as to time or place of the origin of the rubber ball. However, it may be significant that the very early people of high cultural attainment in Mexico were the Olmecs (dating prior to 500 B.C.) whose name is usually considered to mean "rubber people," as suggested by the Mayan word *olli*, rubber. It is intriguing that a word of similar sound—*uol* or *uolol* in Mayan— means a round thing or a ball. So perhaps the Olmecs had a round thing—the rubber ball for playing a game.

But where was the most probable place for rubber to have been discovered? My guess would be where rubber grew best. The finest kind of rubber tree, *Hevea brasiliensis*, is found in the forests of the Amazon River valley, its tributaries, and other river systems with similar ecology. I picture some nomadic Amerind of three or four thousand years ago wandering through the tropical forests of the Amazonas territories of Brazil, Venezuela, or Colombia looking for food. With a sharp-pointed hand-ax he hacked into the bark of a rubber tree, perhaps hoping to extract juicy grubs. Noticing a milky liquid oozing from the cut he dipped his fingers into it and tasted. Not at all good and very sticky! Perhaps his hand became covered with the gooey stuff and he tried to rub it off on his hip, the most convenient way to get rid of it. There it dried quickly and he felt as though he had an extra skin on his thigh. Rubbing his thigh again he found that the dried film rolled up easily into a mass which he threw away. It hit a tree or rock and, to his amazement, bounced off in such a lively manner that, curious, he picked it up and threw it again. Once more it bounced. This was too interesting not to be shared. Carrying it back to the campsite he showed his discovery and demonstrated its lively behavior by throwing it on the hard ground around the huts. It bounced and rebounded while the village children chased it delightedly. Clearly this was a magic substance. Everyone wanted to touch the strange stuff, to throw it and leap after it, the more boisterously as they pitched it harder. By this time the mass had become more or less rounded into the shape of a ball. It was thrown, caught, and returned, and the more the villagers became accustomed to the wonder of it, the more the ball established itself as their favorite plaything.

Other people went to the tree and collected their own supply of the magic stuff. And from this village the knowledge of rubber and its wonderful qualities spread to neighboring areas. It was not just the children who played with it. Grown men and women responded to the liveliness of the rubber ball as well. Everybody wanted one and it was easy to supply the demand from the available trees. Perhaps one of the village families, making a long canoe trip down river, stopped overnight at a group of huts. Talk would be exchanged even though the language varied a bit, and there would be trading. Red jasper stones and beads might be exchanged for the red feathers of the cock-of-the-rock, or river fish for an agouti to make a nourishing *barbasco* (from which we get the word barbecue). But for that magic rubber ball the hut dwellers would exchange almost anything.

It could have taken hundreds of years before rubber was introduced into Mexico by traders going northward along the west shore of the Caribbean to villages already well established on the Gulf of Mexico. Also, traders coming south from Mexico may have encountered people, perhaps in Venezuela, playing with the rubber ball. They acquired some of these fascinating objects and carried them back to Mexico, thereby "diffusing" the game from South America.

This is, of course, a conjectural reconstruction of how the rubber ball may have been discovered, its game potential realized, and how the ball and the game may have spread into Mexico. But it is a reconstruction typical of the accidental manner in which many of man's discoveries have taken place, and the method of diffusion is in agreement with increasingly accepted theories concerning early trade routes in the areas involved. Slowly evidence has been accumulating that trading was much more extensively practiced than previously had been thought possible. Trade routes were probably well established between the Gulf of Mexico and South America at a quite early date, possibly several hundred years B.C.

The extent to which trading developed may be indicated by the statement in the Codex Mendoza that twenty-two towns paid sixteen thousand rubber balls annually in tribute to the court of Mexico in Tenochtitlan. All the towns mentioned lie on the slopes of the Oaxaca mountains and in the alluvial plain watered by a multitude of rivers flowing into the Gulf of Mexico south of Vera Cruz. It is rich country, and was once the home of the Olmec nation. I do not know whether the Oaxaca region was producing rubber in Aztec days, but I am told that no forms of rubber grew in the adjoining Toltec-Aztec country. It seems likely then that rubber was being traded extensively along the so-called H-shaped diffusion route from the South American rubber forests to both Mexico and the Antilles.[8]

Further support of this H-shaped diffusion route is furnished by the description, made by three Spanish priests, of the ballgame as played by Amerinds in the eighteenth century in South America—specifically the Otomac of Venezuela, living near the junction of the Rio Apure and the Orinoco. The Apure originates near the Colombian border and flows through western Venezuela. Indeed, this could have been a very likely route along which Arawaks (or Amerinds who later would be known as Arawaks) migrated some three thousand years ago on their way to the llanos of eastern Venezuela.

Three missionaries—Gumilla, Gilij, and Bueno—describe the Otomac ballgame. Gumilla (in 1747) said the ball was kept in play by use of the right shoulder only. Gilij (in 1784) said the ball could be hit with the head as well as the right shoulder. Bueno (in the late 1700's) said players used elbows and buttocks as well as head and right shoulder. This indicates a slow modification of the game over a period of a hundred years, apparently in much the same manner as the game changed in Mexico through the two thousand years it was played there.[9]

No ball courts have as yet been identified on any of the Leeward or Windward islands, but Professor Rouse has called to my atten-

Fig. 90. Possible ball court at Indian Creek, Antigua (1967).

tion the fact that in the 1920's Gudmund Hatt found a typical ball court at Salt River, St. Croix, in the Virgin Islands. In the 1950's, Dick Richards found a fragment of a ball belt not far from Salt River.

On Antigua two sites have been found where ceremonial plazas or ball courts may have existed. One is at Marmora Bay and the other at Indian Creek, about a mile inland. At Marmora Bay there is a large rectangular area, about five hundred by two hundred feet, from which we have excavated a few ritual objects: a ceramic female fertility figure (Figure 29), two pottery stamps, and two flat stones cut to the same shape and standing on edge, although buried some eighteen inches underground. These flat stones line up with what would seem to be the outer edge of a possible ceremonial plaza or ball court, and although much smaller they resemble somewhat the flat limestone slabs that edge the ball court at Capá. The two pottery stamps presumably were used in applying body decoration by dipping in dye, such as that obtained from roucou weed or bixa.

One, bearing a heart-shaped face, was probably a "head stamp," applied to the forehead of all members belonging to a single clan participating in the arietos or games.

The Indian Creek site gives promise of being the most important Arawak site in Antigua, both because of the variety of artifacts revealed on the surface and also the five extensive mounds which, fortunately, appear to be of widely varying dates. On one flat area a narrow stone, about three feet long, was found embedded in the surface and resembling the "pillar stones" Professor Rouse described as markers for the smaller ball courts of Puerto Rico. Three similar stones were located, just barely buried in the surface of the ground. Raised to a vertical position, they marked out a rectangle about thirty feet long by twenty feet wide, and we could not resist the inference that they *might* mark the outline of a ball court (Figure 90). The rectangle, the size, and the location of the stones were similar to what we had seen at Capá, although none was incised with petroglyphs.[10]

Comparing this site with the well-defined courts of Puerto Rico, it would seem that the Capá courts belonged to a "major league" class, whereas the Indian Creek court, if such it should prove to be, would just make the "sand-lot" category. Since Yale will shortly dig Indian Creek it was important not to disturb the spot. Therefore the stones were carefully returned to the troughs they had occupied for hundreds of years. These stones were not geologically native to the spot; evidently they had been carried there for a definite purpose and at some effort—perhaps for a ball court! It will take only one broken fragment of a belt or elbow stone found on the site to identify it thus.

XI

Visit to an Arawak Community *ca.* A.D. 1490

ABOUT a quarter of a million Arawak artifacts of pottery, shell, and stone have now been collected over a period of sixteen years. A considerable amount of information has been gleaned from these artifacts about the habits of the Arawaks. Sites have been visited on twenty-five islands of the Lesser and Greater Antilles and also in South America, particularly in Surinam and Venezuela.

It has always been the actual living people using these artifacts whom I was striving to visualize and understand. Two small museums were established for these artifacts, one at Mill Reef in Antigua and the other at Guilford, Connecticut. Over a period of several years many hundreds of people have visited these museums and contributed much by their knowledge and questioning. I now feel encouraged to try and create an imaginary community as it might have existed in 1490, just before the Spaniards came and the world of the Arawaks declined, and to suggest what made up their day-to-day life in an Arawak village.

For this imaginary community I have selected a site in the center of Puerto Rico, about halfway between Arecibo and Ponce (Map 8), a region surrounding the present town of Utuado and containing the ceremonial site of Capá. I shall also call upon findings from many other places in describing the community.

When Juan Ponce de Leon arrived in Puerto Rico in 1508 he found a number of settlements or villages scattered over the length and breadth of the country. Each was under the command of a chieftain or cacique. Eighteen of these settlements have been identified in Puerto Rico by name and location, together with the name of the chieftain at the time, and we know that the region now called Utuado was named Otoao by the Arawaks. The difference in the names is slight. The chieftain of our settlement in Columbus' time was Guarionex and his domain was a beautiful stretch of land surrounded by low hills from which emerge occasional limestone cliffs that form a dramatic containment of the broad fertile valley. What appears to be a lovely valley is actually a plateau in the central mountains of Puerto Rico, and the streams which collect the rain falling on the mountains run northward into the Atlantic.

Early in the present century the archeologist John Alden Mason made a trip into the valley by horseback and his notebooks describe an Arawak site he called Capá, a few miles west of Utuado on the Rio Tanamá. More recently, in 1967, I made the same trip by car. No road map I have seen bears the name Capá and the natives I asked knew of no such place, but it will serve to identify our imaginary settlement.

Capá was once a well-established ceremonial center, its great extent indicating that it must have been used by a large number of people. Mason, however, in reporting his 1914 excavations, made no reference to any associated village sites, and no extensive middens have been found which would proclaim a longtime residence by the Arawaks. In the absence of evidence one is led to assume that in some of the broad valleys leading from it there were villages where perhaps several hundred Arawaks dwelt and cultivated their manioc patches.

Drawing upon the vivid journals of that entertaining Spanish padre, Father Gumilla, who lived and worked among the Otomac tribe on the Orinoco in Venezuela about A.D. 1750, let us step back several centuries and join the villagers of Capá one morning as the sun is about to rise.

Just before daybreak the shaman awakes, goes outside his hut, and calls in a loud voice "laden with misery" to the spirits of his ancestors. Then from every thatched hut the people pour into an open area, probably similar to the sandy space I had seen in the Arawak village of Powakka in Surinam (Map 1). All join in the wailing, bemoaning the departure of the great ones of the tribe. This is to make sure that the powerful ancestor spirits are adequately propitiated so they will not wreak vengeance on the tribe for neglecting to pay proper tribute.

With the rising of the sun the tone changes from misery to joy, and as the day gathers strength steps quicken into a wild dance. The fearsome spirits have been vanquished. By this time the entire village is out; old people are standing and clapping their hands to the rhythm; the children are romping in their own groups—all cooperating to launch the day's activities with zest and friendliness.

In due time the women drop out of the dance, go back to their huts, and start to prepare the morning meal of cassava bread dipped in pepper pot soup. The dancing stops at a signal from the chieftain, who then makes his announcements for the day, specifying which groups will hunt, which will go to the fields, and stating any other duties to be performed.

Immediately after breakfast the men depart to their assigned tasks. Those who have not been given any chore for the day make their way to the ball courts.

Here their first task is to sweep the courts with faggotlike brooms, to insure that the playing areas are smooth, level, and free of stones. The care exercised in cleaning the surface is vivid testimony to the fact that each man knows the hazards of the game as players leap into the air repeatedly to hit the ball, then slide with bare bodies, usually on their hips, over the surface of the ground.

Groups separate to each of the five practice courts, some to perfect special plays, such as jumping in the air and swinging their torsos to give a powerful hip blow to an oncoming ball. This is an almost incredible acrobatic stunt, tried again and again with such eagerness that it seems incomprehensible how a man could continue such violent expenditure of energy without utter exhaustion.

A match has evidently been agreed upon by rival local factions. Two groups quickly line up for play on the main court, six men on each team facing each other. The referee bounces the ball on a flat stone embedded in the center of the court. Instantly the players scatter, two from each side racing toward the ball as it rebounds from the stone. The nearest man leaps into the air and with a rapid rolling motion strikes the ball with his thigh, sending it eight to ten feet into the air toward his opponents' goal. The ball, made of black dried-rubber latex, sails about twenty feet. It is intercepted by an opposing player, who jumps high and returns the ball with his elbow. This time the ball goes bouncing along the ground, a teammate adding to its forward motion with a spinning blow from his hip. The games and the practicing continue all morning.

But what about the working groups? One team of men is making a canoe, so important in securing the fish which provide much of the protein in the Arawak diet. A tree, measuring about twenty-four inches in diameter and twenty feet long, has already been felled and is on the ground. On top of the trunk a series of small fires, about a foot apart, have been burning for several hours. Now the charcoal is being scooped out with conch-shell celts. The ridges of charred wood remaining between the fire pits are being split off by stone adzes. The cutting is "with the grain" and the charred wood is brittle. By burning, chipping, and adzing, the work will continue until sufficient wood is removed from the center of the log to allow the walls to be stretched enough to receive the thwarts. The leader of the group knows this large fishing canoe will take at least six moons to finish before it can be paddled down the river to the sea.

Along the edge of the river men are mending fishing nets. Others are collecting a shrub which contains a fish poison.[1] One man is pounding the roots and stems until they are in shreds like hemp. Some of this mass is thrown into a large pool near the shore of the river. In a matter of minutes fish begin to rise and float on the surface. Young boys wade in, gleefully picking up the fish and bringing them ashore.

Next a couple of men take their canoe down the river to a deeper pool. Again some of the pounded root mass is tossed into the water. This time nets are used to bring in the fish as they rise to the surface.

Another group of men, who have just spent several days at the coast, are bringing back a canoe-load of turtles from the ocean. They have caught the turtles with the aid of remora fish.

At the end of the village pottery is being made by the women. At one spot a brush heap is slowly burning out and the pots lying on the embers are almost fully fired. A few more branches are put on the fire to finish baking the pots.

Nearby two women are kneading the reddish plastic mass they have brought from the valley where good potter's clay is found not far from the river. Small amounts of water and sand are being added until the clay has the desired consistency. Experienced hands roll long rods of clay, about the thickness of a finger, which they coil layer by layer until the basic pot shape is formed. Smooth disks of stone, which they have picked up on the beach, are held snugly in the palm of the hand and the coils rubbed down until the ridges disappear and the bowl takes on a satinlike surface on both the outside and inside walls.

Two types of pottery are being made today: large cooking vessels and cassava griddles. The cooking pots are sixteen inches in diameter and ten inches deep and have a wide mouth. One potter is giving some extra finishing touches to her pot. She is making handles in the shape of an agouti head. She pats a half-inch thick piece of clay into a three-by-three inch square. Deftly she models the head with her fingers, but uses a sharp stick to incise the ears, eyes, mouth, and the tuft on the bridge of its long nose. Actually she makes two of them and thoroughly works them onto each side of the pot, dampening the rim to ensure a firm bond for the handle.

Another woman is making a cassava griddle. She first forms a large flat disk about half an inch thick and twenty-four inches in diameter. The upper surface is rubbed smooth and a slightly raised rim is added to contain the cassava crumbs and give a bread disk about a quarter of an inch thick. The flat griddle has no legs like those found on Antigua, but is raised above the fire by being placed on three stones. The lower surface which the flames will lick is rough.

At noon several women who have completed their chores arrive at the ball court. Teams are selected, the women opposing the men. The women's team is given two extra players. As an additional advantage each woman is allowed to use a bat, apparently adapted from a canoe paddle. By using two hands, with these bats a woman can hit the ball so powerfully that frequently a man is forced to receive the ball on the broad of his back. Father Gumilla furnishes the note that "hardly a day passes without a back being broken, which these hens celebrate with laughter."

In one hut lies a sick man, ill for several days. The shaman has been summoned and he now is blowing smoke over the sick man, directing it at the point of the pain. The patient is thoroughly familiar with the ritualistic smoking of tobacco by the shaman prior to going into a state of trance, so its use during his treatment is undoubtedly considered to be of special significance in the curing of his disease. The shaman is summoning the good spirits to his rescue.

After the smoke treatment the shaman sucks vigorously at the painful spot directly with his lips. Sometimes he uses a tube. The shaman then rushes out of the hut to spit out the evil matter. If the ailment should be a snakebite, the treatment might easily be the only known effective remedy. But occasionally the chronicles record bits of chicanery in which the shaman produces small pebbles he has hidden in his mouth as evidence of the cause of the pain.[2]

Just beyond the fringe of trees surrounding the village are the fields where manioc is grown. Some of the fields are relatively clean of fallen trees and stumps; these are the ones that have been longest under cultivation. They lie near the stream and are kept fertile when the rains from the surrounding hills flood the area, bringing new silt to the soil. The women are gathering their day's supply of manioc. They bend to feel the size of the tubers at the base of the manioc stem, and when these are considered large enough the plant is pulled up and the tubers loaded into a wicker pack, which they will carry back to their hut when it is full. If the tubers are particularly large and smooth the stem of this manioc plant is put into a pile for later planting. By this process of selecting the stems from plants which have yielded the largest tubers, the improvement of the manioc plant has been going on perhaps for thousands of years.

Additional fields are needed as families grow in size, or as soil, which is not refreshed by flooding, becomes less productive. This is man's work, and a dozen are building fires around the base of trees to eat away the wood until the tree falls. This new field is now a tangle of trees that have fallen in all directions, but before the rains come the slashed area will be burned. At every available space between the stumps and logs short segments—cut from the manioc stem so as to contain two nodes—will be planted. A new plant will grow that faithfully reproduced the characteristics of the parent plant. This is vegetative agriculture as contrasted with seed planting. It is a widely observed feature of human behavior in primitive settlements that seed planters tend to remain growers by seeding, while a society that practices cultivation by cutting portions of stems or roots will continue vegetative planting.

Down a path from a nearby field several women come dog-trotting, each carrying a pack of manioc tubers on her back. Most of them also have a baby strapped to a board fastened to the pack. While each woman jogs along she spins cotton thread that will later be knotted to make fish nets. She has a bundle of cotton fibers wrapped around her left arm. With the fingers of her right hand she pulls from the bundle a small fleck of fibers, rapidly twisting it into a thread which hangs from her right hand and is fastened to a spindle whorl on which it is being wound. She keeps the whorl spinning by tapping it with her left hand. At each jog a little more cotton thread is spun and her baby gets another bump on the back of its head. It is frequently written that a baby's head is flattened for cosmetic reasons, but for these babies flattening is also inevitable.

As soon as the women reach their huts the babies are taken from the packs and placed in their respective hammocks.[3] Each hut has as many hammocks as there are members of the family. They are fastened to the poles that support the roof and the walls and are in orderly stacks. The largest one at the highest position is for the husband. It is easier for him to climb into the top one. The lowest is for the wife because it is her duty to keep the fire going. Baby has the smallest one fastened to the line that supports the mother's hammock.

The manioc tubers are unloaded on the floor and mother, with the help of a daughter, begins to peel off the brown skin, using the sharp edge of a flint knife. The white cores are placed in a wide basket, where they are held ready for the grating process.

At another hut the scraped manioc is being loaded into the woven matapi tube in order to squeeze out the poisonous juice. Later the core of white cassava is removed and screened into crumbs, which will be baked into golden-brown disks of cassava bread. At every hut in the village some part of the manioc process is being carried out, since cassava bread is about 80 per cent of the daily food.

As the afternoon wears on small groups of hunters return to the village. The animals they carry look strange because they are not like the game commonly hunted on the mainland. Puerto Rico, like all the islands of the Antilles, has been separated from the mainland for millions of years, so there are no herds of deer or other ruminants. Nor are there any predators like the jaguar. Indeed, the only mammals are those such as the rice rat, which have chanced to float there on logs carried by the prevailing currents, or those which the Arawaks have brought in their canoes from the mainland to breed for food. These land mammals are mostly rodents, but some of them are quite large. The agouti is perhaps the commonest, about the size of a large rabbit, with five hooflike claws on the front feet and three on each of its hind feet. Many a hut has a tame agouti that the children love to fondle.

At each hut the returning hunter is skinning the animals with flint knives. After cleaning and cutting them into suitable chunks, they are given to the women to add to the pepper pot, which has been cooking for some time. Yams, sweet potatoes, turtle, and other meats are thrown in pretty much as we do today with pot-au-feu. An important ingredient of the stew is the peppers which give piquancy. However, an essential component of every pepper pot is the cassareep syrup, which the women have made by previously boiling down the manioc juice squeezed out by the matapi. When cooked down to a heavy, dark syrup (not unlike soy sauce) the poisonous hydrocyanic acid has been evaporated and the remaining mass is not only safe to eat, but imparts a pungency to the stew, as well as acting as a tenderizer of the meat.

By this time all of the men have returned from their tasks. This is the time for relaxing and going to the river to bathe. Stories of the fishing trip, the hunt, and the ballgame are exchanged. It will soon be time for the evening meal and all men must be ready for it. No man or boy would appear willingly without having washed and been appropriately anointed with oil by wife, daughter, or sister.

Usually the whole body is smeared with an unguent such as turtle-egg oil, or oil obtained from the seed of the crabwood tree (*Carapa guianiensis*). This acts as a mosquito repellant, a skin softener, and also as a vehicle for the desired coloring matter, such as the red arnotta (*Bixa orellana*). Ornamentation in the form of colored lines and patches is usually at the whim of the wearer or the helper doing the painting. It is obviously important, perhaps because people who wear no clothes seem intuitively to seek some individual adornment.

The meal this evening is special because a young neighboring chieftain and his court have come to Capá on a mission from the kingdom of Abacoa, immediately to the north on the coast. The guests had announced their presence as soon as they reached the borders of the territory of Guarionex, and messengers had run to the village to advise the cacique of their coming. Then the ranking nobles of the Capá community hurried to meet the visitors and escort them into the presence of Guarionex.

The entire tribe assembles at the large ceremonial plaza. They gather by families, and the head of each wears his necklace of stone beads with a pendant or gorget comprising a flat circular slab of conch shell, on which is delicately carved the sign of his clan. With him are his sons and the male members who are married to his daughters. Each wears a gorget similar to that carried by the head of the family, but appropriately smaller. His chief wife has a necklace of shells with a pendant disk of conch, but without any clan symbol. In her braided hair are attractive combs of bone crosspieces, into which the teeth, made of finely cut and polished mahogany, are inserted and held in place with thread knotted into intricate patterns and decorated with small colored feathers from the macaw and parrot.

The nobles, who are the heads of the clans, arrange themselves in the center of the plaza; their necklaces are more numerous and of larger stones. Their gorgets, likewise, are larger and carved with their respective clan totems and surrounded by a pattern of small disk plates of conch shell. They are permitted to wear a single circle of feathers around their head. A series of decorative patterns has been printed on their bodies by rolling over their skin an intricately designed pottery cylinder inked with a paste of oil and red pigment.

At the blaring of conch trumpets the groups move into their proper positions and the cacique makes his appearance. In front of and following him come groups of his principal chieftains, each decked out in his special ornaments and status symbols. Each man carries a thin wooden wand, near the top of which is a carved stone mace, his symbol of office, and a cluster of colored feathers. The cacique Guarionex is carried on a litter by six men. He wears a large feather crown of many colors on his head and a necklace of beads carved from onyx, amethyst, carnelian, rock crystal, jasper, and, most precious of all, a pendant of jade in the form of a frog, symbolizing the rain god. The cacique is lifted from his litter and placed on his carved wooden duho[4] in front of the large central slabs bearing the petroglyphs. His chieftains fan out on each side of him.

At a signal from Guarionex the nobles bring in the visitor, who hails his host by calling in a loud voice the five ceremonial names of the cacique: "Guarionex, lord of the rich lands, lord of the river, lord of peace, and lord of fruitfulness." He wishes him great health and great joy.

His retainers bring their gifts to Guarionex: mangoes, fresh conchs from the sea, pineapples, and a small, specially carved wooden box, which is handed to Guarionex personally. The cacique opens the box and on a single white lily petal lies a beautiful large pink pearl—a conch pearl of great rarity.

Guarionex admires the pearl and thanks his visitor for the splendid gift. Then he orders food to be brought. Pottery bowls decorated with elegantly incised lines and modeled with turtle designs are placed before each group.[5] The cacique commands all to be seated and the pepper pot stew is passed. A shallow shell is used by each to spoon out meat, squash, beans, and soup, while pieces of cassava bread are served from a specially woven basket,[6] dipped into the dish, and eaten.

When the food is finished large jars of cassiere wine[7] are brought in, but before any is passed out to be drunk Guarionex asks the visiting chieftain what is the purpose of his mission. The man raises himself to his full height, and with a look of conscious pride he announces that he desires a daughter of Guarionex as his wife. The cacique replies that he knows of the fine lands the chieftain's father possesses to the north since he and his people traverse these lands each time they go to the sea. He also knows well the cacique Arasibo[8] with whom he has long been friendly and with whom he has hunted and feasted many times. Finally he says he will be glad to receive his guest as a son-in-law and he knows that the "bride-price" will be magnificent.[9]

With that the cassiere is drunk by all. Guarionex calls his daughter to his side and places her hand in the hand of her future husband. Both drink from the same cup and at a signal from the cacique they lead off into a dance in which all the ritual rules of both tribes are adhered to with strictness. Everybody joins in the dance, which follows the beat of the drums, the trills of the flutes, and the accent notes of the conch trumpets. Maracas are shaken and the younger men vie with each other to stamp their heels to the ground and to follow each pulse of the rattles with the traditional steps, interspersed with their own innovations. The tempo increases and the figures swirl and weave through the elaborate patterns of the dance.

Suddenly the drums stop and the dance ceases. More cassiere wine is drunk, and as the wine begins to affect the assembly the noise level rises steadily. Men and women talk louder and sing more lustily. The dancing resumes and becomes more intense. All the family groups of the village enjoy this social excitement. Some of the younger men become boisterous and quarrelsome, but are promptly disciplined by the nobles.

The children are taken home and the elders return to their hammocks. The dance continues, but when the moon shows that midnight has arrived the conch trumpets sound and the festivities are over. Guarionex and the son of Arasibo leave the plaza and only then can the nobles and the rest of the people depart to their respective huts.

XII

Origins – from Saladero to the Antilles

THERE is general agreement that the Arawaks who inhabited the Caribbean islands came from Venezuela. But by what route? When did they start from Venezuela, and when did they arrive in the Antilles? Why did they leave Venezuela? Where did the Arawaks come from originally?

I have been struggling with these questions for over ten years and for some of them I have still no answers which satisfy me. Nevertheless, the available evidence does strongly suggest that the Arawak culture began along the upper reaches of the Orinoco River and moved—very slowly—downstream to the Atlantic Coast, then by stages up the chain of islands from Trinidad to Puerto Rico.

The most significant clue enabling us to follow their migration is that the same kind of pottery is found in the earliest layers of middens on each of the islands of the Lesser Antilles as well as in Puerto Rico of the Greater Antilles—pottery of precisely the same type that occurs on the mainland of Venezuela, specifically at the village of Saladero located at the apex of the Orinoco delta.

One carbon-14 date obtained for Saladero pottery is 1010 B.C., the earliest date yet found for any Arawak pottery. For the time being we have to regard Saladero as the point of origin of the Arawaks. On the islands of the Antilles the dates are appropriately later, from A.D. 100 to A.D. 400.

Sherds from the lowest layers of several spots along the route are obviously from well-made pottery, remarkably thin and hard, indicating well-controlled firing techniques at a fairly high temperature. But the outstanding feature is the attractive decoration on the sherds, a sophisticated ceramic style comprising areas of white paint on a red background. The designs are well executed

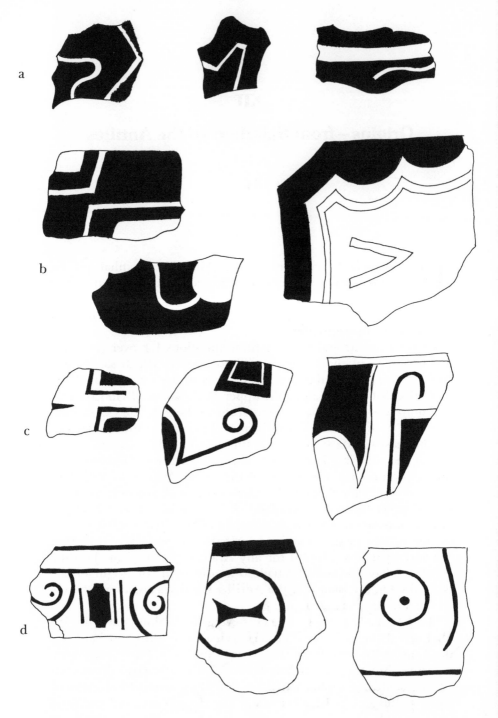

e

f

g

Fig. 91. Saladoid sherds from seven stages of the Arawak migration route.
a: Saladero style from Saladero, Orinoco Delta, 1010 B.C. b: Cedros style
from Cedros, Trinidad, 190 B.C. c: El Mayal style from El Mayal, Peninsula of Paria, A.D. 100–300. d: Mill Reef style from Antigua, A.D. 400–
600. e: St. Croix style from St. Croix, Virgin Islands, A.D. 400–600. f:
Cuevas style from Puerto Rico, A.D. 510–590. g: Hacienda Grande style
from Puerto Rico, A.D. 120–370.

and of high esthetic competence. Indeed, this pottery has become so well recognized that it is commonly referred to by archeologists as "white-on-red" pottery and sometimes simply by the symbol "W-O-R" (Figure 91).[1]

I am conscious of being faced with the serious problem of trying to hold the reader's interest while these sherds are being described in some detail. But we are almost totally dependent on specific features of these broken chips of pottery for our understanding of the migration of the Arawaks. These W-O-R sherds constitute a sort of "calling card" which the Arawaks left along a thousand-mile trail from their earliest known home at Saladero to the northern coast of Puerto Rico. It took them about a thousand years to complete the trail.

An examination of the sherds shown in Figure 91 indicates a steady development in the painted decoration as the Arawaks progressed along their migration route. For example, the W-O-R design on the Antigua sherds (Figure 91d) is more advanced than on those from Saladero (Figure 91a). The same is true for the beautiful bowl from St. Croix (Figure 91e), which is such an elegant and sophisticated design that I think it compares favorably with the ceramic products of other cultures of the same date, about A.D. 400–600.[2] This gradual improvement in design is exactly what might be expected, since the general W-O-R pattern persisted throughout the ten or twelve centuries of their migration, an ample period to permit taste and technique to develop.

Although some archeologists have been studying the migration of the Arawaks for thirty years they are still unhappy about fixing either the course of the migration or the time intervals involved. The main time gaps occur in Trinidad.

But when did the Arawaks leave Venezuela? And why?

The real clue was not discovered until July, 1950, when Professor Rouse and his Venezuelan associate Professor Cruxent made their nine definitive excavations at Saladero (Map 4). It was in the bottom of Excavation 7 that the existence of a pure style of pottery was established. Rouse and Cruxent describe this material as follows: "The sherds are technologically among the best in Venezuela: fine, compact and hard. They ring when struck."[3]

More than 80 per cent of the decorated sherds from Saladero are painted and the design consists of geometric patterns in white on a red background (Figure 91a and Figure 92c). Handles for lifting the pots are very simple, usually just nubbins or tabs on the rims

(Figure 92b). The vessels are generally bell-shaped with thin rims (Figure 92a). "The sherds come mainly from graceful, open mouthed bowls," says Professor Rouse. This then is the description of what Rouse calls Saladero-style pottery (Figure 92).

When pottery closely resembling the Saladero style is found in other locations it is designated as Saladoid, and the potters who made them are called Saladoids.[4]

Professor Rouse's next major observation was that a different kind of pottery appeared immediately above the lowest levels containing the pure Saladero style. This later material was seen to be similar to pottery previously dug at the site of Port Barrancas, half a mile or so downstream, and hence called the Barrancas style. Rouse described these sherds as: "relatively soft and in contrast to Saladero pottery sound dull when struck together . . . it would appear that the Barrancas potters strove more for massiveness and less for grace than in the case of Saladero pottery."

They were, however, not decorated with white-on-red painting such as Saladoid potters used. Instead, the Barrancoid potters made the handles of their pots quite ornate (Figure 93a, b, c). These Barrancoid handles are known, appropriately, as *adornos* (Spanish for "decorations"). The majority are modeled with great skill in the form of animal or bird heads, in contrast with the very simple nubbinlike handles of the earlier Saladoid pottery. Occasionally there are bas-relief human faces applied to the walls of vessels (Figure 93d). The bases frequently have annular rings (Figure 93e), while the rims are flanged and have a triangular cross-section (Figure 93f); both features give added strength to the vessels. About 90 per cent of the decorated Barrancoid pottery lacks any W-O-R painting, but does bear incised designs (Figure 93g, h, i). Thus the Barrancoid pottery varies basically from the Saladoid, both as to techniques and esthetic tradition.

Professor Rouse points out that the Barrancoid potters were a quite different people, who may have come from northwest Venezuela across the llanos. Since he had seen no evidence of destruction in the Saladero middens he suggests that the displacement of the Saladoid inhabitants was not hostile. He also believes that some Saladoids continued to exist there because their painted style of pottery persisted at Saladero for about two hundred years, although in reduced quantity. However, since the women were the potters, this persistence of Saladoid decoration could be accounted for if some of the women had remained or had been held captive when

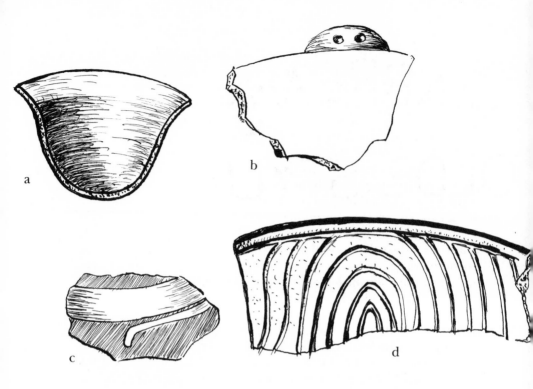

Fig. 92. Saladero-style sherds (from Rouse and Cruxent excavation, Saladero, 1950). a: Flared bell-shaped bowl. b: Nubbin handle. c: W-O-R. d: Incised groove.

the main body of the Saladoids moved on to Trinidad and the Antilles.

Three carbon-14 dates are given by Rouse for the Saladero style pottery at its homesite, viz.: 1010, 900, and 830 B.C. He also gives three dates—985, 955, and 930 B.C.—for the Barrancoid pottery he dug at the same site.

Thus it is indicated that the earliest Barrancoid potters were at Saladero only twenty-five years after the arrival of the first Saladoid potters. This figure is almost without statistical significance since each carbon-14 determination is reported with a plus or minus deviation of about a hundred years. There is, however, clear-cut stratigraphical evidence for the prior occupation by Saladoid potters, in that the Barrancoid sherds lie in layers *above* the Saladero-style pottery and in some excavations are separated from the under-lying Saladoid sherds by a layer of sterile soil.

Personally, I am inclined to the view that the Barrancoids *did*

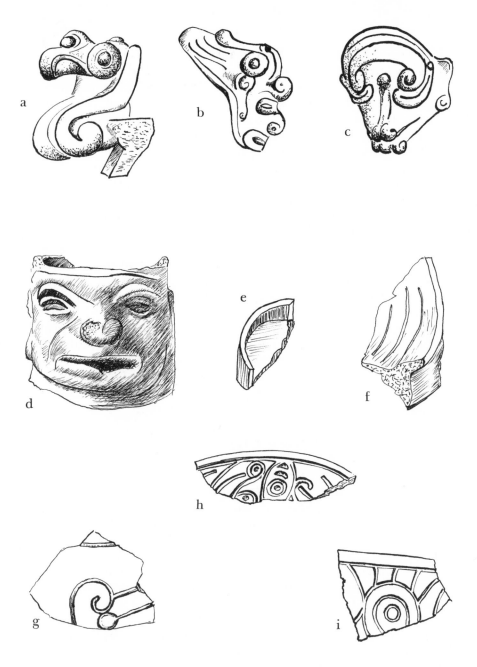

Fig. 93. Barrancoid sherds excavated at Saladero. a, b, c: *Adorno pot handles.* d: *Bas-relief face on side of vessel.* e: *Annular base.* f: *Flanged rim.* g, h, i: *Incised groove decorations.*

displace the Saladoids, perhaps to a major degree. This could have been by hostile action, persuasion, or through timidity on the part of the Saladoids. My reason for believing that the great migration that peopled the Antilles must have been initiated *solely* by Saladoids is that the earliest pottery on every island is almost pure Saladoid, with little or no Barrancoid traits.

It would appear that since Saladoids ventured alone into the islands there must have been some basic cause for the separation of the Saladoids from the Barrancoids. My guess is that the invading Barrancoids were either more numerous or more aggressive. Rouse's comment that he had seen no evidence of destruction when the Barrancoids arrived at Saladero might be explainable on the basis that such traces would be exceedingly difficult to discern with people who occupied perishable thatched houses and practiced no masonry to leave permanent records.

In my judgment it is of major significance that it took about a thousand years for the Saladoid potters to reach the Antilles from their Orinoco home at Saladero. This would have given them plenty of time to develop the culture of manioc and to build up their population. Throughout this long period they preserved their pottery techniques intact and adhered to the white-on-red decorative designs they had used when they lived in Saladero. This, I contend, would be very unlikely if they had been long associated with the Barrancoid potters, who made technically much poorer quality ceramics that Professor Rouse describes.

I am amazed at the tenacity with which the Saladoids maintained the high quality of their technical practices in producing ware of such thinness and hardness throughout the thousand years of their migration. These physical characteristics could only have been obtained by a rigid control of the preparation of the clay and the conditions of firing. Perhaps even more significant was the retention of the design features of the white-on-red pottery. True, there were variations and developments of the decoration, but a thousand years is a long time for a style or fashion to persist.[5] On the other hand, at Saladero during those same thousand years the early Saladoid features disappeared completely and the pottery became characteristically Barrancoid. I am emphasizing this point because it will be important in assessing the degree to which a later Barrancoid influence swept through the islands.

It is this thousand-year gap between the departure of the Saladoid potters from their Orinoco home and their arrival in the

Antilles that has caused me considerable concern. Where were these Saladoid Arawaks and what were they doing for that length of time? As the crow flies, it is only about three hundred miles from Saladero to Grenada. But it may have been a very long and difficult journey for the Arawaks.

An examination of the map suggests three likely routes (Map 3). I have given much thought as to which of these three routes was the most likely way that the Saladoid potters could have taken. Also I have traveled over several portions of them and my strong feeling is that the water route is the most probable one for the people who had spent many generations on the great Orinoco River and had become skilled in the use of dugout canoes. This is the Route 3 shown on Map 3.[6]

Good paddlers leaving Saladero could probably have reached the mouth of the Orinoco in a few days. But the truth is, we have no idea how long they took on the journey. All we can say is that Arawak Saladoids left the apex of the delta possibly before 900 B.C. and were in the Lesser Antilles a thousand years later, about A.D. 100 to 300. Looking at the map, I would guess that they spent most of the time in Trinidad. Unfortunately, not a single carbon-14 dating has been obtained for pottery in Trinidad (as of July, 1969). Nor, for that matter, do we have any trace of sites occupied by Saladoids along the Orinoco after their departure from the apex of the delta.

If the move had happened in flood time, when the water at Saladero rises forty feet above the low level of the river, then most of the land downstream to the Boca Grande would have been flooded, with very little nearby hilly country to which the travelers could have escaped. Presumably they could have moored their canoes at night to the trees. Fish could have been obtained from the river and starch from the core of the moriche palm, even as the Amerinds do today. I was told the land is usually flooded for only about one month each year. If the journey was *not* at the time of high water there would have been plenty of camping sites available.

It is quite possible that the Saladoids took their time in making this journey, cutting manioc fields on the lowlands along the delta and growing sweet manioc (Yuca dulce) in the highly fertile alluvial soil. As I have said in Chapter V, more than two thirds of the banks of the whole length of the Orinoco River up to Puerto Ayacucho, where the major rapids begin, are flooded almost every year. The conditions on this lowland were favorable for the Yuca dulce type of manioc, but whether or not they cultivated manioc as they moved down the delta lands of the river is pure speculation since no trace of their campsites has yet been discovered.

When the Arawak Saladoids reached the Boca Grande of the Orinoco they would have faced the huge expanse of the Atlantic Ocean. As skilled boatsmen they would have been quickly aware that the Orinoco current was sweeping northward, and they would have discerned the broad junction line between their own brown muddy current and the blueness of the encompassing ocean. I can picture their growing uneasiness when, accustomed to satisfy their thirst by scooping up a gourd full of water, they realized the growing saltiness of the water. To be surrounded by undrinkable water must have been a truly frightening experience.

Presumably they would have hugged the shore along the eastern coast of Venezuela, camping wherever they found a beach in between stretches of mangrove swamp. For more than fifty miles north from Punta Barima on the Boca Grande the coast is studded with islands and the water is generally shallow for several miles offshore—most of the way the ten-fathom line is twenty-five miles out to sea. In general, it should be a fairly safe shore where no rocks, shoals, or dangerous currents would be encountered. In the event of storms canoes could seek the safety of the many small rivers or the lee shore of the numerous islands.

It is less than 150 miles from Saladero to the Boca Grande and less than two hundred miles from there to Cedros (Map 3) on Trinidad. If the Arawaks had made only "overnight" camping stops, the whole trip from Saladero to Trinidad could perhaps have been accomplished in a month. If, instead, they had taken even a hundred years for the journey, they would have had ample time to experiment with temporary living on such pieces of land as appeared attractive to them for the growing of manioc or as campsites.

As they approached the Serpent's Mouth they would have been aware of the increasing roughness of the water. The Atlantic Ocean currents become turbulent in the funnel-shaped wedge formed by the coast of Venezuela running northwest and the southern coast of Trinidad, which is almost due east and west. At Erin (Maps 11, 12) on Trinidad, where the Serpent's Mouth is only eleven miles wide, the coast of the new land would have been readily visible to the paddlers even if they had hugged the Venezuelan shore. Many landing places, such as that near the Cedros site, could have been spotted easily.

The Arawak site of Cedros has been known for some time. Rouse dug it in 1946 and the pottery was sufficiently different from any style with which he was acquainted to warrant his naming it the Cedros style. He described it as thin, hard, and decorated with white-on-red painted designs (Figure 91b). He had, of course, no idea at that time that these would be the diagnostic features of the Saladero-style pottery he would discover four years later (1950) at the apex of the Orinoco delta, features which were to become the basis of the now-famous Saladoid pottery—the hallmark of the early Arawaks. From that time on it would be by systematic digging for evidence of Saladoid pottery that the migration route of the Arawaks would be traced. I feel justified in asserting that we know the Arawaks reached Cedros *because* of the Saladoid white-on-red sherds found there. Moreover, Cedros has the added importance of being a likely spot for the first arrival on Trinidad of such Arawaks as might have traveled downstream from Saladero after their displacement by the Barrancoid invaders.

More and more I have come to realize that it is crucially important that Cedros be redug. Charcoal samples must be obtained from the lowest layers containing Saladoid sherds, to establish positively the time of arrival of the Arawaks in Trinidad.

There is a second site, known as Palo Seco (Maps 11, 12), some twenty miles or so to the east of Cedros, that also begs attention. As far back as 1919, long before the present system of classification was worked out by Rouse, the late Professor Bullbrook had dug at Palo Seco and obtained the major part of his Arawak sherd collection. I have seen specimens of Bulbrook's Palo Seco material on several visits to the Royal Victoria Museum at Port of Spain, Trinidad, of which he was the director. It varies sufficiently from Cedros pottery to be classed by Professor Rouse as a different style or "tradition"—the Palo Seco style—but belonging to the same general Saladoid series.

Since the bulk of the Bullbrook collection had been sent years ago to London, Professor Rouse and I, in the spring of 1965, decided to examine all the Trinidad sherds in the British Museum. While Rouse sorted the sherds according to the taxonomic system which he had developed, I photographed them for record.

Rouse also had dug in Palo Seco, in 1946, the same year he excavated the Cedros site but twenty-seven years after Professor Bullbrook had discovered Palo Seco. Rouse noticed sherds in the lowest layers of Palo Seco that were identical with the Cedros style, but many of the sherds in the next higher layers were what had been designated as the Palo Seco style. Hence the Palo Seco style was later than, and possibly a development of, the Cedros style. From this 1965 examination of the Bullbrook material in the British Museum, Professor Rouse confirmed his earlier conclusion that both Cedros and Palo Seco styles belong to the Saladoid series.

Since the 1965 visit to the British Museum, I have given much study to our photographs of the Bullbrook Palo Seco sherds and of the Cedros material obtained by Rouse. I have long had a growing uneasiness about the conclusion generally offered, that the Palo Seco represents a style produced by Saladoid potters who had "deteriorated" from the time they made the Cedros material. What bothers me most is that large numbers of the Palo Seco style sherds were *not* thin and hard like the Cedros style material Rouse had found throughout his excavation at Cedros and in the lowest layers of Palo Seco. Instead, they were coarse, soft, and twice as thick. The W-O-R painting, characteristic of Cedros, is present, but, as Rouse says, "scarce and apparently on its way out of existence." Several of the Palo Seco style rim-sherds have broad flanges, decorated by red paint or curved line incision. Lugs or handles in the form of animal heads occur which are much more varied and complicated than the simple nubbin handles found in Cedros pottery.

To my eye, the Bullbrook Palo Seco style yielded so many sherds showing Barrancoid influence that it suggested a major intrusion of Barrancoid potters rather than just a diffusion of Barrancoid traits through the acquisition of trade pieces by local Saladoids. It seemed to me the condition at Palo Seco rather strongly resembled that at Saladero when the Barrancoid potters moved in on the original Saladoids about 900 B.C. A next logical step was to assume that history was repeating itself and the Barrancoids, after living almost a thousand years on the Orinoco, advanced once more into Saladoid territory at Palo Seco. Obviously the point is crucial and I could not let it pass.

To satisfy myself I felt it was necessary to make a much clearer analysis of the available data. I hoped to define more precisely just what constituted the difference between Saladoid and Barrancoid pottery and how to determine the degree to which a sample of sherds exhibited changes due to influences exerted by the Barrancoids. If the influence should be found to be great, it would be reasonable to assume an actual invasion by Barrancoid people. If it was slight, then the change could plausibly be attributed to "trait diffusion" by traders. For this we would need clear-cut criteria for each style. It would be necessary to closely scrutinize the only data we had, namely the artifacts, almost exclusively potsherds, which the Arawaks had left from place to place as they journeyed through Trinidad into the Antilles. To help in the more detailed analysis of Saladoid and Barrancoid pottery styles I know of no better yardsticks to apply than the crucial distinctions laid down by Professor Rouse when he made the original classification of these two styles of pottery found in his excavations at Saladero in 1950.

I have studied all the data on Saladoid and Barrancoid pottery given in the various technical reports by Professor Rouse, and in the two books written on Venezuelan archeology by Rouse and his associate Professor J. M. Cruxent. I have attempted to organize this material so that the precise differences between the Saladoid and Barrancoid seem reasonably clear to me. I am placing my analysis in Table 1[7] hopeful that any future visitor to Arawak sites will thus be able to differentiate between Saladoid and Barrancoid potsherds and to assess the degree of Barrancoid influence existing in any pottery considered to be basically Saladoid.

Next I studied the pottery from twelve locations along the migration path of the Arawaks, from Saladero through Trinidad and the Lesser Antilles to Puerto Rico, in terms of the most significant characteristics. A second tabulation has therefore been made by which the degree of Barrancoid influence can be detected at each successive site. Thus Table 2 is also to be found in note 7 of this chapter.

It seems obvious that potsherds should be called Saladoid if they exhibit a preponderance of characteristics which occur in the Saladoid column of Table 1. This is generally quite simple to decide, but difficulties arise when sherds are found bearing features that are both Saladoid and Barrancoid. For example, I have noted the tendency of several workers, when sorting potsherds, to regard the pottery as being Saladoid merely if it contains white paint on top of red. They do this even though the sherds are thick and soft and the white areas have been painted directly and somewhat crudely on the red base. Decoration of this kind is in marked contrast with the sharply defined areas so adeptly painted by the early Saladoid artists using their meticulous technique of removing areas of the white slip to reveal the red surface below.

From these two tabulations it seems fair to draw the following conclusions about the pottery from the various early Arawak sites.

Cedros

The pottery from the Cedros site in Trinidad is almost pure Saladoid, as shown in Table 2 and as judged by the W-O-R decoration shown in Figure 94a and by the nubbins (Figure 94b), both typical of the Saladero style. It is probably several hundred years later than the pottery from the Arawak homesite at Saladero, so it is natural to expect some changes that sprang directly out of native inventiveness. The main difference between the Cedros and Saladero styles is the presence of the "zoned-incised-cross-hatched" (Z-I-C) decoration on several of the Cedros sherds (Figure 94c). This Z-I-C designation means exactly what it says—the design on the sherds has *zones* (Z) clearly surrounded by a grooved line; the area in these zones is covered with fine *incised* (I) lines of *cross-hatching* (C). No Z-I-C sherds have been found at Saladero or at any associated sites on the Orinoco.

I consider the Z-I-C design a logical innovation for a Saladoid potter to make, since she could have used the same sharp-pointed tool for marking the fine cross-hatched lines of the Z-I-C design as for scratching off the white areas to reveal the red coating below in the W-O-R designs. Moreover, the Z-I-C designs would have the advantage that it is not necessary to apply either the burnished red undersurface or the white marl overcoating. This might have seemed a desirable simplification of the process, especially in places where marl was absent.

For all we know, the Z-I-C technique may have been an invention of Saladoid potters at Cedros, but to me it seems more likely that it was a trait that diffused eastward, possibly from a source as remote as Ecuador or Colombia, where, as I shall show later, very early examples of Z-I-C sherds have been found. If so, the trait definitely skipped Saladero on its diffusion route—a matter discussed in Chapter XIV.

Unfortunately, no carbon-14 datings had been obtained for Cedros because Professor Rouse dug the site before this dating technique was developed. Yet it would appear that Cedros is an earlier site than El Mayal on the Peninsula of Paria (Map 3, and also Table 2), for which we do have carbon-14 dates of A.D. 100 and A.D. 300, because Cedros has none of the modeled heads such as occur on the handles of El Mayal pottery. In a personal communication Professor Rouse comments, "I wouldn't be surprised if, when we do

Fig. 94. Saladoid sherds, Cedros style. a (top): *W-O-R (red indicated by fine vertical lines).* b (middle): *Nubbins.* c (bottom): *Z-I-C (Cedros, Trinidad).*

obtain radiocarbon analyses for the Cedros style of pottery, it turns out to be somewhere in the first millenium B.C."

PALO SECO

The next Trinidad site in Table 2 is Palo Seco. The pottery from this site is considered to belong to the Saladoid series, but it differs from the Cedros style and from the original Saladero styles by changes which suggest Barrancoid influence.

First of all the sherds are thicker and softer. Rouse says the sherds are so soft that they "sometimes disintegrate upon excavation, like mud." Thus they do not have the characteristic Saladoid feature of being hard enough to give a metallic ring when struck. "There is some polychrome white-on-red painting in the Palo Seco style, but it is on its way out of existence," says Professor Rouse (see Figure 95a). Nubbin handles do occur, but are giving way to heads

239

Fig. 95. Saladoid sherds, Palo Seco style. a: W-O-R sherds. b: Nubbin-type head. c: Incised and with nubbin. (Palo Seco, Trinidad).

(Figure 95b, c), and also there are flanged rims, both of which features are generally considered to be typically Barrancoid. In spite of these Barrancoid traits the pottery is still classified as basically Saladoid. Unfortunately, as of July, 1969, no carbon-14 datings have been determined for the Palo Seco style.

At Erin, a site on the southern coast of Trinidad (Map 11), a few miles west of Palo Seco, the pottery is definitely Barrancoid (Table 2).

At El Mayal and Irapa, both on the Paria Peninsula, the pottery is Saladoid, since white-on-red painted sherds are found and also the Z-I-C style of incision is present (Table 2). Early El Mayal (Figure 96) resembles Cedros very closely, but Irapa (Figure 97) is later than El Mayal and shows more Barrancoid influence in the modeling of the heads used as pot handles.

SITES IN THE ANTILLES

There is very little difference between the earliest pottery of Grenada, Guadeloupe, Antigua, St. Croix, and Puerto Rico. It is all Saladoid, judged by the tell-tale W-O-R decoration on thin,

240

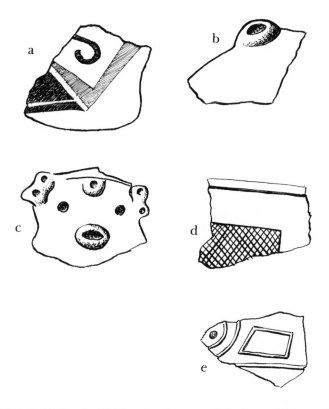

Fig. 96. Saladoid sherds, El Mayal style. a: *W-O-R.* b: *Nubbin.* c: *Handle made of nubbins, an incipient adorno.* d: *Z-I-C.* e: *Incised.*

hard sherds (Figure 91d, e, f) and sufficiently resembles the El Mayal style (Figure 96) to suggest that migration through the Antilles may well have begun from El Mayal. This migration feature is supported by the fact that the Z-I-C design and also nubbin handles occur abundantly at the Grenada, Guadeloupe, and Antigua sites.

At this point we are perhaps ready to speculate about the roles played by the two component families of the Arawaks, the Saladoids and the Barrancoids, in the occupation of Trinidad and their migration into the Antilles. Clearly, the character of the pottery at the three sites—Cedros, Palo Seco, and Erin—located in a twenty- to thirty-mile stretch of coast in the southwest part of Trinidad, could be explained in either of two ways. The first possibility is

241

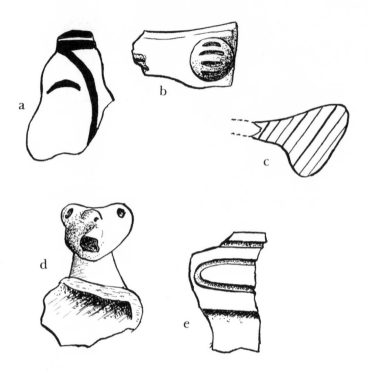

Fig. 97. Saladoid sherds, Irapa style. a: *W-O-R.* b: *Nubbins.* c: *Flanged rim.* d: *Adorno.* e: *Incised.*

that the Saladoids, after their expulsion from Saladero by the encroaching Barrancoids, migrated down the Orinoco and settled in Cedros and then advanced eastward along the southern coast of Trinidad to Palo Seco.

In the course of time traders arrived bearing Barrancoid pottery and the Saladoid potters were influenced to modify their techniques. Perhaps they liked the sculptural adornos on the Barrancoid vessels. Presumably this advent of the traders occurred *after* the Saladoids had left Cedros, since there is no evidence of any Barrancoid influences in Cedros pottery. I would guess that it happened shortly after the Saladoids settled in Palo Seco because Professor Rouse found pure Cedros-style sherds at the lowest layer at Palo Seco when he dug the site in 1946. I recalled, too, that when we were at the British Museum studying the Bullbrook collection of Palo Seco sherds excavated in 1920, Rouse had pointed out to me that the lowest layer at Palo Seco bore Cedros-style sherds showing no trace of Barrancoid influence. However, in the layers above the pottery was gradually "contaminated" with material showing Barrancoid influences, resulting in thicker, softer pottery with prominent modeling and a reduction in the W-O-R painting. Furthermore, the rims become flanged, which is a pronounced Barrancoid trait.

A second possibility is that traders bearing Barrancoid pottery actually settled at Palo Seco, perhaps displacing some of the Saladoids, who moved farther east along the coast. Although we have no carbon-14 dates for Cedros, Palo Seco, or Erin (as of July, 1969), the changes in these three styles are progressively more Barrancoid and therefore would suggest a time sequence in that order. As Professor Rouse states, "The Barrancoid pressure was a steady one and more and more Barrancoid traits were absorbed." His use of the word "pressure" is compatible with a greater aggressiveness on the part of the Barrancoids. But whether the pressure was in the form of more frequent trading or involved actual settling at Palo Seco and Erin, with the subsequent ousting of the Saladoids, has not yet been determined.

If the Barrancoids actually drove out the Saladoid men it is possible that they retained some of the Saladoid women, who would have contributed to the continuance of some features of Saladoid pottery, even though it was constantly changed to include more Barrancoid characteristics as required by their new masters. Either of the two explanations seems plausible and both should be studied in light of the data revealed by other sites.

It seems reasonable that either population pressure or the prodding by the Barrancoids resulted in the continued movement of the Arawaks along the southern and eastern coasts of Trinidad and later northward along the west coast.

Some thirty pottery sites have so far been located in Trinidad (Map 11), indicative of a protracted occupation of the island. But for none of them are there any carbon-14 dates (as of July, 1969). Less than half of these sites contain Cedros-style pottery (Figure 94), so it seems fair to discount the idea of a large population expansion of the Saladoids. Many of the sites contain solely Barrancoid-type pottery, which to my mind strongly supports the idea of increased migration of Barrancoids from the Orinoco.

The displaced Saladoids may have taken a water route from Cedros or Palo Seco across the Gulf of Paria. As we sailed the relatively calm waters of the Gulf of Paria in the S. S. *Poseidon* (Chapter V) I became impressed that this large body of sheltered water might easily have been the place where the maritime skills of the Arawaks were developed during the hundreds of years they presumably lived in Trinidad or on the Venezuelan side of the Gulf of Paria prior to their adventure into the Antilles.

The presence of Saladoid pottery on each island of the Lesser Antilles and on Puerto Rico, more closely related to the El Mayal style than to any other, favors the initial occupancy of the Antilles by Saladoids from the northern shore of the Peninsula of Paria. Professor Rouse has suggested that the first Saladoids might have been blown by storm to Grenada or possibly to Guadeloupe while fishing off Margarita Island. I like this suggestion. I feel that the men who had survived the first trip in storm-driven canoes would presumably have had the homing instinct to retrace their passage to Venezuela and persuade their wives and neighbors of the desirability of the newly discovered islands.

Professor Rouse has often mentioned to me that the Z-I-C sherds serve as a kind of "time-marker," roughly indicating a period of A.D. 100 to 300. I have personally found Z-I-C sherds on Grenada,[8] Guadeloupe, and Antigua, and am inclined to the view that the Arawaks settled in all these islands rather rapidly.

The Saladoid-type of pottery continued in the Lesser Antilles and in Puerto Rico for two or three hundred years, but by about A.D. 400–500 the pottery was markedly thicker and softer; the white-on-red negative painting disappeared; flanged rims and annular bases occurred; more elaborately incised decoration developed; and even more pronounced were the realistically modeled heads of humans, birds, reptiles, and fish decorating the handles of their vessels. All of these are strong Barrancoid trends superimposed upon the basic Saladoid pottery.

Whether these changes are due to "trait diffusion" of Barrancoid pottery by traders or to an increasing flow of Barrancoid migrants remains for further archeological research to discover. Almost certainly this will involve a meticulous excavation of potsherds, their precise stratigraphic classification by means of the yardsticks for Saladoid and Barrancoid features as shown in Tables 1 and 2 (Note 7, Chapter XII), and perhaps of equal or even greater importance the carbon-14 testing of charcoal directly associated with the potsherds.

XIII

When Did the Arawaks Arrive in Trinidad?

IN seeking an answer to the question posed in this chapter, it is clear that carbon-14 dates for the Cedros and Palo Seco sites are crucial. Furthermore, the dates are also essential for establishing whether the inhabitants of the El Mayal and Irapa Arawak sites on the Peninsula of Paria (Map 3) were the recipients or the suppliers of Saladoid pottery techniques from Trinidad.

At a meeting with Professor Rouse I made the comment that I was willing to redig the sites at Cedros and Palo Seco for charcoal if only I knew their location. He promptly offered to join me, and when Professor Cruxent, who at that moment was visiting Yale, heard of this he also volunteered to be one of the party.

Arrangements were quickly made and the three of us, after a morning of preparation in Port of Spain, proceeded to Cedros and Palo Seco at the southwest corner of Trinidad in July, 1969.

THE CEDROS SITE

Professor Rouse had no trouble locating the Cedros site (Map 13), although it was in the thick of a large coconut plantation. His field notes were obviously good and his memory keen, even though it had been twenty-six years since he first dug the site. After a couple of exploratory test pits we staked out a two-meter square only a few feet away from Rouse's original excavation. Immediately we were in a large mass of empty chip-chip shells (*Donax striata*, a small clamlike bivalve and a favorite Arawak food). Sherds appeared with the first shovelfull on the screen. They were clearly Saladoid—thin and hard, with a metallic ring when struck, several with the char-

245

Fig. 98. Cedros-style sherds showing Z-I-C variations at different levels. a, b, c: top layer, 0–25 cm. d, e, f: intermediate layer, 25–50 cm. g, h, i: bottom layer, 50–75 cm. (Cedros, Trinidad).

acteristic white-on-red decoration. Since our main objective was to obtain charcoal, particularly from the earliest level, the gathering of potsherds was really only incidental, although we were delighted when any choice specimens came to light displaying the definitive white-on-red (W-O-R) or zoned-incised-cross-hatched (Z-I-C) decoration. Actually we encountered W-O-R sherds at every level (Figures 91b and 94a), and also a liberal supply of Z-I-C sherds (Figure 94c). Characteristic Saladoid nubbin pot-handles gave further evidence that these potters were Saladoid Arawaks (Figure 94b).

Figure 91a-f will show how the Cedros style of Saladoid W-O-R sherds fits into the series of Arawak pottery styles, stretching from Saladero on the Orinoco to Puerto Rico and covering a span of over a thousand years.

We found no pockets or chunks of charcoal, as is frequently the case when we came across ancient cooking hearths in Antigua middens. Instead, the charcoal was in granules about the size of a grain of wheat or smaller. It was necessary to go through each spadeful of earth, separating it a handful at a time while Rouse, Cruxent, and I collected any piece of charcoal bigger than the head of a pin from the damp and sometimes wet soil. It was tedious and messy work. It took us two days digging with four helpers to reach sterile ground at a depth of 70 centimeters.

It seemed to me, in comparing the sherds from the various layers at Cedros, that there were hints of a development in the complexity of the Z-I-C design, being simpler in the lowest levels and somewhat more intricate in the upper levels (Figure 98). This suggested that the Saladoids had arrived at Cedros during the early stages of the Z-I-C design, and perhaps had developed the more complex Z-I-C features right on the spot. I realized, however, that there might be too small a sampling of Z-I-C sherds to warrant such an assumption. Everything depended on what carbon-14 tests would show. We obtained what appeared to be two satisfactory samples of charcoal—one in the lowest layer and the other in the middle layer. We did not take charcoal from the surface layer since this would almost certainly have been contaminated by recent cultivation of the coconut plantation.

The Palo Seco Site

We also dug the site at Palo Seco (Map 12), which Professor Bullbrook had first excavated in 1919 and again with Rouse in 1943. Ben was again successful in pin-pointing his previous digging of twenty-six years earlier, and this time it took us three days to reach sterile ground because we had to go to a depth of 125 cm. Again we obtained charcoal samples from each 25-cm layer below the top one and by the same tedious process. Also we established a sequence of ceramic styles similar to what Rouse had found previously.

The bottom layer (100–125 cm) fortunately contained a cassava griddle sherd (Figure 99a) thereby proving that the Arawaks had grown manioc in Trinidad during their earliest occupation of Palo Seco. Most of the pottery from this lowest level was unquestionably early Saladoid—thin, hard, and with W-O-R decoration (Figure 99b, c, d) and typical Saladoid nubbins (Figure 99e, f, g), and even

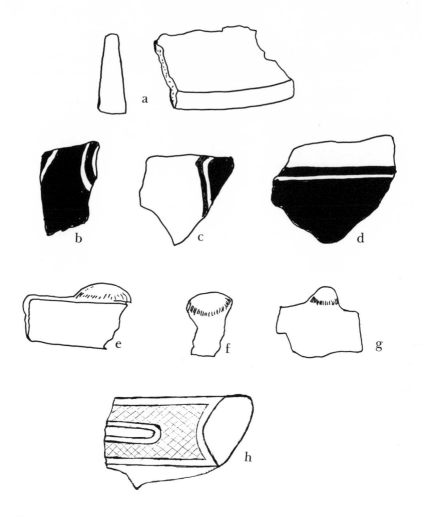

Fig. 99. Cedros-type sherds in lowest layer at Palo Seco. a: Griddle sherd. b, c, d: W-O-R sherds. e, f, g: Nubbin handles. h: Z-I-C.

some Z-I-C sherds (Figure 99h). These features are clearly compatible with occupation by the same kind of Arawaks that had been living at Cedros, and we concluded that the bottom layer at Palo Seco contained Cedros-style pottery.

A difference was discernible in the next-to-bottom layer (75–100 cm). Most of the sherds were still readily classifiable as Saladoid since the W-O-R design was present (Figure 100a) and also the two nubbin sherds (Figure 100b, c). But it was evident that the Cedros-

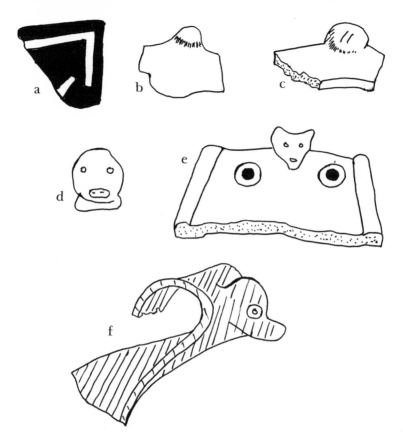

Fig. 100. Palo Seco sherds in intermediate layer. a: *W-O-R.* b, c: *Nubbin handles.* d, e, f: *Zoomorphic handles.*

type sherds were giving way to the style that had been named "Palo Seco" when previously dug by Bullbrook and Rouse many years earlier. These sherds were moderately thick and soft, and the nubbins showed more modeling, sometimes with distinctly zoomorphic heads. Heavy flanges of triangular cross-section had been added to the rim. Rouse says of these modifications, "These Saladoid sherds indicate Barrancoid influence, probably a good example of trait diffusion, not necessarily indicating any actual migration of Barrancoid potters."

I am intrigued by this idea of Barrancoid men, who came presumably as traders bringing their pottery to the Palo Seco Saladoids. This hints that trading was perhaps common at these early times.

This change to the Palo Seco style can probably be illustrated most clearly by referring to the "evolution" of the nubbin style of decoration. We have seen that at Saladero, at Cedros, and even in the earliest levels at Palo Seco the nubbin was a simple tab on the rim (Figures 99e, f, g and 100b), serving no doubt as a primitive handle for picking up the vessel. The simplest kind of change is shown by the sherd in Figure 100c, where the nubbin is decorated with nothing more than a couple of small indentations, perhaps made by slight jabs with a pointed stick while the clay was sufficiently plastic. Both of these Palo Seco nubbins (Figure 100b, c) are similar in form to those of the Cedros style, but the sherds are thicker, softer, and lack the metallic ring of true Cedros pottery. A later change in the nubbin is illustrated by the Palo Seco-style sherd (Figure 100d) where the form suggests a head, but of no discernible animal. The blob of clay had been subjected merely to two jabs to provide eyes and a dragged jab to give a mouth and can be considered as a modified nubbin.

Next in the line of development comes the sherd shown in Figure 100e which is quite elaborate, comprising two heavy side ridges, two ringed perforations, and a modeled head of an animal, even though it is not identifiable.

Still later in this series of handles is the Palo Seco-style sherd (Figure 100f). Here the loop handle of the vessel has been ornamented with a still more sculptural treatment until the "head" takes on an added touch of realism, proclaiming the animal to be a duck. However, all three of these sherds (Figure 100d, e, f) are characteristically Palo Seco style, even though the duck head is well on its way to the totally sculptural adornos so typically Barrancoid, as shown in the Erin style heads found in the top layer of the Palo Seco site (Figure 101a, b). These Erin-style adornos display an animal head (Figure 101a); a human head (Figure 101b) and a highly stylized handle of the complete vessel found as a grave furnishing for a burial whose skeleton we were lucky enough to excavate at Palo Seco (Figure 101c). My feeling is that the Erin style is so strong in the upper layers at Palo Seco that I would guess these sculptural achievements were the work of actual Barrancoid potters in residence at the Palo Seco site rather than due to more extensive trading. Professor Rouse, however, points out: "Alternatively, these could be objects made at Barrancas and brought into Palo Seco by the traders mentioned above. This would be my interpretation."

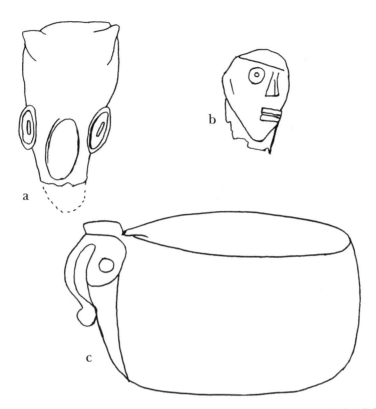

Fig. 101. Erin-style sherds in top layer at Palo Seco. a: *Animal head adorno.* b: *Human head adorno.* c: *Complete pot found as grave furnishing.*

Great as was this concern with sculptural effects, as revealed by these advanced examples of modeled handles found at Palo Seco, the Barrancoid art did not reach its highest development in Trinidad. Indeed, it was several hundred years later, about A.D. 800, in their homesite at the village of Los Barrancos, half a mile or so downstream from Saladero, that the finest examples of Barrancoid sculptural attainment were found. An elegant and highly imaginative head of an animal is shown in Figure 102a, while Figure 102b illustrates well-advanced realism—a parrotlike adorno.

When the sherds we had just obtained at the Cedros and Palo Seco sites were compared with those found many years earlier at the same places, Professor Rouse commented that we had found a wider variety of Z-I-C sherds than he had secured at Cedros. He also

Fig. 102. Barrancoid adornos from Los Barrancos. a: *Imaginative animal head, one of finest examples of Arawak sculpture.* b: *Realistic parrot with "baroque" modeling.*

felt that the Erin-style sherds in the upper layers at Palo Seco were even more strongly Barrancoid than was indicated by his former excavation.

It is noteworthy that the "traders" who brought the Barrancoid traits to the Palo Seco site evidently had failed to make contact with the Saladoid Arawaks at Cedros, only about thirty miles to the west, because at no time during the several hundred years that the Saladoid Arawaks presumably occupied Cedros did their pottery show any of the Barrancoid traits found in the Palo Seco style.

Since Professor Cruxent's laboratory at Caracas was well equipped to make carbon-14 tests I was delighted that he personally supervised the collection of the charcoal samples at each site. At the end of November, 1969, the results arrived. Altogether we have six carbon-14 values, the earliest dating for Cedros being 190 B.C. and for Palo Seco 180 B.C. The latest date for Cedros is A.D. 100 and for Palo Seco A.D. 470. These seem quite reasonable values and suggest that what we had always suspected was now established: that after leaving the Orinoco the Saladoid Arawaks had spent several hundred years in the bountiful island of Trinidad before embarking on their migration to the Antilles.

As I interpret these data:

(1) The Saladoid Arawaks were at Cedros in southwestern Trinidad as early as 190 B.C. and remained there for almost three hundred years before they reached El Mayal on the northern shore of the Peninsula of Paria in A.D. 100. This is compatible with the idea of an Arawak migration from Saladero by the water route down the Orinoco to the Boca Grande and northward along the eastern coast of Venezuela to the Serpent's Mouth, with a landing at Cedros about 190 B.C. (Route 3, Map 3). In my estimation this tends to invalidate the overland route 2B and 2C straight north from Saladero to the Peninsula of Paria shown on the same map.

(2) We can only conjecture why the Saladoids left Cedros about A.D. 100. I think the best hint comes from what happened at nearby Palo Seco.

In the lowest layer at Palo Seco (100–125 cm) only Cedros-style sherds were found (Figure 99). In the next higher layer (75–100 cm) were the Palo Seco-style sherds (Figure 100) in which the Saladoid pottery had been gradually subjected to the influence of traits of Barrancoid pottery, probably as the result of "trait-unit diffusion." The evidence for this Barrancoid influence is most clearly shown by the coarser, softer paste and the greater concern over modeling. "The Palo Seco style was being generated," as Rouse suggests—an example of trait diffusion, probably by the advent of Barrancoid traders.

Since there is no trace of any Barrancoid influence at Cedros it is my feeling that the Cedros inhabitants chose to leave their location when they became aware of the coming of the Barrancoid traders at Palo Seco. They may have remembered their ancestors' tales of their displacement from Saladero by the Barrancoids. The Cedros Saladoids probably made their way northward around the eastern shore of the Gulf of Paria, through the Dragon's Mouth and westward along the coast of the Peninsula of Paria to El Mayal (route marked +++++ on Map 3). It is perhaps not without significance that the earliest date for El Mayal is A.D. 100, precisely the date of the ending of occupation at Cedros. Moreover, the pottery is the same at Cedros and El Mayal at the same dating (Figure 94 and 96).

(3) Irapa pottery was later than El Mayal, both stylistically and by carbon-14 dating, namely A.D. 200 (Figure 97). It is my suggestion that this was the result of a somewhat later exodus of Saladoids, this time perhaps from Palo Seco, since the Irapa sherds more closely resemble the later Palo Seco style (Figure 100) rather than the Cedros style (Figure 94). The Palo Seco inhabitants may have gone directly across the Gulf of Paria landing at Irapa, which is near Yaguaraparo (route marked ΔΔΔΔΔ on Map 3).[1]

(4) It would thus appear that the displacement of Saladoids from Saladero early in the first millennium B.C. by the Barrancoids was perhaps repeated roughly about a thousand years later in southwestern Trinidad.[2]

I am, of course, aware of two major points that these perhaps oversimplified hypotheses fail to explain. First is the time gap which still exists. Prior to our recent findings we were puzzled by a gap of a thousand years between the exodus from Saladero, about 900 B.C., and the arrival at El Mayal or the Antilles, about A.D. 100. We have now reduced this gap to seven hundred years because of the carbon-14 dating of 190 B.C. for Cedros. We still have no evidence of where the Arawak Saladoids were or what they were doing during this stretch of seven hundred years. At the moment I see two possible avenues of investigation: we must look more closely for additional Saladoid sites having earlier dates than 190 B.C.; or we must consider the possibility that the arrival of the Saladoids at Cedros may be shown to be earlier than 190 B.C.

With respect to the first possibility, any further knowledge must await the results of investigations that future archeologists will make for sites earlier than Cedros in Trinidad, or perhaps along the delta land between Saladero and Trinidad. At the moment I know of no such projected studies.

I am a bit more hopeful about the possibility of earlier dates for Cedros. My reason is that the carbon-14 dates for Cedros were actually 190 B.C. for the *intermediate* 25 to 50 cm layer, and A.D. 100 for the *lower* 50 to 75 cm layer—the reverse of what we would expect. I personally saw Professor Cruxent collecting the charcoal samples and am satisfied he was meticulously careful about the packaging and labeling. Hence, unless the samples were switched in the carbon-14 laboratory, I think we must accept these dates for the two layers as correct, despite the seeming contradiction.

I can think of one possible rational explanation. It has been mentioned that the Cedros site was in a dense coconut grove (Map 13), where the trees were generally spaced at fairly uniform intervals. Obviously we did not dig in a place where we would damage the roots of the trees. We selected a site in the most open spot, as judged by a noticeable gap in the canopy of palm fronds. This was most likely a place where a young coconut tree had failed to root during the original planting of the grove, but where a hole had been dug to accommodate one. My assumption is that the digging and refilling of the hole during the planting had mixed some of the original layers of the soil. The net result would be that the oldest charcoal would be contaminated with younger material so that the carbon-14 dating of 190 B.C. would be more recent than that of charcoal from the original lowest layer.

We must thus await another redigging of Cedros, forewarned of the possibility that layers could be mixed during the planting operation. A site should be selected between two coconut palm trees that clearly involves no break in the canopy where an original seedling had failed to develop. I would not be surprised if the earliest dating for Cedros is eventually pushed back, perhaps to 400–500 B.C.

The second feature still unexplained is the origin of the Z-I-C sherds, since their presence at Cedros and their absence at Saladero implies either that the design was invented by the Saladoids between the time they left Saladero and their arrival at Cedros, or that the intrusion of the Z-I-C trait by diffusion from somewhere unknown occurred during that same interval. The possibility of Z-I-C trait diffusion will be examined in the next chapter.

Some observations made as we finished our work at Cedros are, I think, pertinent here. Professor Cruxent had completed his measurements for the preparation of the map of the site (Map 13) and I was paying off the four workers as they filled in the holes and tidied up. I badly needed a swim because the heat had been intense and I was thick with dust from the screening. But, sentimentally, I wanted to step into the water the Arawaks had frequented two thousand years ago and get more intimately the feel of the location. Perhaps I would be able to discover some reason why Cedros had been the first occupation site in Trinidad.

The Cedros site was only a quarter of a mile from the sea, which could be glimpsed through gaps in the forest of coconut palms. As we approached the shore I noticed it was littered with a great pile of driftwood, including many heavy logs. The beach was also strewn with a quantity of spherical objects looking like a mass of golf and tennis balls. Closer examination revealed that they were nuts of the moriche palm, which grows plentifully in the Orinoco delta lowlands but which I had seen only occasionally in southwest Trinidad. We could easily recognize the low coast of Venezuela, perhaps seven to ten miles away, and the rollers were pounding into the Cedros shore quite heavily. The water was definitely muddy from the Orinoco current and it felt about 83° or even a bit warmer. Nevertheless, I was glad to dive into the breakers. It was obvious immediately that a very strong current was running westward toward Icacos Point—the current into the Serpent's Mouth. I recalled that Columbus had mentioned the turbulent water of this entrance to the Gulf of Paria.

It is a primary precaution in strange waters to first swim against the current, and I found I was being driven backward even when using all my strength in trying to move eastward along the shore. I turned toward the shore until I could touch bottom, but was unable to walk against the current when more than waist deep in water.

It seemed evident that the driftwood and the moriche nuts had been carried from the delta lands of Venezuela to the southwest coast of Trinidad, and I pictured that any Arawak dugout starting from the delta would, willy-nilly, be carried by the strong current to land upon the Trinidad shore. There are many suitable landing spots along the western end of the south shore, so it was not difficult to understand the Arawak settlement at the three ancient sites of Cedros, Erin, and Palo Seco.

I remembered also the stories of men who had escaped by boat or raft from the penal colony of French Guiana some seven hundred miles to the southeast. They had hoped to reach friendly Venezuela, but almost inevitably the Orinoco current swept them onto Trinidad, where they were returned by the British government to the French authorities.

In short, rather than a planned trek, it would seem possible that the Arawak "migration" to Trinidad may have been promoted by such natural forces as strong ocean currents and later to the Antilles even by hurricane winds quite beyond the control of the sturdy paddlers. But it is conceivable that the Arawaks may have preferred, and so deliberately chosen, the somewhat higher land of the Trinidad southern coastline to the lowlying shore of the Venezuelan delta. Either hypothesis is tenable.

256

XIV

Origins – Peru, Ecuador, or Colombia?

MUCH of the difficulty in tracing the migration of the Arawaks springs from the fact that there were two distinct groups of Arawak people: the Saladoids, who were displaced from Saladero about 900 B.C., and the Barrancoids, who did the displacing. I am designating these two groups of people as Arawaks because their affairs were closely interwoven for about two thousand years. Also, I am regarding as Arawak territory all lands occupied by either the Saladoids or the Barrancoids.[1]

Nothing is known positively about the origin of the Arawaks prior to their occupation of Saladero about 1000 B.C. I now propose to seek out clues which may provide a reasonable basis for speculation as to the earlier homelands of both the Saladoid and the Barrancoid components of the Arawaks.

Since it was the Saladoids who developed the islands of the Antilles into the home of the Arawak "nation," perhaps a couple of million people at the time of Columbus, it follows that the Saladoids are of prime importance in any consideration of Arawak origins. The Barrancoids for their part were responsible for the hegira of the Saladoids from their Orinoco homeland and presumably influenced the Saladoids during their stay in Trinidad and in the Lesser Antilles prior to the coming of the Caribs. Consequently, it is necessary to examine the backgrounds of each of these groups.

The case for the Barrancoids appears fairly simple. Evidence offered by Professor Reichel-Dolmatoff[2] suggests that the Puerto Hormiga pottery in Colombia (Map 14) was the prototype for the Barrancoid ceramic techniques and decoration style. He made the following statement about the sherds he had found at Puerto Hormiga: "As the radiocarbon dates obtained from organic material associated with the sherds place this complex at the very beginning of the third millennium B.C., this would be the earliest pottery anywhere in the New World, a fact which is of considerable importance." He also says: "We know nothing at present about the origin of Puerto Hormiga pottery . . . . The Barrancas phase of the lower Orinoco River in Venezuela, beginning about 900 B.C., probably derives its characteristic biomorphic and incised ceramic decoration from the Colombia pottery tradition originating at Puerto Hormiga."

In his book *Colombia*, Professor Reichel-Dolmatoff illustrates two adornos from Puerto Hormiga (Figure 103a, c) which are similar to the animallike heads occurring on pot handles fabricated by Barrancoid potters at the apex of the Orinoco delta (Figure 103b, d). The Barrancoid heads, however, were made about two thousand years later than those found at Puerto Hormiga. It is on this resemblance that he postulates either the migration of the Puerto Hormiga potters from Colombia to the Orinoco or the diffusion of their pottery. This seems plausible since not only would there have been ample time—two thousand years—for the transfer to have taken place, but the route seems quite feasible. The bearers of the pottery could have gone upstream along the Magdalena River from Puerto Hormiga toward Bogotá, then cut across the plateau to the Rio Meta or the Rio Apure, tributaries of the Orinoco—a relatively easy journey (Map 5).

It was not only the highly developed adornos that indicated the similarity between Puerto Hormiga and Barrancoid pottery; both had thick walls of lightly baked clay which gave no metallic ring when struck. In all these features the Barrancoid and the Puerto Hormiga wares were not only similar to each other but differed markedly from Saladoid pottery.

It is about fifteen hundred miles from Puerto Hormiga to Saladero by land and river, and the migrant Amerind bearers of the pottery could have reached Saladero by 1000 B.C. by averaging less than one mile per year if they had left Puerto Hormiga some time shortly after 3000 B.C.

I first met Professor Reichel-Dolmatoff when he visited Professor Rouse at Yale in April, 1969. To my inquiry as to whether any griddle sherds had been found with the earliest Puerto Hormiga pottery, he replied that none was present anywhere in Colombia for almost two thousand years following 3100 B.C., the earliest radio-

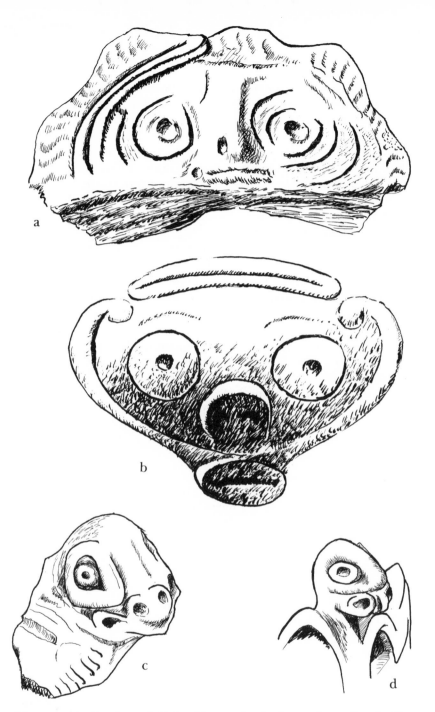

Fig. 103. Comparison of Colombian animal adornos from Puerto Hormiga (a, c) with Barrancoid handles from the Orinoco (b, d).

259

carbon date given for Puerto Hormiga pottery. Then about 1120 B.C. griddle sherds appeared suddenly at Malambo,[3] only a few miles from Puerto Hormiga (Map 14). He explained the occurrence of these griddle sherds by suggesting that Puerto Hormiga potters had migrated into Venezuela (perhaps about 2000 B.C.), where they learned the technology of manioc. Then, for some reason or other, they had returned to their homeland, taking with them the cassava process. If true, the carrying of pottery between Colombia and Venezuela was not a one-way journey from west to east—the cassava griddle was taken west.

This was indeed exciting news for at least two reasons. First, because it strongly suggested an early Arawak linkage with Colombia; and second, because the date of 1120 B.C. for their return from Venezuela to the Malambo site in Colombia was only about a couple of hundred years *before* the people we now call the Barrancoids arrived at the Orinoco delta to displace the original Saladoid Arawaks. It hinted that the Puerto Hormiga-Barrancoid potters might have lived in Venezuela for several hundred years before some of them returned, about 1120 B.C., to Colombia, while others moved on to Saladero around 985 B.C. My hunch, based upon my Orinoco River trip in 1965, is that the intermediate home of these pre-Saladero Barrancoid potters will eventually be found somewhere east of the junction of the Rio Apure with the Orinoco, perhaps around Caicara (Map 5).

The group returning to Malambo produced a pottery somewhat similar to, but slightly advanced over, the original Puerto Hormiga ware, apparently due to added Barrancoid features they had learned or developed in Venezuela. These changes were mainly in the zoomorphic adornos (Figure 104a, b) and elaborately modeled decorations for the walls of vessels (Figure 104c). Later Arawak sherds show these same Barrancoid features (Figure 104d, e, f). This, I think, argues strongly for the association of Barrancoid potters with Colombia, and also suggests that similar Barrancoid traits will someday be found in a Venezuelan site earlier than the 985 B.C. date of Barrancoid pottery in Saladero.

This return of potters from the Orinoco to their ancestral home on the Colombian coast, and specifically to the great Magdalena River basin, somewhat similar to the Orinoco River system, also suggests a vivid memory pattern of their earlier eastward migration or a consciousness of trade routes quite beyond anything previously suspected for that date and location.

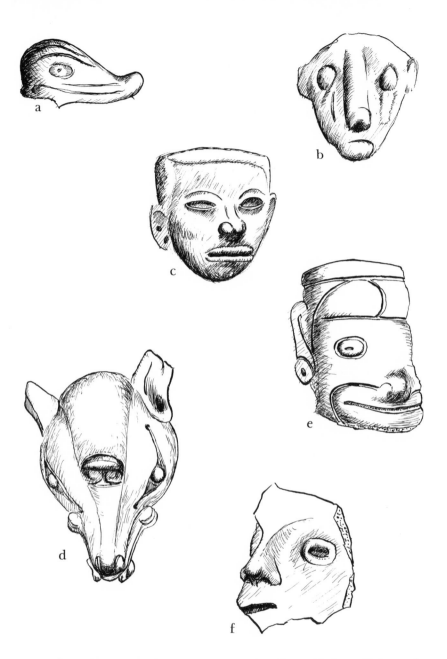

Fig. 104. Barrancoid-type adorno pot handles and bas-reliefs. a, b: Zoomorphic pot handles, Malambo. c: Human head bas-relief on wall of vessel, Malambo. d: Pot handle from Barrancas. e: Bas-relief on wall of vessel, Barrancas. f: Bas-relief on wall of vessel, St. Lucia.

261

Almost simultaneous with this criss-crossing of the South American continent by the Puerto Hormiga-Barrancoid-Malambo potters was the movement of the Saladoid potters. Unfortunately, we have no direct evidence as to where they originated, but their reaching Saladero about 1010 B.C. is of crucial significance to the Arawak story. Saladoids were cognizant of manioc technology because we find griddle sherds in the earliest layer at Saladero. Also they were much more highly skilled at pottery-making than any contemporary people in Venezuela. They had probably occupied territory farther up the Orinoco for some hundreds of years, and I should not be surprised if the Saladoids had come in contact with those migrants from Colombia, whom Reichel-Dolmatoff suggested had learned about manioc in Venezuela and then returned to Colombia to settle at Malambo in 1120 B.C.

Why had these Puerto Hormigans turned around and gone back home? And why had some of them gone downstream to Saladero by 985 B.C.?

I am suggesting that the intermingling of the pre-Saladero Arawaks and the Puerto Hormiga-Barrancoid people, strangers to each other and from widely separated origins, may have resulted in tensions that became more and more strained, even to the point of a confrontation, resulting in a split of the people from Colombia into two groups that for one reason or other went in opposite directions. There is, of course, no direct evidence of such an occurrence. But the fact is that an extensive settlement of Saladoids did exist at Ronquín, a village site near Caicara on the main stream of the Orinoco, just below the point where the Rio Apure enters as a mighty tributary coming from Colombia (Map 6). It is a strategic point geographically since the river banks are high enough to be well above any flood and would attract settlement not only by Amerinds coming down the Rio Apure from Colombia, but also by those journeying down the Orinoco from the Brazilian Rio Negro and even from the more remote Amazon tributaries in Peru. Likewise, people from Ecuador could have come down the Rio Meta, which separates Colombia from Venezuela, to join the Orinoco at Puerto Paez just a little upstream from Ronquín. Indeed, I know of no more likely spot for such widespread travelers to have met.

Unfortunately, no carbon-14 dates exist for Ronquín. I feel just as strongly about the necessity of redigging Ronquín for charcoal samples to give carbon-14 datings, so essential to the clarification of this early Arawak prehistory, as I did about getting dates for Cedros and Palo Seco in Trinidad. My hunch about a meeting between pre-Saladero Arawaks and the pre-Barrancoid Colombians would be greatly supported if we should find at Ronquín, among the known W-O-R sherds of Saladoid pottery, some pot-handle adornos like those found at Puerto Hormiga, and still more so if these could be shown to be earlier in style or in date than the Barrancoid adornos of 985 B.C. found at Saladero. In the meantime I shall guess an earlier date for Ronquín than the 1010 B.C. of the Saladero site, namely 1200 B.C., sufficiently early to permit the Puerto Hormiga-Barrancoid group to return to Colombia by 1120 B.C.

But where were the Saladoids prior to this guessed date of 1200 B.C. at Ronquín? In 1963, Rouse stated that their origin is a mystery. After puzzling over this problem for several years and trailing up many blind alleys, I embarked on an extensive study of the literature relating to all the ceramic sites in South America and Middle America (from Panama to the Mexican-U.S. border) having a date earlier than the first known date of the Saladoids—1010 B.C. at Saladero. This study included an examination of pottery collections from several of these sites.

What I was looking for was pottery with the following Saladoid features: (a) thin and hard; (b) decorated with white-on-red designs, preferably made by some kind of "negative" painting; (c) decorated with zoned, incised cross-hatching—the Z-I-C design—although I recognized clearly that this feature was not present at Saladero in 1010 B.C., but made its first appearance in Arawak pottery in Trinidad, at Cedros, in 190 B.C.

Betty Meggers and Cliff Evans, archeologists of the Smithsonian Institution, were very helpful and made available data showing that a thin, hard type of pottery occurred in the Valdivia style in Ecuador more than a thousand years earlier than at Saladero on the Orinoco. Thin, hard sherds were also found in such later styles as the Machalilla and Guangala from the same Valdivia site; so evidently, this making of very thin vessels and firing them at high temperatures was a long practiced technique in Ecuador.

However, I found no description anywhere in the literature of Middle or South American pottery earlier than 1010 B.C. having the kind of "negative" painting as practiced by the Saladoids on their W-O-R pottery. I did notice that the Ecuadorian Machalilla and Guangala styles, mentioned above, exhibited quite elaborate geometric polychrome ware that was also thin and hard, which may have been the prototype for the geometric W-O-R design even if it did not use the same kind of "negative" painting technique so characteristic of Saladoid pottery.

The Z-I-C design, I was astonished to learn, had appeared quite early in many places. The earliest Z-I-C sherds in the Americas are found in the Valdivia style pottery (Figure 105a, b, c, d) with a dating of about 2500 B.C. and continuing into the later Machalilla style of about 1500 B.C. (Figure 105e, f).[4]

The net result of these studies was an awareness that much unscrambling of the data was needed before any hypothesis could be formulated about the origin of the two branches of Arawaks and of a reasonable explanation as to how they acquired their pottery-making techniques. Nevertheless, the odds seemed to favor the Barrancoids as coming from Colombia and the Saladoids from Ecuador. Therefore I determined on a new approach. I would visit the sites of Valdivia and Puerto Hormiga in the hope that by actual encounter with these ancient centers of imaginative ceramic craftsmanship some kind of rapport might be established with those early talented artists and a clearer understanding obtained of their work.

As an added lure, there appeared about this time a provocative publication by Meggers and Evans[5] suggesting a classification of the aboriginal migrants from Mexico to South America into two groups: nonagriculturalists (prior to about 3000 B.C.) who had sought permanent homesites along the seacoast which were rich in shellfish; and agriculturalists (of somewhat later dating, possibly about 2000 B.C.) who practiced the "milpa" system of slash-and-burn farming devoted to the seed crop corn.

As Meggers and Evans explain it, the first impulse is to regard the nonagriculturalists as the earlier and less developed of the two groups, but *both* had one thing in common: they formed communities and tackled the problems of communal living. A sedentary life is apparently a prerequisite for pottery-making, and both groups could be expected to take up pottery at some stage in their development. This is, of course, precisely what they did.

Meggers and Evans also describe these two groups in terms of their climatic preferences. The nonagriculturalists seem to have kept to almost desert-dry lands—"xerophytic regions," as Meggers and Evans call them. (I am inclined to doubt this for reasons I shall explain later.) On the other hand, the seed farmers stuck to

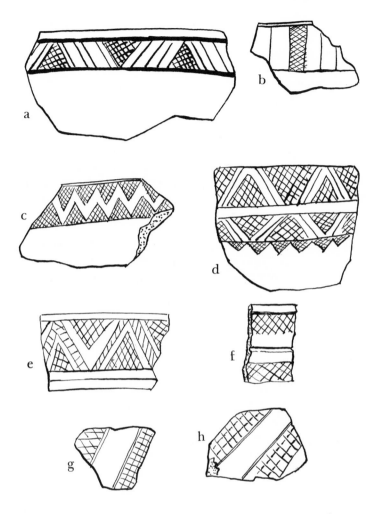

Fig. 105. a, b, c, d: *Valdivia-style Z-I-C sherds from Ecuador,* ca. *2500 B.C.* e, f: *Machalilla-style Z-I-C sherds from Ecuador,* ca. *1500 B.C.* g, h: *Jomon-style Z-I-C sherds from Japan,* ca. *3000 B.C. or earlier.*

the tropical rain forests, where rainfall was frequently over forty inches per year.

It was the nonagriculturalists, whose discarded shells formed the great shell mounds, who were the first potters in the Americas. The sites are at Puerto Hormiga in Colombia and Valdivia in Ecuador, both originating pottery about 3000 B.C. (Map 5). The agriculturalists are most readily identified as the corn-growers, who originally had domesticated corn possibly between the valley of Mexico and Chiapas, perhaps near Tehuacan, about 5000 B.C.[6] Their pottery development, at about 2000 B.C., was probably a thousand years later than that of the shell-mound builders.

I was somewhat familiar with the agricultural sites of Mexico and Guatemala, where the Mayans to this day practice the slash-burning of tropical forest for growing corn, but I had not seen the xerophytic regions where the people whose long time dumping of empty shells and other garbage had produced the shell-mounds where they had developed their splendid ceramics. It seemed that a desert region would be a strange place to begin communal living, but I determined to see for myself.

In April, 1969, I flew to Mexico City accompanied by my wife and Brad Endicott, my enthusiastic associate at Antigua. We spent about a week in Mexico, visiting the excellent anthropological museum and with side trips to the pyramids at Tenayuca, Tula, and Teotihuacan. Then to Guatemala where we had been invited by Edwin Shook who, after digging for several years at Tikal, was excavating Monte Alto near the Pacific Coast of Guatemala. I was eager to see this site because Monte Alto is near the line separating the rain forest from the xerophytic regions and might have been on the path ancient migrants had traveled on their way from Mexico to Panama and Colombia. It could even be the route that ancestors of the Arawaks had used in reaching Venezuela from Mexico, but frankly I did not expect to find any artifacts in Guatemala that could have any possible relationship with the Arawaks.

We were lucky in reaching Monte Alto (Map 1) just after Ed Shook had unearthed several large, globular stone figures with what seemed to be distinct Olmec affiliation, and also a few days after a farmer's bulldozer had exposed a double pottery vessel containing a real treasure—a large jade-green head, *intact*!

Exciting as these recent finds were archeologically, they could in no conceivable way be associated with the Arawaks. But when Ed Shook started to show me the potsherds he was unearthing with these strange figures I was quite unprepared to come across clear-cut examples of Z-I-C sherds (Figure 106) resembling those found in Cedros and other Arawak sites. There were dozens of specimens having zoned areas, finely incised cross-hatching, and at the same time were hard and thin. Asked about their date Ed said they were around 500 B.C. Further searching among the trays of sherds revealed negative painting, although not quite the same technique as

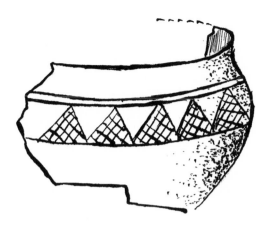

Fig. 106. Z-I-C sherd (Monte Alto, Guatemala).

used by the Saladoids. Here were two features exemplified on Guatemala sherds which resembled those on Saladoid pottery. Noting my excitement, Ed offered to take me to the museum at Guatemala City to see the sherds he had dug about twenty years earlier at Kaminaljuhu, now a suburb of Guatemala City. There I saw dozens of sherds with Z-I-C designs and with negative painting dating possibly 1000 B.C. to 500 B.C. There is no doubt about the popularity of these two forms of decoration; however, the dates are hardly early enough to have been a likely source of the Saladoid white-on-red painting techniques. It seems more probable that both the Saladoid and the Guatemala styles of sherds were derived from some other center of diffusion—perhaps in Ecuador or Colombia.[7]

From Guatemala we flew to Quito and then on to Guayaquil on the Ecuador coast. Betty Meggers and Cliff Evans had kindly furnished names of friends who might be able to show me the archeological sites at Valdivia, but one was on a business trip to Denmark and all the others were out of town. I did have a note that Richard Zeller, an amateur archeologist, had a vacation house at Palmar near Valdivia, so a taxi was hired for a three-day jaunt from Guayaquil to Punta Salinas and then northward along the coast to Valdivia. I was gambling that Zeller might be spending the weekend at Palmar since he did not answer his Guayaquil phone.

Around Guayaquil the land was lush with vegetation and trees two feet in diameter and fifty feet high were common. Obviously this was good farming country and would probably have been rich in food during prehistoric times, judging by the abundant bird life. However, as we drove westward some thirty miles to the long north-south stretch of the Pacific Coast of Ecuador, the trees were smaller and less numerous. Approaching the coast, the vegetation became more scrubby and the soil noticeably drier, until finally there was nothing but thorny brush and cactus. Clearly we were reaching the xerophytic conditions about which Meggers and Evans had written.

The taxi driver admitted he had never heard of Palmar, and the road map didn't show it. But near Valdivia we met people on the roadside who did know of Palmar, so without incident we reached the tiny village. An open-air barber told us that Richard Zeller was at home and a boy climbed aboard to guide us to his house. Explaining that I was a friend of Cliff Evans and Betty Meggers, I was welcomed and soon Mr. Zeller was showing me sherds he had found recently near Valdivia.

A mention of my interest in Z-I-C design and "negative" painting brought out many specimens, some in the form of partially reconstructed pots. My spontaneous interest in some of the sherds resulted in their being offered to me, and I accepted a few with delight. He also offered to show us the Meggers and Evans sites at Valdivia.

Driving northward up the coast I was reminded of a trip several years earlier along the Peruvian coast from Lima to Paracas. At both places there were long stretches of desert-dry gray sand and dust with only an occasional dwarfed shrub, even though the waves were breaking only a few yards to the west. The present spot looked like an improbable place for finding sherds, but I had thought the same thing in Peru, where sherds and pots couldn't be more abundant if you knew where to look for them.

Valdivia is a fishing village, its neatly built houses raised on posts so that the living floor is six to eight feet above the ground.[8] Goats, donkeys, and chickens live under the houses.

We had barely entered the village of Valdivia when Zeller stopped the car and pointed to the main site where Meggers and Evans had dug a trench about twenty feet deep. It was now only about ten feet deep and the whole site looked like recently bombed ground. The local people had been digging to find the little pottery figurines so much desired by visitors and collectors (Figure 107).

We clambered up the hillside into a sea of dust. Sherds were everywhere. These bits of broken pots were evidently of no interest to the natives or to the visitors with eyes only for figurines, but they

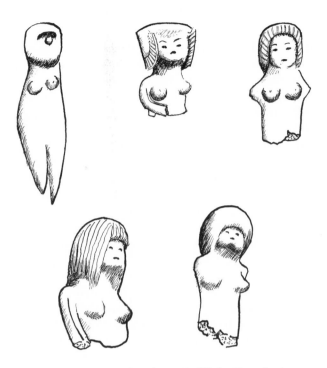

Fig. 107. Pottery figurines (Valdivia, Ecuador).

were precisely what I wanted. I had done my homework and was well versed in the various types of ceramic decoration Meggers and Evans had classified during their many years of excavating at Valdivia. It didn't take more than a few minutes to realize that here, in wild profusion, were fine examples of many types of pottery covering a period of about four thousand years. No sooner had I picked up a dozen or so sherds than I was surrounded by several delighted youngsters whose sharp eyes spotted at once the kind of sherds in which I was interested. Because of their long experience on the site the children were also able to find other specimens I might never have seen.

After I had secured and packaged in plastic bags enough sherds to represent a good cross-section of the various types that Meggers and Evans had classified, I did a few minutes' additional skirmishing to look for sherds of what they had designated as resembling the Japanese Jomon pottery.

I hadn't been at the site more than an hour before I had the feeling of being alert to the environment of those ancient potters in a way that would have been impossible otherwise. No amount of reading, discussion, or analysis of artifacts could have substituted for this wonderfully vivid firsthand experience.

The site was amazingly rich. Frequently, Brad Endicott and I exchanged glances as we picked up sherds of such thinness, hardness, and fine quality that they brought a strong reminder of our own Saladoid finds, even to the metallic clink when two sherds were struck together. Nevertheless, I was conscious that, apart from these characteristics, the sherds did have some major differences from the earliest Saladoid sherds. There was no trace of any white-on-red painting which so strongly characterized our Saladoid pottery. There was, however, one other feature of resemblance between Saladoid and Valdivia sherds, namely the Z-I-C design.

At Valdivia there was evidence galore of the early use of Z-I-C decoration. Meggers and Evans had furnished the dating. Sherds with Z-I-C designs occurred as early as 2500 B.C., amply early for the Z-I-C feature to have diffused to Cedros in Trinidad by 190 B.C. However, I was acutely conscious that a feature which had occurred over a period of two thousand years in regions as far separated as Ecuador, Peru, Guatemala, and Trinidad (not forgetting the Meggers and Evans suggested relationship with Japanese Jomon) might not be indicative of migration or even diffusion. It might mean that the Z-I-C design was so simple or so obvious as to have been "invented" independently by many potters.[9]

I puzzled over these ideas as I stood on this main site at Valdivia. But a still stronger, more persistent line of thought intruded, prompted by a basic point that Meggers and Evans had raised. The Valdivian potters, they said, belonged to a group that preferred xerophytic conditions rather than the rain forest environment of the seed-planters. The region we had passed through in reaching Valdivia was certainly desertlike, but to my amazement when we explored the village of Valdivia we came upon a number of lush gardens, including one of the richest crops of watermelons I had ever seen. I tasted them and their flavor surpassed that of the melons we normally purchase in the States, but the superb quality of "Sandia" in Colombia and Ecuador is widely known. Watermelons like plenty of sun, but they also require abundant water for their growth. After all, a watermelon is a melon with a vast water content. It became evident that Valdivia was situated at the mouth of the Rio Valdivia, one of the few streams entering this long stretch of desert coast from Esmeraldas in the north to Salinas in the south, a waterway so small that I had heard no mention of it, nor was it shown on any of the maps I had been studying.

Oddly, there was no water visibly flowing along the riverbed of the Rio Valdivia into the Pacific Ocean, clearly in sight a few yards west of the main road passing through the village. The natives saw to it that no drop of the precious water of the Rio Valdivia was wasted by running into the sea. It was being pumped out of wells in the riverbed into their beautiful gardens. I wondered if early dwellers in this region had used the Valdivia river for irrigation, just as the people in Peru to the south had carried water, sometimes through many miles of stone aqueducts, to make livable large areas of coastal desert. Perhaps some kind of agriculture had been practiced also in Ecuadorian sites along the Rio Valdivia, although no trace of the early domestication of plants has as yet been found.

Zeller took us upstream for several miles and pointed out a nearly continuous stretch of ancient sites. We had picked up Jaime Dominguez, a fine young Amerind who, I was told, had worked for Meggers and Evans. Jaime was very knowledgeable and apparently spent most of his time looking for new sites, of which he had found a dozen or more since Meggers and Evans had left the region. When he saw Zeller hand me some sherds he had picked up, I immediately became the recipient of Jaime's skilled attention. He would give me a couple of sherds and pronounce them "Machalilla" or "Guangala," as the case might be, even correcting Zeller's prior designation at times. Both these styles are later than the Valdivia Phase, Machalilla lasting from about 2000 B.C. to 1500 B.C., and Guangala much later, about 400 B.C. to A.D. 400. However, they are important indications that occupation of this area had been continuous for more than three thousand years. Both styles contained Z-I-C sherds as well as thin, hard, polychrome ware.

We progressed upstream past the villages of Cinthal, Barcelona and La Ponga to Loma Alta, whose name signaled that we were at a high spot, although the *loma* was a hill only a few hundred feet above sea level. From the top we could see the valley of the Rio Valdivia winding its way into a distant higher range of hills. The path of the river was marked by a lush rim of vegetation along both its banks.[10]

I couldn't help wondering if the Valdivian middens had been the seasonal locations of people who had actually lived in the hilly regions but who came down perhaps during their rainy season to gorge themselves on the protein of the bountiful shellfish deposits. in the lagoons along the seacoast. Surely they would not have spent all their time in the desert coastal region living on shellfish alone when this nearby river valley would most likely have been a rich source of bird or animal life and also of vegetation. People who made such splendid pottery as did the Valdivians were evidently inventive and resourceful to an unusual degree.

Then on to Cartagena[11] in Colombia, the nearest town to Puerto Hormiga where Reichel-Dolmatoff's excavations had yielded the earliest pottery of the New World with a date of 3100 B.C. No one we met in the city had heard of Puerto Hormiga, and I doubt that we would have reached the site without the pencil sketch Professor Reichel-Dolmatoff had given me. Our taxi man was unenthusiastic about the whole project, and I had to assume full responsibility for our route before he would even start. Actually we had no trouble, and when we reached the Hacienda Pomares, at the precise point shown on the map, we met a young man who said he had dug with Reichel-Dolmatoff and knew exactly where the shell mounds, "Los Concheros," were located. He agreed to guide us.

As we were leaving Cartagena I noticed that we were surrounded by lush vegetation, but as we progressed the terrain changed, just as it had done between Guayaquil and Valdivia, to a sparser growth until, within a mile or so of the shell middens, we were in a xerophytic region—mostly scrub bush and cactus. This was the same kind of desert region Meggers and Evans had said was preferred by the earliest potters in America.

Suddenly our guide announced we had arrived. I saw nothing to suggest a shell midden, but fifty yards or so off the road was a heap of shells rimming a shallow area. There was no sign of any deep excavations, but perhaps they had been filled in to avoid injury to grazing cattle. All I could see were low depressions, not more than one or two feet deep, but exhibiting clam shells packed tightly along the banks—thousands of them lying all over the place. Not a pottery fragment was in sight. I was sure, however, that a sherd or two would have been overlooked even by the most thorough of excavators, and after several minutes of close search I came across one, about two inches square. It was crude, porous, and fired at a low enough temperature to leave a thick black core.

It was unmercifully hot in the bright sun with no available shade, and after ten minutes of bending over my glasses were so covered with sweat and dust that it was difficult to distinguish anything. Nevertheless, I did find a dozen or so sherds and by this time our guide and our driver, noting what I selected, began to help. So did Florence, Brad, and Dean Blanchard, the ornithologist from the Galapagos trip, who had come with us to photograph "an archeological expedition," as he called it. We finished up with three dozen sherds, none with any decoration but some which clearly revealed needlelike tubes from which fine grass and Spanish moss, used for tempering, had burned out.

Brad noted that there were several shell mounds arranged in a circle. This checks with Reichel-Dolmatoff's statement that, as the population grew, new families leveled off mounds as foundations for their houses and the circle widened as the years passed. This circular arrangement of the houses was in all likelihood for companionship. We found later that occupation of Puerto Hormiga had lasted only for about 500 years, and no evidence of repeated building has been discovered.

Returning to the car, we headed toward the Canal del Dique (Map 14), a working canal originally built by the Spanish colonists to connect Cartagena with the Rio Magdalena. Actually the Magdalena River had entered the Caribbean Sea at Cartagena three or four thousand years ago, but the river silted up leaving lagoons and ox-bow lakes and changed its course to the present port of Barranquilla, about seventy-five miles to the northeast.

We rested on the slopes descending to the canal, under the canopy of a huge ceiba tree, and had lunch of cheese and bananas. We were in quite a lush spot, alive with birds. Dean Blanchard pointed out the glossy ibis, the screeching goose, black gallinule, and a number of others unfamiliar to me. This was evidently one of the lagoons from the ancient riverbed of the Magdalena they called *cienagas* (sea-*ane*-ah-gaz) and are rich in game, fish, fruit, and a nearly inexhaustible source of shellfish. Regardless of the stretches of desert, thorn, and cactus lands we had seen along the coast, here was an oasis teeming with edible material. The similarity between this area and the Valdivia site was apparent.

I began to wonder again about Meggers and Evans's classification in which the nonagriculturalists had been attracted to the xerophytic or desertlike coastal areas where the shellfish lagoons existed. I felt rather that people had congregated at places like Valdivia and Puerto Hormiga because they combined a rich supply of shellfish in the lagoons, which happened to be in a desert coastal area, with nearby river localities rich in vegetable and animal food. As a consequence they became sedentary, evolved a community existence, and developed a fine brand of pottery. I was aware, too, that this was the place where Puerto Hormiga potters had produced the earliest pottery in the New World. It was here they had developed the animal heads which served as handles for their pots—the adornos that constituted the first evidence of their later relationship with the Barrancoid potters.

I know of no archeologist who has denied this derivation of the Barrancoid type of early Arawak pottery. I recalled Reichel-Dolmatoff's pictures of sherds bearing well-modeled heads that displayed strong Barrancoid affiliations (Figure 103). Yet here at the site of this excavation I had not found a single sherd showing the characteristic Barrancoid decoration. I was, admittedly, disappointed. True, the three dozen sherds we had picked up were of the same thick, coarse, soft ware that we had found in Barrancoid sites on the Orinoco, but there were none of the typically modeled heads to seal the comparison. This was not the sherd-rich site we had seen at Valdivia. I was about to quit our spot near the Canal del Dique, when I realized I had not yet seen the village of Puerto Hormiga which had given the name to this style of pottery.

An inquiry brought the surprising information that we had been sitting in Puerto Hormiga all during our lunch hour.

"But where are the houses?" I asked our guide.

"They used to be at this spot," he said, pointing to several flat rectangular patches where the vegetation was obviously different from that of the rest of the area. These spots were where the houses had been located, our guide informed us. Then, a few years ago, the owner of the land had decided that the people should no longer occupy his property and ordered them off. The Colombian government came to their rescue, purchased about seventy-five acres of land half a mile or so away, and moved the ousted squatters there.

"There is no longer any Puerto Hormiga," added our guide, Miguel Marugo. "The new village is named Puerto Vadel, after the governor of the Department of Bolívar in which it is located."

Miguel took us to the village, which lay just beyond the fringe of trees hugging the shores of the Canal del Dique. Obviously it had been laid out quite recently and comprised only two or three blocks of wattle-and-daub huts along straight wide roads which were no more than parallel lines in the desert, marked off as streets.

Stark desert, even though it was just a few minutes' walk from the lush canal!

Miguel led us to a house where soft drinks were for sale and in no time we were surrounded by youngsters, delighted at the novelty of visitors. Holding up a couple of sherds, Brad asked, in Spanish, if they had seen anything like these. Most shook their heads, but two lads scampered off and in a minute were back, eagerly displaying a few potsherds. One had a slightly wavy rim, probably from finger indentation. Another showed rows of punctation. Then came a surprise: an adorno with a nice bird's head, looking very much like a Barrancoid pot handle—perhaps even more Barrancoid than the adornos illustrated in Plate I of Reichel-Dolmatoff's book *Colombia*, which I have shown in Figure 103.

I told Brad I would like to buy the fragment. The boy was obviously eager to sell, but didn't know what to ask for it. Someone suggested "Uno peso." Another shook his head and called "Cinco pesos." A third raised it to "Diez." The soft-drink dealer chimed in with "Cincuenta." It was a game now, and Brad himself called out "Cien." The dealer laughingly shouted "Mil" and clapped his hands, whereupon Brad upped the bidding to "Un million." Everyone was laughing and dancing in glee, but this seemed to exhaust the fun. There was a moment of silence. I turned to the boy and gave him twenty-five pesos (about $1.50). He was clearly delighted and clenched the money tightly in his fist. Dean wanted to photograph the lad holding the bird's head, and I wanted to examine the object more closely. It was no bird's head, as I had first thought, but that of a reptile, perhaps a turtle or even an alligator. I turned it around. There was an unmistakable alligator's foot, a front foot with five claws (Figure 108a). It was very likely a direct modeling of the reptiles the ancient dwellers along the Rio Magdalena had seen frequently and hunted avidly some five thousand years ago.

This alligator head had all the precision of modeling displayed by the Barrancoids two thousand years later at the apex of the delta of the Orinoco. Thought of such a direct transfer from the Magdalena to the Orinoco gave me a strong emotional charge, although I realize more soberly, as I write of the incident, that it will require a vast amount of research before any such migration or diffusion route can be settled.

From Cartagena we flew to Bogotá. After a couple of days in the refreshing coolness of the eighty-five-hundred-foot altitude with

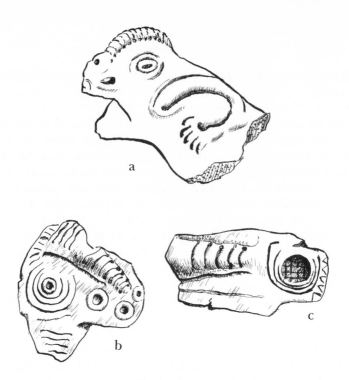

Fig. 108. Alligator sherds. a: *Obtained by author at Puerto Hormiga, Colombia.* b, c: *From Puerto Hormiga, collection of Professor Reichel-Dolmatoff.*

visits to the magnificent display of ancient Colombian gold artifacts in the Museo del Oro at the Banco de la Republica, we got in touch with Professor Reichel-Dolmatoff. We were immediately invited to tea at his home, which is full of Colombian artifacts and books on art and archeology.

The sherds he had dug at Puerto Hormiga were at the Museum of Anthropology, he explained. With his permission to photograph them, I took a set of twenty-six pictures of sherds from Puerto Hormiga, Canapote, Barlovento, and Momil (Map 14), covering an almost complete sequence of early Colombian ceramics from 3000 B.C. to 1000 B.C.[12]

It was with a distinct feeling of satisfaction that I noticed, in the very first tray of Professor Reichel-Dolmatoff's Puerto Hormiga sherds, an alligator head very much like the one obtained from the little boy at Puerto Vadel. The right foot of the alligator was visible, fashioned with the same care as the left foot of my specimen. As I continued photographing I came across two other alligator heads (Figure 108b, c). Apparently the alligator was a favorite food of ancient Puerto Hormigans, just as it is with the Arawaks in Surinam to this day. The realism of the reptiles was conveyed as clearly as on the Barrancoid sherds at the Orinoco site. I was strongly impressed with the probable validity of Reichel-Dolmatoff's hypothesis that these early Colombian potters were the producers of the prototypes for the Barrancoid sculptors. Moreover, this Puerto Hormiga pottery, at present considered the earliest in the Americas, obviously represents a sufficiently good quality of pottery to have required perhaps a thousand years of previous ceramic experience. As to where that experience was developed and by whose agency and instigation, we have not the slightest trace of evidence.

However, equally strong was the conviction that the Saladoids must have had a different origin. They were painters rather than sculptors. Their beautiful white-on-red pottery derives its esthetic competence from the deep concern of the Saladoids with geometric forms set off in color. Even when Saladoids used a more bulky nubbin as a handle, it was only roughly in the shape of a head and indistinguishable as belonging to man, bird, or reptile. Not so with the Barrancoid potters. They were realists in art and delighted in incorporating precise recognizable features—a characteristic which presumably they had acquired from their Puerto Hormiga predecessors.

Thus in Colombia there were Amerind sites covering a wide range of shellfish locations, mostly around the lagoons of quiet seawater close to the Pacific Ocean. These spanned a couple of thousand years of the second and third millenia B.C., and it was during this period that the Z-I-C type of sherds appeared, any of them early enough to have been a possible source for the Z-I-C design to have diffused to Cedros by 190 B.C. The river routes via the Magdalena and the Orinoco river system could have provided paths for diffusion.

I felt richly rewarded by my trips to both Valdivia and Puerto Hormiga. Now I had before me the pleasant task of organizing all the bits of information I had accumulated into a plausible hypothesis to link the artifacts left by the Saladoid and Barrancoid Arawaks in Venezuela and in the Caribbean islands with the work of earlier artisans in Colombia and Ecuador.

XV

The Findings to Date

THE adventures in searching out the Trail of the Arawaks have resulted in the following tentative conclusions—or perhaps it might be better to say hypotheses.

1. The Arawaks consisted of two component peoples, the Saladoids and the Barrancoids, probably of widely different origins.

2. The Saladoids were painters, judging by the high technical and esthetic competence of their ceramic ware as early as 1010 B.C., at which time it was the most sophisticated pottery in Venezuela (Figure 91). The Barrancoids, on the other hand, were sculptors, whose elaborate vessels were decorated with beautifully modeled handles, often showing a high degree of realism, which sometimes permit ready identification as animals such as alligators, parrots, or even human beings (Figure 93).

3. The earliest pottery in the Americas has been traced to Colombia and to Ecuador, going back to 3000 B.C. or possibly somewhat earlier. Specifically, the sites are at Puerto Hormiga in Colombia and Valdivia in Ecuador, both occupied by preagricultural people, largely consumers of shellfish and generally described as living in typically xerophytic or desertlike regions, but also having easy access to lush lands where vegetation, birds, and mammals were available.

4. The Barrancoid component of the Arawaks probably stemmed from the Colombia Puerto Hormiga potters because of the close resemblance between the handles on pottery found at Puerto Hormiga, dated about 3000 B.C., and the adornos on Barrancoid pottery found at the apex of the Orinoco delta in the first millennium B.C.

5. Another convincing piece of evidence linking the Venezuelan Barrancoids with Colombia is the finding of cassava griddle sherds

dated 1120 B.C. in a midden at Malambo, not far from Puerto Hormiga. According to Professor Reichel-Dolmatoff, Colombian potters made their way via the Magdalena and Orinoco river systems
into eastern Venezuela, where they learned manioc technology
which they carried back to their Colombian homeland. The Malambo sherds (Figure 104) associated with these griddle sherds display
a quality of sculptural modeling that was an advance over what the
Puerto Hormiga potters had produced about 3000 B.C. and well
along the road to the still more elaborate adornos of the Barrancoid
potters at the apex of the Orinoco during the first millennium B.C.

This date of 1120 B.C. at Malambo is the basis for my hypothesis
that there may have been a confrontation of the Puerto Hormiga-
Barrancoid potters and the Saladoids somewhere near Caicara, just
east of the junction of the Rio Apure and the Orinoco (Map 5, 6),
perhaps a little earlier than 1120 B.C., resulting in the partition of
both groups. Apparently the Saladoid group split, part of them
going upstream to Cotua (Map 6) not far from Puerto Ayacucho
on the upper Orinoco and the remainder going downstream to arrive at Saladero about 1010 B.C. Likewise, part of the Puerto Hor-
miga-Barrancoids returned to Malambo, while the remainder
proceeded more slowly downstream, arriving at Saladero about 985
B.C. This hypothesis would be supported if further digging of the
Saladoid Ronquín site at Parmana, near Caicara, furnishes charcoal with a date about 1120 B.C. or somewhat earlier.

6. These Barrancoids displaced the Saladoids they found at Saladero, sending them on their journey to Trinidad and the Antilles,
while the Barrancoids continued to occupy the sites at Saladero and
other nearby locations for about two thousand years.

7. The tracing of the Arawak Saladoids prior to their occupancy
of Ronquín is much more tenuous than the relation of the Barrancoids to Colombia. Our search for the white-on-red decoration so
characteristic of Saladoid pottery has so far turned up no sherds
earlier than the Saladero pottery of 1010 B.C. Indeed, the technique
of "negative" painting—involving the meticulous scraping away
of the outer white coating to reveal a red design below—seems to
be a unique invention of the Arawak Saladoids. Even the white-on-
red design, regardless of the technique of application, is not found
on Ecuadorean pottery until the period Betty Meggers calls the
"Regional Development Period," which begins about 500 B.C.,
much too late to be a prototype for the Saladoid W-O-R pottery.
Actually Meggers, Evans, and Estrada, in their comprehensive vol-

ume on the excavations at Valdivia, show *no* painted pottery in their eighty-nine plates illustrating the Valdivia style which lasted until about 1700 B.C. Painted sherds (not W-O-R) do appear in styles later than Valdivia at about 1500 B.C., and these may have been early enough to diffuse painting techniques to various groups, including the Saladoids, during their early wanderings in Venezuela, from which they could develop their apparently unique white-on-red decoration by 1010 B.C.

Actually I am equally concerned with the thin, hard vessels made by the Valdivian and Machalilla potters of about 2000 B.C., which was amply early to provide the technique to the Saladoids who made the same type of thin hard ware.

We may be on much firmer ground when we consider the features of the Z-I-C design, which showed up in Saladoid pottery for the first time at Cedros about 190 B.C. (Figure 98). Similar Z-I-C designs are found on Valdivia-style pottery as early as about 2500 B.C. and were continued in the Machalilla style of 1500 B.C. (Figure 105a-f). From Valdivia the Z-I-C feature probably diffused south to Kotosh in Peru about 1000 B.C. and north to Colombia, where it is found in the Barvolento and Momil styles, also about 1000 B.C. Any of these dates are early enough for the Z-I-C feature to have diffused to Cedros by 190 B.C. Moreover, diffusion routes could have been provided by the river systems of the Magdalena, Orinoco, and Amazon from either Colombia, Ecuador, or Peru to Trinidad. Consequently, I consider trait diffusion of the Z-I-C feature from the Pacific Coast to Trinidad by 190 B.C. as being quite plausible.

I have the feeling, too, that this discrimination between the "pure" Saladoid features of early Arawak pottery and the encroaching Barrancoid influence, whether due to "trait diffusion" or to actual physical interference (i.e., to "site-diffusion," the current archeological term) by the Barrancoids, may likewise enable us to reassess our earlier findings on the Arawak religion, their manioc culture, the ballgame, and the complex development of their tools.

8. No artifacts relating to Arawak religious practices have been found in Venezuela, with the possible exception of the Barrancoid burial urns discovered in the upper layers of the Saladero site. Neither do I know of any Barrancoid zemies or deities.

However, the Saladoids did develop a pantheon in the Antilles. Conch zemies representing the volcano, which presumably was the home of the male god Yocahú, possibly originated in Guadeloupe as early as A.D. 220. These volcano-shaped zemies have been found on all of the Lesser Antilles islands in a variety of forms, from the small ones cut from the prong of a conch shell to the large carved stone figures—all, however, keeping the volcano shape.

The Yocahú cult apparently reached its climax, perhaps about A.D. 1200, in Puerto Rico and Hispaniola. However, the pottery remained Saladoid in its early Hacienda Grande and Cuevas styles but did show Barrancoid "trait diffusion" influence in its later Chicoid style. Nevertheless, we have no evidence of actual intrusion by Barrancoids and hence have no reason for assuming that the Barrancoids had any effect upon the Arawak religion.

The prominence of the female deity Atabeyra as the goddess of moving waters and childbirth, and of the dog deity Opiyel-Guaobiran, the third member of the Arawak trinity, has been well documented in the early Spanish chronicles and supported by the discovery of many stone and shell artifacts from Haiti to Antigua and Guadeloupe. In both the Lesser and Greater Antilles the Arawaks developed an elaborate ritual involving shrines, beautifully carved stone zemies, and other appurtenances. The number of different kinds of zemies or deities indicates the complexity of the rituals. These were originated by the Saladoids and presumably experienced no Barrancoid influence.

9. The cultivation of manioc and its conversion to cassava were shared by Saladoids and Barrancoids as shown by the ubiquitous griddle sherds. It seems probable that it was the perfecting of manioc culture that was mainly responsible for the growth and development of the Arawak nation in the Antilles.

That manioc was an Arawak discovery is suggested by the name given by the Saladoids to their principal deity, Yocahú, which means "giver of manioc." We guess, therefore, that the Barrancoids may have learned manioc technology from the Saladoids, whom they encountered at or near Ronquín in pre-Saladero days and which they carried back to Malambo in Colombia about 1120 B.C.

10. We have found no evidence of any participation by Barrancoids in the ballgame. But the sport was known to the Saladoids because numerous ball courts have been found in Puerto Rico and we know of no "site-diffusion" by Barrancoids there. The chronicles also testify that the ballgame was being played in Haiti at the time of Columbus. Complete stone belts and elbow stones have been found in Puerto Rico. Fragments of both have been excavated at several ball-court sites there, and also in St. Croix, indicating

that these stone artifacts were actually used in playing the game. This supports the idea that the complete belts were not just ceremonial trappings, as appears to have been the case with the handsomely carved Mexican yokes found in pristine condition at Vera Cruz, in contrast with the much-scuffed state of the Arawak belts.

I shall not be surprised if ball courts, with fragments of playing equipment, are discovered in Antigua, Guadeloupe, and other islands of the Lesser Antilles.

It still seems plausible that the rubber ball and the game itself were invented near the source of rubber, perhaps along the tributaries of the Amazon and Orinoco rivers. Admittedly, the Arawak ballgame reached its height in Puerto Rico and Hispaniola, which has led some to suppose that the game diffused from Mexico by way of Yucatan. However, if ball courts are found in the Lesser Antilles this might furnish evidence that the game had diffused independently from the mainland of South America into the southern end of the Antillean chain. This would be established if carbon-14 datings should prove to be earlier in the Lesser Antilles than in Puerto Rico or Haiti for the courts or the equipment for the game. Indeed, references have been made by early Spanish padres, such as Gumilla, to the ballgame being played along the Orinoco.

11. The relation of the polished petaloid celts occurring in both the Lesser and Greater Antilles to the ground axes found in St. Vincent and other islands of the Lesser Antilles is still indeterminate. Petaloid celts of high polish are found wherever Saladoids were present in the Antilles. The ground axes, frequently with lugs for hafting, are later than the polished celts; although quite numerous in the range of islands from St. Vincent northward to St. Kitts, these ground axes are scarce in Puerto Rico and Hispaniola and, where studies have been carried out, are made of igneous rocks of the Lesser Antilles. This occurrence hints that the polished petaloid celts are of Saladoid development and that the ground axes may be a Barrancoid or even a still later Carib innovation.

Recently I became acquainted at firsthand with the remarkable stone double-bladed axes attributed to the Ciboney in northern Haiti. They are surprisingly well fabricated, and what is quite astonishing is their shape: they resemble the double-bitted axes for which the Minoans were famous. For a Meso-Indian tribe, apparently without knowledge of either agriculture or ceramics, the Ciboney achieved an extraordinary proficiency in stoneworking. Many of their axes are sculptural gems.

It has long been recognized that Meso-Indian artifacts occur in Trinidad, the Virgin Islands and the Greater Antilles but none had been found in the Lesser Antilles. In March, 1970, a pre-ceramic site was discovered at Salt Pond, near Deep Bay in north-west Antigua, where large, fine quality flint blades and scrapers were found. This was followed, in April, 1971, by the discovery of an extensive flint "factory" on Long Island to the north of Antigua. These are presumably Ciboney sites and hint that other Meso-Indian locations will eventually be found in other islands between Trinidad and the Virgin Islands.

Since no polished petaloid celts have been found in Saladero we are now in a position to suggest that the Saladoid Arawaks learned to make their tools from the Meso-Indians they encountered in Trinidad and the Antilles.

The only instance of which I have direct knowledge where petaloid axes have been dated was our find, at Mill Reef, Antigua, of two large celts associated with charcoal of a burned house-pole, which yielded a carbon-14 date of A.D. 600.

Hafting axes with lugs or grooves were evidently of later date since they occur mostly on the surface, but at what date we really don't know because no matte-surfaced ax with lugs for hafting has been found with charcoal to give a carbon-14 date.

I have looked for evidence of Barrancoid association with the ground hafting axes, but so far without success. If a mainland source of the ground ax could be established it would encourage further search to ascertain if the Barrancoids were the ones who brought the ground ax to the Lesser Antilles after, say, A.D. 500. If so, they might also have been directly responsible for the growing trend of Barrancoid features in the late pottery of the Lesser Antilles, thereby suggesting actual migration rather than just trait diffusion of the pottery, as is generally assumed.

My years of wanderings along this tortuous trail of the Arawaks have led me to Colombia as the probable site from which Barrancoids originated, and to Ecuador as the possible homeland for the Saladoids. Admittedly, the Arawaks were not recognized as a "nation" in the course of European man's affairs. In 1492 the history of man, as it was then being recorded, covered little outside the interests of "Western" man living in an oval-shaped block of land that included most of Europe, a little of western Asia (the so-called Near East), and a slice of North Africa. The rest of the world was peripheral and its doings were almost totally ignored by Western man. But the great Aztec empire of Meso-America, the Inca empire of Peru, and the tiny "nation" of the Arawaks were actively and intensely living out their lives, despite the fact that Western man was without knowledge of these events.

The Arawaks, whose remains we had stumbled on in Antigua, were almost a homogeneous and an isolated culture. I have made much of the distinction between the Saladoid and Barrancoid components of the Arawaks. But apart from the differences between the potsherds they scattered in their respective middens, and the possibility that the Saladoids were less aggressive than the Barrancoids, they were probably as alike as two beer drinkers in a London pub.

These Saladoids lived more than a thousand years ago on what, to me, are the loveliest of islands, in an equable climate and with abundant food at hand. In all probability they were exposed to occasional Barrancoid traders, whose well-sculptured pottery decoration proved a compelling attraction. Or perhaps these Barrancoids did more than just trade and kept displacing the Saladoids out of their Lesser Antilles homes, some time after A.D. 500. But no Barrancoids appear to have physically migrated to the Greater Antilles. "I don't believe there was any *site-unit* diffusion to the Greater Antilles," says my scholar-friend and mentor, Ben Rouse. "I do believe there was *trait-unit* diffusion. Plenty of it," he adds. So perhaps the Barrancoids, like the later Caribs, were stopped at Puerto Rico.

It was the size of Puerto Rico and Hispaniola, together with their soil wealth, that were major elements contributing to the great development of these islands of the Greater Antilles. There the Arawak culture thrived. Their carved stonework outstripped the sculptural qualities of the products of the Lesser Antilles. Their ceremonial practices became richer, as the vast caches of ritual objects testify.

The Arawaks also worked out an elaborate social structure involving a hierarchy of caciques and a supporting staff of chieftains, to the extent that there were nine separate "kingdoms" in Puerto Rico prior to 1492, each with its own cacique.

Then came the downfall at the hands of the Spaniards—devastatingly rapid and complete. Their expulsion from the islands of the Lesser Antilles by the Caribs had taught the Arawaks no lesson of resistance. Perhaps all their men had been devoured by the Caribs, with none escaping to the Greater Antilles. It is estimated that there were a couple of million Arawaks in Hispaniola and Puerto

Rico, which would seem to be enough to overpower the handful of men Columbus had brought. But the Arawaks had no background of world history to impart knowledge of self-preservation. On the other hand, Cortes, with only 500 men, defeated the entire Aztec nation, who had lifted warfare to a height that would have delighted Bismarck. The permissive many succumbed to the aggressive few.

These Arawaks have become very close to me, almost entirely through their fragments of potsherds, their discarded tools, and the many ritual objects we luckily discovered. This intimate contact with their artifacts for seventeen years has given me a feeling of almost being able to visualize the men and women who used them in their daily life on these islands. I am deeply concerned by the factual evidence of their complete annihilation, and I wonder if we, who can computerize the orbital movements of manned satellites, can guide our own paths away from destruction.

Epilogue

WHILE this manuscript was being examined by the publishers, Professor Rouse called my attention to Donald W. Lathrap's book, *The Upper Amazon*, published in 1971. This splendid book suggests answers to some of the questions raised in my chapters on the origin of the Arawaks.

In those chapters I had concluded that the Arawak potsherds we had encountered could be explained as being the product of two distinct groups of migrants—the Saladoids and the Barrancoids—each producing characteristically different types of pottery. Professor Reichel-Dolmatoff had pointed out the similarities between the Barrancoid sherds of the first millennium B.C. found at the apex of the Orinoco delta and those from the Puerto Hormiga site in Colombia of the third millennium B.C. He suggested that the Venezuelan ware was most likely the work of potters who had migrated from Puerto Hormiga to Barrancas. The migration route from the upper reaches of the Magdalena to the tributaries of the upper Orinoco seemed easy to delineate. Consequently, the possible origin of the Barrancoid component of the Arawaks appeared to be reasonably well indicated.

It was the Saladoid pottery that was difficult to trace to sites earlier than Saladero, with its date of 1010 B.C. From a study of several thousands of sherds and from dozens of Arawak sites, I had decided that the most significant features of Saladoid pottery were the W-O-R (white-on-red) and the Z-I-C (zoned-incised-cross-hatched) designs used so frequently in decorating their ceramic ware in Saladero, Trinidad, and the Antilles. Admittedly, the Z-I-C aspects had appeared several hundred years later than the W-O-R. This Z-I-C design occurs first on Arawak pottery at Cedros in Trinidad about 200 B.C., along with the conventional W-O-R design.

By A.D. 100–300, Z-I-C sherds show up at El Mayal on the northern shore of Venezuela and then along the migration route on several islands of the Lesser Antilles, specifically in Grenada, Guadeloupe, and Antigua.

It now seemed necessary to search for evidence of W-O-R and Z-I-C sherds throughout the early sites of South America. It seemed a huge task, involving the study of sherds from all sites in Colombia, Ecuador, and Peru, as well as from the almost endless mesh of tributary river systems of the Amazon and Orinoco (Maps 1 and 5). I have described my findings in Ecuador and Colombia, but I knew nothing about the sites in the great Amazon basin (Map 15). Fortunately, Donald Lathrap's book discusses the ceramic products from more than a hundred sites on the Amazon-Orinoco complex. He leaves no doubt that the producers of Barrancoid type of pottery were widely distributed throughout the great river systems.

Even more broadly, Professor Lathrap points out that "Languages of the Arawakan stock had a far greater geographical range in South America than those of any other stock or family." He suggests that the origin of the Arawaks may have centered on that part of the Amazon into which several of the great tributaries flow: the Negro and Putumayo from the north and the Madeira, Purus, and Jurua from the south (Map 5). From such a center the "Proto-Arawakans" could have migrated *upstream* about 3000 B.C., reaching the Orinoco, says Lathrap, by 2000 B.C. and northern Venezuela by about 500 B.C.

The earliest pottery used by these speakers of Arawakan he locates in the upper Amazon at the Tutishcainyo site on the Rio Ucayali (Map 15) in Peru at about 2000 B.C. The next earliest pottery was found about 150 miles southwest of Tutishcainyo, at the Wairajirca site near Kotosh, also in Peru, on the Rio Huallago, a branch of the Maranon tributary of the upper Amazon. This Kotosh pottery is dated 1850 ± 110 B.C. and Lathrap adds, "The earliest preceramic occupation here must date well back into the third millennium B.C." He points out that both the early Tutishcainyo and the Kotosh ceramics are very closely related stylistically and apparently the work of the same kind of people. Both have some Barrancoid features.

As I understand Professor Lathrap's theory, some tribes of "Proto-Arawakans" found themselves in the huge valley system of the middle Amazon perhaps early in the third millennium B.C. He suggests that originally they were a preceramic people, who may have practiced a form of agriculture involving the vegetative cultivation of manioc. Presumably their deep concern with the fermentation of cassava starch to produce a manioc beer for fiesta purposes, as well as the use of cassava starch as a bread or gruel, had stimulated their invention of large pots for the fermentation of the beer; of smaller drinking vessels—possibly ornamented for use in their fiestas—together with food vessels for cooking and serving cassava gruel and even the flat griddles ("comals") for baking cassava cakes.

Lathrap makes no mention of any "hearth" in the whole Amazon River system bearing a date earlier than the 2000 B.C. of the Tutishcainyo site or the 1800 B.C. for Kotosh. Neither does he offer any evidence of pottery being invented at the confluence of the Amazon tributaries, which he considers to be the homeland of the Proto-Arawakan, from where it might have diffused upstream to Tutishcainyo or Kotosh. Consequently, it seems to me, some weight must be given to the existence of two pottery sites *outside* the Amazon complex that are a thousand years earlier than these two Peruvian sites. I refer to Puerto Hormiga, near Cartagena in Colombia with a date of 3100 B.C., and to Valdivia, on the coast of Ecuador and roughly the same date. I have described my visit to these two sites and discussed certain features of the Puerto Hormiga pottery, particularly the adornos, which strongly resemble those found on Barrancoid pottery from the apex of the Orinoco delta. Indeed, their discoverer, Professor Reichel-Dolmatoff, has suggested not only that the Venezuelan Barrancoid pottery was derived from the Colombian ceramics, but has postulated the migration of Puerto Hormiga potters to Venezuela, where they learned the manioc process, and their subsequent return to their homeland bearing their newly acquired griddles for cooking the cassava. His evidence lies in the cassava griddle sherds first discovered in Colombia at the Malambo site, dated 1120 B.C., not far from Puerto Hormiga, in a ceramic context containing pottery similar to that found in Puerto Hormiga but with modifications derived from their sojourn in Venezuela.

Reichel-Dolmatoff has also shown that for a span of about 2000 years Colombian potters developed the original Puerto Hormiga style (3100 B.C.) so that a continuous series of changes can be illustrated in the ceramics found in a string of associated Colombian sites: Bucarelia (3000 to 2000 B.C.), Canapote, Barlovento, Malambo, and Momil (Map 14). These ceramics show Barrancoid features, including elaborately modeled adornos. Also important is the

presence of the Z-I-C design in the Momil style, a feature characteristic of Saladoid pottery.

It has been suggested by Professor Rouse and others that the two
components of the Arawaks found in Venezuela and Trinidad, the
Saladoids and the Barrancoids, were quite different peoples. I prefer to distinguish them by the difference in their skills. The
Saladoids were painters and the Barrancoids were sculptors. The
Saladoids painted their hard, thin ware with white-on-red geometric
designs, done with meticulous craftsmanship. On the other hand,
the Barrancoid potters demonstrated their sculptural qualifications
by an extensive use of well-modeled decoration. In this they ran
the gamut of forms from realistic representations of birds, fish, and
humans to forms so highly stylized as to defy identification, although their sculptural competency is apparent. Even when the
Barrancoids made use of geometrical designs similar to those employed by the Saladoids, they carved well-excised grooves either
straight-lined or curved. The Barrancoids reached their most elaborate forms in the Los Barrancos style of about A.D. 600–900 on the
Orinoco.

Even when Barrancoid trade pieces began to exert their influence
in Trinidad or the Lesser Antilles, a Saladoid potter's attempt at
modeling resulted in little more than pellets of clay being attached
or appliqued to give an indeterminate form. Correspondingly,
when a Barrancoid potter attempted any painting it consisted of
mere streaks of white paint applied somewhat clumsily on top of
a red base, rather than the accurate removal of the overlying white
slip to bring out the red design, as practiced by the Saladoid
painters.

I find myself strongly impressed by the importance of the very
early date of about 3000 B.C. for the Puerto Hormiga and Valdivia
sites. It can hardly be without significance that both of these sites
have carbon-14 dates earlier than any other pottery in the Americas. Moreover, both are geographically feasible locations from
which migration or diffusion to the Amazon and Orinoco river
systems could occur (Map 5).

I am also inclined to emphasize the occurrence of the Z-I-C ornamentation on both early Colombian and Ecuadorian vessels, suggesting a possible diffusion to Tutishcainyo and Kotosh (Map 15)
in Peru about 1800 B.C.; then to Cedros, Trinidad, by 200 B.C.; and
finally to the middens along the Arawak migration route from El
Mayal in northern Venezuela to Grenada, Guadeloupe, and An-

tigua in the Lesser Antilles about A.D. 100. This persistence of the Z-I-C motif for about two thousand years and over a stretch of territory across the entire width of the South American continent entitles it to be regarded as a very important "hallmark" of these Amerind migrants, who are later designated as Saladoid Arawaks and who may have been of Arawakan stock for much of that span of time.

Thus it would be my preference to trace the Proto-Arawakans back much farther than the central Amazon region, to coastal Ecuador and Colombia. They were probably ever on the alert for the "flood-plain" areas Lathrap describes. They would have experienced these in the lower Magdalena River in Colombia; in the Rio Valdivia and even the Guyas River delta in Ecuador (Map 5); then in the huge areas at the confluence of the Amazon with its major tributaries; and finally on the Orinoco. They were looking for places that would provide not only the protein of fish and shellfish, but also fertile land on which to grow their vegetative plants such as yuca (or manioc). Perhaps it will be found someday that these ancestors of the Arawaks knew about root crops as early as, or even before, the Mexicans had learned the cultivation of maize.

During this same period of editing this book, the excavation of the Indian Creek site on Antigua by Yale University has taken place. Professor Irving Rouse, who first guided our amateur archeological efforts at Mill Reef in 1956, and who has been my mentor ever since, started this dig during the last week in May, 1973. The work was financed by the Antigua Archeological Society, with the aid of a grant from the National Science Foundation.

The plan laid out by Dr. Rouse involved digging a series of trenches, and this was completed over a period of nine weeks. Unfortunately, Professor Rouse suffered a heart attack at the end of a month and was hospitalized for four weeks in Antigua. He was then considered sufficiently recovered to make the return flight to the U.S. for checking by his personal physician in the New Haven Infirmary.

For the first three days of his illness, the digging schedule was halted in the hope that Dr. Rouse might recover and be able to direct the work. As soon as this appeared unlikely, I consulted with the President of the A.A.S., Desmond Nicholson, and we decided to continue the excavation along the lines already established by Rouse. It became quickly apparent that the five workmen under the competent foremanship of John W. Meade, a former senator in the Antigua Legislature, had been so thoroughly trained during their month's teaching by Professor Rouse that they could proceed with the program satisfactorily. This decision seems to have been justified by the fact that work was maintained on schedule throughout the time of the excavation.

Professor Rouse had laid out a plan for digging seven trenches each eight meters long by two meters wide and, of course, of a depth sufficient to ensure reaching ground sterile of artifacts. These trenches were in an oval pattern, going clockwise from the southwest corner of the site, northward along the higher slope of the ground and sweeping in a broad curve along the east-west boundary and then southward, parallel to the old bed of Indian Creek. The reason for this schema was that there were five or six mounds, suggesting a series of occupation sites based upon the differences in pottery styles of sherds found on the surface.

The position of the number one trench at the southwest corner was chosen because its surface sherds were the earliest, as judged by the occurrence of typical white-on-red Saladoid sherds accompanied by early conch zemies. At no other part of the site were these two features of W-O-R sherds plus conch zemies displayed on the surface so we agreed that it was best to start with the earliest material. None of us knew, nor had we any basis of "accurately" guessing how far the early occupation layer revealed at the surface of trench one might spread. We just hoped the W-O-R sherds and conch zemies might show up in the lower layers of some of the trenches on the eastern downward slope of the site.

As it turned out, our hopes were fulfilled in a quite spectacular manner. The lower layers of trenches five and six proved to be incredibly rich in fine examples of classic W-O-R sherds. Perhaps I had better clarify what I mean by the term "classic," attached to the white-on-red type of sherds. I am referring to the elegant geometric patterns of W-O-R decoration where red areas of the design were frequently disclosed by a unique technique of meticulously removing portions of the upper coating of white slip to reveal the burnished red surface below. This separation of the white coating from the underlying red layer is a form of "negative" painting and is a quite sophisticated process.

In addition to this "removal" technique, the use of "direct" or "positive" painting can also be seen on other sherds. As an example, a single white line may occur on the broad sweep of red color on the neck of a bowl (Figure 109), which would obviously be easier to produce by accurately painting a white line than by removing excessively large areas of white paint. Examination with a lens confirms that no scratching had occurred on the neck of the bowl whenever the design comprised a single white line on a large red surface. Furthermore, instances are found where portions of the design have deliberately been produced by "direct" or "positive" painting of small areas of white (Figure 109c). All of the types shown in Figures 109a, b, c are found among W-O-R sherds of the earlier Saladoid period, *ca.* A.D. 300–700. In later Saladoid pottery the painting tends to be carelessly drawn bands frequently in a chevron pattern (Figure 109d).

While the excavation was still in the earlier stages, viz from trenches one to three, I was much interested in the comments of Professor Rouse that the site was yielding a plentiful supply of artifacts. For my part, I was quite disappointed, and said that this site was turning out to be more like the Mill Reef site, where W-O-R sherds were quite sparse. Trench four showed slightly richer yields. But it was only in trench 5 that the supply of W-O-R sherds became lavish. It was during the digging of the first two layers of trench five that Dr. Rouse became ill (June 24), and it was not until August 15, 1973 that I was able to show him several hundred slides which revealed the riches of the lower layers of five or of the subsequent trenches six, seven, and eight. In the bottom meter of each of these trenches hundreds of W-O-R sherds appeared, some of them large enough to show clearly the complicated shapes of the vessels and the intricate patterns of their decoration (Figure 110). In several instances the upper part of the pot showed the classic W-O-R geometric design, but below the keel of the side wall the design would change to polychrome areas of a more baroque form. There was no question but that this pottery was really elegant—the product of Saladoid Arawaks with a high degree of esthetic sensitivity and also of great technical competence.

An abundance of charcoal was obtained from each layer so we anticipate a quite complete series of radiocarbon datings. It would not surprise me if the duration of this classic W-O-R production was several hundred years, possibly from A.D. 300 to A.D. 600. But it is quite striking that these rich layers of W-O-R pottery peter out in the upper layers, perhaps from A.D. 600 to A.D. 1000, their place being taken by pottery quite sparse in decoration and simpler in form. I have no explanation to offer for this change. The pottery still looks Arawak. I did note however that before the W-O-R de-

a

b

c

d

Fig. 109. W-O-R sherds from Indian Creek. a: Classic W-O-R design; white surface scratched to reveal underlying red. b: White line applied directly to red surface. c: Small white areas painted directly on red base. d: Chevron style, late Saladoid.

sign ceased, there was an interim period, perhaps of two or three hundred years, in which white chevrons were painted directly on the red vessels, but this painting was never of the "negative" style and consisted of quite crudely drawn bands, frequently of uneven width (Figure 109d), and totally lacking the precision so characteristic of the classic W-O-R (Figure 109a).

Naturally I must await the expert analysis of these ceramic sequences by Professor Rouse, and also the carbon-14 datings, before any valid conclusions can be drawn as to the causes of change in the cultural habits of the residents of the Indian Creek site. In the meantime, I shall content myself with the mental picture developed during the day-by-day watching of the excavating, followed by the washing and classification of the sherds. These experiences stimulated in me no hypothesis of any "catastrophic" change in the cultural patterns of the occupants. The observed variations in the pottery could just as easily be explained by their loss of interest in a W-O-R style after practicing it for several hundreds of years, or by the minor year-by-year adjustments in technology that might suggest themselves naturally to artisans subjected to little if any outside influences.

However, we did encounter some exciting experiences, the most important of which occurred during my efforts to find evidence for the existence of a ball court in Antigua.

In Chapter X reference was made to the generally held view that the Arawak ballgame, as evidenced by the ball courts in Puerto Rico and Hispaniola, was derived from Yucatan, coming eastward to Hispaniola and finally to Puerto Rico. The great Yucatan court at Chichén Itzá, with its stone rings tenoned into walls thirty feet high and with temples at various parts of the court, is dated about A.D. 1200. The feeling is that the Puerto Rico courts should be about A.D. 1250 or 1300, and recent carbon-14 dates support this. No ball courts have been discovered south of the Virgin Islands, and I have often heard the comment that no ball courts are likely to be found in the Lesser Antilles, since diffusion from Yucatan would be too late to reach the islands before the Caribs came.

My basic objection to this view is that I find it difficult to believe that anyone could bring the quite complicated concept of the ballgame from Yucatan to Puerto Rico without the suggestion of the masonry walls that dominate Chichén Itzá.

I have seen no example where any ancient Arawak has ever placed one stone on top of another to build a wall.

My picture has long been similar to that of Theodore Stern, *The Rubber Ball Games of the Americas*, namely that the rubber ball probably originated where rubber is found, for example, along the Amazon tributaries, moving as a trade object—the magic bouncing ball—up the Orinoco and north through the islands of the Antilles.

Fig. 110. Elegant specimens of W-O-R sherds from trench six, a: *level five and* b: *level six.*

Also it could have traveled to Honduras, Guatemala, and Mexico by a parallel route along the west of the Gulf of Mexico.

With no ball court in the Lesser Antilles, this remained an unsubstantiated hypothesis. For ten years I searched for traces of ball courts in Antigua.

In Chapter X, I mentioned finding at Indian Creek a long pointed stone lying partly buried in the earth, which suggested to me a ball court marker similar to those seen in Puerto Rico. Describing the game briefly to some visitors, it was only a matter of minutes for the group to find three other stones, which, when raised to a vertical position, marked the corners of a rectangle. The site was photographed in March 1967 (Figure 90) and the four stones laid carefully in the holes from which they had been raised,

in the hope of concealing the site until the time of the Yale excavation. I admitted that these four stones did not prove the site to be a ball court, but added that, in my judgment, it would be proved by finding even one fragment of a stone belt which the players had worn. Broken ball belts have been encountered frequently in Puerto Rico and I have three fragments in my collection (Figure 111).

On June 26th, 1973, I searched the Indian Creek area for the "ball court" found in 1967. Only two of the original corner stones were located, the right rear and front stones (Figure 112). John Meade and the five workmen told me they were not surprised that the other two stones were missing, since they are of just the size used for tethering cattle, allowing them some wandering in their search for food. Presumably cows had sought relief from the hot sun and dragged the missing stones to a nearby shade. We hope to find them soon.

Recently Desmond Nicholson showed me a small cylinder of

Fig. 111. Fragments of stone ball belts and elbow stones (Puerto Rico, ca. A.D. 1300).

stone, whose ends showed ancient breaks, but for which he could think of no probable use. I recognized immediately that it was just like one of the fragments of ball belts I had obtained from Puerto Rico. He had picked it up "somewhere" on the surface of the Indian Creek site. This fragment, to my thinking, greatly increased the probability of the existence of a local ball court, but we needed to find a specimen "in situ." I showed photos of the ball belts, and also Desmond's fragment, to each of John Meade's workers, so that they could be on the watch for similar stones.

Early in July, 1973, a group of government officials, including Basil Peters, Minister for Education and Culture, under whose sanction the excavation was being conducted, were making their first visit to the site. About five minutes before the group reached the ball court site one of the workers handed me, from a low layer of trench five, an oval cylinder of stone—obviously a ball belt fragment. It was made of the local "green-stone" from nearby hills (Figure 113).

This dramatic find made a definite impression upon the visitors and a few minutes later, Sydney Prince, Minister of Public Works,

298

Fig. 112. Indian Creek ball court, June, 1973.

came to me with a much larger fragment he had picked up on the surface about forty yards from the ball court. I recognized it as a broken piece of a "massive" ball belt, which would probably weigh about forty pounds and be worn by the back field player.

An important feature is that the green-stone fragment came from the fifth layer down (about fifty inches deep) of trench five (Figure 114). This layer had produced a mass of early Saladoid pottery—the fine, hard, white-on-red material—that could be as early as A.D. 300–500 (carbon-14 date A.D. 582 ± 85 years, [September 1973]). This fragment furnishes evidence that the ball game was played in Antigua hundreds of years earlier than the A.D. 1250–1300 date attributed to the Puerto Rico courts; and also that the migration of the game probably was not eastward from Yucatan but northward through the Lesser Antilles.

Recalling that my reporting at the Fourth International Congress at St. Lucia in July, 1971, of newly-found preceramic sites on

299

Fig. 113. Ball belt fragments found at Indian Creek.

Fig. 114. Trench five, Indian Creek where fragment of ball belt was found at depth of fifty inches.

a

b

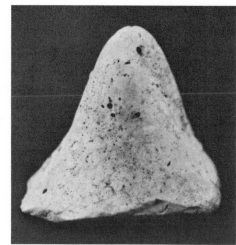

c

*Fig. 115. Conch zemies from Indian Creek.
Left to right, a: Proto zemi, trench five, layer
five (A.D. 582). b: Proto zemi, trench five,
layer six (A.D. 477). c: Carved conch zemi,
trench five, layer four (A.D. 860); d: Bases of
zemies shown in b, c, a.*

d

Antigua with Meso-Indian flint and ground stone tools was followed by the discovery of twenty or more similar sites elsewhere in the Lesser Antilles, I am now predicting that the announcement of the Antigua ball court at the Fifth International Congress held in Antigua in July, 1973, will be followed by the finding of ball courts on other islands of the Lesser Antilles perhaps before the end of 1973.

During the last two weeks in July two more ball-belt fragments were found on the Indian Creek site, bringing the total to five specimens.

Our good luck continued. The zemies that had been so scarce in trenches one to four showed up significantly in trench five. In layer four an elegantly carved conch zemi (Figure 115c) was found. Then in layer five (not far from the ball-belt fragment) a very simple conch zemi (Figure 115a) with well-cut flat base occurred. No working of the sides of the conch prong was visible. So evidently we had found a "proto-zemi" similar to the earliest one Edgard Clerc had dug in Morel II. A foot or so lower down, in layer 6, a second proto zemi appeared (Figure 115b), just a plain uncarved prong but with a flat base. Figure 115d shows the flattened bases of the zemies in Figures 115a, b, c. Thus we had once more the evidence of the early stages in this evolution of the Yocahú zemi. Recently (September 1973), carbon-14 results have been obtained from these three bottom layers of trench 5, namely A.D. 477, 582 and 860 (with a plus or minus of 85 years), so the Antigua zemies are later than the corresponding forms at Guadeloupe.

Even in the later stone zemies of A.D. 1400 from Puerto Rico, which show the human head of Yocahú, the characteristic volcano cone of the earliest conch zemies is retained in the pointed hump of his back. The evolution of this sculptured form of the volcanic cone is thus traceable for a thousand years. The coming of the Caribs is perhaps responsible for the broken stone zemies found in late occupation layers in Guadeloupe and in Antigua, possibly also for the absence of zemies in the topmost layers of some of the excavations in Guadeloupe.

Apparently the Christian-Judaic concept of God making man in His own image was somewhat changed by the Arawaks who created their main god Yocahú in the form of the ubiquitous volcano in their newly found island paradise.

Maps

BAHAM

CUBA

Chichen Itza

YUCATAN

JAMAICA

HA

MEXICO

GUATEMALA

GREATER ANTILLES

HONDURAS

CARIBBEAN

Monte
Alto

Copan

EL SALVADOR

NICARAGUA

Barranquilla —

Mala

Cartagena.

COSTA RICA

Puerto
Hormiga

PANAMA

Rio Magdalena

B

COLOM

Quito

ECUADOR

Valdivia —

Guayaquil

PERU

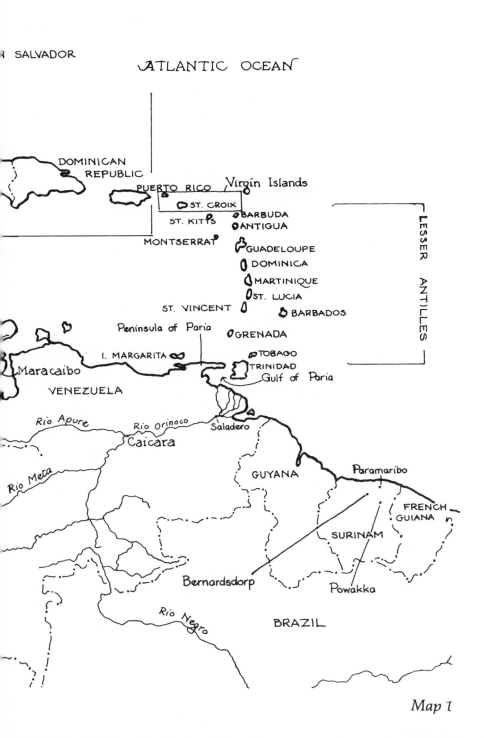

SALVADOR

ATLANTIC OCEAN

DOMINICAN
REPUBLIC

PUERTO RICO   Virgin Islands

ST. CROIX

ST. KITTS   BARBUDA

MONTSERRAT   ANTIGUA

GUADELOUPE

DOMINICA

MARTINIQUE

ST. LUCIA

ST. VINCENT

BARBADOS

Peninsula of Paria   GRENADA

I. MARGARITA   TOBAGO

TRINIDAD

Maracaibo   Gulf of Paria

VENEZUELA

LESSER ANTILLES

Rio Apure   Rio Orinoco

Caicara   Saladero

Rio Meta

GUYANA   Paramaribo

FRENCH
GUIANA

SURINAM

Bernardsdorp   Powakka

Rio Negro   BRAZIL

Map 1

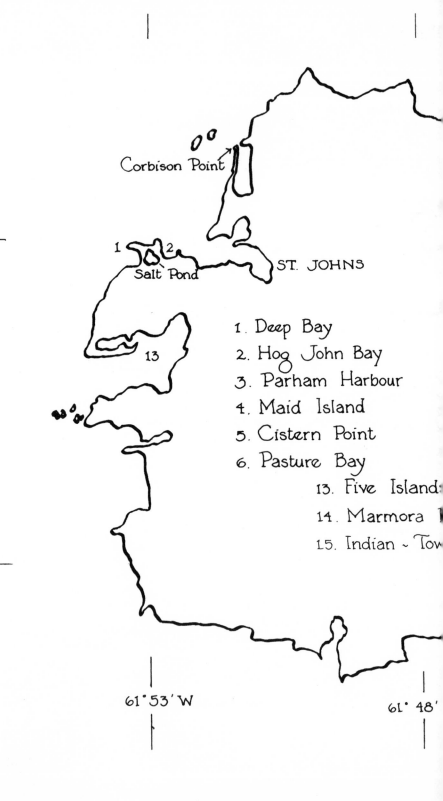

Corbison Point

ST. JOHNS

Salt Pond

1
2

13

1. Deep Bay
2. Hog John Bay
3. Parham Harbour
4. Maid Island
5. Cistern Point
6. Pasture Bay

13. Five Island:
14. Marmora
15. Indian - Tow

61°53' W

61° 48'

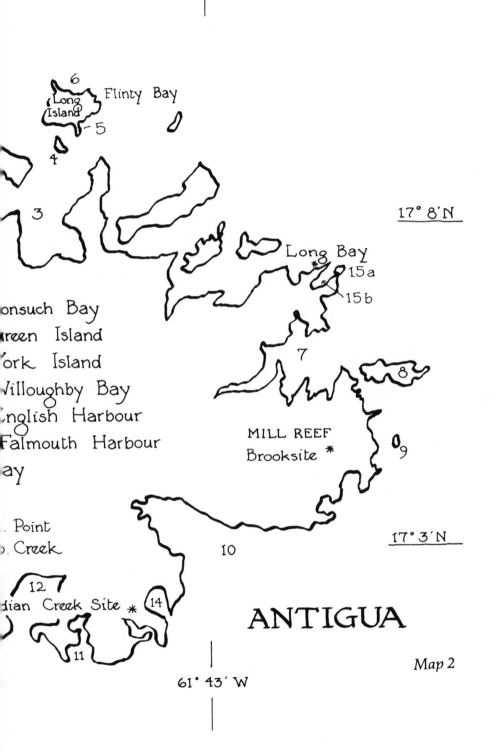

6

Long
Island

Flinty Bay

−5

4

3

onsuch Bay

reen Island

ork Island

Villoughby Bay

English Harbour

Falmouth Harbour

ay

Point

Creek

12

dian Creek Site *

14

11

Long Bay

*

15a

15b

7

8

MILL REEF
Brooksite *

9

10

ANTIGUA

17° 8'N

17° 3'N

61° 43' W

Map 2

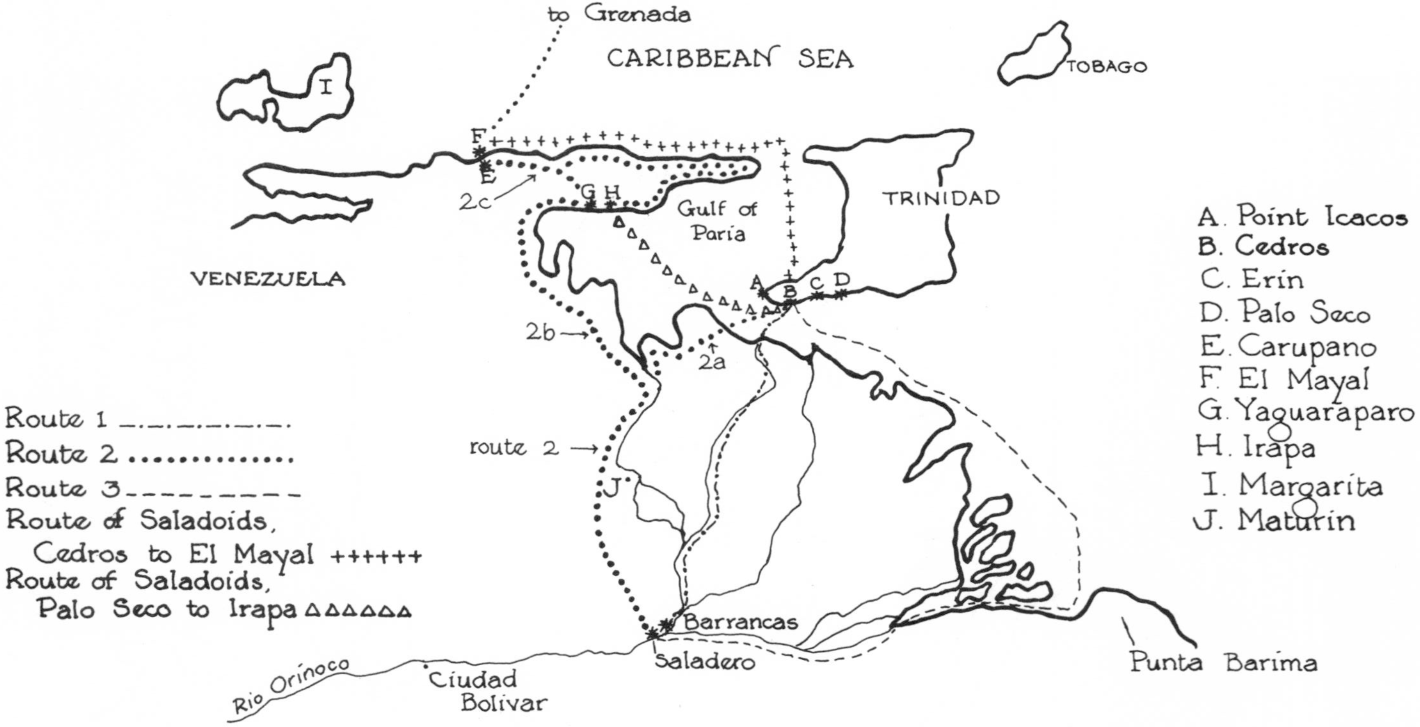
to Grenada
CARIBBEAN SEA
TOBAGO
I
TRINIDAD
Gulf of
Paria
VENEZUELA
A
B
C
D
E
F
G
H
J
2a
2b
2c
route 2
Barrancas
Saladero
Punta Barima
Rio Orinoco
Ciudad
Bolivar
A. Point Icacos
B. Cedros
C. Erin
D. Palo Seco
E. Carupano
F. El Mayal
G. Yaguaraparo
H. Irapa
I. Margarita
J. Maturin
Route 1 _._._._._._
Route 2 ....
Route 3 _ _ _ _ _ _ _ _ _
Route of Saladoids,
Cedros to El Mayal ++++++
Route of Saladoids,
Palo Seco to Irapa ΔΔΔΔΔΔ

MAP of POSSIBLE ARAWAK MIGRATION ROUTES FROM SALADERO to TRINIDAD & GRENADA

Map 3

Map 4

309

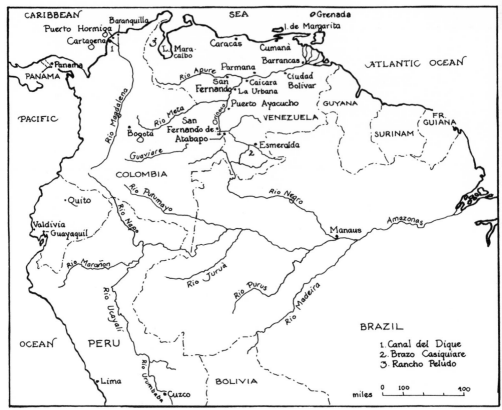

MAP of the VALLEYS of the AMAZON, the ORINOCO, & the MAGDALENA

Map 5

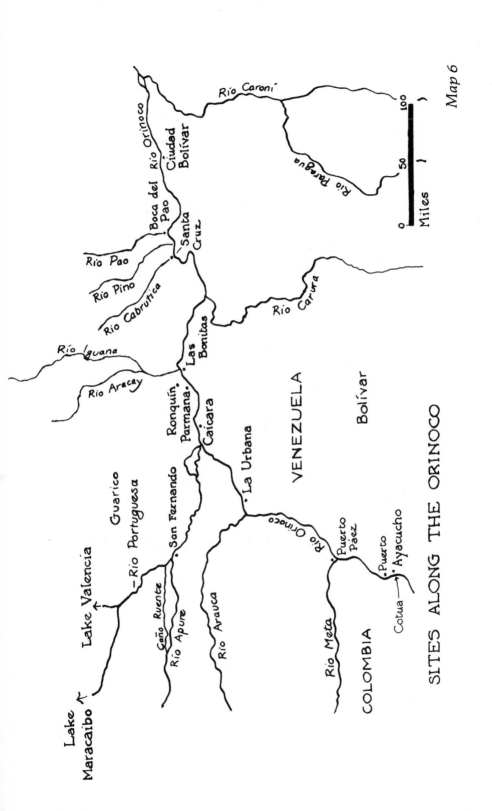

Map 6

SITES ALONG THE ORINOCO

CARIBBEAN SEA

GUAJIRA

PARAGUANA

Muaco Springs

Rio Guasare

Coro

Rancho
Peludo
Maracaibo

Rio Pedregal

El Jobo

LAKE
MARACAIBO

VENEZUELA

0   30   60

miles

RANCHO PELUDO & MUACO SPRINGS

Map 7

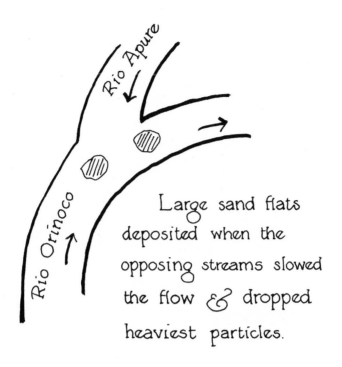

Large sand flats deposited when the opposing streams slowed the flow & dropped heaviest particles.

Map 8

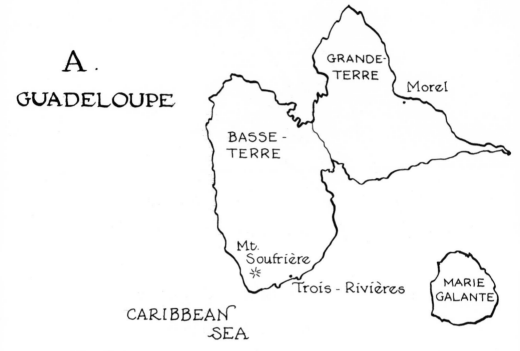

A.
GUADELOUPE

GRANDE-TERRE

Morel

BASSE-TERRE

Mt. Soufrière

Trois - Rivières

MARIE GALANTE

CARIBBEAN SEA

Map 9a

B.
ST. VINCENT

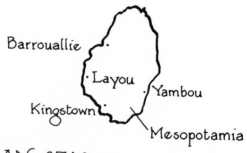

Barrouallie

Layou

Yambou

Kingstown

Mesopotamia

CARIBBEAN SEA

Map 9b

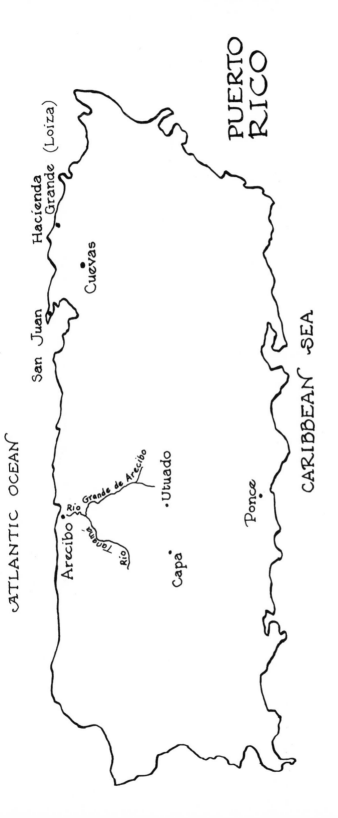

ATLANTIC OCEAN

San Juan

Cuevas

Hacienda
Grande (Loiza)

Arecibo

Rio Grande de Arecibo

Rio Tanamá

Utuado

Capá

Ponce

CARIBBEAN SEA

PUERTO
RICO

Map 10

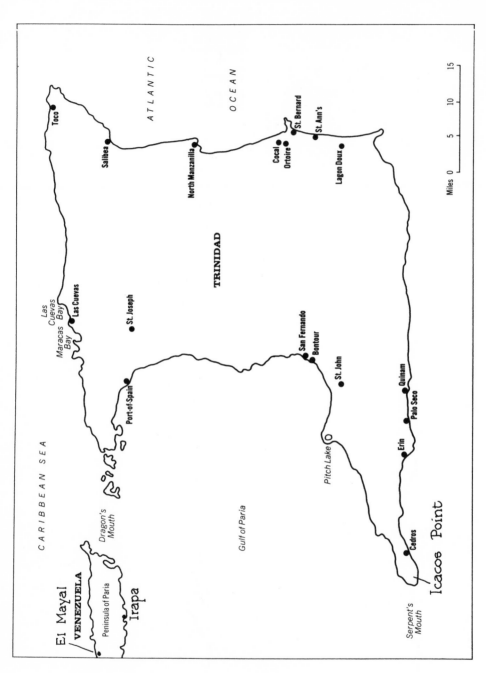

CARIBBEAN SEA

El Mayal
VENEZUELA
Peninsula of Paria
Irapa

Dragon's
Mouth

ATLANTIC

OCEAN

Toco

Salibea

North Manzanilla

Las
Cuevas
Maracas Bay
Las Cuevas

St. Joseph

Port-of-Spain

Gulf of Paria

TRINIDAD

San Fernando
Bontour

St. John

Pitch Lake

Quinam
Palo Seco

Erin

Cedros

Serpent's
Mouth

Icacos Point

Cocal
Ortoire

St. Bernard

St. Ann's

Lagon Doux

Miles 0   5   10   15

316

Map 11

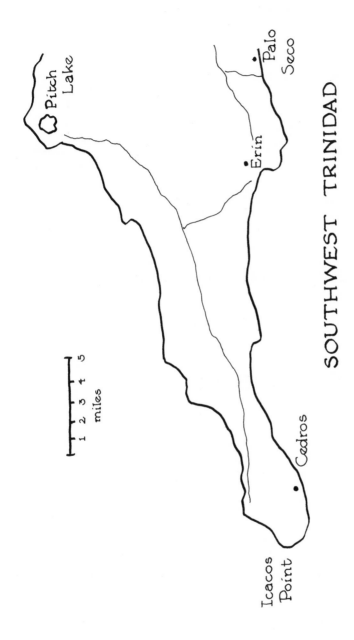

SOUTHWEST TRINIDAD

Map 12

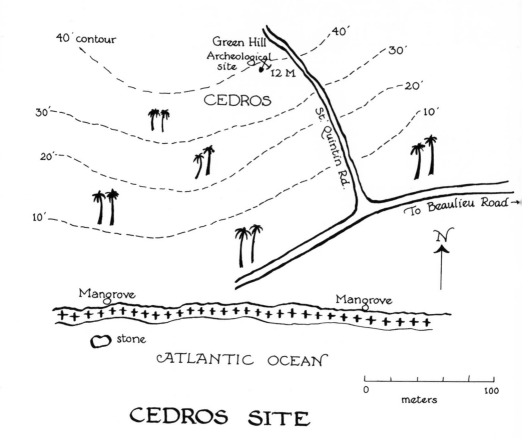

40' contour

Green Hill
Archeological
site
12 M

CEDROS

40'

30'

20'

10'

30'

20'

10'

St. Quintin Rd.

To Beaulieu Road →

N

Mangrove

Mangrove

＋＋＋＋＋＋＋＋＋＋＋＋＋＋＋＋＋＋＋＋＋＋＋＋＋＋＋＋＋＋＋＋

stone

ATLANTIC OCEAN

0   100
meters

CEDROS SITE

Map 13

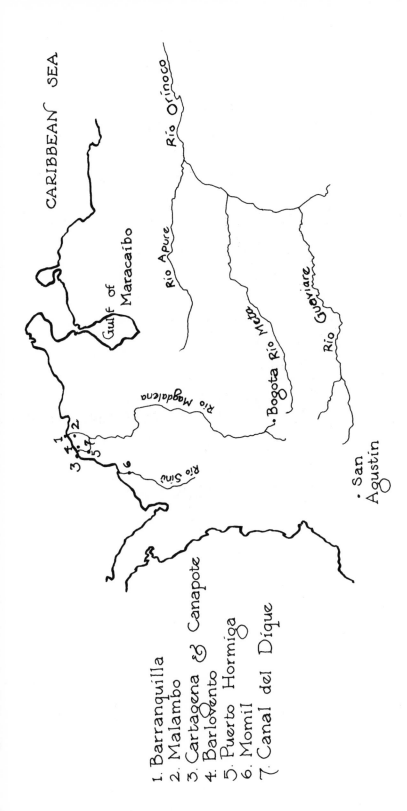

CARIBBEAN SEA

Gulf of Maracaibo

Río Orinoco

Río Apure

Río Magdalena

Bogotá Río Meta

Río Guaviare

Río Sinú

San Agustín

1. Barranquilla
2. Malambo
3. Cartagena & Canapote
4. Barlovento
5. Puerto Hormiga
6. Momil
7. Canal del Dique

ARCHEOLOGICAL SITES IN COLOMBIA

Map 14

Map 15

Notes

Chapter I

1. From the air San Salvador, the most easterly of the Bahamas, resembles a sand or mud flat, and indeed this is characteristic of most of the island cays over which one flies coming from Nassau. The island's elevation is so low that about half the interior is covered with brackish lakes. The rest of the land has only a shallow layer of soil, so that the plantations of a couple of hundred years ago could hardly have been very fertile. Ruins of "great houses" as well as of tiny abandoned native huts are seen in many places. Scrub brush has reclaimed much of the land from the futile attempts to farm it, so that the scars of man's earlier efforts are now covered and much of the island must be reverting to what it was when Columbus landed.

Chapter IV

1. David J. Rogers, *Studies of Manihot Esculenta Crantz and Related Species*, Bull. Torrey Botanical Club, Vol. 90, Jan. 1963.

2. Tupi-Guarani is the name of a broad spectrum of languages used by several hundred tribes extending from Brazil to Colombia. As pointed out by Donald Lathrap, "Next to Arawakan, Tupi-Guarani is the most widely distributed linguistic stock in South America."

3. See next page.

4. The possible origins of the world's important domesticated plants have been studied intensively, especially wheat and barley, since these two grains have been the mainstay of several Asiatic and European peoples for many millennia. Through close cooperation experts in several scientific disciplines—including botany, archeology, paleobotany, cytology, and genetics—have collaborated to trace the origin of wheat and barley to the Fertile Crescent in Asia Minor, extending from Mesopotamia to Palestine and Anatolia. Similar studies have been made on the origins of maize, and the earliest maize has been traced by MacNeish

CHARACTERISTICS OF SWEET AND BITTER MANIOC

Variety	Leaflets		Petioles		Stems		Leaf Scars	
	number	size*	color	size*	color	markings	nature	distance apart*
White Stick				SWEET CASSAVA				
Sample 1	5–7 mostly 7	1¼ x 5	green: red near base	7–9	green	longitudinal	heavy	1
Sample 2	5–7	1 x 3½	green: red at base	3–4	green	none	heavy	1
Sample 3	all 7	1½ x 6	green: red at base	8–10	green	longitudinal (slight)	heavy	1
Sample 4	5	2 x 6	green: tinge red at base	5–6	green	none	heavy	½–1
Butter Stick								
Samples 5 and 6	3–5	1¾ x 5	bright red throughout	5–7	green (pale)	none	heavy	¾
Black Stick								
Sample 7	3–5	1½ x 4	dark purple all over	5–6	green (dark)	none	very heavy	1
Sample 8	all 5	2 x 6	dark red all over	6–7	green (dark)	longitudinal	heavy	1
				BITTER CASSAVA				
Sample 9	all 7	1½ x 7 sharp-pointed	green: red at base	9	gray-green	longitudinal	heavy	¾
Sample 10	**5–7	1½ x 6 sharp-pointed	brownish-green	5	gray	longitudinal	heavy	1

* In inches.
** Possibly the five leaflets would become seven when the young leaflets matured.

only recently to lands lying at elevations of five thousand feet or so in the Tehuacan Valley, with a dating about 5000 B.C. Unfortunately, the evidence for the development of manioc is so meager that I have had to look for further clues among the origins of agriculture on a world-wide basis before trying to pinpoint the hearth from which manioc sprang.

In the late Pleistocene era of the Old World, Paleolithic man, from about 50,000 to 15,000 B.C., was a hunter of large animals such as the mammoth. When these animals became extinct, perhaps about 12,000 B.C., possibly through excessive hunting, Mesolithic man of the Old World turned to small game such as the antelope family, the wild pig and even rodents, perhaps augmenting his diet by gathering fruits and roots. Throughout these two eras of hunting man knew nothing of agriculture. It is likely that one of his favorite hunting devices was to lie in wait at some runway leading to a lake, river, or spring, and then club, spear, or stone the animals as they came to drink.

From this increasing familiarity with locations near water man turned to fishing, and more and more became an eater of fish and shellfish, acquiring the skills needed for life on the river, lake, and later the sea. Permanent campsites would be established at the most favorable spots, such as the junction of a tributary with a river, the mouth of a river entering a lake, and especially protected waters on the seacoast such as inlets, bays, and lagoons.

Food-getting was then no longer a matter of long nomadic journeys over land following herds of wild animals; the fish came either up or down the rivers to these suitably selected campsites and the supply of shellfish in certain places was apparently inexhaustible. Some anthropologists believe that these fisher-folk were the earliest planters, and that the first to be cared for around the campsites may not have been food plants, but those used in producing fiber for fishnets and lines. Vines yielding gums and resins would have been brought to the campsite area for treating the spun cords to give them increased strength, flexibility, and waterproofing. This care of plants yielding fibers and gums, and their conversion to nets, would probably be men's work. The women may have followed suit by introducing their favorite food plants. This stage of man's development occurred in the late Mesolithic era, a period during which stone and other implements of a much wider variety and precision were required for the increased complexity of his activities. The bow and arrow were invented (but Arawaks presumably did not know of them until the Caribs came); also the elaborate lanceolate flint points, together with fishhooks and harpoons of stone or bone. Mesolithic man in the Old World is dated from about 15,000 to 10,000 B.C.

Sauer makes a strong case for the theory that the fishing communities on the lakes, rivers, and shores of Southeast Asia were first to practice propagative planting of food stuffs. This achievement is attributed to

Neolithic man of about 10,000 to 7,000 B.C. It was at this time that the cultivation of such vegetative plants as taro, yams, banana, breadfruit, and citrus may have been accomplished by selecting the best plants and making propagative cuttings from their stems or roots. While this method of planting was being developed, the domestication of the pig, dog, and fowl occurred probably somewhere around the eastern shores of the Indian Ocean. These Southeast Asian fisher-folk from Burma, Malay, Thailand, or Vietnam are thus nominees for the world's earliest agriculturists and animal domesticators.

It is possible that the Japanese islands should be included in this brief survey of the earliest incipient "civilizations," since pottery-making (Jomon pottery) seems to be as early, and possibly even more ancient (if current carbon-14 datings are accepted), than the pottery of any other part of the world—about 7,000 B.C. This Jomon pottery was apparently some thousands of years earlier than any agricultural activity in Japan. Ancient Japan was essentially a fish and shellfish food economy.

These fisher-folk of Southeast Asia were thus incipient agriculturists. Man had become a sedentary creature. He was tied to his chosen sites, near great beds of shellfish or at his favorite fishing spot, where his accumulation of needed plants for nets or for food and his growing stocks of tools and other artifacts were located. Perhaps, too, he had mentally staked out the territory that he would defend against predators or trespassers, whether animal or human. The understanding or acceptance of these territorial rights between neighbors was probably the basis for the development of community life.

Seed planting was apparently later than vegetative propagation, and it seems probable that rice was originally found in taro patches as a weed, which was removed and planted elsewhere, so that even rice culture had an associated vegetative origin.

Perhaps the cradle of seed plants was also in Asia. Millets and peas have been traced back to central India. Wheat and barley probably had their start in the foothills of the Zagros Mountains overlooking the Mesopotamian Valley. From there they moved west along the Fertile Crescent to the Mediterranean and east into the Indus Valley. This activity in seed planting occurred from 9000 B.C. to 6000 B.C. and perhaps south to Egypt a millennium later.

With the development of seed plants came the domestication of goats, sheep, and cattle, perhaps centering, like wheat and barley, in the foothills of the Zagros Mountains, dating about the sixth or seventh millennium B.C. As Sauer states, "The household animals I have associated with vegetative planting in origin: the herd animals belong with seed farming." By household animals he means the pig, dog, and fowl of Southeastern Asia, and by herd animals the goats, sheep, and cattle 'in the hill country around Mesopotamia.

In the New World the Paleo-Indian hunting of big game, such as the mammoth, giant sloth, and the horse, has been dated at Muaco Springs, Venezuela, as early as about 15,000 B.C. Vegetative planting may also have preceded seed planting, as it did in Asia. Professor Rouse gives a dating of 5000 B.C. to 1000 B.C. for the Meso-Indian, who practiced vegetative improvement of plants such as manioc. The earliest date established for the use of manioc by the Arawaks is 1010 B.C. at Saladero, but it was used considerably earlier, since both Rouse and Cruxent have discovered the earliest pottery in Venezuela at Rancho Peludo (northwest of Maracaibo) dated about 1900 B.C. Griddle sherds were also found, but no specific date was assigned to them, although presumably appreciably earlier than the 1010 B.C. dating for Saladero. Thus the tribes who fished the large rivers like the Orinoco and its tributaries stretching up into Colombia, and who took their carbohydrate food from the manioc tubers found in the llanos, may have been the New World's first farmers.

However, the relative dates for seed and vegetative culture in the Americas have not been thoroughly worked out. At the moment the dates for primitive corn cobs in Chiapas, about 5000 B.C., are actually earlier than any established for manioc or other root plants, such as the potato, in the Peruvian Andes. But where the two cultures do impinge upon one another, as west of the north-south line at Caracas, the Venezuelan manioc growers are at lower levels than the maize growers, who presumably encroached upon them from Mexico or Colombia.

CHAPTER V

1. Professor Rouse says that this erosion has been accelerated by the recent heavy traffic of iron-ore boats. The waves generated by these large ships have undermined the site, especially during periods of high water. "Between the time of our first visit in 1950 and our last in 1957 a strip of the site some two meters wide has disappeared into the river." Figure 10 shows the effects of a recent landslide.

As we walked along the edge of the bank I had noticed several large pieces of rusty machinery scattered among the ranchos. It turned out that many years ago some German had chosen this high spot, well above flood level, as a site for a plant to treat beef from the nearby llanos. The Spanish word for a place for salting beef is "Salador." Hence the name Saladero.

2. This way of making mandioca is similar to the practice of the Bush Negroes in Surinam, who soak the grated manioc in a cloth bag in the river for two or three days, possibly to remove more of the poison but perhaps also to start a slight fermentation. The bag is then squeezed to remove the water and the starch is heated in a large open pan. It is

stirred continuously until it is golden colored. In this state the dry crumbs are called "kwak." They taste like Grapenuts and are a standard food in Surinam.

3. But if no clear-cut examples of acceptable antecedents of Saladoid or Barrancoid pottery are discovered in Peru, Ecuador, or Colombia, then the vast intervening territory between these western lands and Saladero must be critically examined (Map 5). This will mean a very difficult exploration to search for ancient Amerind sites along every tributary of the Amazon, Magdalena, and Orinoco drainage basins—a tremendous undertaking probably best started along the streams in Peru belonging to the Urubamba, Ucayali, Napo, Marañon, and Putumayo tributaries of the Amazon. And since the Napo, Marañon, and Putumayo also have branches initiating in Ecuador, this would cover the likely parts of western South America except Colombia.

Colombia divides naturally into three portions: the western part, drained by the Magdalena running north into the Caribbean; the northeast part, drained by the Meta and other Orinoco tributaries; and the southeast drained by the Caqueta and other Amazon tributaries. The land along all of these streams would need examining for early sites which, hopefully, would give evidence of Saladoid prototypes.

Whenever any Saladoid features are discovered among the artifacts of these intervening tribes, their positions should be plotted on suitable topographical maps. A study of these locations might reveal that they lie along river routes which could have served as migration paths leading to Saladero. Their extrapolation backward may then suggest potential origin sites. These centers could then be subjected to more intensive search for antecedents of Saladoid pottery.

4. My first choices of probable ancient Arawak living sites at which I would like to see excavations made would be the high banks of the Orinoco as follows (Map 6): (1) Between Boca del Pao and Santa Cruz de Orinoco, about fifty miles west of Ciudad Bolívar, where the tributaries Rio Pao, Rio Pino, and Rio Cabrutica enter. (2) At Las Bonitas, about two hundred miles west of Ciudad Bolívar, on the south bank, where the Rio Iguana and the Rio Aracay enter from the north. Ronquín, near Parmana, is only about five miles to the west, on the north side of the river. It was dug in 1943 by Howard and yielded Saladoid pottery with griddle sherds and should be redug for charcoal samples. (3) At Caicara, a few miles east of the entry of the Rio Apure, and also up the Apure to see if the Arawaks came down river from Colombia. (4) At La Urbana between the entry of the Rio Arauca and Rio Capanaparo. (5) And at Puerto Paez at the mouth of the Rio Meta, and up the Rio Meta with Venezuela on its left bank and Colombia on its right. This

might give weight to Colombia as a place of origin of manioc-growing Arawaks.

CHAPTER VI

1. Friends had told me of a fine collection of Arawak artifacts belonging to Miss Cecil Stevens in Puerto Rico, so I decided to visit her at her home in Hyde Park near San Juan. I found her to be a frail, gentle person with a sweet manner, becoming blind with cataracts and quite dependent on her companion, Miss Huber. But it was evident that she had once been a woman of vigor and resourcefulness. Over tea she said she had come to Puerto Rico right after the Spanish-American War in 1898 and was one of the first American women on the island. A teacher, she later became head of the school system. From the beginning, she had been interested in the Indian lore of Puerto Rico and had collected stones once used by the Borinquens, as the Arawak tribe of Puerto Rico was called.

Miss Huber handed the stones to Miss Stevens, who no longer could see well enough to find them, but as she held them her face lit up in recognition of each piece, her fingers reconstructing for her the story of its acquisition and the interpretation of its significance. It was obvious that she lavished affection on these stones, but there was no mawkish sentimentality involved, just a vivid recollection of the part each piece had played in her sixty years of collecting. "Everybody calls them 'Stevie's stones,' " Miss Huber explained. I inquired cautiously whether they were for sale. "Oh, I'm afraid not," Miss Huber said. "Stevie wouldn't want to part with them." Later Miss Stevens asked me about my own collections.

"I understand you send them on loan to various colleges in the States," she said. "Tell me something about this."

I explained that I had a dozen exhibitions travelling a circuit of colleges in the United States. Half of these were of contemporary paintings and sculpture and the remainder were collections of the art of earlier cultures. "Such as Chinese and Egyptian?" she asked. A collection of Chinese paintings, bronzes, and sculpture was at that time on the road, I told her, adding that the Egyptian material was mostly Coptic. "Do you charge the schools for the loan of the objects?" she wanted to know. I said we didn't, but appreciated having transportation and insurance costs met by borrowers able to afford it. She continued her questioning, particularly about our relationship with educational institutions. "But if you get no money from the schools, why do you send such valuable material to them?" she asked. I explained that I hoped to stimulate interest in esthetic and cultural material not ordinarily available to students, adding that I would also rather share the material than keep it hidden in a storeroom. Miss Stevens put her hand on my arm and there were tears in her eyes as she said, "Oh, my! And I have been so selfish all these years, keeping my stones in my own house! If you want my collection, you may have it." I made an inventory of the material and applied approximate appraisal to each of the better pieces, then offered her a sum which she seemed quite satisfied to accept.

I told her that part of the collection would be used to bring a knowledge of the Arawaks, in whom we were both so much interested, to the young men and women of our own United States, and that part would be set aside for circulation to acquaint the people living in the Caribbean with these early components of their own cultural heritage. Arawak exhibits that are shown either in the United States or in any of the islands bear reference to Miss Cecil Stevens.

2. The islands of the Lesser Antilles are volcanic, except Barbados which is geologically part of South America. The humpbacked zemi figure is therefore a common sight to anyone sailing the islands and familiar with the Arawak zemi concept.

3. The meticulous Ferdinand Colón (Columbus) had listed the manuscript *Historia de la Inuencion de las Yndias* in the card index of his library as coming from Pérez de Oliva in 1528 and relating to the life and works of Columbus. It was described as being in nine parts and the reference quoted a few words from the beginning and the ending of the book. The Yale copy is in nine parts and begins and ends with the same words, although with some very slight modification in spelling and word order, which Ferdinand himself may have made while preparing the card index.

Professor Arrom's book was published in Spanish in Bogota in 1965, and from it I learned that Pérez de Oliva was the rector of the University of Salamanca. He had translated Plato and other important books from Greek and Latin into Spanish. His stated purpose was to promote the use of Spanish as an adequate literary medium and he contended that recourse to Latin was no longer necessary. Professor Rouse recently told me that the material in the Pérez de Oliva manuscript stems back to a Spanish priest, Ramon Pané, who had been commissioned by Christopher Columbus, on his second voyage, to make a study of the Arawak religion, which had greatly intrigued him. Rouse pointed out that this was the first anthropological research in the New World. He said that Father Pané had carried out Columbus' order and produced a manuscript on Arawak religion. Unfortunately this manuscript disappeared, and until recently we have known it only through a summary made by Pedro Martir (or Martyr) de Angleria, through extracts published by Father Bartolome de las Casas, and through a complete transcript made

330

by Ferdinand and included in his biography of Admiral Don Christopher Columbus.

When Ferdinand died in 1539 his manuscript and that given him by his friend Pérez de Oliva were included in his library which he gave to the Cathedral of Seville. Both manuscripts disappeared from the Cathedral collection. Fortunately an Italian translation of Ferdinand's book had been made by Alfonso de Ulloa, published in 1571, and is still in existence. The Pérez de Oliva work was completely lost until the copy was found at Yale. Although known as early as 1528, it bears a date of 1583, which is the time when Pérez de Oliva's nephew, Ambrosia de Morales, made a collection of the works of his uncle. A comparison of the versions by Pérez de Oliva and Peter Martyr shows that Pérez de Oliva freely invented dialogue which he put into the mouths of the Indians. His style of writing is evidence of the debate current in Spain at that time as to whether or not the Indians were human beings. It is clear that Pérez de Oliva was on the side of those who believed that Indians were human and should be treated as such.

4. Atabeyra was undoubtedly a great favorite with the Arawaks since there were three more figures among the Stevens collection from Puerto Rico. One of these (Figure 116) is a splendid example of the sculptor's ability to convey monumentality in a small figure. The piece, only five inches tall, is a "Mutter Erde" type, carved from black basalt.

5. I asked Mr. Drinkwater, the owner, where he had found the piece, and he said he had stumbled upon it while working in his garden. He showed me the location, and within a few minutes I found several potsherds that were obviously Arawak, so it was an ancient site.

Drinkwater is a tall man, as are so many of the inhabitants of Barbuda. The island had been established by Lord Codrington, who owned sugar plantations in Antigua in the seventeenth century, as a breeding place for slaves. He must have selected magnificent specimens. At his death, he bequeathed the island to the slaves, making them free and independent. Barbuda has remained so continuously. There are few places in the world where people can be found more stalwart physically or more independent mentally. Mr. Drinkwater was typical.

6. In addition to the parrot grinder the Barker collection contained half a dozen other grinders which seemed to have strong stylistic affiliations. These include: Figure 117a, a frog grinder about the same size as the parrot, apparently made of the same kind of sandstone and possibly the work of the same sculptor; and Figure 117b, a similar grinder in the form of an animal which I am unable to identify. It may represent a man or a dog or even a turtle. The large number of these grinders suggests

Fig. 116. Monumental figure of Atabeyra (Puerto Rico).

that the grinding of narcotics may have been an important feature of shamanistic rituals.

7. Possibly used as votive offerings are the small pottery animals we occasionally find. They are clearly distinguishable from the animal heads that occur so frequently as handles for vessels, since there is no broken surface where the latter were attached to pots. These animals are obviously designed to stand on a flat surface and their small size, only one

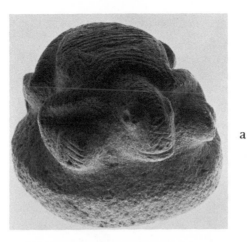

Fig. 117. Narcotic grinders in the form of a: frog and
b: dog (Trois Rivières, Haiti).

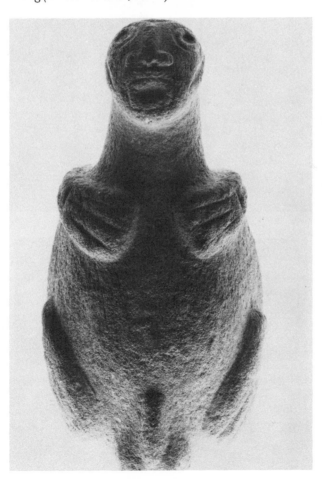

Fig. 118. Votive offerings. a: Dog. b: *Agouti.* c: *Bird.* d: *Monkey.* e: *Manatee.*

or two inches each, suggests their use as votive offerings. Typical are: Figure 118a, probably a dog; Figure 118b, perhaps an agouti; Figure 118c, a bird; Figure 118d, a monkey, probably a fetus; and 118e, a manatee, a much-sought Arawak food.

The next most numerous group of figures found at Cadet comprises fishes, many of which are rather easy to identify by anyone familiar with tropical waters; for example, an angel fish (Figure 119a) poised motionless as they are often seen on the reefs, with slightly turned tail. The fishes shown are possibly a grouper (Figure 119f), a killer whale (Figure 119b), a turtle (Figure 119c), and a shark (Figure 119e), but many are so stylized that I cannot identify them. These figures, I suggest, were votive offerings made by local fishermen from the nearby bay, now known as Port-de-Paix where fishing is still carried on.

8. The Paul Barker Haitian collection also contained two elegantly carved conch figures (Figure 35). I guessed that they might be dogs, but instead of standing upright on their hind legs, like the dog deity from Trois Rivieres (Figure 32), these are "sitting up," as dogs do when begging for food. The heads show typical dog features, although there is no evidence of the dentition as shown on the Antigua conch shell dog deity. A hole bored crosswise through the head of each shows these pieces to have been amulets. Perhaps the shaman occasionally visited a home where death had occurred, wearing the dog deity as a pendant to a necklace. This may have satisfied the needs of the family concerned with the whereabouts and status of the spirit of the immediately deceased.

CHAPTER IX

1. While on a photographic safari in East Africa, I called on Professor L. S. B. Leakey in Nairobi, briefly explaining my interest in Arawaks and offering him a small collection of Arawak artifacts, mostly tools, which he gladly accepted. He proceeded to show me some interesting things about the tools which I had not noticed but which his trained eye spotted immediately. One of the flints, he told me, was a knife with a serrated edge. When I expressed surprise he handed me a lens which immediately revealed the sawtooth edge. Picking up another piece of flint he showed me how the serrations could have been made. He held the thin-edged flint blade in one hand and nicked out a tiny piece with his thumbnail; then, with the nail of his index finger, he snapped out another micro-V-shaped notch. Alternating thumb and finger pressures, he quickly gave the whole length of the flint a sawtooth edge. Turning to me with a smile he commented that the Arawaks knew how to make the same kind of serrated edge that today's housewife likes for cutting bread. Looking at my safari schedule he pointed out that I would be only

Fig. 119. Votive offerings of fish. a: *Angel fish.* b: *Killer whale.* c: *Turtle.*
d: *Unidentified.* e: *Shark.* f: *Grouper.*

fifteen minutes' flight from Olduvai en route from Serengeti to Lake
Manyara, and kindly offered to have a Land Rover meet the plane and
bring me to the gorge. I could not have been more delighted.

Olduvai Gorge itself is a magnificent spectacle. It is thrilling to see
the upward sweep of two hundred feet of sedimentary deposits spanning
a major segment of man's evolution. Perhaps even more impressive is the
lowest layer, Bed I, showing habitation sites of earliest man nearly two
million years ago, where thousands of bones of long-extinct animals lie
exposed, bones of animals he had killed and eaten and then broken open
to extract the marrow. At that early period this was not a deep gorge
as we were now experiencing it, but a wide level plain bordering on a
lake which may have been the extension of what is now Lake Victoria,
the world's third largest inland body of water. Here the long struggle
of our ancestors against an ominous environment had taken place.

Soon I spotted a pebble chopper with a bifaced knife edge (Figure
48a) among a whole cluster of white fossil animal bones. The guide
handed me the piece, and as I held it I visualized Homo habilis chopping
his way into the hidebound package of protein of a small antelope he
had just caught. Then I realized that this was actually the site where
Zinjanthropus had been found. So perhaps this stone was a tool used
by one of those "ape men," near relatives of our ancestors. It made the

continuity of that long chain of evolutionary changes seem still more closely linked. The bones of Homo habilis had been found only a matter of yards away, so perhaps he had even lived in some kind of harmony with the man-ape Zinj and had built upon the results of the accumulated knowledge of those "near men." This stone tool might be a link connecting "ape man" with true man.

Professor Leakey had found some seven thousand of these stone choppers in the lowest level, Bed I, of the area excavated around the Zinjanthropus bones. It seemed like an enormous concentration of tools, perhaps even a tool factory, until he pointed out that the layer at which we were looking had been deposited over a period of more than one hundred thousand years. So the simultaneous activity of Zinj and Homo habilis in fabricating the same kind of chopper tools seemed to be quite possible.

I asked my guide to show me some Acheulean-Chellean-type hand axes which I recalled had been found in Bed IV, the top layer of the gorge. They were quite large, well designed, and well fabricated (Figure 48b, c).

Holding the earliest Bed I pebble chopper in one hand and the Bed IV hand ax in the other, the picture was vividly clear. It had taken almost one and a half million years for man to invent his way from the simple biface pebble chopper to the multifaceted hand ax. Even though the hand ax was admittedly a better tool, it did seem like an incredible length of time to effect such a small change. Yet if man had not made that crucial step of improvement, followed by thousands of similar steps, we would not have been able to send men to the moon. Nothing has ever given me such a vivid and sweeping picture of the incessant obstacles which frustrated our earliest ancestors. With almost infinite patience they had struggled to adjust themselves to a fantastically difficult, almost overpowering environment.

Homo habilis had picked up a pebble which fitted his small hand (he was only about four feet tall) and had cracked off a few chips in a minute or so to produce his hand chopper. Acheulean-Chellean man had taken perhaps an hour to flake his ax. An Arawak man probably took months to polish his stone petaloid celt. Just what functional advantage would these successive tools have had for developing man? The multifaceted Acheulean hand ax could slash its way through the hide of even an elephant, just as the pebble chopper of Zinj or Homo habilis could cut through an antelope. But the Acheulean pointed ax could also be used as a digging tool to extract roots from the ground much faster than could be done with fingernails. Man the hunter needed the carbohydrate food his arboreal ape and monkey predecessors had lived on, and roots provided the starch possibly better than any other type of food.

2. I have further divided the 29 per cent useful flints, separated from

Fig. 120. Flint cores and waste material (Mill Reef, Antigua).

the 71 per cent cores and waste materials (Figure 120), into eight categories as follows:

	Figure Number
15 per cent sharp-edged flints	
3 per cent knives and saws	67
5 per cent chisels	66a, b
7 per cent scrapers	66c
12 per cent sharp-pointed flints	
5 per cent projectile points	121a, b
7 per cent burins	68, 121c
2 per cent miscellaneous	
1 per cent hand choppers	71
0.5 per cent awls	122b
0.5 per cent draw knives	122a

Fig. 121. a: *Bird and fish spear-points.* b: *Manatee, turtle, or shark spear-points.* c: *Burins. (All Antigua.)*

Sharp-pointed flakes (Figure 121a, b, c) might serve as projectile points when attached to suitable rods, smaller ones (Figure 121a) being useful for spearing birds and fish. Sharp-pointed flakes too large for fish inside the coral reefs (Figure 121b) might serve as powerful spears for manatee, presumably plentiful in pre-Columbian days, or for sharks, turtles, etc. Many of these (Figure 121c) might be used as burins for cutting or engraving cavities in wood, shell, or stone. Of the 2 per cent miscellaneous flints, hand choppers (Figure 71) might have been used to cut up turtle or conch meat, or roots such as yams, or to sever strands of vines to make baskets. The draw knives (Figure 122a) have a sharp-edged, semicircular notch that could be drawn along a straight stick to convert it into a rod or spear shaft. Awls (Figure 122b) are self-explanatory since on each tool there is a long, sharp point which would be twisted like an awl or drill. Apparently awls were not so important to the Arawaks as to European man, who needed them for piercing holes for sewing or lacing furs and skin clothing for protection against the winters. Arawaks had no need for clothes.

339

Fig. 122. a (upper): *Draw knives.* b (lower): *Awls. (Both Antigua.)*

3. I found confirmation for my speculation about this technique of chiseling out short lengths of wood when I saw in the museum at Port of Spain, Trinidad, an ancient Arawak paddle that had been recovered undamaged from Pitch Lake in Trinidad (Figure 123a, b). The paddle was unfinished, and my guess is that an Arawak craftsman had split a log with wedges until he had a plank of suitable size. This was then shaped with chisels driven by hammer stones. What may be saw marks can be seen about an eighth of an inch deep, cut into the handle at intervals of about a quarter of an inch (Figure 123b). The saws could have been flint knife blades serrated as Professor Leakey showed me in Kenya. The ridges of wood remaining between the saw cuts had probably been removed by a chisel or small adze. I was told that the paddle

was of very hard wood, perhaps lignum vitae or purple heart, so the cross-cuts had been only a quarter of an inch apart to facilitate the chiseling.

4. The visit to Surinam had shown that present-day Arawaks live on about 80 per cent carbohydrates, mostly from manioc, and the numerous griddle sherds are compatible with a similar predominance of manioc in pre-Columbian days. The screening of the soil from the middens had made us aware of fish vertebrae, bird and mammal bones, but these were relatively small in quantity compared to the great masses of shells. True, the shells seemed much more numerous in some layers than in others, but this might have been just a chance result of where the bulky shells had been pitched after they had been cracked open and the meat extracted. Actually it was Professor Clayton Ray, the Harvard biologist, who had pointed out, to my embarrassment, that we had not been paying proper attention to these fish and other bones in our eager search for potsherds. So we began collecting all the bones we came across and were greatly aided by the generous labors of Professor Elizabeth Wing, of the Florida State Museum, who identified the animals from which the bones had come.

I was surprised to learn that among the food of the Arawaks there were so many rice rats, an animal of which I had not even heard. It is a large rodent, about the size of a rabbit, an aquatic animal possessing peculiar characteristics which permitted it to reach the islands from the mainland of South America. It could ride a floating log, going into a comatose state resembling the hibernation of bears and other animals. It remained in this state while the log drifted in the currents, possibly for several months. When the floating log bumped against the shore, the rice rat became alert, "jumped ship," and went ashore to take up habitation in a new land. The rice rat is still common in South America where it is regarded as a pest in the rice field, hence its name. But it is no longer found in Antigua. It may have been hunted to extinction by the Arawaks, as suggested by David R. Harris of the University of California, Berkeley. If there were any survivors they probably were destroyed by the ubiquitous mongoose, introduced by the planters.

The guinea pig bones were identified as belonging to *Cavia porcellus*. The only way this animal could have reached Antigua would seem to have been in the canoes of the Arawaks, presumably to be bred for food. Guinea pigs had been domesticated in Peru by the Incas, or earlier tribes. While visiting the restored fortress of Puruchuco, near Lima, I saw pens where guinea pigs had been raised in pre-Columbian days. It was said that the bones found there belonged to *Cavia cutleri*, but I have not been able to find how *Cavia porcellus* differs from *C. cutleri*. It is another hint of a possible early linkage of Arawaks with Peru.

a

b

341

Fig. 123. a: *Wooden paddle (Pitch Lake, Trinidad).* b: *Close-up of handle.*

The only other pre-Columbian land mammal known to have been on several of the islands is the agouti, *Dasyprocta agouti*. The agouti, like the rice rat, is about the size of a rabbit. It is a night-feeding forest animal, living on nuts, fruit, roots, and leaves, which probably accounts for its being regarded as good eating. Quite plentiful in Guyana bush villages, it is a common pet of Amerind children, which suggests that it might have been brought to the islands by the Arawaks and bred for food.

In a similar manner monkeys may have been brought to the islands by the Arawaks from South America. To this day they are a prized item of food by Amerinds in the Guyanas. In Grenada they became so well established that hunting parties have to be arranged periodically to keep them from becoming too serious a menace to agriculture. Presumably monkeys were not brought to Antigua since none of their bones have been found in the middens. It is said that on islands where monkeys live there are no parrots, because monkeys diligently seek out the parrot eggs. The chroniclers mention no monkeys on Hispaniola, so there probably weren't any. It will be recalled that when Columbus landed at Guanahani the Arawaks presented him with parrots, and this plentiful supply of parrots is consistent with the absence of monkeys.

Bird bones are not so frequent as fish or mammal bones and comprise mainly the Audubon shearwater (which I have never seen on Antigua shores) and the dove. Perhaps they were more difficult to catch. Birds may have been brought down by slingshot (Figure 124) since round pebbles and even small pottery spheres are found in the middens. I was told in Surinam that Arawaks are so skillful with the sling that they can hit a flying bird three times out of five. Unfortunately, I never witnessed the performance.

Iguana bones belong to *Iguana delicatissima*, whose name suggests it is a tasty food, and I regret never having had an opportunity to try it.

The green turtle, *Chelonia mydas*, was probably as welcome to the Arawaks as it is to us since it is excellent meat. Today the native fishermen throw a net over a swimming turtle, but the Arawaks had an ingenious way of catching them. Noting that the remora or suckerfish, *Echeneis naucrates*, attached itself to the body of a shark or other larger fish by means of a suction disk in its head, the Arawaks caught, fed, and tamed the remora, training it to tolerate a light cord fastened to its tail and gill frame. When a turtle was sighted the remora was released. Immediately it swam to the turtle, attaching its suction disk to the under side of the carapace. The canoe followed the turtle, the Arawak angler holding a firm line on the remora which, in turn, held tightly to its quarry until the turtle could be gaffed or tied to the canoe. The remora was then suitably rewarded. While snorkeling among the reefs I have

Fig. 124. Stone slingshot (bolas) from Haiti.

seen a remora "taking a ride" on a fish such as a big blue parrot fish. The remora was accepted or even welcomed by the other fish for removing crustaceans from their skin.

Forty-one species of fish were found, by far the greatest quantity of bones belonging to the coral feeders—parrot and surgeonfish—accounting for 63 per cent of individuals found. Another 20 per cent of bones were of carnivores—groupers, snapper, crevalli, etc.—but a goodly number of barracuda and shark bones also were present. The barracuda were small, hinting that the Arawaks might have had the experience that fish poisoning (ciguatera) is more likely with larger carnivores.

5. Summarizing the findings given in *Vertebrate Remains from Indian Sites in Antigua, West Indies*, by Elizabeth S. Wing, Charles A. Hoffman, Jr., and Clayton E. Ray (Carib. S. Sci. 8(3–4) Sept.–Dec. 1968), the relative abundance of animal bones found at Mill Reef is:

Fishes:	coral feeders—parrot and surgeonfish	829
	grouper, snapper, crevalli, etc.	252
	barracuda, shark, gar	137
	others	76
		1294
Mammals:	rice rat	257
	agouti	36
	others	17
		310
Birds:	Audubon shearwater	117
	dove	14
	others	18
		149
Reptiles:	iguana	48
	turtles	31
	others	11
		90

6. That these whorls were used for making twine for nets and lines rather than thread for weaving into clothes is adduced from the statements of Columbus that the natives were naked, and also from the fact that after examining thousands of sherds with a lens I have seen no imprints of woven cloth, as would most likely be the case if women potters had worn a garment while shaping or smoothing a vessel held in the lap. Fibers for making thread or cord could have been readily obtained from the seed of wild cotton or from the leaves of the dagger plant.

7. I recalled the lessons I had learned so vividly at Olduvai Gorge, that it had taken one and a half million years for the bifacial or pointed pebble choppers (Figure 48a) of Homo habilis in Bed I to evolve into the Acheulean-type of faceted hand ax (Figure 48b) in Bed IV—an almost incredibly long time for such a small change in an artifact.

But perhaps this is not proper reasoning. These vast stretches of time are possibly only significant when we are considering the basic steps in the progress of the genus Homo. They are probably not applicable to the local developments of individual tribes. Nevertheless, the migration of Mongoloids across the Bering Bridge was a major movement of Homo sapiens. Even though many anthropologists appear to favor the end of the Wisconsin glaciation as the period of the heaviest transfer of people from Asia, there is a sufficient number of artifacts that date back to

15,000 B.C. or earlier to suggest important transfers of men from Asia during the various interstadials of the Wisconsin ice stage. Moreover, pebble tools of the Oldowan or Abbevillian styles have been found scattered over most of Asia, including Mongolia, more than a hundred thousand years before the Wisconsin glaciation. The more developed Acheulean bifaced hand axes and a wide repertory of flint tools had been diffused throughout Asia by the time of the first Wisconsin era, about 60,000 B.C. Man, therefore, came to America whenever that may have been, with an extensive system of flint and stone techniques, though possibly without knowledge of grinding or polishing. Hence we need not be puzzled about there being men in Trinidad about 200 B.C. with an adequate know-how for making flint blades and simple stone axes, adzes, and chisels.

8. The Caribs are said to have told the Spaniards that they had arrived in the islands only "a short time" earlier. The Arawaks confirmed this by talking about the terrible Caribals (a Spanish word slurred into "cannibals") who had recently attacked them so brutally. It will be recalled that Columbus found Arawaks being eaten on Guadeloupe, perhaps indicating that the occupation of Guadeloupe was still underway in 1493, or that the Arawaks captured on other islands were brought to Carib headquarters in Guadeloupe. Furthermore, unpolished stone axes are particularly prevalent in St. Vincent, Guadeloupe, and St. Lucia, all of which were Carib strongholds.

9. Allegedly there is one exception to this statement, namely a very fine hafting ax attributed to Antigua, although no specific provenance can be assigned to it since the original owner is no longer alive. It is on loan to the Old Mill Museum at Mill Reef, lent by Dr. Zoltan Wisinger, of St. Johns, Antigua. It is an amazing specimen, a splendid example of matte-surfaced ax (Figure 125) with well developed lugs for applying cordage, such as might be made from fiber-producing plants like the dagger plant (*Agave karatto*) or the yucca. These lugs are the type generally described as the "crested bird head," and the name fits this ax. Even the bird's eye is incised. In addition it has a strange and, as far as I know, unique triangular perforation. I have suggested that this opening may have had an animistic significance—to let the spirits fly through. Undoubtedly the Arawak ax-wielder found it a very slow and tedious task to fell a tree even with the aid of fire. Perhaps he attributed this difficulty to the presence of spirits who had chosen the tree as their abode and resented the destruction of their house, so did all in their power to thwart the efforts of the woodsman. However, the resident spirits recognized the magic of the triangular hole and accepted it as a proper means to effect their escape.

Fig. 125. Stone ax with crested bird lugs and triangular opening.

10. Knowing that St. Vincent was the home of some of the finest matte-surfaced axes, I visited the island but found no place where they might have been made. We had to cross a rough channel to the neighboring

Fig. 126. These stone pieces fall into the "problematical objects" category (Puerto Rico).

small island of Bequia before we found an ancient ax "factory," consisting of deep grooves in a rock at the edge of the sea. It was not hard to envision the tedious back-and-forth rubbing of the ax blade in one of the grooves, while every couple of minutes a wave gently washed over the rock clearing the grooves of rock dust.

I wondered why the factory was in such an isolated spot rather than on the main island of St. Vincent where so many stone axes and "problematical stones" are found. Perhaps these axes were secretly made, which could account for a slow progress of the techniques through the islands. Axes may have been made in the Bequia factory for a couple of hundred years before the Caribs arrived and killed off the Arawak men, not only on St. Vincent but on other islands, thus effectively shutting off diffusion of the stone ax concept to the Greater Antilles.

Collectors and students of Arawak artifacts are familiar with the strange carved stones found at a small village on Fancy River, on the northernmost coast of St. Vincent. Fancy has throughout historic times been in Carib country, so the artifacts are almost invariably called "Carib stones"—or, more cautiously, "problematical objects," because many of them are exceedingly difficult to identify. From my own collection I could add several examples of carved stones which fall into the category of "problematical objects." I have no explanation for the three pieces shown in Figure 126. They are intriguing examples of stone sculpture, but do not fit into the context of any Arawak activities with which I am acquainted. The piece in Figure 127, I am guessing, might have had something to do with puberty rites. It could possibly have been used for deflowering virgins, and if there is any merit in this suggestion it may be related to two of the problematical objects from Fancy illustrated by J. Walter Fewkes, in his book *A Prehistoric Island Culture Area of America* (Smithsonian Institution, 1912–13, Plates 26–E and 52–B).

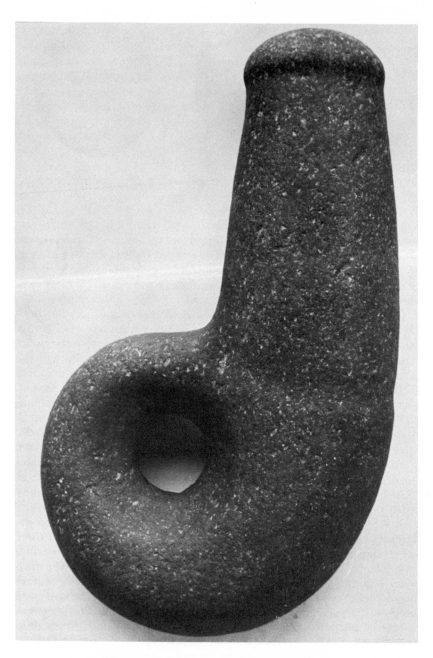

Fig. 127. Puberty rite stone (Puerto Rico).

Chapter X

1. Fewkes puzzled about the use of these "horse collars" and listed half a dozen theories which he considered to be the "most reasonable": (1) insignia of office worn on the person; (2) sacrificial objects; (3) idols for animal worship—serpents, lizards; (4) idols for tree worship, especially yuca; (5) to assist in childbirth—representation of female organ of generation; (6) collars for men and women dragging canoes. Fewkes inclines "to combine the third and fourth theories as the nearest approach to a correct interpretation of the stone collar."

2. The stone belts for the Arawak game are of two sizes: one, about fifteen pounds, usually known as a "slender" belt; and the other, about fifty pounds, called "massive" (Figure 81). That the fifteen-pounder could have been used in actual play was acceptable, but it was hard to believe that a man, however vigorous, could engage in a violent game weighted down by a fifty-pound belt. To test their practicability, several belts—both slender and massive—were taken to the Yale University gymnasium. There the famous swimming coach, the late Robert Kiphuth, had his young athletes try them in a simulated game, using a modern basketball instead of the Arawak solid-rubber ball and striking it with the projecting knob of the stone belt. After a few minutes of play, one athlete said that the sweat on his thumb made a suction-tight fit in the oval-shaped cup of his "slender" belt which greatly helped him to guide the belt in hitting the ball.

Moreover, a man wearing one of the fifty-pound belts did not find it uncomfortable riding on his hips. Indeed, the heavy belt gave him a feeling of unexpected stability when positions close to the floor had to be taken to hit a low bouncing ball, probably because the added weight lowered his center of gravity. Presumably these heavy belts were used by backfield players who could make a shot from either the right or left side because of the two large protuberances. Such shots would be used to drive the ball (estimated at six to eight inches in diameter and about six to ten pounds weight) a much greater distance than could be effected by a blow with shoulder or elbow. The slender belts had their single knob placed differently for use by right or left wing players. Thus the Arawak stone belts were probably used in active play rather than for ceremonial usage because several fragments of Arawak belts exhibit ancient broken surfaces. These belts are carved from tough igneous rock and presumably were broken in accidents occurring either when players came into violent collision or when they made a flying leap to strike a low bouncing ball and crashed to the ground. Several broken pieces of Arawak belts have been unearthed during systematic excavation of Puerto Rican ball courts and nearby middens. Both the fragments and whole belts show signs of considerable abrasion, such as might result when players slid along the ground to make shots.

In addition to the stone belts, the Arawaks had L-shaped stones which fitted over the elbow and were fastened to the upper arm and forearm by thongs passing over grooves in the stone. It is easy to imagine the added force that could be applied to the ball by this sturdy protective elbow stone. That such stones were also used in actual play is deduced from finding whole elbow stones as well as fragments during excavations of ball courts. No elbow stones have been found in Mexico; as of now they are classed as uniquely Arawakan.

3. The principal authors who have discussed the Amerind ballgame (see Bibliography) are: Theodore Stern, F. J. S. Grace, Gordon Ekholm, Stephan F. de Borhegyi, and Ricardo E. Alegria.

4. Professor Enrique J. Palacios, in his *Architectural Guide to Chichén Itzá* (Secy. Publication, Mexico, 1935), does not accept the story that it was the losing captain who was decapitated. "One must remember," he says, "that the deity of the earth also symbolized Vegetation, that is, Agriculture. Sumptuously clad, the victim is shown decapitated in such a way that his blood bathes the disk. Seven serpents are shown, but these are clearly not Plumed Serpents (Quetzalcoatl) but Serpents of Blood (Ezcouatl) . . . . The ceremony is a plea for abundant crops, and since the Ball Game represented the movements of the Sun, and the Sun was recognized as master of the crops, this offering of man's most precious possession, his blood, was properly represented on the Ball Court."

This suggestion that the ball represents the movements of the sun is intriguing. Could it be that the stone rings tenoned into the wall at Chichén Itzá also signify the earth, which is shown as a disk in the bas reliefs? If so, the ball could then be the sun, and the supreme act of the players would be to make the sun penetrate the ring, thus fertilizing Mother Earth perfectly. To accomplish this end man puts forth his greatest effort, even to the giving of his life, as exemplified by the spurting streams of blood.

5. In Aztec days warfare probably developed from the accelerating need for sacrificial victims to meet the demands of a priesthood engulfed in the necessity of propitiating deities who, they said, would respond only to an ever increasing flow of human hearts and blood. No blood, no rain. No hearts, no full ears of maize. To keep up the supply of victims raids on neighboring tribes became essential. But it was a two-way invasion. Neighboring tribes had an equal need for blood. In one sense, this system of punitive slaughter was effective, since fewer mouths to feed was equivalent to a richer harvest.

6. Play is common to both men and animals. Most animals exhibit playfulness and even casual observation reveals their sense of decorum and rules. On safari in East Africa I saw lion cubs wrestling, biting, and pounding one another, but always short of drawing blood or damaging eyes. If a cub got too rough, the lioness-umpire would administer a sound cuff as penalty. So man's playfulness frequently seems like an extension of animal play. The jumping and scampering become a dance. The dance evolves into a ritual. The game and the ritual may eventually become a major part of a religion.

The priest or shaman of ancient tribes undoubtedly recognized that games were an intimate and natural expression of the people and gradually incorporated them into the religious practices, or even inserted the rituals into the games.

Some phases of the Arawaks at play are described by the early chroniclers who saw them in Hispaniola, decorated with paint and feathers, dancing while drums were beaten and conchs blown. Frequently the Arawaks engaged in such activities for the sheer joy of participating in boisterous, rhythmic exercise, just as young people have done through the ages. When the dances were part of a ritual the Spanish writers referred to them as *arietos.*

In much of this Arawaks and other Amerinds did not differ markedly from tribes in other parts of the world, but in one of their activities they were unique. They played a game with a rubber ball several hundred years before a rubber ball was known to Europeans. Indeed, it was not until about two hundred years after Columbus that a rubber ball was used by Europeans. Whenever I make this statement I am challenged by people who think back to early ballgames of which they have read— Drake finishing his game while the Spanish Armada was off Plymouth; Henry V who, as young Prince Hal, played tennis and received a gift of tennis balls from the sneering Dauphin; Odysseus returning to consciousness after being cast ashore from a shipwreck and spying on the lovely Nausicaa playing with a ball. I have no idea what kind of ball Nausicaa played with, but it certainly was not rubber. Drake probably played with a wooden ball, and the tennis balls of Prince Hal were most likely cork and wool wrapped with fine twine. No rubber was used in Europe until the end of the eighteenth century. Moreover, the first rubber of commerce came from India and was called "India rubber" because it was used to rub out pencil or other marks.

7. These Codices are picture books, prepared by Mayan and other Amerind authors in pre-Columbian times. Although the Maya invented the concept of zero and were sufficiently advanced in astronomy to develop a calendrical system more accurate than our own Julian calendar, they did not devise an alphabetic form of writing. In these Codices

glyphs are used to denote the names of people, but for numerical data they had an orderly arrangement of dots and dashes. The stories of people, places, and events were painted pictorially on a long strip, folded accordian-wise into a book about eight by ten inches.

The Maya books were made of *amatl* (Fig bark) paper, coated with a gessolike base upon which the clear, brilliant pictures were painted in panels from left to right to denote sequence of events, somewhat in the manner of our own comic strips. When one side was completed the strip was turned over and the reverse painted. Aztec Codices were also amatl paper, but the Mixtec books were painted on animal skin, perhaps tanned deer hide. Some of the Aztec texts read from right to left.

Early members of Cortes's invading forces commented on the vast number of books existing at that time. Many "libraries" were destroyed at the sacking of Tenochtitlan, and, equally distressing, Bishop de Landa ordered that all such "pagan" writings in Yucatan be gathered and burned. About a dozen of these books remain, only three of them in the Mayan language. They are now stored in important libraries and facsimiles have been made. Scholars have made partial translations, a few published in English.

The running series of pictures depict a wide range of events. In several, the Mixtec and Aztec for example, each individual was identified by a name-glyph; but the Maya Codices related to gods and cult heroes rather than to mortals. The drawing was meticulous, in keeping with established conventions, and though facial features were not depicted to show personal likeness it was essential to use the correct form of status symbols, such as headgear, nose or ear ornaments, which applied to each individual. Costumes were altered to indicate whether the wearer was at war, traveling, or performing some ritual. Towns, mountains, rivers, and roads were given general stylized shapes, but the place-name glyph was added so the location could be identified.

The Codices are certainly not easy reading since every symbol must be recognized and properly translated. But since conventions were adhered to strictly there is usually relatively little ambiguity. Every hand and finger position is significant, and a vast assemblage of equipment must be recognized as to shape, color, and position. Whenever I have made the effort to follow recent scholarly commentators through the detailed description of each page, I have felt definitely rewarded, even when the commentary was in Spanish, French, or German and therefore involved double translation. I have developed great admiration for the painstaking skill not only of the original painters of the Codices, but also of the specialist interpreters.

The first two such Codices to reach Europe were given by Moctezuma to Cortes, who sent them with jewels and other articles from Vera Cruz on July 10, 1519, to Charles V of Spain.

The Florentine Codex is perhaps the most famous of the Aztec Codices: Fray Bernadino de Sahagun's extensive *General History of the Things of New Spain*, written in parallel columns of Spanish and phonetic Aztec and copiously illustrated by Aztec artists. The Aztec ballgame is called Tlachtli; its amusement aspect is stressed and the following reason given for engaging in the sport:

The ruler, when he beheld and knew that the common folk and vassals were very fretful, then commanded that the game be played, in order to animate the people and divert them. He commanded the major-domo to take out the rubber ball, and the girdles, and the leather hip guards, and the leather gloves with which the ruler's ball players were dressed. And things were arranged on the ball court; there was sprinkling, there was sanding, there was sweeping. And all that the ruler was to wager in the game—the valued capes, the duck feather capes, the costly breech clouts, the green stone lip plugs, the golden ear plugs, the green stone necklaces, the golden necklaces, the wrist bands with precious green stones upon them, and all the precious capes and bedding—the major-domo brought out and placed in the ball court . . . and all that the poor folk placed for the ruler were old capes like those the vassals wore.

Plate 91 of this Florentine Codex pictures an H-shaped court with a ring on each side wall. Two players are actively posturing and the large black rubber ball is in motion. In spite of the fact that the major-domo was ordered to provide hip-guards, girdles (yokes?), and gloves, the players are not wearing them. Perhaps the artist, feeling crowded for space, omitted these pieces of equipment because any Aztec looking at the picture would know that they would be worn. Their omission is a pity, since this is the only picture in any of the Codices that shows the actual playing of the game. All other scenes show ceremonial use of the ball court.

In the Codex Borgia there are seventy-five pictures and in four of these ball courts are shown. In one of these (Figure 128a) an H-shaped court, the fierce Aztec god, Texcatlipoca, occurs in his two forms, the figure at left of the court is the day deity, the one at right is the night deity. Texcatlipoca in his night form is heavily equipped. On his back are his shield, quiver of atlatl darts, and pennant. On his right forearm he carries his hip-guard made of jaguar skin, so obviously he has not yet started to play. Texcatlipoca, on the left, the day god also carries his hip-guard in his right hand and holds the ball with which they will play the game. Each figure gestures with clenched hand from which the thumb and index finger point directly at the opponent. But the game presumably cannot begin until they remove some of the impedimenta and don at least their hip-guards.

In the center a naked figure is being slain (Figure 128a). The obsidian

Fig. 128. a: *Codex Borgia: ballgame between god of day* (left) *and god of night* (right). b: *Codex Borgia: day god* (left) *victorious over night god* (right).

knife has penetrated his breast from which blood spurts copiously. Directly in front of the victim is a large rubber ball being drenched liberally with his blood. The ball, which must be sanctified by blood before it is fit for use by the gods, is held in the coil of a serpent which, from the shape of its tail, seems to be a rattlesnake. Below the ball is the victim's heart. The court, like the one at Chichén Itzá, is equipped with two rings shown above and below the victim.

The night deity is depicted as black and much larger than the day deity, to indicate that he will win this particular game, bringing on the darkness of night. In Figure 128b Texcatlipoca on the left is now the day god, is larger and has red bars on his face. He is already the victor of the game. Morning has come. Here the successful day god is discharging a bolt of lightning which shatters a large tree and startles a vulture roosting in the branches. The advance of the day is symbolized by the progress of the red deity whose striding across the morning hours is indicated by footprints on the path. The day deity is also shown as the merchant or provider whose pack-sack is filled with goods for distribution to the people.

These Codices not only give information about the ceremonial significance of the game, but also illustrate some of its accessories. We get confirmation of the shape of the court and an idea of the relative size of the ball. The importance of hitting the ball with the hip is indicated by the frequency with which the leather hip-guard is shown being carried by the players. Otherwise, the Spanish chroniclers are vague about the nature of either the Mexican or the Arawak game. They certainly were not sportswriters and they leave us with a very limited picture of the actual mechanics of play.

I am still puzzled about the manner of serving. The only hint I have found is that a flat stone was inserted in the center of some of the playing alleys. It may be that the game was started by the "umpire" dropping or bouncing the lively ball on this stone plate, the contestants then putting the ball into play with elbow, hip, etc. I saw such a stone in the court in Copán in Honduras and was told it was a *botadero*, a hitting stone. The court at Monte Alban has a similar stone at its center.

Before the rings such as those at Chichén Itzá became popular, the object of the game apparently was to keep the ball moving from player to player as long as possible. Fray Diego Duran, a Spanish padre in Mexico and one of the few eyewitness observers, says that the game was played with such dexterity that, on occasion, the ball remained in flight from one end of the court to the other for a whole hour without a shot being missed. This sounds like volley ball or even lawn tennis, but with an unbelievably long interval of play for a single point. Possibly the ball was lobbed more in the earlier game the Mayans called Pok-ta-Pok than in lawn tennis, where smashing drives tend to make more balls unplayable.

Commenting on this hour-long play for a single point, Fray Duran states that in Mexico the ball was hit only with the knees and the buttocks and not (as in the Arawak game described by Oviedo) with elbow, shoulder, and head. So the techniques of the game apparently varied with the locale where it was played.

However, Fray Duran clearly indicates the fun character of the sport when he describes games in which "a great multitude of nobles and gentlemen took part, and they played with much contentment and joy." From time to time others would enter the field to replace those leaving, so all might have an opportunity "to enjoy the pleasure of the game, and were so content with the play that the sun would go down before they knew of it." This was obviously not the kind of game where the losing captain was decapitated.

The old padre was apparently an aficionado with an eye for the finer plays, for he says, "Some were so outstanding in playing the game and made so many elegant moves that it was worth seeing; and I will especially relate one which I saw done by Indians who had practiced it. When they saw the ball in the air coming toward them, they were so quick in leaping toward it and timing precisely the moment at which to give a sharp thrust with their knees or buttocks that they returned the ball with extraordinary velocity. With these blows they suffered great damage on the knees and the thighs, so that those who used these trick shots too much got their haunches so mangled that they had to have the accumulations of clotted blood cut out with a small knife." This, of course, was the reason for the knee and thigh pads.

Moreover, fatalities were frequent. Fray Duran relates that "some were carried dead out of the place, and the reason was that as they ran after the ball from one end of the court to the other, tired and out of breath, they would leap in the air in order to reach it first before the others, and if the ball should hit them in the pit of the stomach they fell to the ground and some of them died instantly."

8. It is currently the practice among anthropologists to refer to the migration and diffusion routes in the circum-Caribbean area as being H-shaped. The west vertical of the H connects Mexico with Colombia and Peru. The east vertical joins the Antilles with the Amazonian regions. The horizontal of the H covers a wide band comprising the region between the northern coastline of South America and a rather diffuse east-west line through the entanglements of the Amazon and Orinoco drainage basins. It seems likely that the two vertical routes—the Peru to Mexico and the Venezuela to the Greater Antilles—may have been

independent. I know of no definite evidence of any diffusion of the ball-game from Mexico to the Greater Antilles.

9. The ballgame was played also in the southwestern United States. The Hohokam culture and the ball court at Snaketown, Arizona, have been described in several technical papers by Professor Emil W. Haury, of the University of Arizona, and illustrated in color in an article by him in the May, 1967 issue of the *National Geographic* magazine. Presumably the game as played in Arizona was diffused from Mayan sources through Nayarit and played up the west coast of Mexico. The use of high-banked walls bearing wicker rings at Snaketown suggests a game similar to the Yucatan version.

The possible persistence of techniques of the original ballgame into modern versions of other North American games should not be overlooked. For example, lacrosse was originally an Amerind game with points scored when the ball crossed the opponent's back line. In lacrosse this is now a space of six feet, called a goal and designated by a frame of posts. The rubber ball is carried or thrown by a racket shaped like a bishop's crozier, as long as the player is able to retain possession of the ball. He may pass it to a teammate, who accepts it only by use of his lacrosse stick. The opponents, of course, strive to obtain the ball at every moment with their own sticks. Lacrosse, therefore, bears some relationship to the ballgame depicted in the Nayarit model (Figure 88), except that a racket is the propelling medium instead of the shoulder, elbow, hip, and knee. Lacrosse, as any player or spectator knows, is a very fast and exciting game.

In a paper prepared in 1954, F. J. S. Grace gathered and interpreted the scanty data on the techniques of the ballgame as given by the early chroniclers. He compared these rules of play with those of the various ballgames that have been preserved in Mexico and played there within the past fifty years. His reasoning was that the ballgame as played recently, especially in more remote localities, might contain relics of the rules of the original game. For example, Grace selected the first description of the Arawak game, Batey, as given in 1535 by Oviedo, and adds: "One side serves, putting the ball into the air; waits until some player on the other side strikes it, whereupon whoever is nearest of the serving side plays it, and so it continues with the utmost activity. The object is to put the ball across the other side's back line. Play continues until the ball rolls along the ground, whether due to poor timing by a player, or failure to make the ball bounce, or, there being no player near enough, the ball dies or stops by itself. This constitutes a point [presumably against the side in whose territory the ball goes dead] and the side now serves which had previously received. So the game continues until the score agreed upon at the beginning of the game."

This Arawak game seems to be similar to volley ball, or even a little like lawn tennis without rackets, in that the ball is hit into the opponents' territory on each play, then back to the other team until either the player fails to return it, the ball goes dead, or is driven past the opponents' base line. There was, of course, no net, and only occasionally is reference made to a center line dividing the court into halves.

Grace compares this ancient Arawak game with several forms of pelota as played in Mexico in recent years. They involve variations in rules of penalties and scoring based upon a plan of serving a ball by striking it with the hand so as to cross a central line and being returned by the opposing team, whose players hit the ball only by hand, either on the fly or after one bounce. In broad terms, the modern pelota resembles lawn tennis, except that the hand is used instead of a racket and a center line replaces the net.

10. Many years ago I acquired a beautiful large stela from a New York dealer who said it came from Teotihuacan and was a Tlaloc monument (Figure 129a). It has attracted the attention of hundreds of visitors, including several distinguished scholars of pre-Columbian art, many of whom have expressed their delight at this beautiful piece of abstract sculpture.

Professor George Kubler examined the stela on various occasions and recently brought to my attention an article ("The Teotihuacan Stela from La Ventilla," by Luis Aveleyra Arroyo de Anda, Museo Nacional de Anthropologia, Mexico, 1963) covering an important discovery made in February, 1963, during excavations at Teotihuacan. It described a handsome carved stone stela dug at the Ventilla ranch on the southeast boundary of Teotihuacan. The significance of this monument was not clear until the murals of Tlalocan, at the nearby site of Tepantitla, were examined. Tlalocan, as Sahagun tells us in the Florentine Codex, was the site of "the earthly paradise where the souls of the dead rejoice and have comfort and no sorrow whatever." High among these joys was the ballgame, and one of the murals, though fragmentary, gives a vivid idea of the game. Each player carried a bat with which to strike the ball, the only indication I have come across where sticks were used in a Mexican ballgame. Professor Kubler estimates that this mural dates about A.D. 300, which suggests that hitting the ball with a bat may have been an earlier stage than the elaborate technique of striking it with the hips. It adds one more indication of the wide variation in playing styles that occurred over a considerable space of time and geographical range—especially if we are justified in considering the Mexican, the Arawakan, and the South American tribal methods of play as being variations of the same general type of ballgame.

But the mural shows something else that is perhaps more important.

358

At each end of the court there is a stone boundary marker quite similar to the Teotihuacan stela. Both the marker depicted in the mural at Tepantitla and the actual stela from La Ventilla have a large disk at the top with a ring of carved feathers, such as are frequently found on statues of the rain god, Tlaloc. The Teotihuacan stela is almost certainly a marker for locating the goal line of a ball court. That stela now graces the anthropological museum in the gardens of Chapultepec Park in Mexico City.

At the museum there is also a pottery disk showing in strong relief the face of Tlaloc surrounded by the same ring of feathers (Figure 129b), and described as part of a ball-court marker. It took only one glance at this ceramic specimen to recognize its close resemblance to the design on the stone disk forming the top element of the stela which, for many years, has had the place of honor at the entrance to my small museum in Guilford, Connecticut. This "three-eyed" Tlaloc stone with fierce jaguar mouth and a crown of feathers is evidently an ancient Teotihuacan ball-court marker.

CHAPTER XI

1. The shrub is *Lonchocarpus nicou*, a member of the senna family. The shredded material contains a poison which temporarily desensitizes the locomotor nerves of a fish so that it is unable to swim and therefore suffocates from lack of oxygen. One of the interesting taboos of this fishing process was that women were not allowed to participate in poisoning the water, possibly because of the widespread ancient belief that their menses were equally poisonous.

2. Another pain-relieving practice used by the Amerinds is the chewing of coca leaves (*Erythroxylon coca*). Two hundred species of Erythroxylon are known in the tropics and four species are indigenous to Puerto Rico and other parts of the Antilles. The coca leaves contain several other alkaloids in addition to cocaine, which are only released by the chemical action of the lime which is chewed with the leaves. Their joint effect is a desensitizing against pain, relief from hunger, and a marked increase in ability to perform hard work.

3. Not only has the word "hammock" been taken into our language from the Arawaks, but the hammock itself was adopted by many of the navies of the world after the Spaniards learned its use from the Arawaks and saw how little space it occupied in their tiny cabins.

4. These duhos are elegantly carved seats and attributes of the rank of the owner. I was exceedingly fortunate in securing a fine example

a

b

Fig. 129. a: *Ball-court marker showing face of Tlaloc, the rain god, with ring of feathers. From Teotihuacán, Mexico (collection of author).* b: *Pottery disk showing face of Tlaloc surrounded by ring of feathers, once part of a ball-court marker (Teotihuacán Museum, Mexico).*

(Figure 65c) from a cave discovered in 1957 on the island of Gonave in the Gulf of Gonaïves, Haiti. It shows some signs of decay after more than five hundred years of existence and its heaviness indicates it was made of some specially dense wood.

5. The turtle bowl (Figure 130) was assembled from numerous sherds. The finding of the head gave the clue to the nature of the bowl, but it was only after weeks of sorting, selecting, and finally of making several mock-up bowls of plasticine, to which were attached the sherds of the same thickness, color, and texture, that I realized the broadly incised grooves comprised the front and back flippers of a turtle. The small

361

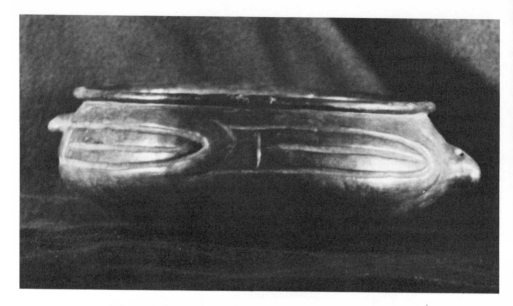

Fig. 130. Ceramic turtle bowl, ca. A.D. 800 (Antigua).

stubby tail was the item which completed the identification. The turtle bowl is a splendid example of pottery showing Barrancoid influence. It came from a layer of a Mill Reef site that yielded charcoal of A.D. 750. Turtles are still highly prized meat by the natives and visitors alike. The elegant turtle design was not merely for decoration, but to provide an attractive habitation for the spirits of slain turtles, which would presumably be content to occupy this turtle form and not seek revenge upon the slayer.

6. The basket with four wooden legs and a lid (Figure 131), was the gift of the Prime Minister of Guyana, the Honorable Forbes Burnham, who had spent his honeymoon at Mill Reef early in 1967. It is of modern fabrication, but preserves the tradition of ancient Arawak tribes. In olden times it was found only in the hut of the cacique of the tribe and contained cassava "cakes" to be offered to visitors.

7. Cassiere wine, or more accurately beer, is made from cassava. A group of older women gather in the afternoon and sit around a large earthenware jar. Each chews a piece of cassava bread, and when thoroughly mixed with saliva the charge is accurately spit into the jar. This is the occasion for neighborly women to chat. The mass in the jar ferments for two or three days and is then ready to drink. The alcohol content is lower than our beer, but it is drunk in quantities that produce

Fig. 131. Basket with four legs and a lid. Kept in chieftain's house and contains cassava cakes for visitors (contemporary Arawak from Guyana).

various degrees of intoxication. I have witnessed the operation of making the beer in jungle villages in Surinam, but so far I have not had the courage to taste the brew. In Peru and Ecuador the drink is called *chicha* and is made in the same manner, but using corn bread or crushed maize instead of cassava.

8. The present city of Arecibo preserves the name of the ancient cacique Arasibo.

9. There is no dowry paid by the father of the bride. Instead the suitor must furnish a "bride price" compatible with the station of the bride and the position of the groom. Legends contain stories of the exploits the suitor was required to perform in order to "win" the girl and establish not only his competence as a provider but also his courage, strength, and resourcefulness.

CHAPTER XII

1. Perhaps just as important as the design feature of the white-on-red style was the technique by which the pattern was executed. The surface of the vessel was first burnished to a smooth finish with red oxide of iron. This red surface was then coated with a slip of white pigment, possibly pulverized marl dispersed in water containing some plant sap such as cactus juice to make it stick well. When dry, the lines or areas that were to appear red in the finished design were developed by meticulously scraping off parts of the white surface layer, perhaps with a pointed stick or more probably a sharp piece of flint. I have found hundreds of sharp flint engravers or burins in every Arawak site in the Antilles. Indeed, the edges of the white-on-red areas are so precise and the red lines so thin that it is inconceivable that they could have been produced by any direct painting technique.

This scraping can be easily detected with a hand lens, which clearly reveals the marks of the tool. It is actually an example of "negative" painting, since the red design is developed by removal of areas of the white coating. I know of no other tribe contemporary with the Arawaks who practiced this kind of negative painting, so I consider both the W-O-R design and its technique of application to be unique with the Arawaks.

2. Three of the samples shown in Figure 108—those from Saladero and El Mayal in Venezuela and from Hacienda Grande and Cuevas in Puerto Rico—I photographed from sherds in Professor Rouse's collection at Yale. Those from Cedros in Trinidad and from Antigua I helped to collect. The beautiful vessel from St. Croix was reconstructed from

sherds which Dick Richards kindly furnished from a site not far from his home on St. Croix, to which he had introduced me in 1960.

Cuevas is a village on the Rio Grande de Loiza, about eleven miles, as the crow flies, southeast of San Juan, Puerto Rico. Professor Rouse says that it is on a very fertile flood plain, where the river leaves the foothills. It "must have been an ideal location for an Indian village," he added. They could have grown their manioc well and obtained fresh water readily.

Hacienda Grande is a site at Loiza near Cuevas, and is the earliest known place in Puerto Rico occupied by the Saladoid Arawaks; its ceramic style is closest to that of Cedros.

3. Cruxent and Rouse, *An Archeological Chronology of Venezuela*, (Washington, D.C.: Pan American Union, [1958], I, 216).

4. This is in keeping with current practice among archeologists, who prefer to call people by the site name used to designate the type of pottery they made, rather than to try and pin some tribal name on them. This is certainly a precise and unambiguous system of nomenclature. However, I have chosen to refer to the people who inhabited the various locations where Saladoid pottery is found as Arawaks because I am trying to determine the origins of those Arawak people whose artifacts I have been digging in Antigua and other islands. I, too, am willing to pin-point those Arawaks who made the W-O-R pottery as Saladoids, whenever the purpose is to distinguish them from other types of potters.

5. This is not unlike my own experience with Sialk pottery from the Zagros Mountain region of Iran, which from 5500 to 3000 B.C. remained practically unchanged. Perhaps the main reason for the lack of change in both Sialk and Saladoid pottery is that both cultures were relatively undisturbed by alien intruders with strange ideas affecting their pattern of living. In my collection of Persian pottery from Sialk, I had half a dozen bowls covering the years 5500 B.C. to 3000 B.C., each bearing a painted basket weave design and showing only minor innovations over the twenty-five-hundred year span. The first of these bowls was perhaps one of the earliest known pieces of pottery with painted decoration. It is tempting to speculate. Is the basket weave painted on the pots a hint that the much earlier containers were baskets used by food-gathering tribes for collecting seeds? Possibly the baskets were at one time sealed by clay to give more secure retention of the seeds. The early food-gatherers probably observed that the clay, originally supported by the weave, was a better seed container, and so clay eventually displaced the baskets, a change perhaps expedited by chance baking of the clay as a reinforced basket was placed too close to the fire.

6. Route 1 would reach Trinidad by going directly north from Sala-, dero along one of several branches (caños) that make up the extensive delta of the Orinoco (Map 3). Route 2 is an overland path, roughly northward, across the llanos to the Gulf of Paria. Route 3 is the all-water journey from Saladero down the Orinoco, then north by sea along the east coast of Venezuela to Trinidad.

Route 1 seems the most direct and obvious way of reaching Trinidad. However, oceanographers have found that none of the branches of the delta flowing north to the Gulf of Paria, or to the Serpent's Mouth, existed prior to about A.D. 1000.

In *Venezuelan Archeology*, Professor Rouse says: "Shortly after the beginning of Period IV, (i.e., A.D. 1000) the Orinoco River broke through to form the Boca Vagre and began to discharge for the first time into the Gulf of Paria, killing the coral communities which could no longer exist there because the Orinoco's waters caused a marked decrease in the salinity of the gulf" (p. 52). Hence Arawaks, who might have left Saladero about 900 B.C., had no such waterways to Trinidad available to them. We must therefore discard Route 1.

Route 2, the land passage, would appear to have no such disqualifications. There are, at present, many small streams which run through this overland route. I have flown over several of them and even traveled by automobile across a hundred miles of the llanos lying northwest of Saladero. I know of no study by modern geographers that would indicate whether these many streams existed unchanged about three thousand years ago, but from any data now available this land route seems an entirely feasible one. The rivers are small and would be easy to cross. They would provide convenient sources of water and fish for the migrating Saladoids. The llanos would contain animal and bird life, and if the Saladoids had chosen to remain in any desirable spots for a few years they could have grown their manioc, which requires the long spells of drought following the rainy season characteristic of the llanos.

When they reached the south shore of the Gulf of Paria by Route 2, the Arawak Saladoids would have had the choice of turning either east or northwest. If they took the eastern course, which I am naming Route 2A, eventually they would have come to the Serpent's Mouth and been in sight of the southwest tip of Trinidad. Presumably they might have made their way across the seven- to ten-mile stretch of sea to Point Icacos and thence to Cedros.

If, however, they had turned northwest on Route 2B, they could have gone along the west coast of the Gulf of Paria to the point where the coastline swings eastward. They could then have followed the south shore of the long neck of land, called the Peninsula of Paria, pointing directly at the northwest tip of Trinidad. The Dragon's Mouth, connecting the Gulf of Paria with the Caribbean Sea, separates Venezuela from Trinidad and is about eleven miles wide with several intervening islands. Land is easily seen looking in either direction across it. I learned this when I made the trip on the *S. S. Poseidon* from Port of Spain through the Dragon's Mouth and around the north and east coasts of Trinidad to Ciudad Bolívar on the Orinoco.

Route 2B is thus a possible route for the Arawak Saladoids to have traveled to reach Trinidad, but no site bearing Saladoid pottery has as yet been discovered on the northwest part of Trinidad. At Irapa, on the road running east along the south shore of the Peninsula of Paria, one Saladoid site was found, which encourages a search for other sites on this coastal route.

There is a variant of Route 2B that must be considered. When the Saladoids reached the point where the coast line swings due east along the northern shore of the Gulf of Paria, they would probably have been impressed by the imposing range of mountains a few miles to the north, forming the backbone of the long Peninsula of Paria. They might have been tempted to try the obvious gap in the mountain range north of Yaguaraparo. This low pass runs northwest and would have led them to the shore of the Caribbean Sea. The significance of this passage through the mountain range, which I am calling Route 2C, is that Arawak sites are found along the Caribbean shore, a short distance to the west of the mountain pass, near the present city of Carúpano. One of these sites is the well-known El Mayal, where Saladoid pottery findings have carbon-14 dates of A.D. 100 to 300, a period covering the beginning of the migration through the Antilles. We are therefore encouraged to consider El Mayal as a possible "take-off" point for the crucial journey to Grenada.

I consider the aforementioned Route 2A an entirely feasible one, especially as the Cedros site, perhaps the first Arawak site on Trinidad, is only a few miles east of Point Icacos. However, a possibly strong objection to Route 2 is that the riverine Arawaks might have shunned a land journey after having in all probability lived for many generations on the Orinoco. The llanos would have appeared to them, as indeed they did to me as I drove over them, an endless, bewildering stretch of grassland.

I realize that Paleolithic man had walked from Asia to Venezuela. Charred bones—broken to extract the marrow of such animals as the mastodon and megatherium—have been carbon-14 dated at 15,000 B.C. at Muaco Springs, near Coro, west of Caracas (Map 7). Furthermore, Junius Bird, of the American Museum of Natural History, has dated Paleo-Indians in Tierra del Fuego at 8000 B.C. Undoubtedly groups of early men had scattered over a great deal of South America.

Professor Rouse gives the following classification of Amerinds in South America:

367

Paleo-Indian	15,000 B.C. to 5000 B.C.
Meso-Indian	5,000 B.C. to 1000 B.C.
Neo-Indian	1,000 B.C. to A.D. 1500

The Paleo-Indians were big-game hunters. The Meso-Indians ate sea-food and their middens show vast quantities of shells and fish bones. They knew neither pottery-making nor agriculture, but fabricated good flint and stone tools. The Neo-Indians were both potters and agriculturists.

It has been known for several years that Meso-Indians were at Ortoire in eastern Trinidad (Map 11) in 800 B.C. Recently Professor Rouse has told me of Jose Cruxent's obtaining a date of about 3000 B.C. for Meso-Indians in western Trinidad. It is quite probable they too had reached there by walking rather than by canoe; Trinidad was then part of the mainland since the Serpent's Mouth had not broken through from the Atlantic to the Gulf of Paria prior to that time.

As yet we have no dating for any campsite on the Orinoco earlier than 1010 B.C. It seems reasonable to assume, therefore, that when the Saladoids left their home at Saladero about 900 B.C., being displaced by the encroaching Barrancoids, they may not have had any contact with Meso-Indians who could have informed them of the Boca Grande and the Orinoco current swinging northward through the Atlantic to Trinidad.

7. That this pottery is definitely Barrancoid, I am basing on Professor Rouse's description of the Erin-style pottery that he and Professor Bullbrook excavated at Erin Bay in 1946. He states that the Erin-style sherds are very thick; the W-O-R design is absent; zoomorphic lugs are particularly elaborate; and the modeling more expertly delineates the features of the animals. A good description of Barrancoid pottery!

On the Peninsula of Paria the two important sites of El Mayal and Irapa are both Saladoid (Map 3 and Table 2). El Mayal is somewhat the earlier and resembles Cedros in many respects, such as W-O-R sherds (Figure 96a) and the presence of nubbins (Figure 96b). Z-I-C sherds are particularly prominent (Figure 96d). The earlier El Mayal style also has no flanges, although they do occur in later El Mayal.

Barrancoid influence is perhaps most readily detected in the marked increase in the decoration of the nubbins, which are frequently arranged as if intended to suggest a head (Figure 96c). They remind one of a beginning of the typical Barrancoid adornos.

There are two carbon-14 dates: A.D. 100 and A.D. 300 for El Mayal.

The Irapa style is also similar to El Mayal with W-O-R sherds (Figure 97a and Table 2), but the Barrancoid influence is even more strongly present. There are still nubbins (Figure 97b), but more frequently the

TABLE 1.

Criteria for Distinguishing Saladoid and Barrancoid Pottery (Figs. 91–94)

Pottery Features	Saladoid	Barrancoid
Physical structure		
Wall thickness	Thin (average 6 mm)	Thick (average 12 mm)
Hardness	Hard, metallic ring when struck	Soft, dull sound when struck
Surface	Fine and smooth	Coarse, uneven, though sometimes scraped and polished
Color	Tan to light gray, sometimes almost white	Tan to reddish brown and black
Tempering materials	Sparse amounts of fine grit, difficult to see with naked eye	Sparsely tempered with particles of coarser grit, large enough to be seen by naked eye
Shape of vessels		
Contour	Graceful, open-mouthed bowls, flaring or bell-shaped, few jars and bottles, round bottoms, no boat-shaped vessels	Open-mouthed bowls, jars, and bottles common, boat shapes common
Rims	No flanges	Large, heavy flanges, often with triangular cross-section
Bases	Rounded or flat, no annular rings	Annular rings common
Size of vessels	Average diameter 24 cm, maximum 46 cm	Average diameter 25 cm, maximum 70 cm
Decoration		
Painted design	83 per cent of decorated sherds have white painted design on red background; frequently elegant, made by "pseudo-negative" technique in which white coating has been scraped off with great precision to reveal underlying red	Painting rare [designs perhaps copied from Saladoid; usually broad white lines applied directly but ineptly rather than by precise negative painting]*
Handles	Usually strap or D-shaped applied vertically; small tabs or nubbins common; usually undecorated; when knob is large enough to suggest an adorno the modeling is simple and animal, bird, or human head not distinguishable	Elaborately and imaginatively modeled handles known as adornos in form of animal, bird, or human heads frequently modeled in bas-relief on outside wall of vessel
Incised	Only about 10 per cent of sherds decorated with simple incised lines, usually as grooves	Incised decoration frequent and elaborate; in early Barrancoid incised lines thin and less surely drawn; later are frequently Baroquelike designs

* Material in brackets added by author.

TABLE 2. Comparison of Saladoid and Barrancoid Pottery Characteristics from Sites along the Probable Migration Trail of the Arawaks

Pottery Characteristics	ORINOCO	TRINIDAD			PENINSUL
	Saladero	Cedros	Palo Seco	Erin	El Mayal
Thin, hard, with metallic clink	Yes	Yes	Moderately thick and soft	Thickest	Yes
White-on-red negative painting	Yes	Yes	Continues, but less negative	None	Yes
Nubbins, lugs common on rims	Yes	Yes	Some modeling	Elaborately incised and modeled	Yes
Modeled animal head adornos	No	No	Zoomorphic heads occur	Yes	Nubbins sometimes arranged like heads
Flanges on rim	No	No	Yes	Heavy flanges	None early, but some late
Incised linear design commonest form of decoration	No	No	Simple incised lines	Yes	Some incised design
Zoned-incised cross-hatched (Z-I-C)	No	Yes	Rare	No	Yes
Strap handles present	Yes	Yes	Yes	Yes	Yes
Strap handles with modeled heads	No	No	Some	Yes	Some
Carbon-14 dating	1010 B.C.	600 B.C (est.)	A.D. 200 to 400 (est.)	A.D. 600 (est.)	A.D. 100 to 300

370

TABLE 2.—*Continued*

Paria	Grenada	Guadeloupe	Antigua	St. Croix	Puerto Rico	
apa	Pearls	Morel	Mill Reef		Hacienda Grande	Cuevas
s	Yes	Yes	Yes	Yes	Yes	Yes
s	Yes	Yes	Yes	Yes	Yes	Yes
s	Yes	Yes	Yes	Yes	Yes	Yes
s	Zoomorphic heads occur but mainly nubbins arranged like heads	Nubbins arranged like heads but not modeled elaborately	Slight	Slight	Nubbins but not modeled heads	Some modeling
s	No	No	No	No	No	No
s	Slight	Some	Slight	Slight	Slight	Yes
w	Yes	Yes	Yes	Yes	Yes	Slight
s	Yes	Yes	Yes	Yes	Yes	Yes
s	Slight	Some	Slight	Slight	Some	Yes
. 220 570	A.D. 100 to 300 (est.)	A.D. 17 and 190	A.D. 100 to 300 (est.)	A.D. 100 to 300 (est.)	A.D. 120 to 370	A.D. 510 to 590

371

handles are adornos with realistically modeled heads (Figure 97d). Several flanged rims occur (Figure 97c), and there is an increased amount of incised decoration (Figure 97e). Z-I-C sherds have almost disappeared. Actually, Irapa is more like Palo Seco and may indeed be a variant of it. Irapa has carbon-14 dates of A.D. 220 and A.D. 325.

There are many suitable landing spots on the southern shore of the Peninsula of Paria, and if the Arawaks made their way to Yaguaraparo (Map 3) they could have crossed through the gap in the mountains to settle at El Mayal on the Caribbean coast. The slightly later date of the site at Irapa, near Yaguaraparo, might be regarded as supporting the water route by way of the Dragon's Mouth rather than the route through the mountains to El Mayal. On the other hand, it might have been a later group that migrated to Irapa, perhaps from Palo Seco, than the ones who had reached El Mayal from Cedros, as I have suggested.

It must be granted that the Arawaks occupying Irapa, particularly El Mayal, were typical Saladoids. Their pottery is only Barrancoid enough to favor a diffusion of Barrancoid traits into these sites rather than a displacement by Barrancoid invaders.

The appearance of Saladoid pottery (with dates of A.D. 220, 325, and 570) at Irapa (Map 3) on the northwest coast of the Gulf of Paria and at El Mayal on the Caribbean coast of Venezuela at A.D. 100 to 300, brings up again the question as to whether the Arawaks had wandered there after their hegira from Saladero by the Route 2 overland trail or by Route 3, the all-water passage to Cedros, both shown on Map 3. If they took the overland route, where did they spend the thousand years between leaving Saladero at 900 B.C. and arriving at El Mayal and Irapa about A.D. 100 to 300? There are no campsites known on that overland passage. Dates for Cedros and Palo Seco would of course help to establish the feasibility of the Trinidad route.

At the moment all we can do is to speculate whether or not Barrancoids pushed the Saladoids out of Cedros or Palo Seco and started them on their way to the northeast section of Venezuela. The Saladoids may have moved up the west coast of Trinidad until they reached the northwest corner of the island and there crossed the Dragon's Mouth to the Peninsula of Paria and then westward to El Mayal. Sufficient data from campsites on the western coast are not available to provide the answer.

8. Although an abundance of Saladoid pottery has been found at Grenada, I know of no carbon-14 dates for that island. But we do have a much better picture of what happened in Guadaloupe. Two early dates of A.D. 170 and 190 have been assigned to Saladoid pottery from Morel I, the lowest layer in the Morel site (on the eastern coast of the Grande Terre section of Guadeloupe, Map 7). Moreover, two supporting dates of A.D.

240 and 260 have been obtained from the bottom of the layer imme-diately above, Morel II. I should not be surprised if further carbon-14 findings will eventually show dates earlier than A.D. 170 since the Morel I layer is thick enough to suggest that it may have required two hundred years or more for its deposition, which would favor Arawak occupation of Guadeloupe perhaps as early as A.D. 1.

CHAPTER XIII

1. The site at El Mayal has an earlier date of A.D. 100 than the A.D. 220 for Irapa. A study of the ceramics from El Mayal and Irapa reveals that the differences in stylistic features are compatible with these two datings. At El Mayal the characteristic features of Saladoid pottery are distinctly in evidence: the W-O-R decoration and the Z-I-C ornamentation. On the other hand, the sherds at Irapa, although possessing an appreciable amount of the W-O-R pottery, definitely show more Barrancoid in-fluence, such as more pronounced sculptural adornos, heavy triangular flanged rims, and a reduced representation of Z-I-C sherds. The El Mayal pottery more closely resembles the Cedros style, whereas the Irapa is more like the Palo Seco style.

2. In the opinion of Professor Rouse these two situations at Saladero and Palo Seco are not comparable. He points out that "site-unit" dif-fusion (his technical name for what I am loosely calling "migration") took place at Saladero, but only "trait-unit" diffusion at Palo Seco. He cautions that, "A new group of people is not the same as the arrival of traders!" But it seems to me it would be similar if the "traders" decided to settle in this lush new land and then to displace the Saladoids from their Palo Seco home. It would appear that the Saladoids thereupon migrated across the Gulf of Paria to Irapa.

I realize I have been heading into a tricky and controversial subject of "migration" versus "trait diffusion." But at least some of the basic criteria for migration are present since the Saladoid occupation *did* terminate about A.D. 100 at Cedros and the Saladoids *did* appear sud-denly a couple of hundred miles across the Gulf of Paria, also about A.D. 100, at El Mayal, where they produced ceramic material closely similar to that at Cedros.

I see no reason for inventing a more complex explanation for the oc-currence of Saladoid pottery at three distinct locations (Saladero in 1010 B.C., Cedros in 190 B.C., and El Mayal in A.D. 100) than that migra-tion occurred along this path. Whether or not the motivation for the migration was displacement by the Barrancoids is by no means estab-lished, but the possibility certainly merits consideration.

Chapter XIV

1. Professor Rouse reminds me that the term Arawak is also used to include people who speak the Arawakan language. There are many such people: the Indians of the Guajira peninsula, west of the Gulf of Maracaibo, for example. Also certain people in the Amazon Basin and in the Guianas speak Arawakan. Likewise there are many Indians who call themselves Arawaks. I met several of these groups in Surinam. Indeed, I suspect that these may have been fairly recent arrivals in the Guianas.

Specifically the people I am describing in this book are those who lived on the migration route from the Orinoco to the Antilles and who produced the Saladoid and the Barrancoid types of pottery. The Arawak areas I am considering are:

The apex of the Orinoco delta, reached first by the Saladoids about 1010 B.C. and after 985 B.C. by the Barrancoids, who remained there until A.D. 1000 and possibly much later.

The Peninsula of Paria region of northern Venezuela, as exemplified by the El Mayal site near Carúpano, which was occupied by the Saladoids and from which they may have made their exodus to the Antilles about A.D. 100–300.

Trinidad and Tobago, which at first were Saladoid and presumably became more and more Barrancoid after about A.D. 100.

The Lesser Antilles, which were purely Saladoid from about A.D. 100 to A.D. 500, perhaps with only diffusion of Barrancoid traits until the takeover by the Caribs "shortly" before the arrival of the Spaniards.

The Greater Antilles, occupied solely by the Saladoids (with the exception of parts of Haiti and Cuba that remained in the hands of the Ciboney people until the time of Columbus). The Saladoid pottery of Hispaniola and Puerto Rico shows only the same kinds of Barrancoid trait influences as were present in the El Mayal style.

2. Professor Gerardo Reichel-Dolmatoff is the outstanding authority on the archeology of Colombia. He was born in Austria, educated in Vienna, Munich, and at the University of Paris. He is author of the splendid and readable book *Colombia* (New York: Praeger, 1965). This book was the result of thirty years of research in Colombia, culminating in the discovery of the Puerto Hormiga site which, Reichel-Dolmatoff points out, may be the home of the earliest pottery-makers in the New World.

3. Malambo is a village about six miles south of Barranquilla (Map 14), located on a cienaga or shallow lagoon connected by canos with the

374

Magdalena River. Pottery dating 1120 B.C. has been found there with strong Barrancoid features. The excavation was carried out by Carlos Angulo Valdes, Director of the Institute of Ethnological Studies, University of the Atlantic, Barranquilla (*Evidence of the Barrancoid Series in North Colombia*, University of Florida, 1962). Professor Angulo shows that the pottery had the well-known Barrancoid characteristics of zoomorphic adornos or handles, elaborately incised linear decoration, and applied work (Figure 104). But what was also highly significant was that these Malambo potters practiced manioc culture.

4. Unquestionably, one of the most exciting finds of very early pottery in South America was made by Evans, Meggers, and Estrada in 1959. They dug at Valdivia, a fishing village in Ecuador just north of the Gulf of Guayaquil, on which Guayaquil is situated (Map 5). This was essentially a shell midden in which pottery occurred without any indication of agriculture, and in an archaic environment where the inhabitants supplemented their main diet of fish and shellfish with animal protein food from the mangrove swamps and river valleys and with the gathering of various food plants.

This condition is perhaps similar to that described by Michael D. Coe in his *America's First Civilization: Discovering the Olmec*. Professor Coe speaks of these associated regions of food resources as "microenvironments": the seashore where crabs and mollusks abound; the lagoon areas where fish are abundant; the mangrove swamps surrounding the lagoons, with oysters and mussels clinging to the mangrove roots and birds and small animals in plentiful supply; and finally, the nearby higher ground, forested and supplying edible vegetation, fruit, and nuts. Later, when I visited Ecuador and Colombia, I saw that each of these microenvironments existed around the Valdivia and the Puerto Hormiga sites, and presumably it was the aggregate of these environments that had attracted the early Amerinds.

I recalled that in several eastern hemisphere locations it was the domestication of plants that had led to permanent living locations favoring the development of pottery. However, on the Valdivia site it was the existence of an apparently endless supply of shellfish which had caused the people to maintain their occupation of this favorite spot from about 3000 to 1500 B.C. During their long tenure the shell mounds built up to such a degree that Evans and Meggers had to dig trenches at Valdivia about twenty feet deep before they reached layers devoid of pottery. They assign a carbon-14 date of 3200 B.C. to their earliest pottery, which is thus a little earlier than the 3090 B.C. figures given by Reichel-Dolmatoff for the pottery at Puerto Hormiga. On this basis Meggers and Evans suggested that the Valdivian pottery is the oldest yet found in the Americas.

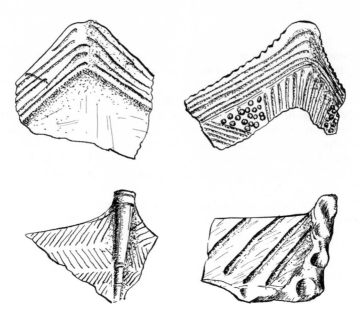

Fig. 132. Comparison of Jomon (left) and Valdivia (right): castellated rims (above); turreted points (below).

However, there are a few points raised by some critics against these early dates. They point out that Meggers and Evans obtained twenty-one radiocarbon dates for Valdivia, thirteen of which came from their earliest Period A. Twelve of these range between 2150 and 2670 B.C., while the thirteenth is 3200. In discussing this matter with Professor Rouse, he reminded me that "the accepted procedure in radiocarbon dating is to throw out a date which does not fall within the normal range, since the technic is a statistical one and subject to various errors." Other workers in this field prefer a dating for this type of Valdivian ceramics between the 2150 and 2670 B.C. dates given by Meggers and Evans, rather than the extreme one of 3200 B.C. Thus they consider the Valdivian pottery of the Meggers and Evans's Period A as later by several hundred years than the Puerto Hormiga pottery in Colombia.

The real excitement about their discoveries was, of course, the resemblance they saw between the sherds from the lowest layers at Valdivia and the Jomon pottery from Japan. When they found Valdivian sherds that exhibited decoration known as "castellated rims" and "turreted points" (Figure 132), outstandingly Jomon characteristics, they were faced sharply with the possibility that this Valdivian pottery had such strong affinities with Jomon pottery as to suggest the possibility of its Japanese origin. Jomon pottery has a long history in Japan, the earliest varieties dating from about 9000 B.C. and continuing for about

376

seven thousand years, thus making it a contender for the title of the world's earliest pottery. The Middle Jomon period, to which the Valdivia style pottery appeared to be related, is placed at about 5000 to 3000 B.C. by Japanese archeologists.

Cliff Evans explained that they had been very reluctant to imply a Japanese origin for the Valdivia pottery and felt the need of a much more intimate knowledge of Jomon pottery characteristics. Both he and his wife proceeded to Japan and examined the extensive collections of Jomon pottery in the great Japanese National Museum, as well as those in the provincial museums and private collections of Honshu and Kyushu. As a result of their studies they concluded that there were about seventeen criteria which were shared by Jomon and Valdivia pottery and that they knew of no other pottery than Jomon which could show a similar close relationship with the Valdivia pottery. They have published these shared characteristics, together with excellent photographic illustrations. Among these controversial seventeen-point comparisons the one that interests me most is the Z-I-C design, which occurs prominently in both the Jomon and Saladoid types of pottery. This might indicate an extremely early and astonishingly distant origin of the Z-I-C feature, should a relationship be established between the Valdivian and Japanese pottery.

I find the arguments of Meggers and Evans regarding this seventeen-point correspondence between Ecuadorean and Japanese pottery features to be very persuasive, although I am also impressed with the scholarship of those opposed to it. But it is no obligation of mine to enter this polemic. Rather, I shall content myself with noting the similarities between the Z-I-C design of Jomon pottery of 3000 B.C. with Valdivia pottery of about 1500 to 2500 B.C. and with Saladoid Z-I-C pottery of 190 B.C. at Cedros in Trinidad. I shall watch with deep interest for further evidence of anyone "bearing" pottery by sea from Asia to South America in the first millennium B.C. or earlier, but I shall be even more concerned with other discoveries of Z-I-C sherds at locations between Ecuador and Trinidad.

As a first step in this possible diffusion I noted that the technical literature seems to reveal that the Z-I-C design moved south from Valdivia to Peru, where it is found at the Kotosh site about 1000 B.C., still early enough for the Z-I-C design to reach Cedros by 190 B.C. from Peru via the Amazon and Orinoco tributaries to the mainstream of the Orinoco.

Evans and Meggers explain that they were forced to the conclusion that the comparison between Jomon and Valdivian pottery was too close to be attributed to chance. They say that they were obliged, therefore, to postulate that some Japanese craft had been blown off course from Kyushu in one of the many typhoons that strike the islands of Japan, and that the vessel had then been driven by the prevailing winds and currents somewhat north of Hawaii, then eastward toward the coast of North America, where it would enter the currents flowing south toward South America. The bulge of Ecuador would have provided an effective landfall, the mariners going ashore at what is now the village of Valdivia. There they may have met friendly fisher-folk, who would have looked familiar since both groups were of Mongoloid stock. To these native people the visitors presumably taught the art of making Jomon-style pottery.

Meggers, Evans, and Estrada answered the question as to when this might have occurred by quoting the carbon-14 dating of 3200 B.C. for the lowest layer of Valdivia. This fitted nicely into the range of Jomon pottery being made in Japan at that period.

I had my own personal adventure with this hypothetical Japanese origin of pre-Columbian Amerind pottery when I visited Kyoto in 1965 and obtained a fine fragment of Jomon pottery. I am showing this piece beside an Arawak sherd (Figure 133a, b) that I found at Saladero. (More specifically, it was from Guarguapo, a village a little over a mile west of Saladero, and is derived from the Arauqinoid Series and hence related to the Barrancoid pottery.) The correspondence is tantalizing, but, I admit reluctantly, apparently without any valid relationship.

5. Betty J. Meggers and Clifford Evans, "Speculation on Early Pottery Diffusion Routes Between South and Middle America," in *Hombre y Cultura*, I, 3, (Panama: University of Panama, December, 1964).

6. Although the present evidence of the earliest agriculture in the Americas favors the seed-growers who originated corn, it would not surprise me if later studies support an even earlier origin of root crops grown by vegetative propagation. At Rancho Peludo, northwest of Maracaibo, the earliest pottery in Venezuela, recently discovered by Professor Cruxent, is associated with griddle sherds with a dating of 1970 B.C., which encourages the viewpoint of still earlier sources of the root crop manioc.

7. In Guatemala I saw a collection in the village of Patzun containing a complete bowl with fine Z-I-C decoration. It came from Quezaltenango from the ruins at Salcaja, which Ed Shook placed as pre-Classic, about 1 A.D. (Figure 134).

8. I noticed a most interesting construction feature. Bamboo was evidently available, though where it came from in this desert country I didn't know. These ingenious Amerinds had made use of it by crushing the four-inch diameter stems to yield boards almost a foot in width.

Fig. 133. Comparison of Jomon and Guarguapo pottery heads. a: Jomon pottery from Kyushu, Japan, ca. 3500 B.C. b: Guarguapo (Arawak) pottery ca. A.D. 1000. Both fragments with raised eyebrows, coffee-bean eyes and mouth, and snubbed nose.

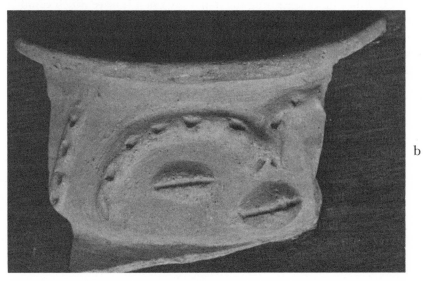

Fig. 134. Complete Z-I-C bowl (Salcaja, Guatemala).

9. I was uneasy about the fact that *no* Z-I-C occurs on any pottery found at Saladero. How did the Z-I-C trait reach Trinidad and bypass Saladero? I wondered if my emphasis on Z-I-C sherds might be unwarranted. In suggesting the Valdivia pottery as a prototype for the Saladoid Z-I-C, I may be exaggerating the importance of a feature which could be just a chance correspondence. I recalled my recent encounter with Z-I-C sherds dug by Ed Shook in Guatemala, albeit of rather too late a date to have qualified as a possible ancestor of Cedros pottery of 190 B.C. A feature which occurred over such a wide range of time and location might simply be one that was easy for many craftsmen to invent.

10. In this connection I was much interested in being introduced to two new plants. One was evidenced by bundles of "straw" which we saw hanging up to dry at various houses. This was *Paja toquilla*, the straw for making Panama hats, which I was told are made much more extensively at Guayaquil than in Panama. The other plant was *Carrizac*, a wild pineapple, which made an effective living fence around various properties.

11. We took a side excursion on the *S. S. Romantica* and went ashore at about a dozen islands of the Galapagos. I took over two thousand pictures of the extraordinary wildlife that had given Darwin his basis for

the *Origin of Species*. The theory of evolution was vividly demonstrated every day, and no one could fail to see the striking changes that birds, reptiles, and plants had undergone in their adaptation to this much secluded environment.

No woodpeckers had reached the islands, so some of the finches developed longer beaks, one of them with the ability to break off a cactus needle or a sharp thorn which it held like a toothpick to probe for insect life under the bark of trees. This toolmaking finch had found an ecologically satisfactory niche, normally occupied on the mainland by the woodpecker, and had evolved to perform like a woodpecker.

The sea lions were delightfully playful, and it was great fun to snorkel and have them joyously join us by diving and swimming under us, through out legs, and coming up gleefully in front of us, touching their noses to our masks and apparently laughing.

Our ship went through the Panama Canal and we spent a day in the San Blas Islands with the colorful Cuna Indians, whose gayly sewn *molas* (blouses) make fine wall hangings. The Cuna seem to me to have some Carib characteristics, the tight bands binding their legs below the knees resembling those I had seen on Caribs in Surinam.

12. This turned out to be a treasure trove of Colombian artifacts. Professor Reichel-Dolmatoff was most gracious in permitting me to photograph the results of his many years of research on Colombian archeology.

After the Puerto Hormiga style came the Canapote (Map 14), found at the site of that name in a suburb of Cartagena and covering a period of 2000 to 1500 B.C. The Barlovento site is just a few miles north of Cartagena, on the way to Barranquilla. Here the decoration was largely broad grooves, frequently of parallel curves in geometric arrangement and occasionally with some red paint. In a few cases a sherd showed a highly stylized human head, not as part of a handle but worked in very low relief on the outer wall of a vessel—later a common characteristic of Barrancoid pottery. Then I saw what appeared to be a Z-I-C sherd, possibly the earliest one I had observed from Colombia (1500 to 1032 B.C.). My eyes were not sharp enough to identify the cross-hatching while I was doing the photography. Later, a careful examination of the transparency with a lens showed that it was *not* incised cross-hatching, but an extraordinarily accurate arrangement of tiny punctations in precise straight lines which gave the appearance of cross-hatching. I am deeply impressed by the meticulous accuracy and draftsmanship of these potters, and am inclined to regard this style of punctation as a possible progenitor of the Z-I-C technique.

The next series was the Malambo, about which Reichel-Dolmatoff had told me during his visit to Yale. He had no Malambo sherds to show

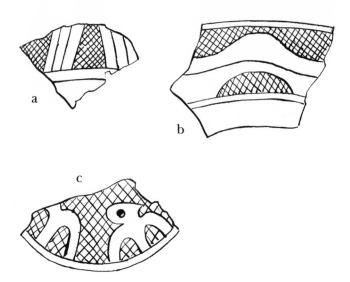

Fig. 135. Z-I-C sherds also occur in Momil-style pottery.

me, saying that they were to be seen only at the museum at Barranquilla (Figure 104).

The final series shown to me was from Momil on the Sinu River (Map 14), located a little over a hundred miles south of Puerto Hormiga and dated about 1000 B.C. It was immediately obvious that here were potters producing highly sophisticated polychrome pottery with the same kind of flair for geometric precision that characterized the Saladoids. Also, on the very first tray of Momil handed to me, I spotted half a dozen Z-I-C sherds (Figure 135a, b) quite similar to those Saladoid sherds from El Mayal, Cedros, Guadeloupe, and Antigua. Geometric areas were clearly zoned and these zones were filled with fine incised cross-hatching. Next came a series of well-made circular plaques, thin, hard and black, with outlines of birds and possibly other animal figures, the spaces or zones surrounding these figures being filled with incised fine-lined cross-hatching (Figure 135c). This was a new and puzzling innovation which I had not seen in any Saladoid decoration. The zones were not geometric but zoomorphic; the cross-hatching was not within the zoned figures but *surrounded* the zones. It almost looked as if Saladoid potters making their hard pottery had been influenced by Barrancoid-type potters to create animal designs instead of geometric ones, then decided to leave the animal shapes blank and fill in the background with their characteristic incised cross-hatching, thereby giving greater emphasis to the figure. It may be, however, not without significance, that this skillfully employed cross-hatching was perhaps several hundred years *earlier* than any Trinidad or Venezuelan cross-hatching. The Guatemala Z-I-C pot-

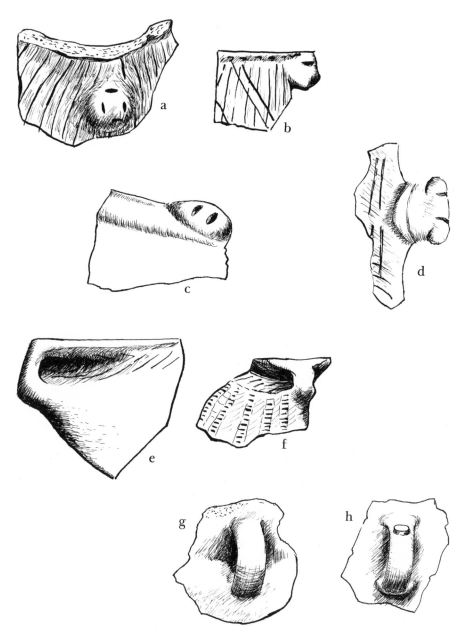

Fig. 136. Comparison of Valdivia and Saladoid styles of pottery. a, b Nubbin handles (Valdivia, Ecuador). c, d: Saladoid nubbin handles (Orinoco). e, f: Strap handles (Valdivia, Ecuador). g, h: Saladoid strap handles (Orinoco).

tery from Monte Alto (Figure 106) may be roughly contemporaneous with the El Mayal, Cedros, and Antillean Z-I-C sherds.

Having established to my satisfaction the early presence of such important Saladoid features as the thin, hard ware, the polychrome painting, and now the Z-I-C design being present in Valdivian pottery, I again studied the Ecuador sherds for additional details of resemblance. Suddenly I realized that they shared another important Saladoid characteristic: slight nubbinlike projections on the bowls, possibly serving as small handles (Figure 136a, b). Frequently these Valdivian nubbins were slightly nicked or even arranged to give a crude resemblance of a head, not however distinguishable as human, bird, or mammal, but quite similar to the nubbins found in the Cedros or El Mayal styles of Saladoid pottery (Figure 136c, d). They were in striking contrast to the elaborately modeled Barrancoid heads of clearly zoomorphic form. Furthermore, both Saladoid and Valdivian pottery frequently used the same form of strap handles (Figure 136e, f, g, h).

When I noticed among the various types of pottery from the Valdivian site sherds displaying negative painting, I thought this might be evidence of where the Saladoids learned their technique for the white-on-red painting. However, Cliff Evans pointed out that the sherds I was examining were much later, and that no negative painting was found in either the Valdivia or the Machalilla styles until 500 B.C. to A.D. 500, much too late to have been the prototype for Saladoid pottery of 1000 B.C.

I have suggested that the Saladoid potters may have invented their own type of negative painting since I know of no other ornamentation produced in this manner. In discussing this feature with my friends I find more than a little confusion as to just what comprises negative painting. One of them, however, is quite definite on the matter. Cliff Evans wrote me: "Please do not use the name 'negative painting' with reference to anything in the Valdivia or Machalilla cultures. If you want to use the name 'pseudo-negative,' okay. But true negative technique, done by a resist of some sort, does not occur in the Ecuador sequence until the Tejar period, about 500 B.C. Nor does true negative appear in the Saladoid material or anywhere in the Antilles to our knowledge. Be sure you do not mix one technique, that is negative with a resist, with a design that gives a negative effect."

In the "true negative" operation, as mentioned by Cliff Evans, the vessel is usually coated before firing with a layer of red oxide of iron and burnished to a fairly high polish with a smooth stone. A design is then painted on this red coating, usually with some organic material that will "resist" the adherence of the subsequent white coating. We don't know what material was used by the ancient potters, but tribes in Surinam and Guyana today use water dispersions of a tree gum to which the subsequently applied white slip will not adhere. This white slip is spread over the whole surface where white is to occur, leaving "windows" wherever the tree gum design has been applied. Firing burns off the tree gum, allowing the primary coat of iron oxide to show through as a red pattern against a white surface. This is technically a white-on-red design, but usually the demarcation between the white and red surfaces is not sharp. The red areas appear with a "soft-edge" effect that is frequently quite attractive.

In contrast, the Saladoid potters produced a "hard-edge" effect. This hard-edge terminology is well understood today because many contemporary painters pride themselves on the precision with which the sharp edges of two colored areas on the canvas are delineated. The ancient Saladoids achieved their precision by an ingenious device as described in Note 1, Chapter XII.

Admittedly, this Saladoid technique of pseudo-negative painting is not the "true negative" method as Meggers and Evans define it since no resist material is used. Nevertheless, the design *is* achieved by the *removal* of the white coating and this is a form of *negative* treatment.

Bibliography

Alegría, Ricardo E. "The Ball Game Played by the Aborigines of the Antilles." *American Antiquity*, 16.4:348–352. Menasha. 1951.

———. "On Puerto Rican Archaeology." *American Antiquity*, 31.2:246–249. Salt Lake City. 1965.

Angulo, Carlos V. "Evidence of the Barrancoid Series in North Colombia." Pp. 35–46, 7 plates, in *The Caribbean: Contemporary Colombia*, edited by A. Curtis Wilgis. Gainesville: University of Florida Press. 1962.

Anonymous. *Antigua and the Antiguans: A Full Account of the Colony and Its Inhabitants.* 2 vols. Vol. 1, xiv, 345 pp.; Vol. 2, viii, 355 pp. London: Saunders and Otley. 1844. Reprinted 1967, London and Colchester: Spottiswoode, Ballantyne and Co., Ltd.

Arrom, José Juan. *Hernan Perez de Oliva; Historia de la Inuencion de las Yndias.* (Publicaciones del Instituto Caro y Cuervo, XX.) 126 pp. Bogota. 1965.

Arroyo de Anda, Luis Aveleyra. *La Estela Teotihuacana de la Ventilla.* 26 pp., 12 figs. Museo Nacional de Antropologia e Historia. Mexico. 1963.

Barbotin, Père Maurice. "Arawaks and Caraïbes a Marie-Galante." Reprinted from *Boletín de la Societé d'Histoire de Guadeloupe*, No. 11–12. [1971.]

Bennett, Wendell C., and Junius B. Bird. *Andean Cultural History.* (American Museum of Natural History, Handbook Series No. 15.) 1960.

Blom, Frans. "The Maya Ball-game *Pok-ta-pok* (called *Tlachtli* by the Aztec)." Middle America Research Series, *Publication No. 4*, pp. 485–530. Tulane University, New Orleans. 1932.

Borhegyi, Stephan F., and Suzanne de Borhegyi. "The Rubber Ball Game of Ancient America." ("Lore Leaves," No. 8; reprinted from *Lore*). Milwaukee Public Museum. 1963.

Brinton, Daniel. "The Arawack Language of Guiana in its Linguistic and Ethnological Relations." *Transactions of the American Philosophical Society*, 14:427–444. Philadelphia. 1871.

Bullbrook, J. A. *On the Excavation of a Shell Mound at Palo Seco, Trinidad, B. W. I.* (Yale University Publications in Anthropology, No. 50.) 114 pp. New Haven. 1953.

―――. *The Aborigines of Trinidad.* (Occasional Papers No. 2.) 60 pp. Royal Victoria Institute Museum, Port-of-Spain, Trinidad. 1960.

Bullen, Ripley P. *The Archeology of Grenada, West Indies.* (Contributions of the Florida State Museum, Social Sciences, No. 11.) 67 pp., 25 plates. Gainesville. 1964.

Bullen, Ripley P., and Adelaide K. Bullen. "The Lavoutte Site, St. Lucia: A Carib ceremonial center." Pp. 61–86 in *Proceedings of the Third International Congress for the Study of Pre-Columbian Cultures of the Lesser Antilles, St. George's, Grenada, 1969.* Grenada National Museum, Grenada. 1970.

Bullen, Ripley P., and Frederick W. Sleight. *The Krum Bay Site, a Pre-ceramic Site on St. Thomas, United States Virgin Islands.* (The William L. Bryant Foundation, American Studies, Report No. 5.) iii, 46 pp. Orlando: Central Florida Museum. 1963.

Clèrc, Edgard. "Sites precolombiens de la Grande-Terre de Guadeloupe." Pp. 47–60 in *Proceedings of the Second International Congress for the Study of Pre-Columbian Cultures in the Lesser Antilles, St. Ann's Garrison, Barbados, 1967.* Barbados Museum, Barbados. 1968.

―――. "Les Trois-Pointes des Sites Precolombiens de la Cote Nord-Est de la Grande-Terre de la Guadeloupe." Pp. 73–81 in *Proceedings of the Fourth International Congress for the Study of Pre-Columbian Cultures of the Lesser Antilles, Reduit Beach, St. Lucia, 1971.* St. Lucia Archaeological and Historical Society. Castries. 1973.

Coe, Michael D. *Mexico.* (Ancient Peoples and Places, Vol. 29.) 245 pp. New York and Washington: Frederick A. Praeger. 1966.

―――. *The Maya.* (Ancient Peoples and Places, Vol. 52.) 252 pp. New York and Washington: Frederick A. Praeger. 1966.

Cruxent, José M. and Irving Rouse. "Venezuela and Its Relationships With Neighboring Areas." Pp. 173–83 in *Actas del XXXIII Congreso Internacional de Americanistas, San Jose, 1958,* Tomo 1. San Jose, Costa Rica: Lehmann. 1959.

―――. *An Archeological Chronology of Venezuela.* 2 vols. (Social Science Monographs, VI.) Vol. 1, 1958, xiv, 277 pp.; Vol. 2, 1959, ix, 223 pp., 104 plates. Washington, D. C.: Pan American Union. 1958, 1959.

―――. "Early man in the West Indies." *Scientific American,* 221.5:42–52. New York. 1969.

Dockstader, Frederick J. *Indian Art in Middle America.* 221 pp. Greenwich: New York Graphic Society. 1964.

Ekholm, Gordon F. "Puerto Rican Stone 'Collars' as Ball-game Belts." Pp. 356–71 (Essay 24) in *Essays in Pre-Columbian Art and Archeology,* by Samuel K. Lothrop and others. Cambridge: Harvard University Press. 1961.

―――. "Transpacific Contacts." Pp. 489–510 in *Prehistoric Man in the New World*, edited by J. D. Jennings and E. Norbeck. Chicago: University of Chicago Press. 1964.

Estrada, Emilio, and Betty J. Meggers. "A Complex of Traits of Probable Transpacific Origin on the Coast of Ecuador." *American Anthropologist*, 63.5(Part 1): 913–39. 1961.

Evans, Clifford, and Betty J. Meggers. *Archeological Investigation in British Guiana*. (Smithsonian Institution, Bureau of American Ethnology, Bulletin 177.) xxi, 418 pp., 68 plates. Washington. 1960.

―――. "Transpacific Origin of Valdivia Phase Pottery on coastal Ecuador." Pp. 63–67 in *XXXVI Congreso Internacional de Americanistas*. Seville. 1966.

―――. *Archeological Investigations on the Rio Napa, Eastern Ecuador*. (Smithsonian Contributions to Anthropology, Vol. 6.) xvi, 127 pp., 94 plates. Washington: Smithsonian Institution Press. 1968.

Evans, Clifford, Betty J. Meggers, and José M. Cruxent. "Preliminary results of archeological investigations along the Orinoco and Ventuari Rivers, Venezuela." Pp. 359–77 in *Actas del XXXIII Congreso Internacional de Americanistas, San Jose, 1958*, Tomo 2. San Jose, Costa Rica: Lehmann. 1959.

Farabee, William Curtis. *The Central Caribs*. (University of Pennsylvania, University Museum Anthropological Publications Vol. X.) 299 pp., 40 plates. Philadelphia. 1924.

Fewkes, Jesse Walter. *The Aborigines of Porto Rico and the Neighboring Islands*. Pp. 3–296 in 25th Annual Report of the Bureau of American Ethnology, . . . 1903–04. Washington. 1907.

―――. *A Prehistoric Island Culture of America*. Pp. 35–281 in 34th Annual Report of the Bureau of American Ethnology, . . . 1912–13. Washington. 1922.

Flint, Richard Foster. *Glacial and Pleistocene Geology*. xiii, 553 pp. New York: John Wiley and Sons. 1957.

Grace, F. J. S. " 'Pok-ta-pok' or 'Tlachtli.' " Translated by F. J. S. Grace. New York, courtesy of *Gentry Magazine*. [photocopy of manuscript] 1954.

Haag, William G. "The Lesser Antilles: Their ecological setting and function as a diffusion route." Pp. 87–92 in *Proceedings of the Second International Congress for the Study of Pre-Columbian Cultures in the Lesser Antilles, St. Ann's Garrison, Barbados, 1967*. Barbados Museum, Barbados. 1968.

―――. "The Identification of Archeological Remains with Ethnic Groups." Pp. 121–24 in *Proceedings of the Second International Congress for the Study of Pre-Columbian Cultures in the Lesser Antilles,*

St. Ann's Garrison, Barbados, 1967. Barbados Museum, Barbados. 1968.

————. "Stone artifacts in the Lesser Antilles." Pp. 129–38 in *Proceedings of the Third International Congress for the Study of Pre-Columbian Cultures of the Lesser Antilles, St. George's, Grenada, 1969.* Grenada National Museum, Grenada. 1970.

Harris, David R. *Plants, Animals and Man in the Outer Leeward Islands, West Indies: An Ecological Study of Antigua, Barbuda, and Anguilla.* (University of California Publications in Geography, Vol. 18.) ix, 164 pp., 18 plates. Berkeley and Los Angeles: University of California Press. 1965.

Hawkes, Jacquetta, and Sir Leonard Woolley. *Prehistory and the Beginnings of Civilization.* (History of Mankind, Vol. 1.) xlvii, 813 pp. New York and Evanston: Harper and Row. 1963.

Hoffman, Charles A., Jr. "Implications from the Mill Reef, Antigua; Sugar Factory, St. Kitts; and Palmetto Grove, San Salvador, Sites." Pp. 95–106 in *Proceedings of the Third International Congress for the Study of Pre-Columbian Cultures of the Lesser Antilles, St. George's, Grenada, 1969.* Grenada National Museum, Grenada. 1970.

Howard, George D. *Excavations at Ronquin, Venezuela.* (Yale University Publications in Anthropology, No. 28.) 90 pp., 7 plates, 11 figs. New Haven. 1943.

Im Thurn, Everard F. *Among the Indians of Guiana; Being Sketches Chiefly Anthropologic from the Interior of British Guiana.* London: Kegan Paul, Trench and Co. 1883. Reprinted 1967, New York: Dover.

Jennings, Jesse D., and Edward Norbeck (editors). *Prehistoric Man in the New World.* x, 633 pp. Chicago: University of Chicago Press. 1964.

Josselin de Jong, J. P. B. de. *Archeological Material from Saba and St. Eustatius, Lesser Antilles.* (Mededelingen van het Rijksmuseum voor Volkenkunde, Leiden, No. 1.) Leiden. 1947.

Keen, Benjamin (translator). *The Life of the Admiral Christopher Columbus by his Son Ferdinand.* 271 pp. London: The Folio Society. 1959.

Kidder, Alfred II. *Archaeology of ·Northwestern Venezuela.* (Papers of the Peabody Museum of American Archaeology and Ethnology, Vol. 26, No. 1.) viii, 178 pp., 18 plates. Cambridge, Mass. 1944.

Kidder, A. V., J. D. Jennings, and E. M. Shook. *Excavations at Kaminaljuyu, Guatemala.* (Publication No. 561.) Carnegie Institution of Washington, Washington, D. C. 1946.

Kirby, I. A. Earle. *Pre-Columbian Indians in St. Vincent, W. I.* St. Vincent Arch. and Hist. Soc. 1971.

Krickeberg, Walter. "Das Mittelamerikanische Ballspiel un seine religiose Symbolik." *Paideuma,* III:118–90. 1948.

Lathrap, Donald W. *The Upper Amazon.* (Ancient Peoples and Places, Vol. 70.) 256 pp. New York and Washington: Praeger. 1970.

Leakey, L. S. B. *Olduvai Gorge 1951–61,* Vol. 1, *A Preliminary Report on the Geology and Fauna.* xiv, 118 pp., 97 plates. Cambridge: University Press. 1965.

Lopez de Velasco, Juan. *Geografia y Descripcion Universal de las Indias. . . . Desde el Ano de 1571 al de 1574.* Madrid. 1894.

Loven, Sven. *Origins of the Tainan Culture, West Indies.* IX, 696 pp., 19 plates. Goteborg: Elanders Bokfryckeri Akfiebolog. 1935.

McKusick, Marshall B. *Distribution of Ceramic Styles in the Lesser Antilles.* Ph.D. dissertation in Anthropology, Yale University. New Haven. 1960.

MacNeish, Richard S. "Ancient Mesoamerican Civilization." *Science,* 143.3606:531–37. Washington. 1964.

———. "Domestication of Corn." *Science,* 143.3606:538–45. Washington. 1964.

———. "The Origins of New World Civilization." *Scientific American* 211.5:29–37. New York. 1964.

Mallery, Garrick. *Picture-writing of the American Indians.* Pp. 3–822 in 10th Annual Report of the Bureau of American Ethnology, . . . 1888–89. Washington. 1893.

Martin-Kaye, P. H. A. *Geology of the Leeward and British Virgin Islands.* Castries, St. Lucia: Voice Publishing Company. 1959.

Mattioni, Mario. "Etude Theoretique des Couches Archeologiques aux Petites Antilles sur la Base des Migrations Arawak et Caraibe." Pp. 139–46 in *Proceedings of the Third International Congress for the Study of Pre-Columbian Cultures of the Lesser Antilles, St. George's, Grenada, 1969.* Grenada National Museum, Grenada. 1970.

Mattioni, Mario, and Ripley P. Bullen. "A Chronological Chart for the Lesser Antilles: Sites dated by ceramic typology." Pp. 1–3 in *Proceedings of the Third International Congress for the Study of Pre-Columbian Cultures of the Lesser Antilles, St. George's, Grenada, 1969.* Grenada National Museum, Grenada. 1970.

Meggers, Betty J. *Ecuador.* (Ancient Peoples and Places, Vol. 49.) 220 pp. New York and Washington: Frederick A. Praeger. 1966.

———. "The Theory and Purpose of Ceramic Analysis." Pp. 9–20 in *Proceedings of the Second International Congress for the Study of Pre-Columbian Cultures in the Lesser Antilles, St. Ann's Garrison, Barbados, 1967.* Barbados Museum, Barbados. 1968.

Meggers, Betty J., and Clifford Evans. "An Experimental Formulation of Horizon Styles in the Tropical Forest Area of South America." Pp. 372–88 in *Essays in Pre-Columbian Art and Archaeology,* by Samuel

K. Lothrop and others. Cambridge: Harvard University Press. 1961.

———. "Machalilla Culture: an Early Formative Complex on the Ecuadorian Coast." *American Antiquity*, 28.2: 186–92. 1962.

———. "Especulaciones sobre rutas tempranas de difusion de la ceramica entre Sur y Meso-america." [Speculations on Early Pottery Diffusion Routes Between South and Middle America.] *Hombre y Cultura*, 1.3:1–15. Panama. 1964. (Reprinted 1971, *Revista Dominicana de Arquelogia y Antropologia*, 1.1:137–49, Santo Domingo.)

———. "Beginnings of Food Products in Ecuador." Pp. 201–207 in *XXXVI Congreso Internacional de Americanistas*. Seville. 1966. (Reprinted from *American Antiquity*, 28, 1962.)

———. *Potsherd Language and How to Read It*. iii, 74 pp. Washington, D. C.: Smithsonian Institution. 1967.

Meggers, Betty J., and Clifford Evans (editors). *Aboriginal Cultural Development in Latin America: An Interpretive Review*. (Smithsonian Miscellaneous Collections, Vol. 146, No. 1.) vi, 148 pp. Washington: Smithsonian Institution. 1963.

Meggers, Betty J., Clifford Evans, and Emilio Estrada. *Early Formative Period of Coastal Ecuador: the Valdivia and Machalilla Phases*. (Smithsonian Institution Contributions to Anthropology, Vol. 1.) xix, 234 pp., 196 plates. Washington. 1965.

Morban Laucer, Fernando A. *Pintura Rupestre y Petroglifos en Santo Domingo*. (Universidad Autonoma de Santo Domingo, Vol. 147; Coleccion Historia y Sociedad No. 4.) Santo Domingo. 1970.

Morison, Samuel Eliot. *Admiral of the Ocean Sea: A Life of Christopher Columbus*. xx, 680 pp. Boston: Little Brown. 1942.

———. *European Discovery of America: the Northern Voyages, A.D. 500–600*. xviii, 712 pp. New York: Oxford University Press. 1971.

Morison, Samuel Eliot (translator and editor). *Journals and Other Documents on the Life and Voyages of Christopher Columbus*. xvi, 417 pp. New York: Heritage Press. 1963.

Morison, Samuel Eliot, and Mauricio Obregon. *The Caribbean as Columbus Saw It*. xxxv, 252 pp. Boston and Toronto: Little, Brown. 1964.

Olsen, Fred. "Petroglyphs of the Caribbean Islands and Arawak Deities." Pp. 35–46 in *Proceedings of the Fourth International Congress for the Study of Pre-Columbian Cultures of the Lesser Antilles, Reduit Beach, St. Lucia, 1971*. St. Lucia Archaeological and Historical Society, Castries. 1973.

———. "Did the Ciboney Precede the Arawaks in Antigua?" Pp. 94–102 in *Proceedings of the Fourth International Congress for the Study of Pre-Columbian Cultures of the Lesser Antilles, Reduit Beach, St. Lucia, 1971*. St. Lucia Archaeological and Historical Society, Castries. 1973.

————. "On the Trail of the Arawaks: When Did They Arrive in Trinidad?" Pp. 181–91 in *Proceedings of the Fourth International Congress for the Study of Pre-Columbian Cultures of the Lesser Antilles, Reduit Beach, St. Lucia, 1971*. St. Lucia Archaeological and Historical Society, Castries. 1973.

Osgood, Cornelius. *The Ciboney Culture of Cayo Redondo, Cuba*. (Yale University Publications in Anthropology, No. 25.) 61 pp., 6 plates. New Haven. 1942.

Osgood, Cornelius, and George D. Howard. *An Archeological Survey of Venezuela*. (Yale University Publications in Anthropology, No. 27.) 153 pp., 15 plates, 27 figs. New Haven. 1943.

Petitjean-Roget, Jacques. "Etude d'un Horizon Arawak et Proto-Arawak a la Martinique: A Partir du Niveau II du Diamant." Pp. 61–68 in *Proceedings of the Second International Congress for the Study of Pre-Columbian Cultures in the Lesser Antilles, St. Ann's Garrison, Barbados, 1967*. Barbados Museum, Barbados. 1968.

————. "En Maniere d'Introduction." Introduction to *Martiniquan Archeology*. Paralleles 36/37, pp. 4–9 (in French), pp. 48–51 (in English). Martinique. 1970.

Petitjean-Roget, Jacques, and Henri Petitjean-Roget. "Recherche d'une Methode pour l'Etude de la Decoration des Ceramiques Precolombiennes de la Martinique." Pp. 151–56 in *Proceedings of the Fourth International Congress for the Study of Pre-Columbian Cultures of the Lesser Antilles, Reduit Beach, St. Lucia, 1971*. St. Lucia Archaeological and Historical Society, Castries. 1973.

————. "Etude Comparative des Tessons Graves ou Incises." Pp. 157–73 in *Proceedings of the Fourth International Congress for the Study of Pre-Columbian Cultures of the Lesser Antilles, Reduit Beach, St. Lucia, 1971*. St. Lucia Archaeological and Historical Society, Castries. 1973.

————. "Etude de la Decoration des Vases Precolombiennes de la Martinique." Pp. 174–80 in *Proceedings of the Fourth International Congress for the Study of Pre-Columbian Cultures of the Lesser Antilles, Reduit Beach, St. Lucia, 1971*. St. Lucia Archaeological and Historical Society, Castries. 1973.

Rainey, Froelich G. "Porto Rican Archaeology." *Scientific Survey of Porto Rico and the Virgin Islands*, Vol. 18, Part 1, pp. 1–208, 6 plates [whole volume]. New York Academy of Sciences. New York. 1940.

Ralegh, Sir Walter. *The Discoverie of the Large and Bevvtiful Empire of Guiana by Sir Walter Ralegh*. Edited by V. T. Harlow. London. 1928. (Originally published 1596, London: Robert Robinson; reprinted 1966, Cleveland: World Publishing Co.)

Reichel-Dolmatoff, G[erado]. *Colombia*. (Ancient Peoples and Places, Vol. 44.) 231 pp. New York: Frederick A. Praeger. 1965.

Rogers, David J. "Studies of *Manihot Esculenta* Crantz and Related Species." *Bull. Torrey Botanical Club*, Vol. 90, Jan. 1963.

Roth, Walter Edmund. *An Introductory Study of the Arts, Crafts and Customs of the Guiana Indians.* Pp. 25–745 in 38th Annual Report, Bureau of American Ethnology, . . . 1916–1917. Washington. 1924.

Rouse, Irving. *Prehistory in Haiti: A Study in Method.* (Yale University Publications in Anthropology, No. 21.) 202 pp., 5 plates. New Haven. 1939. (Reprinted 1964, New Haven: Human Relations Area Files Press.)

———. "An Analysis of the Artifacts of the 1914–1915 Porto Rican Survey." Pp. 273–301, plates 18–19 (Appendix) in *Scientific Survey of Porto Rico and the Virgin Islands*, Vol. 18, Part 2. New York Academy of Sciences. New York. 1941.

———. *Archeology of the Maniabón Hills, Cuba.* (Yale University Publications in Anthropology, No. 26.) 184 pp. 26 plates. New Haven. 1942.

———. "Prehistory of Trinidad in Relation to Adjacent Areas." *Man*, 47.103:93–98. London. 1947.

———. "The Arawak." Pp. 507–46 in Vol. 4, *The Circum-Caribbean Tribes*, of *Handbook of South American Indians*, edited by Julian H. Steward. Smithsonian Institution, Bureau of American Ethnology Bulletin 143. Washington. 1948.

———. "Petroglyphs." Pp. 493–502, plates 49–52 in Vol. 5, *The Comparative Ethnology of South American Indians*, of *Handbook of South American Indians*, edited by Julian H. Steward. Smithsonian Institution, Bureau of American Ethnology Bulletin 143. Washington. 1949.

———. "Areas and Periods of Culture in the Greater Antilles." *Southwestern Journal of Anthropology*, 7.3:248–265. Albuquerque. 1951.

———. "Porto Rican Prehistory: Introduction; Excavations in the West and North." *Scientific Survey of Porto Rico and the Virgin Islands*, Vol. 18, Part 3, pp. 397–460 [whole volume]. New York Academy of Sciences. New York. 1952.

———. "Porto Rican Prehistory: Excavations in the Interior, South and East; Chronological Implications." *Scientific Survey of Porto Rico and the Virgin Islands*, Vol. 18, Part 4, pp. 463–578 [whole volume]. New York Academy of Sciences. New York. 1952.

———. "The Circum-Caribbean Theory: An Archeological Test." *American Anthropologist*, 55.2:188–200. Menasha. 1953.

———. "On the Correlation of Phases of Culture." *American Anthropologist*, 57.4:712–22. Menasha. 1955.

———. "The Inference of Migrations from Anthropological Evidence." Pp. 63–68 in *Migrations in New World Culture History*, edited by Raymond H. Thompson. (University of Arizona, Social Science Bulletin 27.) Tucson. 1958.

――――. "The Classification of Artifacts in Archaeology." *American Antiquity*, 25.3:313–323. Salt Lake City. 1960.

――――. *Entry of Man into the West Indies*. (Yale University Publications in Anthropology, No. 61.) 26 pp. New Haven. 1960.

――――. "Recent Developments in American Archeology." Pp. 64–73 in *Men and Cultures*, edited by Anthony F. C. Wallace, (Fifth International Congress of Anthropological and Ethnological Sciences, Philadelphia, 1956.) Philadelphia: University of Pennsylvania Press. 1960.

――――. "The Bailey Collection of Stone Artifacts from Puerto Rico." Pp. 342–55 (Essay 23) in *Essays in Pre-Columbian Art and Archaeology*, by Samuel K. Lothrop and others. Cambridge: Harvard University Press. 1961.

――――. "The Caribbean Area." Pp. 389–417 in *Prehistoric Man in the New World*, edited by Jesse D. Jennings and Edward Norbeck. Chicago: University of Chicago Press. 1964.

――――. "Prehistory of the West Indies." *Science*, 144.3618:499–513. Washington. 1964.

――――. "The Place of 'Peoples' in Prehistoric Research." *Journal of the Royal Anthropological Institute of Great Britain and Ireland*, 95 (Part 1):1–15. London. 1965.

――――. "Mesoamerica and the Eastern Caribbean Area." Pp. 234–42 (Chapter 11) in *Archaeological Frontiers and External Connections*, edited by Gordon F. Ekholm and Gordon R. Willey, (Handbook of Middle American Indians, Vol. 4). Austin: University of Texas Press. 1966.

――――. "Terms Used in Caribbean Archeology." Pp. 9–13 in *Report of the Conference on Archeology, New World Museum, San Salvador, 1966*. New Haven: Department of Anthropology, Yale University. 1966.

――――. "Seriation in Archeology." Pp. 153–195 in *American Historical Anthropology: Essays in Honor of Leslie Spier*, edited by Carroll L. Riley and Walter S. Taylor. Carbondale: Southern Illinois University Press. 1967.

――――. *Introduction to Prehistory: A Systematic Approach*. xvii, 301 pp. New York: McGraw-Hill. 1972.

――――. "Observations on the Indian Creek Excavations, Antigua." *Proceedings of the Fifth International Congress for the Study of the Pre-Columbian Cultures of the Lesser Antilles*. In press.

Rouse, Irving, and Jose M. Cruxent. *Venezuelan Archeology*. (Caribbean Series, 6.) xiii, 179 pp. New Haven and London: Yale University Press. 1963.

Ruiz, Carlos Morales "Informe Sobre Tres Grupos Petroglíficos." *Revista Dominicana de Arquelogia y Antropologia*, 1.1:57–63, 28 figs. Santo Domingo. 1971.

Sanoja, Mario, and Iraida Vargas. *La Cueva de "El Elefante."* (Proyecto Orinoco, Informe No. 2.) 59 pp. Estado Bolivar, Venevuela. 1969.

Sauer, Carl Ortwin. *Agricultural Origins and Dispersals.* (Series 2.) v, 110 pp. New York: American Geographical Society. 1952.

———. "Middle America as Culture Historical Location." Pp. 115–22 in *Actas del XXXIII Congreso Internacional de Americanistas, San Jose, 1958,* Tomo 2. San Jose, Costa Rica: Lehmann. 1959.

———. *The Early Spanish Main.* xii, 306 pp. Berkeley and Los Angeles: University of California Press. 1966.

Smith, Bradley. *Columbus in the New World.* Garden City, New York: Doubleday. 1962.

Stern, Theodore. *The Rubber-Ball Games of the Americas.* (Monograph of the American Ethnological Society, No. 17.) New York: J. J. Augustin. 1949. (Reprinted 1966, Seattle and London: University of Washington Press.)

Stevens, Cecil E. *Before Columbus.* New York: Silver, Burdett and Company. 1928.

Vareschi, Volkmar *Orinoco Arriba: A Través de Venezuela Siguiendo a Humboldt.* 202 pp. Munich: F. Bruckmann. 1959.

Willey, Gordon R. "Historical Patterns and Evolution in Native New World Cultures." In *Evolution After Darwin,* Vol. 2. Chicago: University of Chicago Press. 1960.

———. *An Introduction to American Archaeology.* 2 vols. Vol. 1, 1966, *North and Middle America,* xiv, 526 pp.; Vol. 2, 1971, *South America,* xiv, 559 pp. Englewood Cliffs, N. J.: Prentice-Hall. 1966, 1971.

Wolper, Ruth G. Durlacher *A New Theory Identifying the Locale of Columbus's Light, Landfall, and Landing.* (Smithsonian Miscellaneous Collections, Vol. 148, No. 1; Publication 4534.) vii, 41 pp. Washington. 1964.

Wormington, H. M. *Ancient Man in North America.* 4th edition, revised. (Popular Series, No. 4.) XVIII, 322 pp. Denver: Denver Museum of Natural History. 1957.

Index of Figures

399

General Index